THE CATHOLIC UNIVERSITY OF AMERICA

STUDIES IN MEDIEVAL AND RENAISSANCE LATIN

VOL. III

THE SYNTAX OF THE VARIAE
OF CASSIODORUS

A Dissertation

SUBMITTED TO THE FACULTY OF THE GRADUATE SCHOOL OF ARTS AND
SCIENCES OF THE CATHOLIC UNIVERSITY OF AMERICA IN PARTIAL
FULFILLMENT OF THE REQUIREMENTS FOR THE DEGREE OF
DOCTOR OF PHILOSOPHY

BY

REV. BERNARD HENRY SKAHILL, S. T. B., J. C. B., M. A.

of the Archdiocese of Dubuque

THE CATHOLIC UNIVERSITY OF AMERICA

WASHINGTON, D. C.

1934

Nihil Obstat:

Rev. JAMES A. GEARY, Ph. D.,
Censor Deputatus

Washington, D. C., July 17, 1934.

Imprimatur:

✠ FRANCIS J. L. BECKMAN, S. T. D.,
Archbishop of Dubuque

Dubuque, Iowa, July 17, 1934.

PRINTED IN THE UNITED STATES OF AMERICA
BY J. H. FURST COMPANY, BALTIMORE, MARYLAND

TABLE OF CONTENTS

iii

PAGE

SELECT BIBLIOGRAPHY

I. EDITIONS

Opera Omnia

Migne, J. P., *Patrologia Latina*, 69, 70. Paris, 1865.

Variae

Mommsen, Th., *Monumenta Germaniae Historica, Auctores Antiquissimi XII*. Berlin, 1894.

II. SPECIAL WORKS ON CASSIODORUS

Dahn, F., *Die Könige der Germanen*, vols. III-IV. Würzburg, 1866.

Heerklotz, A. T., *Die Variae des Cassiodorus Senator als kulturgeschichtliche Quelle*. Heidelberg, 1926.

Hodgkin, T., *The Letters of Cassiodorus, being a Condensed Translation of the Variae Epistolae of Magnus Aurelius Cassiodorus Senator with an Introduction*. London, 1886.

———, *Italy and Her Invaders*, 2d ed. vol. 3, revised. Oxford, 1896.

———, *Theoderic the Goth, the Barbarian Champion of Civilization*. New York, 1897.

Lechler, G., *Die Erlasse Theoderichs in Cassiodors Varien Buch I-V*. Progr. Heilbronn, 1888.

Lehmann, P., Cassiodor-studien, *Philologus*, LXXI (1912), 278-299; LXXII (1913), 503-517; LXXIII (1914), 253-273; LXXIV (1917), 351-383.

Nickstadt, H., *De digressionibus quibus in Variis usus est Cassiodorus*. Marburg, 1921.

Schmidt, L., Cassiodorus und Theoderich, *Historisches Jahrbuch der Görresgesellschaft*, vol. XLVII (1927), 727-729.

Stangl, Th., Cassiodoriana I. *Blätter für das Gymnasial-Schulwesen*, XXIV (1898): 249-283, 545-591.

———, Cassiodoriana II. *Wochenschrift für klassische Philologie*, IX (1915): 205-214; X (1915), 228-239.

Usener, H., *Anecdoton Holderi, ein Beitrag zur Geschichte Roms in ostgothischer Zeit*. Bonn, 1877.

van de Vyver, A., Cassiodore et son oeuvre, *Speculum*, vol. VI (1931), 244-292.

III. WORKS ON SYNTAX AND STYLE

Arts, Sister Mary Raphael, *The Syntax of the Confessions of St. Augustine*. Washington, 1927.

Bennett, C. E., *The Syntax of Early Latin*, 2 vols. Boston, 1910-1914.

Bonnet, M., *Le latin de Gregoire de Tours*. Paris, 1890.

Draeger, A., *Historische Syntax der lateinischen Sprache*, 2 vols. Leipzig, 1879-1881.

ix

Gagner, A., Studien zur Bedeutung der Präposition Apud, *Uppsala Universitets Årsskrift.* Uppsala, 1931.

Goelzer, H., *Le Latin de saint Avit.* Paris, 1909.

Guillemin, A., *La Préposition " de " dans la littérature latine et en particulier dans la poesie latine de Lucrèce à Ausone.* Dijon, 1920.

Hrdlicka, C. L., *A Study of·the Late Latin Vocabulary and of the Prepositions and Demonstrative Pronouns in the Confessions of St. Augustine.* Washington, 1931.

Juret, P. C., *Étude grammaticale sur le latin de S. Filastrius.* Erlangen, 1904.

Krebs-Schmalz, *Antibarbarus der lateinischen Sprache,* 2 vols., 7th ed. Basel, 1905-1907.

Kühner-Stegmann, *Ausführliche Grammatik der lateinischen Sprache,* 2d ed. Hanover, 1912-1914. Vol. II. 1 and 2.

Lebreton, J., *Études sur la langue et la grammaire de Cicéron.* Paris, 1901.

Leumann-Hofmann, *Stolz-Schmalz Lateinische Grammatik,* 5th ed. Munich, 1928.

Löfstedt, E., *Syntactica, Studien und Beiträge zur historischen Syntax Des Lateins,* Part I. Lund, 1928, Part II, 1933.

——, *Philologischer Kommentar zur Peregrinatio Aetheriae.* Uppsala-Leipzig, 1911.

Lyer, S., Le Participe Présent à Sens Futur, *Revue des Études Latines,* IX (1931), 122-127.

——, Le Participe Présent Exprimant l'Antériorite, *Revue des Études Latines,* VII (1929), 322-333.

McGuire, M. R. P., *S. Ambrosii De Nabuthae, A Commentary with an Introduction and Translation.* Washington, 1927.

Meader, C. L., *The Latin Pronouns, Is, Hic, Iste, Ipse.* New York, 1901.

Nutting, H. C., Note on the Indefinite Second Person Singular, *University of California Publications in Classical Philology,* VIII, 4 (1927), 241-250.

——, Some Tendencies in Post-Augustan Latin, *University of California Publications in Classical Philology,* VIII 5 (1927), 251-267.

Odelstierna, I., *De Vi Futurali Ac Finali Gerundii Et Gerundivi Latini Observationes.* Uppsala, 1926.

Pauly-Wissowa-Kroll, *Real-Encyclopädie der classischen Altertumswissenschaft,* article *Epistolographie,* Supplementband V, 186-220. Stuttgart, 1931.

Peter, H., Der Brief in der römischen Litteratur. Litteraturgeschichtliche Untersuchungen und Zusammenfassungen. *Abhandlungen der Sächsischen Gesellschaft, philol.-hist.* Kl. 20 (1901), 202 ff. Leipzig, 1901.

Riemann, O., *Études sur la langue et la grammaire de Tite-Live.* Paris, 1879.

Salonius, A. H., *Kritische Untersuchungen über Text, Syntax, und Wortschatz der spätlateinischen Vitae Patrum.* Lund, 1920.

Škerlj, S., *Syntaxe du participe présent et du gérondif en viel Italien avec une introduction sur l'emploi du participe présent et de l'ablatif du gerondif en Latin.* Paris, 1926.

Souter, A., *A Study of Ambrosiaster.* Cambridge, England, 1905.

Svennung, J., *Orosiana, Syntaktische semasiologische und kritische Studien zu Orosius.* Uppsala, 1922.

Wackernagel, J., *Vorlesungen über Syntax mit besonderer Berücksichtigung von Griechisch, Lateinisch und Deutsch,* 2 vols. Basel, 1926-1928.

Zucker, L. M., *S. Ambrosii De Tobia, A Commentary, with an Introduction and Translation.* Washington, 1933.

IV. LEXICA

Archiv für lateinische Lexicographie und Grammatik. Leipzig, 1884-1908.

Benoist-Goelzer, *Nouveau Dictionnaire Latin-Français,* 9th ed. Paris, 1922. 10th ed. no date.

Forcellini-Corradini-Perin, *Lexicon Totius Latinitatis.* Padua, 1864-1887.

Georges, *Ausführliches Lateinisch-Deutsches Handwörterbuch,* 2 vols. Hanover and Leipzig, 1913-1918.

Lewis and Short, *Harpers' Latin Dictionary.* New York, 1879.

Liddell and Scott, *A Greek-English Lexicon,* 9th ed. Oxford, 1925 ff.

Neue-Wagener, *Formenlehre der lateinischen Sprache,* 3d ed. Leipzig, 1892-1905.

Thesaurus Linguae Latinae. Leipzig, 1900 ff.

V. GENERAL WORKS

Bardenhewer, O., *Geschichte der altkirchlichen Litteratur,* Vol. V. Freiburg im Breisgau, 1932.

Cabrol-Leclercq, *Dictionnaire d'archéologie chrétienne et de liturgie.* Vol. II. 2. Paris, 1925.

Cambridge Medieval History, Vol. I. The Christian Roman Empire and the Foundation of the Teutonic Kingdoms. New York, 1911.

Ebert, A., *Allgemeine Geschichte der Litteratur des Mittelalters im Abendlande,* Vol. I. Leipzig, 1889.

Laistner, M. L. W., *Thought and Letters in Western Europe, A. D. 500 to 900.* New York, 1931.

Manitius, M., *Geschichte der lateinischen Litteratur des Mittelalters,* Vol. I. Munich, 1911.

Schanz, M., *Römische Literaturgeschichte,* Vol. IV². Munich, 1920.

PREFACE

In spite of the historical significance of Cassiodorus, who, more than any other, gave a scholarly bent to Western Monasticism and played a major rôle in the preservation and transmission of classical literature, his works as a whole have not received the attention which they deserve from modern scholars.

On the textual side, apart from Mommsen's splendid edition of the Variae in the *Monumenta Germaniae Historica,* we must still depend largely on Migne's reprint of the rather poor text edited by the Maurist, J. Garet, and printed for the first time at Rouen in 1679. Much preliminary work has been done by Mommsen, Lehmann, and others on the classification of manuscripts, but a critical edition of the complete works of Cassiodorus still seems remote.

On the linguistic side, too, Cassiodorus may be classed among neglected writers, although this neglect can be explained in some measure perhaps by the unsatisfactory character of the greater portion of the text. Apart from Stangl's *Cassiodoriana I* and *II* and the *Index Rerum et Verborum* prepared by L. Traube for Mommsen's edition of the Variae, we have no studies on the language of Cassiodorus. The two works mentioned, moreover, have their limitations. Stangl is concerned mainly with problems of textual criticism in Cassiodorus' exegetical works and deals only incidentally with questions of vocabulary and syntax. Traube's *Index* is excellent as far as it goes, but it by no means furnishes a complete picture of the linguistic usages of the Variae. Thus it emphasizes unusual and Late words and meanings, but does not pretend to give a complete or systematic historical presentation of Cassiodorus' vocabulary on the basis of its component elements. As regards syntax, Traube calls attention to numerous syntactical peculiarities which are largely confined to Late Latin, but these naturally are presented simply in alphabetical order, and no attempt has been made to systematize and explain the syntactic facts registered. Hence, while the *Index* is very valuable to a student of Cassiodorus' syntax, it can in no sense be regarded as a satisfactory study of his syntax in itself.

My purpose in the present monograph has been to investigate the syntax of the Variae systematically and to present the results of my investigation in a systematic form. I have attempted, therefore, to bring the syntactical phenomena of the Variae into historical relation with the syntax of the Classical, Silver, and Late Latin writers before Cassiodorus. Through such an historical approach it is hoped that a greater insight has been gained into the language of the author and that the present monograph will be of value to all students of Late Latin and early Medieval Latin, particularly to future editors of those works of Cassiodorus for which as yet we have no modern critical texts.

The text used in this investigation is the critical text of Th. Mommsen in the *Monumenta Germaniae Historica, Auctores Antiquissimi, XII.* (Berlin, 1894). I have cited the Variae according to page, paragraph, and line of this text (where only two numbers occur in a citation, they indicate page and line), and Traube's *Index Rerum et Verborum,* by the name Traube and the page.

My study of the historical syntax of the Variae is based mainly on the *Lateinische Grammatik* of Leumann-Hofmann, and in general the order of this work is followed in the presentation of the material. Kühner-Stegmann's *Ausführliche lateinische Grammatik* has also been a valuable aid, as has been the syntactical material in the *Thesaurus Linguae Latinae* and other lexica, notably that of Georges. Furthermore I have utilized the more important monographs devoted to the syntax of Late Latin.

The chief abbreviations and symbols used in referring to works are the following: L.-Hof. = Leumann-Hofmann; K.-Steg. = Kühner-Stegmann; Kr.-Schm. = Krebs-Schmalz; T. L. L. = Thesaurus Linguae Latinae; Hodgkin = T. Hodgkin, *The Letters of Cassiodorus.*

The various periods of Latin Literature are designated as follows: Early, all Latin before Cicero; Classical, the prose of Cicero, Caesar, Sallust and Nepos; Silver, the Latin from the death of Augustus to the death of Suetonius; Late, the Latin after Suetonius. Livy, who forms a connecting link between the Classical and the Silver eras, is regularly mentioned separately.

I wish to express my appreciation to Professor Roy J. Deferrari, Head of the Department of Greek and Latin and Dean of the

Graduate School of Arts and Sciences of the Catholic University of America, for suggesting the subject of this dissertation, for reading the manuscript and offering valuable criticism; to Dr. Martin R. P. McGuire, Instructor in Greek and Latin, for first arousing my interest in the works of Cassiodorus and giving generously of his time in directing the dissertation throughout all stages of its development; to Rev. James A. Geary, Ph. D., Instructor in Comparative Philology and Celtic Languages, for reading the manuscript and offering valuable suggestions.

INTRODUCTION

Flavius Magnus Aurelius Cassiodorus Senator[1] was born at Scyllacium in Bruttium about 485 A. D. By himself and his contemporaries he is called chiefly Senator, by subsequent writers regularly Cassiodorus. His family traced its origin to Syria, but at least three generations of the direct ancestors of Cassiodorus Senator were inhabitants of Scyllacium. The distinguished services of his grandfather and great-grandfather to the Roman state and of his father to the Gothic kingdom are recounted by Cassiodorus in the official letter to the senate (Variae, Book I, Letter IV), which it was the son's duty as quaestor to write in praise of his own father on the occasion of the latter's elevation to the patriciate. Nothing whatever is known about the early education of Cassiodorus. From the learning displayed in the Variae and his other works it can be inferred that he received a liberal training in philosophy and rhetoric, the training usually given to a wealthy and noble young Roman to fit him for service to the state.

His rise to favor with the Gothic king and to power in the Gothic kingdom was rapid. After his appointment at an early age to the office of *consiliarius* to his father, who was then praetorian prefect, he delivered a eulogy on Theoderic which won for him the favor of the monarch and the office of quaestor.

We do not know the dates of his term as quaestor. Mommsen shows that no letter written during his quaestorship can be dated with certainty before 507 and none later than 511. In 514 he became *consul ordinarius*, and in 526 at the death of Theoderic he was *magister officiorum* and continued in this office during the earlier years of Athalaric. Having risen thus by faithful service through the *cursus honorum* of that time, he attained in the year 533 the office of praetorian prefect formerly held by his father. On this occasion he wrote to himself in the name of King Athalaric a beautiful letter of commendation (Book IX, Letter XXIV). Later

---

[1] For the biography of Cassiodorus I have relied chiefly upon Bardenhewer, O., *Geschichte der altkirchlichen Litteratur* (Freiburg im Breisgau, 1932), V, 264-276, Mommsen's *Proemium* in the Monumenta edition of the Variae, pp. v-xii, and Hodgkin's various works.

he attained the dignity of the patriciate as his father had previously done.

We have no exact means of knowing to what extent the sound policy of Theoderic in ruling his kingdom was due to his own prudence and to what extent to the wise counsel of Cassiodorus. Certain it is that the king's task was a difficult one, for he had to reconcile the most diverse characters and cultures, to cause the warlike, lawless Arian Goths and the peaceful, legally-minded, Catholic Romans to dwell together in peace and harmony. Theoderic through the pen of Cassiodorus constantly preaches *civilitas*, which appears to be a combination of the ideas of peace and culture. Not only the word but also the idea seems to be Roman rather than Gothic in origin, and scholars generally assign to Cassiodorus much more than a secretary's part in making it not merely an ideal but also to a considerable extent a fact in this heterogeneous nation.[2]

In 540 the Gothic kingdom virtually came to an end when the Gothic royal city Ravenna fell before the onslaught of Belisarius and the Gothic king Witiges was captured. About the time of this event and possibly as a result of it, Cassiodorus returned to his native Scyllacium, there to found, equip, and govern the monastery of Vivarium, to make scholars of his monks, and by his own labors and those of his associates to make the treasures of Greek and Latin literature available to posterity.[3] In the midst of an extraordinarily busy life at court he had produced, besides his many orations, of which only fragments exist today, his Chronicle, his History of the Goths, the Variae, and the brief treatises *Ordo Generis Cassiodororum* and *De Anima*. Nor did his creative literary ability cease with the transfer of his activities from the court to the cloister. His monastic writings include works of exegesis of the Scriptures, his *Historia Ecclesiastica Tripertita,* his

---

[2] For two widely varying opinions on the extent of Cassiodorus' political influence the reader is referred to the articles of L. Schmidt, Cassiodorus und Theoderich in *Historisches Jahrbuch der Görresgesellschaft*, XLVII (1927), 727-729 and A. van de Vyver, Cassiodore et son Oeuvre, *Speculum*, VI (1931), 244-292.

[3] For details concerning the monastery of Vivarium and the work of Cassiodorus in the preservation of ancient Greek and Latin literature see the article *Cassiodore* in Cabrol-Leclercq, *Dictionnaire d'archéologie chrétienne et de liturgie*, Vol. II, 2, 2357-2365. Paris, 1925.

grammatical treatise *De Orthographia,* completed in his ninety-third year, and the best known and most revered of all his literary works, the *Institutiones quemadmodum divinae et humanae debeant intellegi lectiones, duobus libris,* two books of simple but sound instruction to his monks on their duties as scholars and men of God. In what year Cassiodorus died we do not know. His last work of which we have any knowledge is the *De Orthographia.* Sometime around the year¹ 580 A. D., death came to the ex-praetorian prefect in his monastic cell at Vivarium.

The twelve books of the Variae (sc. *epistolae),* the syntax of which forms the subject of this study, consist of 470 documents (468 letters and formulae and two prefaces) published by Cassiodorus during his prefecture in the year 537. They represent the official letters and documents composed by him for his sovereign and for himself during his years of public activity. Books I-V are written for Theoderic, the first King of the Goths and Romans. Books VI and VII are Formulae of appointments to various offices. Books VIII-X are writen for the successive kings Athalaric, Theodahad, and Witiges, with a few letters written for Amalasuintha, the queen-regent for the young Athalaric, and for Gudeliva, the wife of Theodahad. Books XI and XII are the official correspondence and pronouncements of Cassiodorus himself in his capacity as praetorian prefect.

We have no means of knowing how accurately these documents represent the occasions for which they purport to have been written. They were published and perhaps rewritten, or possibly in some cases composed for the first time, many years after the occasions which some of them represent. Cassiodorus published the Variae, he tells us himself in his first preface, during his prefecture, though it was chiefly during his quaestorship, many years before, that he was the sovereign's official letter-writer.

His own prefaces tell us also what occasioned the publication of the Variae. In the first preface he tells of the importunate pleading of his friends that he give to the world a record of his own achievements and of the benefits conferred by his king. He is influenced also by the desire to have for his own use and to leave for others model letters and formulae, which might serve him for various occasions and might assist others less capable than he when they should have need of a literary form or model. The first ten books of the Variae are then avowed models of official style. The preface to the last two books contains a profuse apology for the style as being that of a busy man and declares (327, 6, 1-4) the purpose of the writer: "I have therefore subjoined two books in which I myself speak in my capacity as Prefect, to the ten in which I have spoken by the mouth of the King; for it seemed absurd to me to be silent in my newly-acquired dignity, who had so often spoken on behalf of others." (Translated by Hodgkin, 450.)

The name Variae was given to the work by Cassiodorus himself, not so much because of the varied nature of the documents it contains as because of the variation in the author's style, though the two are to a certain extent inseparable and the author professes to have adapted his style to the occasion and particularly to the person to whom the document is addressed. He tells us himself in his first preface: "As for the title of all twelve books, the index of the work, the herald of its meaning, the expression in briefest compass of the whole performance, I have for this chosen the name Variae. And this because it was necessary for me not always to use the same style, since I had undertaken to address various kinds of persons. One must speak in one way to men jaded with much reading; in another to those who skim lightly over the surface, tasting here and there; in another (if one would persuade them) to persons who are devoid of a taste for letters, since it is sometimes a proof of skill to avoid the very things which please the learned. In short, the definition given by our ancestors is a good one: 'To speak fitly is to persuade the hearers to accept your wishes for their own.' . . . It must be added hereto that we have sometimes to speak to Kings, sometimes to the Officers of the Court, sometimes to the very humblest of the people. To the last we may allowably pour out our words with some degree of haste, but the other addresses should be deeply pondered before they are delivered. Deservedly therefore is a work entitled Variae, which is subject to so much diversity in its composition." [4]

We may well doubt that Cassiodorus is always successful in adapting his style or the contents of his letters to the recipients. Wit-

---

[4] This translation by Hodgkin, 138-139, though somewhat free, gives a good general idea of thought of the original (Cf. 5, 14, 8-13; 5, 17, 21-25).

ness, for example, Book I, Letter II, in which a dyer of royal robes is rebuked and threatened for not delivering on time a product of his art for the wardrobe of the king and receives, in addition to rebukes and threats, a learned dissertation on the history of dyeing expressed in language (even though it be his native tongue) that only a specialist could read.

He appears even less successful at times in adapting his discourse to the quality of the person for whom it is written. Theoderic could not read or write Latin and was perhaps thoroughly illiterate even in his native Gothic, and yet in the hands of Cassiodorus he is learned enough to quote Tacitus (Book V Letter II) to the Hesti, a German tribe, to explain to them the nature and origin of their own peculiar native product, amber. He can also quote and interpret Homer, Terence, Vergil and other Greek and Latin classics. Cf. e. g., Book II, Letter XL. The boy-king Athalaric, first an effeminate child and later a debauchee, speaks through the pen of Cassiodorus in the words of a statesman and philosopher. Theodahad, "one of the meanest insects that ever crawled across the page of history," speaks as a holy and devout man. We may credit Theodahad, however, with being a clever hypocrite, who perhaps has sufficient intelligence to dictate at least the contents of his letters, and Cassiodorus would be compelled to write as his master ordered. In his writing in the name of Witiges he does better. Something of the character of this rugged untutored fighter appears in the direct blunt style which Cassiodorus uses in the few letters he writes for him.

As a historical source the Variae are valuable, because they furnish the only extensive contemporary record of the relations of Goths and Romans in that most unusual kingdom established by Theoderic and ruled for fifty years by himself and his successors. They throw much light also on the details of official positions and dignities in that elaborate civil service which the Goths inherited from the Romans. As official documents, however, they are so vague and suppress so many essential points, that to some extent they are unsatisfactory as records. Cassiodorus, apparently with design and not through any lack of knowledge or failure of memory, often substitutes for the name of a person or a place, or for an exact date or a number, an indefinite *ille* which hides the exact information from the reader, and his digressions into some very unnatural

natural history, while interesting and amusing, tend to distract the reader and divert his attention from the more important issues of the main part of a letter.

The vagueness is due in part to the formulary nature of the epistles, the author being more interested in furnishing an outline for himself or others to use than in imparting historical information. Moreover the digressions show a defective sense of relative values. In this Cassiodorus may be compared to Cato the Elder who was, as a historian, the despair of Pliny the Elder (Cf. Plin. nat. 8, 11), because he related an entire Roman-Punic campaign without naming the Roman generals, while he discoursed at length and with enthusiasm on the exploits of a Carthaginian elephant named Surus. Cassiodorus too has his elephants, which do strange things, as do his birds, his fishes, his moles, and his salamanders. We should prefer, however, to have him tell us who are the persons *Ille et Ille,* how much money is *illi solidi,* and what date is represented by *illa indictio.*

Cassiodorus possesses a rich vocabulary, partly reflecting the literature of the Golden and the Silver Ages, partly the Christian and Pagan literature of a later day, while many terms are from the current speech of his own time. Our lexica bear witness to a considerable number of words found first in Cassiodorus, and it is mostly the Variae they cite. Many such words, however, were without doubt current in his day and were quite naturally employed by him. Even today monographs on the vocabulary of the late writers and those of the transition period do not exist in sufficient numbers to exclude the possibility that other authors had previously used words cited first for Cassiodorus.

His style is, in general, turgid and bombastic. One is tempted to believe that he never says anything in one word which can possibly be said in two. This wordiness is to a certain extent a characteristic of epistolary style from the time of Pliny and especially of the official style of the Later Empire. (Cf. Laistner, 70, footnote 1). But it appears to be also a personal characteristic of Cassiodorus, who in his other writings exhibits, though in a lesser degree, some of the extreme verbosity of the Variae. His sentences are usually long, complex periods—so long and complex at times that the author gets tangled in his own verbiage, and a rhythmic, full-sounding, but anacolouthic sentence is the result.

Sound no doubt plays a large part in his selection of words and his arrangement of them in sentences; rhythm and cadence he must have, even if clearness of thought is not always present. Neither the vocabulary nor the rhythmic qualities of the Variae have as yet been the subject of a special study. Either field should give a rich harvest to the investigator.

It is the syntax of the Variae, and that alone, which is the subject of the present investigation, but, where rhythm substantially affects the syntax, this factor has not been ignored. That there are serious syntactical difficulties can be inferred from the above general remarks on the style. The Latin language had undergone serious changes between the days of Cicero and those of Cassiodorus, and only the study of the language of the intervening periods can solve the difficulties in an author of the later time. Even after such study, the language of such a writer as Cassiodorus can not fail to present problems of syntax due to his individual peculiarities of style. Hodgkin, who usually grasps the general thought of a letter very well, found a complete translation to be an almost impossible task and contented himself with giving in most cases only an abstract of each letter. "A few important letters," he tells us in his Preface, p. vi, "have been translated, to the best of my ability, verbatim. In the not infrequent instances where I have been unable to extract any intelligible meaning, on grammatical principles, from the words of the author, I have put in the text the nearest approximation that I could discover to his meaning, and placed the unintelligible words in a note, hoping that my readers may be more fortunate in their interpretation than I have been."

The author of the present study is less pessimistic, chiefly for two reasons. First, in the last half-century great advances have been made in the study of the peculiarities of Silver, Late, and Patristic Latin, putting at the disposal of the present-day scholar sources of information concealed from the scholar of the past. Secondly, since Hodgkin's time the publication of Mommsen's excellent text has removed many of the textual difficulties and made intelligible some sentences which had previously refused to yield up their meaning. However, in spite of these aids the language of the Variae remains difficult, and this study is presented in the hope that scholars may find it of some help in interpreting the language of Cassiodorus.

CHAPTER I

GENDER AND NUMBER

I. *Gender*

(L.-Hof. 364-369)

In the Variae divergences from classical usage with respect to gender are few and unimportant.

In 243, 5, 4, *alphabeti* (Gen. Sing.) is masculine, as is shown by the masculine relative, *quem*. T. L. L., I, 1721, 61, gives only the neuter *alphabetum*. This passage, among others, is cited, but without the relative. The Greek, however, is ἀλφάβητος, masculine.

The noun *exormiston*, a kind of fish, is listed by Harpers', Georges, and Benoist-Goelzer as neuter, and Cassiodorus is the only author cited. The citation corresponds to 371, 5, 25, where the modifiers are neuter. The word occurs also, evidently with a feminine adjective, in 362, 1, 20, exormiston Sicula quibuslibet laboribus offeratur. (Harpers' etc. show the Greek equivalent ἐξορμιστόν. Liddell and Scott, 1925 ed., gives it as only neuter, and the only citations are these two from the Variae.)

A masculine pronoun *eum* refers to the neuter noun *praedium* in 24, 2, 9, Si Romani praedium, ex quo deo propitio Sonti fluenta transmisimus, ubi primum Italiae nos suscepit imperium, sine delegatoris cuiusquam pittacio praesumptor barbarus occupavit, eum priori domino summota dilatione restituat. Perhaps the lack of agreement is due to the thought of *ager* or some other masculine noun being present in the mind of the writer. Elsewhere, e. g., 227, 3, 11, the word *praedium* occurs as a neuter noun. Conversely, the masculine noun *agellus* is dealt with as a neuter (*agellum*) in 257, 1, 27, agellum, quod Fabricula nominatur. This is the only occurrence of the word as a neuter noted in T. L. L., I, 1279, 65.

A similar lack of agreement occurs in the use of *ipso* referring to *divinitatis* in 318, 1, 21, Quamvis omnis provectus ad divinitatis est munera referendus nec aliquid constat bonum, nisi quod ab *ipso* dinoscitur esse collatum. . . . Cassiodorus frequently uses the words *divinitas, divina,* or *superna,* in place of *deus,* and it appears

1

that the word *deus* is foremost in his thought here and causes him
to use a masculine pronoun.

Occasionally agreement in gender is according to sense, e. g.,
31, 2, 26, si . . . vox iniusta praesumpserit, noverit se a praefecto
urbis legibus audiendum; 36, 1, 3, congrua videtur esse persona,
qui assumpta domini libertate proficiat.   Elsewhere the author uses
persona, quae, e. g., 56, 3, 31.

Similar examples of agreement according to sense can be found in
classical prose.

II. *Number*
(L.-Hof. 369-372)

1. Abstract Nouns in Plural

Many abstract nouns are found in the plural in the Variae. The
following is a list of plural abstracts which occur in the Variae, but
are not found in the lists of Lebreton, 421 ff., Neue-Wagener I,
628-650, and Riemann, 42 ff. They do not occur in Draeger's
list for Early Latin and for classical prose, p. 11-14, but three of
them, *aequitates, aspectus,* and *aviditates,* occur in his list for
classical poetry, Silver prose including Livy, and Silver poetry,
p. 14.

aequitates 51, 1, 7, benigni quippe principis est ad clementiae commodum transilire terminos aequitatum.
 Plural occurs in Ps. Quint., Itala, and here (T. L. L., I, 1013, 73).
aspectus 114, 3, 16, aspectibus iucundi, usibus gratiores:
 No plural in sense of *species, facies, habitus,* in the examples in
 T. L. L., II, 803, 79.
aviditates 341, 3, 22, qui lucrorum aviditates appetitis.
 Plural in Plin. nat., Heges., Cassiod. Ios. c. Ap. (T. L. L., II,
 1422, 37).
imminutiones } 19, 7, 32, non potestis nomina integritatum dare et
integritates }
 scelestas imminutiones efficere.
 Plural of *imminutio* in Quint., Lampr. (Georges).
 No plural of *integritas* in Harpers', Georges, Benoist-Goelzer, or
 Forcellini-Perin.
iussiones 117, 1, 2, Nullum decet nostras gravanter suscipere iussiones.
 Word is Late Latin. No plurals in Harpers', Georges, Benoist-
 Goelzer, Forcellini-Perin.
nuditates 147, 4, 11, sit nuditatibus expeditus, qui voluntate noluit
esse celerrimus.
 Word is Late Latin. Meaning *bareness* or *want* found in Cod. Th.

No plurals in Harpers', Georges, Benoist-Goelzer, or Forcellini-Perin.

2. Unusual Plural

The plural, *frumenta*, occurs in 33, 2, 16, ut . . . naves frumentis oneret. Also in 33, 2, 22, etc. The plural occurs in classical prose, but usually in the sense of unharvested grain. The collective singular would be regular here, though classical prose occasionally uses the plural in this sense also (Neue-W., I, 584; T. L. L., VI, 1420, 22 ff.).

The plural also occurs in 269, 1, 29, frumenta nobis usualiter natura industria suffragante concedit: passim se vina profundunt: metallum raro proditur. Different kinds of grain and of wine seem to be meant, so the usage is classical (K.-Steg., II, 1, 74; II, 1, 77; Neue-W., I, 607; I, 600). The *metallum* is of one kind, gold, as the context shows.

Commercium in the singular occurs a few times in the Variae, e. g., 63, 3, 29. The word is frequent in Cicero (T. L. L., III, 1872, 4). The plural occurs at least 17 times in the Variae in four different meanings, in none of which is a plural found in a classical prose author. The following examples illustrate the plural use in the various senses:

23, 2, 5, quibus commerciorum sunt commoda deminuta.
52, 1, 20, Si desideriis nostris commercia peregrina famulantur.
> In T. L. L., III, 1874, 59, these two examples are the only ones listed under *quod ex mercatura provenit, latiore sensu, i. q. reditus, fructus, quaestus.*
33, 1, 11, quia iustius est, ut incolis propria fecunditas serviat quam peregrinis commerciis studiosae cupiditatis exhauriat.
> T. L. L., III, 1878, 72, lists this as *i. q. negotium, munus, actio.* Ammianus is the first author listed for the plural.
209, 2, 30 commercia civibus . . . dispone.
> T. L. L., III, 1874, 78, lists this as *in bello, feri i. q. commeatus.* Plin. nat. is the first citation for the plural.
279, 9, 12, Navigiis vecta commercia.
> T. L. L., III, 1874, 17, lists this as *i. q. res emptae venditae-que.* Jerome is the first author cited for the plural.

3. Singular and Plural Indifferently

The singular, *tempore*, and the plural, *temporibus*, are often used indifferently in the ablative of time, e. g., Singular, 72, 17, 32, sapientia vestra eligat praesenti tempore meliorem, 131, 3, 17, sicut Odovacris tempore tributa solverunt, Plural, 86, 3, 15, his egit temporibus continentem, 107, 6, 29, Augusti . . . temporibus orbis Romanus . . . descriptus est.

4. Singular for Plural

The use of *cordi* in the singular in the double dative construction is stereotyped, even in cases where the other dative is plural, e. g., Cic. Att. 5, 3, 3; Caes., Gall. 6, 19, 4. (Cf. T. L. L., IV, 940, 3 ff.) It occurs frequently in the Variae, e. g., 17, 1, 25. The analogy of this construction probably accounts for the use of the singular *cordi* in 281, 2, 19, quatenus cunctorum figatur cordi, though the word is used under circumstances different from those of the *cordi* in the stereotyped expression.

5. Plural for Singular

The plural *bella* is often used in the general sense of war, more frequently than *bellum*, but not to the exclusion of it. *Proelia* often has the meaning of *bellum*, but not the meaning of *proelium* (Cf. Traube, 568, s. v. *pluralis*). To illustrate the usage I quote merely one example of each: 122, 3, 9, ut qui es bello clarus, civilitate quoque reddaris eximius; 164, 2, 32, sic mala pace quasi ludo corruunt, quanti vix potuissent cadere sub necessitate bellorum; 23, 1, 18, quia res proeliorum bene disponitur, quotiens in pace tractatur.

The plural *bella* was thus used by the Augustan poets where the trochaic word fitted better than *bellum*. Late prose, striving for prose rhythm, was influenced by the same consideration (L.-Hof., 371-372; T. L. L., II, 1853, 35). The use of plural forms other than *bella* (*bellorum, bellis*) can be accounted for by analogy.

The singular *certamen* and the plural *certamina* are also used in the meaning of *bellum*, e. g., 329, 12, 14, lacessiti metuerunt cum nostris inire certamen, and 27, 1, 19, Innotescenda sunt magis Gothis quam suadenda certamina.

Sinus is used in the plural four times in various tropical senses. The singular, and not the plural, is used in classical prose as a figurative expression of love, intimacy, or protection. The plural is used in this manner in 179, 2, 29, causarum . . . pondus in eius audientiae sinibus optima securitate reponimus, and 336, 6, 5, in cordis sinibus se omnia non defigant. In the other examples, where the word is used in a geographical sense, 327, 9, 19, omnia in origine sua plenissime vivunt, quae necdum a naturalibus sinibus auferuntur, and 332, 6, 4, confessiones illas . . . Roma felicior in suis sinibus habere promeruit, the plural appears as natural as the singular, and parallels can be found in Tacitus (Harpers', Benoist-Goelzer, Forcellini-Perin).

The plural *animi* is used several times in the sense of *affection* or *understanding* where only one person is indicated. The plural occurs occasionally in classical prose in the sense of a high degree of courage, high spirit, or arrogance (K.-Steg., II, 1, 80; T. L. L., II, 104, 46). No examples of the use of the plural referring to a single person are given in T. L. L., II, 93, 26 or 91, 48, where the use of the word *animus* in the sense of affections or understanding is treated. Examples in the sense of affections or understanding:

12, 3, 26, cum nostris animis singula suaviter inhaesisse cognoscas.
93, 1, 23, qui nostris animis gloriosis actionibus insederunt.
236, 3, 13, animos nostros circa se minores non desiderant effici.
311, 4, 4, quod vestris credidimis animis convenire.
320, 2, 14, apud clementissimi imperatoris animos.
347, 14, devotioribus animis publicae pareat iussioni.

The use of *noster* and *vester* in the above examples is an employment of the possessive in the plural of majesty or of reverence. The affections etc. are those of one person.

It seems probable that, owing to the intimate connection of *animus* with the person, the same influences that occasion the use of the plural of majesty and of reverence serve to make this word plural also.

6. Interchange of Singular and Plural

A singular noun with the adjective *universus* is used as the equivalent of a plural with *omnes* in 150, 2, 31, universum possessorem . . . te iubemus inspicere. I have found no similar use of *universus* in the lexica or grammars.

Conversely, *omnes* is made to serve as the equivalent of a singular, i. e., *quemque* or *unumquemque*, by the use of a singular verb in the subordinate clause in 57, 1, 22, Omnes decet gratanter impendere quod publicas videt utilitates posse respicere. . . .

Alteruter with a singular noun occurs twice where the meaning is not *one or the other*, but *both*, 21, 2, 20, ut alterutro decore fulgentes mutua se gratia qualitatis ornarent, and 31, 3, 2, direximus, quae vobis reserari libenter amplectimur, ut alterutra iussione pensata resarciatur civibus scissa concordia. Traube, 514, suggests *mutuus* as the equivalent of *alteruter* in these passages. The usage of *alteruter* in the sense of *mutuus* begins with Tertullian (L.-Hof., 472; T. L. L., I, 1759, 77 ff.). I should prefer to regard *uterque* as the equivalent in the second example. T. L. L., I, 1759, 72, has examples of *alteruter* from Plin. nat. and Maecian. dig. which are regarded as probably the equivalent of *uterque* (*i. q. uterque?*).

Alternus with a singular noun is the equivalent of a plural in 166, 3, 28, alternae parti indiscreta laude placuisti. The use of *alternus* with plural force is limited to poets and later prose writers and is joined with *geminus, uterque*, etc. (T. L. L., I, 1756, 75).

A noun in the ablative absolute with *se* is employed in the singular in a context where the plural is clearly demanded by the sense in 145, 4, 36, pudoris enim sustinere iacturam nesciunt, qui se prius iudice corriguntur, and in 216, 2, 33, facile enim sequuntur vestigia verbi alieni, qui se possunt monitore compelli. The expression *se iudice* became stereotyped and was applied to the plural.

The plural sense of *quicquid* occasions the usage of the neuter plural gerundive *incorporanda* as a future participle passive in agreement with it in 17, 2, 14, censemus, ut, quicquid a Neoterio . . . te non tam comparasse quam subripuisse cognoscis, incorporanda militi nostro sine aliqua dilatione restituas. . . .

In speaking of the same group of persons, taxpayers, the author changes from singular to plural in 130, 1, 7, nam si fessis minime relevetur onus, necessitate cernitur iacere prostratus. The singular form in the conclusion is probably due to the author's concept of the taxpayers as a unit, so that the idea of *the taxpayer* becomes uppermost in his mind—unless the reading " fesso " of MSS. E and F is to be accepted.

A similar explanation can be given of the use of the singular *curialis* in 56, 1, 20, to which a plural *eos* refers in 56, 1, 22, quod si eos vel ad honores transire iura vetuerunt.

Possessore in 30, 2, 17, would also be the representative of a class if we were to accept the reading *illis* in the same line. Mommsen's reading *illi* in place of the *illis* of the codices brings the pronoun into agreement.

I believe that none of the four examples given above is exactly paralleled in the examples given under *Kongruenz* by Leumann-Hofmann, 631-639.

It is difficult also to explain the use of the singular *cui* in 216, 2, 20, following as it does *illum atque illum*. The successive sentences beginning in 216, 2, 18 are: Quapropter ex officio nostro illum atque illum ad vos credidimus esse dirigendos, ut secundum priscam consuetudinem qui tuis iussionibus obsecundant eos rationabili debeat antiquitate moderari. cui gratiam tuam in conservandis annonis et consuetudinibus suis ex nostra iussione praestabis. debet enim a te diligi, qui a nobis meruit destinari. Lapse of attention on the part of the writer is the best I can suggest here. The entire context and the author's general practice of using a single *ille* for one person make it evident that in this passage he began by speaking of two envoys and ended by speaking of one. For a more complete discussion of this use of *ille,* see p. 77.

A notable example of the non-agreement of a verb with its subject is 134, 2, 2, statim plebis inflammata contentio synagogam temerario duxerunt incendio concremandam, culpas hominum fabricarum excidio vindicantes. . . . Here apparently the verb *duxerunt* agrees in sense with those whose hostility (*contentio*) was inflamed, though grammatically they are represented only by the collective genitive singular *plebis*. Rare examples of such synesis in number occur at all periods of the language, including classical prose (L.-Hof., 635-636).

7. Plural of Majesty
(L.-Hof. 372)

Cassiodorus frequently uses the plural of majesty (i. e., first person) in letters written for the sovereign, in the books of formulae, and in his own letters as praetorian prefect.

Nouns in apposition with a noun or pronoun in the plural of majesty are in the plural also, e. g., 179, 6, 15, ut te tamen rationem credas *nobis iudicibus* redditurum, and 236, 2, 8, in sellam regni sui *nos dominos* collocavit. . . .

Many inconsistencies, however, are noted in the use of plural and singular. Thus, a participle in agreement with the plural subject may be in the singular, e. g., 339, 1, 8, *Sciens* ab eis contrarium posse credi . . . propositi *nostri* votum edictali tenore promisimus, etc.

Subjects in the singular may be accompanied by possessive adjectives, relative pronouns, etc., in the plural indicating the same person, and, conversely, subjects in the plural may be accompanied by possessive adjectives in the singular. Thus, e. g., 301, 1, 11, privata siquidem studia a *nostro* animo probantur exclusa, quia generalis dominus custos *factus sum* deo auxiliante cunctorum; 133, 3, 6, nihil fieri *volumus* incivile, *cuius* cottidianus labor est pro generali quiete tractare; 305, 3, 32, quam *nos probamur* Romano nomini contulisse. reddite affectui *meo* plenissimam caritatem.

At times the plural usage is abandoned in order to put greater emphasis on the individuality of the writer. In the following examples the singular is used for emphasis, where the plural of majesty occurs elsewhere in the same letter or formula, 183, 6, 29, quia in his quae feceris iudex et testis *ero*; 192, 6, 9, diligentius exquirite . . . nam *videro*, etc.; 338, 7, 22, estote devoti, ut *me* provinciarum patrem faciatis esse quam iudicem . . . ; 338, 8, 29, quem iam *coegero*, non *amabo*.

8. Plural of Reverence
(L.-Hof. 372)

The plural of reverence (second person) is used in much the same way as the plural of majesty. It is usually employed in addressing the Eastern Emperor, kings, bishops, and many government officials.

Nouns in apposition with a noun or pronoun in the plural of reverence, or in the vocative accompanying it, are plural, e. g., 98, 2, 15, vobis debet iudicibus terminari . . . ; 310, 3, 2, Sed et vobis, gloriosi principes, . . . aliquid tamen additur.

Inconsistencies similar to those which have been noted in the plural of majesty occur here.

A participle in the plural may be used with a subject in the singular, e. g., 170, 4, 26, ut *aestimantes* omnia, quid fieri in tanta causa oporteat, *providentia vestra* reponat.

Possessive adjectives and relative pronouns may fail to agree in number with the subject, e. g., 171, 4, 20, ut sospitatem *vestram* divina concedant, *cuius* nobis animos validissime cognoscimus esse sociatos; 216, 2, 18, illum atque illum ad *vos* credidimus esse dirigendos, ut . . . qui *tuis* iussionibus obsecundant, etc.; 98, 2, 15, *vobis* debet iudicibus terminari, a *quo* expectanda est magis quam *vobis* imponenda iustitia.

Transitions from plural to singular in different sentences of the same document are more arbitrary than the similar transitions from plural of majesty to the singular. Thus, e. g., no rhetorical reason is evident in the following: 130, 1, 22 ff., Decet prudentiae *vestrae* curam subiectorum negotiis adhibere custodiam, quia *vobis ordinantibus* illa fieri debent quae regiam possunt demonstrare praesentiam. sic enim credimus, quia memor natalium *tuorum a te abicias* omne vitiosum et illa sola diligere *possis*, quae et nos amare *cognoscis*.

2

CHAPTER II

THE CASES

I. *The Vocative Case*
(L.-Hof. 373-374)

In the Variae no notable divergences from classical usage of the vocative case are observed. Where the distinct vocative form exists (in *o*-stem nouns in *-us*) the nominative is never employed for it. No example of the particle *O* with the vocative occurs. *Patres conscripti* is the usual form of address to the senate, as it was in Republican times, and is the most frequently occurring vocative usage. Two vocatives joined by *ac* are found, e. g., in 329, 14, 26, Exultate, Gothi pariter ac Romani. Where the separate vocative form exists, an attributive adjective with the vocative is always in the vocative form, as 319, 1, 17, clementissime imperator; 385, 9, 16, assuete iam bono Ligur.

In general the vocatives of the Variae occupy the normal classical position, i. e., near the beginning of the sentence (Cf. L.-Hof., 611). Usually from one to four words are found preceding the vocative in the sentence. However, in 302, 1, 23, Post primordia nostri imperii vobis feliciter nuntiata congrua nobis contigit, patres conscripti, causa sermonis . . . , ten words, forming an entire clause except for its subject, precede the vocative. The vocative itself is first in 116, 5, 30, parentes publici de clementia nominati, duplex vos ratio benignitatis invitet.

The most striking feature of Cassiodorus' employment of the vocative is the infrequency of its occurrence. Only 124 vocative expressions occur in the 470 documents of the Variae. *Patres conscripti* and words connected by *et* are counted as only one vocative expression. When we consider the nature of the letters, personal and official correspondence, much of it in the second person and embodying commands and prohibitions of the king and his high officials, we conclude that Cassiodorus is extremely sparing in his use of this case. This scarcity of vocatives is, however, due in some measure to the fact that in many instances the employment of a verb in the third person with the title of honor of the recipient of the letter, e. g., *illustris magnitudo vestra,* as subject, turns what is

10

logically a clause in the second person into one which is in the third and obviates the occasion that would otherwise exist for many more vocatives. The titles of honor themselves are never employed in the vocative case.

II. *The Nominative Case*

1. The Nominative as Subject

Aside from the tendency to omit a pronoun subject, even at the expense of clearness, the Variae show no peculiarities in the use of the nominative as subject.

Cassiodorus habitually omits such a pronoun subject where a relative follows, as in 15, 9, 3, Verum haec in illo jure mirentur, qui patris atque avi mores nobilissimos nesciverunt. The relative, as a rule, sufficiently identifies the subject of the main clause. For further discussion of the omission of the pronoun antecedent cf. p. 72.

In many other sentences where the relative plays no part the subject nominative is omitted, where clearness would demand its use. I shall discuss only the two following examples, which are typical of the author's frequent practice.

In 377, 2, 19, non admonitus facit quod vix rogatus impleret et requisitus non potest negare quod is cuius interest se fatetur amisisse, the reader is forced to search through previous sentences to find the subject of *facit, impleret,* and *potest.* Eventually he discovers that it is a *scriba,* the only expression of which occurs in the genitive plural, *scribarum officium* in 377, 1, 15.

A similar example is 84, 3, 19, Atque ideo praesenti auctoritate decernimus, ut, si vera fides est suggerentium nec aliquid publico nunc ornatui probatur accommodum, supra memoratas platonias vel columnas ad Ravennatem civitatem *contradat* modis omnibus devehendas. Here the person serving as subject of the subordinate verb *contradat* does not appear anywhere in the entire letter, and the reader must use context and a knowledge of circumstances gained from study of this and other letters to determine that such a word as *possessor* is to be supplied as subject.

The opposite tendency, viz., that of employing a personal pronoun subject unnecessarily, is discussed under Personal Pronouns,

p. 66. The construction known as the nominative with the infinitive is discussed under the Infinitive, p. 160.

2. *Opus* as Predicate Nominative

The nominative instead of the usual ablative occurs with *opus est* in 179, 4, 1, opus erit praeterea *firmitas* animi, ut a iustitiae tramite nullis muneribus, nullis terroribus auferatur. The meaning is that of *opus erit firmitate*, but the construction of *opus* is that of a predicate noun, with *firmitas* serving as the subject of *est*. This personal construction occurs as early as Plautus and Cato, not only with pronouns and adjectives (Cato, Agr. 143, *quae opus sunt,* etc.), but also with substantives (Plaut. Capt. 164, *milites opus sunt tibi*). Cicero uses this personal construction, but Caesar does not (L.-Hof., 436).

3. The Nominative in Exclamation

Early Latin shows occasional uses of the nominative to express an exclamation. Examples from Plautus, Ennius, and Terence are cited by Bennett, *Syntax of Early Latin,* II, p. 4. This usage continues throughout the Classical Period and into Silver and Late Latin, though the accusative is more frequently employed.

In the Variae both the nominative and the accusative of exclamation are employed, although the use of either case in exclamation is rare. The two cases occur with about equal frequency. In the forms where the case can be distinguished the exclamatory *O* occurs seven times with the accusative and five times with the nominative. In eleven instances the case of the (neuter) noun can not be distinguished. A few examples of nominatives following *en* and *heu* also occur. *Ecce,* where it occurs, is followed by an entire clause, not by an individual word (Cf. T. L. L., V, 2, 30, 75 ff.). The exclamation *pro dolor* occurs about five times.

Examples of the nominative in exclamation:

41, 10, 16, o artis inaestimabilis virtus, quae dum se dicit ludere, naturae praevalet secreta vulgare!
144, 2, 19, O vere vestris meritis electi et auspicio nominis honorati!
170, 12, 2, heu mundi error dolendus!
300, 4, 13, o animi nobilitas singularis! en aequitas mirabilis, quam mundus loquatur.

4. Anacolouthic Nominatives

(A) A nominative or a succession of nominatives can occur as the equivalent of a declarative or exclamatory sentence. These nominatives take no notice of the case of the same or equivalent words in the preceding sentence, but merely place words in the nominative case with no verb whatsoever. They can be resolved into the form of the declarative or exclamatory sentence by the addition of *est* or *sunt*.

Such examples are, 15, 9, 6, antiqua proles, laudata prosapies, cum togatis clari, inter viros fortes eximii; 15, 15, 33, genus in utroque orbe praeclarum; 31, 5, 15, consilium atrox, crudele praesidium, ferina concertatio. Also 19, 3, 4; 38, 3, 28; 48, 4, 21; 68, 4, 18; 72, 14, 16; 105, 3, 20; 174, 1, 4; 195, 3, 30; 213, 1, 9; 213, 2, 29; 241, 8, 5; 362, 3, 30; 367, 1, 4, etc.

The exclamatory nature of these examples is shown by the fact that they all convey the idea of admiration or strong indignation.

(B) Related to the previous group is one in which a new sentence or sentence-equivalent is not formed, but the nominative is found in apposition with a previous word which stands in one of the oblique cases. The construction belongs to Vulgar Latin (Inscr., Chiron) and is based upon the self-explanatory nature of the related word (L.-Hof., 637).

Only a few appositives of this kind occur in the Variae, e. g., 145, 1, 17, omnes enim, quos ad quaesturae *culmen* evehimus, doctissimos aestimamus . . . *dignitas,* quae nec divitiis nec solis natalibus invenitur, and 153, 3, 25, nunc praedictis rebus armamenta procurate, vela praecipue alas navium facientia, lignum volatile, *quidam spiritus* currentium carinarum, etc. Cf. 319, 5, 12; 367, 1, 6; 368, 2, 21, etc.

In a few of the examples noted, the case-transition follows an emphatic *inquam,* e. g., 240, 7, 21, ut . . . vulnera factorum suorum signa susciperet: vulnera inquam, opinio inseparabilis, sine assertore praeconium, propria lingua virtutis. . . . Cf. 287, 3, 22; 351, 3, 13. This would indicate that the writer has lost sight of the previous case-construction and is interested only in presenting the simple noun-idea as vividly as possible. Therefore he uses the nominative. Participles in the nominative in logical agreement with substantives in other cases are discussed under the Participle, p. 177.

(C) Nominative Absolute. The nominative absolute construction also had its origin in anacolouthon (L.-Hof., 409), but in Late Latin had become fixed as a regular usage. The author might then purposely employ it just as he would the ablative absolute with no confusion in his thought and without the consciousness of doing any violence to Latin construction. Its use possibly begins in Early Latin, one example being cited from the Law of the Twelve Tables (C. Mohrmann, in *Glotta*, XXI (1933), 39). It also occurs in Bell. Afr. 25, 1; Calp. his. 27; Lucifer, Chiron, Prisc., Peregr. Ether., Vict. Vit., Ennod., etc., and in inscriptions (L.-Hof., 449). Mohrmann gives several examples from the Sermons of St. Augustine.

Four clear examples appear in the Variae, three with a future participle and one with a present participle.

61, 2, 9, nam si coemptam speciem expensis publicis necessariam non habetis, ab officio vestro suscepta modiatio fideliter distrahatur: eventum rei *ratio fiscalis habitura*.

81, 4, 22, Pendebant quin immo circa eos anxia vota civitatis, crescens supra privatos publicus *amor*.

98, 2, 5, instructam personam ad comitatum nostrum dirigere se promittat, qui apud delegatos motu nostro iudices eius intentionibus valeat praebere responsum: *actor* hic poenam suae *recepturus* audaciae, si contra magnificum virum habuerit falsitatis eventum.

157, 25,   Schola Martia mittat examina: *pugnaturus* ludo, *qui* se exercere consuevit in otio.

For a full discussion of the free or absolute use of the nominative and the psychological background of this usage, see C. Mohrmann, *Glotta*, XXI (1933), *Die psychologischen Bedingungen der konstruktionslosen Nominativi im Lateinischen.*

(D) Another type of anacolouthic nominative appears in 32, 4, 25, definimus, ut *amatores* Helladii, quem de medio saltare praecepimus sine utriusque partis studio, spectandi *eis*, ubi delegerint, libera sit facultas. The nominative *amatores* is given an emphatic position and anticipates the reference to these persons in another case (*eis*) which is to follow (Cf. L.-Hof., 449).

III. *The Accusative Case*

1. Intransitive Verbs Used Transitively
(L.-Hof. 376-378)

Latin inherited from Indo-European a use of verbs with the accusative and a use of verbs with the dative; sometimes the same verb admitted either case. As a general rule the use of the accusative gained ground, until in Late Latin many verbs, formerly simple intransitives or used with the dative or other cases, now took the accusative.

The following verbs are found with the accusative in the Variae. In classical prose they either do not exist or they occur with other cases or are simple intransitives.

considere 64, 2, 18, vastitatem, quam . . . quoddam mare paludestre consedit.
> 195, 3, 33, considis geniatum tribunal.
> No similar example found in T. L. L., IV, 435, 31, under *de rebus*, but T. L. L., IV, 434, 20, notes the passage in 195, 3, 33, as the only example of the accusative with this verb under " de iis penes quos arbitrium est, inprimis de iudicibus."

consuescere, with *the thing to which one becomes accustomed* as object, 27, 3, 32, ne molle otium consuescant.
> No similar example found.

with *the thing which is made accustomed to something* as object, 36, 2, 6, novellos ungues in praedam teneram consuescunt.
> Poetic and Late. Lucr. 6, 397, *bracchia consuescant,* Col., Chiron, Prud., Paul. Petric., Cass., and Ps. Prosp. (T. L. L., IV, 551, 76).

convenire 58, 4, 16, devotio tua praefatum Domitium moderata executione conveniat.
> Cels., Iulian., Venul., Gaius, etc. (T. L. L., IV, 830, 3 ff. This passage cited, 830, 81).

defluere 12, 7, 9, umorem sanguineum defluentia ora.
> Only previous citation is Ambr., 2, 10, 109, *silva quae verbi caelestis alimoniam defluxit.* (T. L. L., V, 363, 37).

deviare 12, 3, 29, mentes ab obstinatione praecipiti deviasti
> Late Latin word (T. L. L., V, 864, 1 ff.); passive in Serv., Cassian. (T. L. L., V, 864, 83).

discurrere 33, 2, 24, solis reflexus australia signa discurrens
> Late Latin usage. Amm., Macr. somn., Arnob., Cass., Eustath., Bas. hex. (T. L. L., V, 1367, 50).

egredi 174, 6, 23, lares proprios etiam calceis auratus egredere.
> *Egredi* with accusative occurs once in Caesar, civ.; once in Sallust,

Iug.; then in Val. Max., Sen., Tac. etc. (K.-Steg., II, 1, 271;
T. L. L., V, 285, 5, 3).

evadere 71, 10, 29, pericula . . . evaderet
Mostly Poetic and post-Aug. prose; not in Cic. Cited for Verg.,
Ov., Liv., Suet. etc. (Harpers').

exire 366, 1, 15, quod iura domini nescit exire
Poetic and post-Aug. prose (Harpers'). Ter., Verg., and especially
Ovid, who uses it with *modum,* in met. 9, 632 (K.-Steg., II,
1, 272).

incurrere, literally, 71, 10, 24, eligebant . . . scopulos incurrere
So used in Sallust. frag. apud Rufin. de Schem. Lex., Tac. ann. 1,
51 (Harpers').
tropically, 23, 2, 24, nec moram fas est incurrere iussionem
Lact., Sid. (Harpers'). Liv. and often in Late Latin. Regularly
with *in* and acc. (K.-Steg., II, 1, 267).

incursare 123, 2, 6, si manus non incursarint exigentum
In with acc. is classical. Acc. alone in Plaut., Liv., Tac. (K.-Steg.,
II, 1, 267).

indigere 54, 4, 28, indiges suffragia. Also 237, 1, 28 and 382, 1, 21.
Cf. use with abl. p. 41. With acc. it is ante-class. Varr. ling. is
only citation (Harpers').

nocere, 90, 4, 8, Castorium . . . nocere temptaverit
Also 251, 3, 16. Found in Sammon. 828; Inscr. Or. 824 and eccl.
(K.-Steg., II, 1, 103), Vulg. Luc. 4, 35 and Act. 7, 26; 18, 10.
Personal passive occurs in Vitr., Sen. Justin., Apul. met., Ulp.
dig., Solin. (K.-Steg., II, 1, 103). Cassiodorus also uses the
dative, e. g., 186, 4, 31.

obstupescere 69, 11, 20, quae . . . obstupescas
Silver and Late. This place only citation (Harpers'). Stat. Theb.
3, 519, silv. 3, 143 (K.-Steg., II, 1, 263).

pavescere 366, 2, 8, chlamides non pavescant
Silver and Late Latin usage. Sil. 16, 127 (Harpers'). Since Tac.
hist. 4, 47; ann. 1, 4 (K.-Steg., II, 1, 263).

perexire 336, 6, 2, non te tamquam vacuam fistulam dicta perexeant.
Harpers' calls the verb neuter and irregular and cites only this
passage. L.-Hof. and K.-Steg. do not mention it. The verb is
not neuter, but active. Occurs thus in Chalcid. Tim. 80 and in
Interpr. Iren. (Georges), also in Pereg. Aeth. IV.

perquirere 161, 1, 32, quem a diversis iudicibus fecimus iusta examin-
natione perquiri.
The passive construction shows that the active would have accusative. Harpers' gives no example of person as object. K.-Steg.,
II, 1, 302, gives only *perquirere ab aliquo,* citing only Cael. 53.

praecedere, literally, 100, 1, 3, supplicationem praecedit humanitas.
Poetic and in post-Aug. prose. Verg., Liv., Sen., Suet., Iust. etc.
(Harpers'; K.-Steg., II, 1, 272).

tropically = *excel,* 175, 4, 25, Praefectorios et aliarum dignitatum
viros praecedit.
> Once in Caes. Gall., 1, 1, 4. Otherwise Silver, Late. Liv., Val.
> Max., Plin., Vulg.

refluere 240, 7, 25, conflictus virorum fortium mutua tela refluit.
> Word is Poetic and in post-Aug. prose. In all citations the
> verb is neuter. Harpers', K.-Steg., and L.-Hof. do not men-
> tion it.

2. The Double Accusative

Exigere occurs frequently governing the double accusative, e. g.,
166, 14, 6, *subvectiones* exigere *eos.* Several other examples occur
with the person as object, or, where the verb is passive, as subject, e. g., 67, 3, 19, nititur *nudatos* exigere and 288, 5, 5, plus
exigitur *heres* bonorum.

The passive use is found in Caecilius and Metellus; the active
first occurs in Late Latin (L.-Hof., 383).

A pasisve form of *exorare* occurs with " retained accusative "
in 61, 1, 27, exorati iustum. The double accusative with this verb
occurs in rare instances from the time of Plautus (L.-Hof., 383).
All citations in Harpers' and K.-Steg., II, 1, 299 are poetic.

A passive form of *commonere* has an accusative of the thing in
34, 2, 26, Illud etiam . . . commonemur. The usage of this verb
with the accusative of a neuter pronoun is mentioned in K.-Steg.,
II, 1, 303 as regular. T. L. L., III, 1932, 79 cites only Plaut.
Pseud. 150 and Aug. trin. 14, 12, 16, in a similar usage with the
passive.

3. The Accusative of Inner Object

Examples such as *vitam vivere* seem to be totally absent from the
Variae. *Reliqua* occurs in 17, 3, 18, *Reliqua* vero . . . ad nostrum
comitatum festinus occurre. L. Hof., classifies this use as one of
inner object after the model of *cetera.* The usage begins with
Iul. Val. and is continued by later writers.

Here too belong the use of *aliquid,* as in 19, 7, 30, aliquid, si
potes, imminue; of *quid,* as in 31, 4, 10, quid enim discrepat a
peccante . . . ?

4. The Accusative of Limit of Motion
(L.-Hof. 386)

The accusative of limit of motion without a preposition with names of towns, with *domum, rus,* etc., does not seem to occur in the Variae. Its absence is to be accounted for, not only by the use of the preposition instead of the simple accusative, but by the total avoidance of expressions which would require its use. Thus names of towns are rare and are usually in adjectival form, e. g., 153, 4, 31, ad urbem Ravennatem, where the use of the preposition is classical. *Domum* and *rus* do not occur.

5. The Accusative of Duration of Time and Extent of Space
(L.-Hof. 381-382)

Ablative uses and prepositional uses have completely usurped the place of the accusative in expressing these ideas. Cf. p. 50 and p. 105.

6. The Accusative in Exclamation
(L.-Hof. 385-386)

Seven examples occur, all with the Interjection *O*. They have been mentioned in connection with the similar use of the nominative, p. 12.

IV. *The Genitive Case*
1. The Partitive Genitive
(L.-Hof. 388-392)

The partitive genitive is found in the Variae depending on nouns, pronouns, adjectives used substantively, and adverbs used substantively. Classical Latin uses the partitive under similar circumstances, and in general Cassiodorus' use of the partitive is classical.

A. With Nouns.

The partitive occurs frequently. A few peculiar uses are noted:

15, 11, 13, in omni consilii parte $=$ *in toto consilio.*

15, 15, 31, in partibus Orientis. Here *partibus* means *regions,* and the genitive is rather one of apposition or a subjective genitive. Cf. Salonius, 95-96.

18, 2, 27, Domestici partis equitum et peditum. Here *partis* means *party* or *class* and is itself a partitive genitive.

143, 1, 6, harum media. The use of *media* as a noun with a partitive genitive is Late Latin.

280, 9, 23, servientium quascumque personas. The indefinite *quascumque* influences the genitive, but the dependence is upon the noun, *personas.*

B. With Interrogative and Indefinite Pronouns. All uses are classical.

3, 2, 8, quid periculi
68, 2, 2, quivis hominum
69, 9, 13, radicum quidam
95, 2, 2, quae enim urbium
157, 24,   quod . . . virtutis
257, 2, 20, si quos Gothorum atque Romanorum
260, 7, 10, aliquas . . . avium
280, 9, 22, quis . . . patriarcharum

C. With Adjectives.

a. Numeral, etc.

29, 2, 13, unus eorum.
        With *unus* the partitive is rare in Caesar and Cicero. Classical Latin regularly uses *de* or *ex*.
135, 4, 26, nullum . . . saionum
178, 1, 12, nullus . . . iudicum
179, 5, 37, nemo iudicum
261, 3, 11, nonnullos fontium. Classical.
319, 1, 19, nemo vestrorum
372, 5, 4, nemo piscium
        Nullus and *nemo* with partitives are rather frequent in Early Latin, rare in Classical. *Nullus* becomes more frequent in the Silver Period (L.-Hof., 391). The use of *nemo* in place of *nullus* with reference to things is Late Latin, e. g., Prud. perist., 10, 744.
270, 3, 13, soli sunt hominum.
        I have found no example elsewhere of the partitive with *soli*.

b. With Superlative (and ellipsis of noun on which the partitive depends). L.-Hof., 390.

213, 1, 25, subtilissima perquisitionis
231, 1, 2, clementissime principum
311, 1, 14, Augustarum prudentissima
342, 3, 10, piissime principum
372, 1, 15, prima urbium

c. With Neuter Plural Adjectives used Substantively. Rare in classical prose, more frequent in Livy and especially in Tacitus (K.-Steg., II, 1, 433).

```
25,  2, 17,  inania verborum
30,  1, 23,  discriminis . . . ultima
87, 18,      ambigua iurgiorum
153, 4, 30,  mundi . . . ignota
223, 1, 12,  subreptionum iniquissima
254, 3, 24,  reliqua . . . patrimonii
275, 1, 10,  saeva discussionis
297, 1,  3,  tristia nuntiorum
349, 1, 11,  laboris incerta
360, 4, 33,  gremiorum celsa
361, 4,  1,  vitiorum humilia
```

d. With Neuter Singular Adjectives used Substantively. Rare in classical prose except in Sallust. More frequent in poets and in Livy and later prose writers (L.-Hof., 389; K.-Steg., II, 1, 432-433).

Examples are few in the Variae, e. g., 4, 9, 18, in obscurum silentii. Cf. Verg. georg. 1, 478, *sub obscurum noctis.*

D. With Adverbs.

282, 3, 5, quocumque loci. A type belonging to Colloquial Latin, where *loci* is used with *ubi, unde, quo,* and other adverbs of place (L.-Hof., 389).

2. The Possessive Genitive

Cassiodorus usually employs this genitive in the classical manner. A few expressions are listed below where the genitive connotes other ideas along with possession. No ellipsis of the nouns denoting the thing possessed occur, as they may in classical Latin, e. g., Cic. Cluent. 94, *Fausto Sullae (filio)* and Ter. Ad. 582, *ad Dianae (fanum).* The full expression without ellipsis appears in 256, 1, 27, Quidilanem Sibiae filium, and in 271, 2, 13, Agenantiam uxorem Campaniani viri disertissimi. A proper adjective is often used in place of a possessive genitive, as in 315, 1, 6, ripam Ticinensem et Placentinam, and in 328, 6, 19, Romani eloquii (Cf. p. 52). *Sui* as a possessive genitive is dealt with under Reflexive Pronouns, p. 86.

In 10, 5, 24, we find the possessive genitive instead of a dative of possession, Romani *regni* unum velle, una semper opinio sit.

In 34, 3, 4, we have the possessive genitive with the added idea of place, Indici *maris* conchae.

In 80, 3, 5, proximarum *gentium* imminentia bella means *cum proximis gentibus imminentia bella.*

In 106, 11, 24, Cetera *circi* Romani (where the genitive may be partitive) the meaning is *cetera de circo Romano.*

In 118, 19, multorum se iniuriis testantur exponi = *injuries to be inflicted by many.*

The predicate use is also classical, as in 130, 1, 5, Providentissimi principis est . . . relinquere, and in 261, 1, 28, Sicut incognita velle nosse *prudentis* est.

3. The Genitive of Definition
(L.-Hof. 394-395; K.-Steg. II, 1, 418-420)

The terms, genitive of definition and genitive of apposition, are employed without clear differentiation in the various grammars (L.-Hof., 394-395; K.-Steg., II, 1, 418 ff.). From one or both of these genitives develops the genitive of identity. I have followed here the practice of Juret, 73, where the divisions are clearly marked. A few examples are cited separately, which do not fall with exactness within any of these three categories. The latter type is mentioned in Leumann-Hofmann, 395, as a development from the genitive of definition, but to be kept distinct from the normal types.

The genitive of definition is a classical construction, used by Cicero and Caesar. It is related to the genitive of possession. The genitive serves the purpose of defining the noun on which it depends, much after the manner of true apposition. (Treatment and examples in K.-Steg., II, 1, 418-419.)

This genitive occurs with great frequency in the Variae. The following examples are typical of the usage:

  5, 16, 20, eloquentis . . . nomen
 19, 5, 20, unciae . . . appellatione
 35, 1, 2, homicidii facinus
 48, 4, 19, virtutum radicibus
 62, 3, 19, Vocabulum principis
 96, 2, 15, vectigal . . . fidei
132, 1, 27, pietatis remedio
146, 7, 21, quaesturae culmine

217, 3, 1, (and elsewhere) comitivae honorem
372, 6, 8, defensio veritatis
Gerunds occur as genitives of definition, e. g., in 71, 6, 3, audiendi epulas, and 201, 2, 10, puniendi remedium.

4. The Genitive of Apposition
(L.-Hof. 394-395)

With the two exceptions noted below, I have limited my usage of this term to the genitive occurring instead of apposition in names of places, as the type *arbor fici* etc., which developed out of this genitive, do not occur in the Variae.

The construction is explained as originally a genitive of possession, the genitive being the name of the deity of the place. It is not found in Caesar or Cicero, but is cited for Bell. Afr., Livy, Verg., Vitruv., Tac., etc. (L.-Hof., 394). Cassiodorus employs it in conformity with the usage of these authors. Examples:

24, 2, 10, Sonti fluenta
28, 2, 10, portum Licini
48, 3, 15, Aonii . . . fonte
64, 4, 27, loca . . . Decemnovii
86, 2, 30, provinciam . . . Samnii
274, 1, 25, Dalmatiarum atque Saviae provincias.

It is probably under the influence of this construction that the name of a people is used in the genitive in 73, 1, 2, gentem Francorum. The same explanation is given by Juret, 73, for the genitive in the name of a book, *librum Sapientiae.* Cassiodorus has in 5, 17, 23, ut merito variarum dicatur. Here there is an evident ellipsis of *liber,* and *variarum* may be regarded as a proper name. This may, however, be a genitive of definition, especially since in 5, 15, 9, he uses the words *variarum nomine.*

5. The Genitive of Identity
(L.-Hof. 395)

Many Late Latin writers frequently added to a noun a definitive or appositional genitive of kindred meaning. This genitive is called the genitive of identity. It differs from the genitive of definition and the genitive of apposition in this that the added genitive in most cases does not serve to define the word to which it is attached, but either the genitive or the word on which it depends is unnecessary. Classical prose has not a trace of the usage. Single examples are found in Lucretius and Catullus, several in Propertius and Vitruvius, while it is frequent in Apuleius, Tertullian, Cyprian and many later writers.

Cassiodorus contributes a considerable number of examples. The following show real identity:

3, 5,16, dictationis eloquium
31, 1,20, voluptatum laetitiam
50, 1, 5, Deliberationis . . . consilium
53, 2, 8, mora tergiversationis
53, 2,17, amplexu copulae
58, 2, 9, aquarum . . . liquores
63, 3,29, commercium negotiationis
90,16, consuetudinis mos
127, 2,19, aedium habitatio
168, 3,27, deceptionis errorem
206, 4, 2, fistularum uberibus
238, 4,11, chlamydum vestis
354, 4,16, necis exitus

These have nearly identical words:

115, 3,28, laboris . . . obsequium
189, 2, 3, monumenta chartarum
334, 1, 4, saporis . . . dulcedinem
348, 8, palmae praemia.

Of the type *vultus furoris*, already occurring in Silver Latin (discussed in L.-Hof., 394, 2) are 70, 4, 24, votum furoris; 102, 1, 21, rixam verborum; 212, 2, 31, necessitas iniustitiae; 306, 6, 34, votum puritatis; 385, 8, 8, praedicationis eventum.

6. The Genitive in Temporal Expressions
(L.-Hof. 395)

The genitive occurs in two types of temporal expressions in the Variae, e. g., in 27, 2, 27, octavo die kalendarum Iuliarum, and in 214, 18, kal. Martiarum diem. Both are classical. The first is on the model of Cic. Sull. 52, *posterum diem nonarum Novembrium*. The second may be regarded as a genitive of definition.

7. The Genitive in Local Expressions

In 188, 2, 15, intra quadragesimum sacratissimae urbis iura custodis, the genitive of the *point of departure* is a Late Latin development from the genitive used in the temporal expressions. It is found first in Eutropius, 1, 15, *usque ad quintum milliarium urbis.* Ellipsis of the substantive denoting the measure is cited first for Macr. sat. 6, 644, and secondly for Cassiodorus (this passage) in L.-Hof., 395, 4.

8. The Objective Genitive
(L.-Hof. 396)

The objective genitive was first used in dependence on abstract nouns derived from transitive verbs. Its use is extended to root-nouns and nouns not related to a verb. It may serve as a substitute for any of the case-relations. Poets and their prose imitators use it freely where classical prose would employ a preposition.

This genitive occurs frequently in the Variae. Examples:

A. Dependent on Verbal Derivatives.

161, 3, 25, defensorem rei publicae
178, 3, 29, imitator . . . antiquorum
225, 1, 18, Institutio divinarum legum

B. Dependent on Nouns not derived from Transitive Verbs.

15, 15, 31, parentum laude
47,   5, 27, fiducia sui
66,   1, 17, supplicii . . . terrorem
119, 3, 19, patrocinium tenuitatis
174, 2, 11, potestas necis
204, 2, 15, fabricandi peritia

C. Instead of Prepositional Phrases.

13,	4,	2,	invidia lucri	= ex lucro
14,	4,	9,	amministrationis introitus	= ad amministrationem
14,	5, 15,	recti persuasor	= ad rectum
16,	2, 20,	fundi controversia	= de fundo
21,	2, 17,	dogmatis opinione	= ob dogma
88,	2, 33,	hostium conversatione	= cum hostibus
100,	1, 16,	cura rerum	= de rebus
108,	8, 3,	finium lis	= de finibus
190,	2, 20,	querela panis [1]	= de pane
271,	1, 31,	pretii . . . contentio	= de pretio
329,	12, 18,	affinium bella	= cum affinibus

---

[1] Cic. Pis. 1, 1 has *querela* with objective genitive.

D. Instead of the Dative.

Cassiodorus uses either the objective genitive or the dative after the words *praefectus* and *praefecturae*. He consistently calls the prefect of the city *praefectus urbis* instead of the common classical *praefectus urbi*, e. g., 31, 4, 9 ; 31, 2, 27 ; 281, 11, 4, and titles of many documents. The praetorian prefect is regularly *praefectus praetorio*. Cf., e. g., 146, 2, 31 ; 154, 3, 23 ; 314, 2, 5 and the abbreviation PPO in the titles of many documents. *Praefectus praetorii* occurs, however, e. g., 59, 2, 21. In the titles of Formulae VII and VIII of Book VII the words *Praefecturae Vigilum* occur. Within the same formulae we find in 206, 2, 30, *praefecturae vigilibus* and in 207, 1, 18, *praefectos vigilibus*.

9. The Genitive of Quality
(L.-Hof. 397-400)

The genitive of quality and the ablative of quality are perhaps of common origin, and, except for minor differences in their usage, their functions are practically identical. Until the end of the classical period the ablative is the more frequent. The genitive gains the ascendancy in Silver and Late Latin. In some authors, not only in the Late period, but even in Silver Latin the ablative has almost entirely disappeared. Cf. K.-Steg., II, 1, 455.

A. With an Attribute. Cassiodorus has the genitive frequently in the adnominal usage, rarely in the adverbial. Scarcely any certain examples of the ablative of quality occur.

Examples of the genitive of quality in the classical manner:

(a) Adnominal.

18, 2, 29, integri ponderis solidos
55, 1, 3, bonae indolis viros
116, 3, 22, unius loci vir
364, 8, 36, homines vel mediocris intelligentiae

(b) Adverbial.

81, 3, 20, cum multae probarentur esse potentiae,
368, 1, 11, Probatae debet esse conscientiae,

The genitive of quality with proper names is very rare in classical prose, but occurs more frequently in Silver and Late Latin and in inscriptions (L.-Hof., 398).

101,1, 7, beatae recordationis quondam Simplicium
122,2, 6, praecelsae recordationis Alaraci praecepta
241,3,31, gloriosae memoriae Theodericum
267,1, 4, divae recordationis Amalafridam
319,2,26, commendatio divae memoriae Amalasuinthae

B. Without an Attribute. The genitive of quality without an attribute does not occur in Early Latin or in classical prose. It occurs in Phaedrus, Ps. Quintilian, Apuleius, Tertullian, and many later writers. Very few examples occur in the Variae, e. g.

14, 8,30, innocentiae virum
32,1,10, viros . . . virtutum
46,3,16, gravitatis factus est filius
258,3, 4, momenti iura

10. The Genitive of the Charge
(L.-Hof. 402-403)

With *verba iudicialia* the charge is often expressed by a genitive. To the usual verbs, *accuso, condemno,* etc., Cassiodorus adds *impeto,* e. g., 124, 3, 27, Et si rei criminis *cuius* impetuntur, fuerint approbati, etc.

With *reus* the same genitive was used. Before Quintilian only *facti* and *capitis* occurred in the genitive with *reus*. Other words denoting the charge or the penalty were added by later writers.

Cassiodorus has *criminis* in the above example, 124, 3, 27. In 124, 3, 11, we find *rei abditi atque secreti*. The understood noun here seems to be *facti*.

11. The Genitive with Adjectives
(L.-Hof. 403-406)

The genitive with adjectives is partly of objective nature and partly a freer use of the genitive of reference.

A. The following, though rather rare, are classical uses:

conscius   326, 3, 14, Facile enim absolutor est alieni conscius sui.
familiaris   341, 2, 20, quod est familiare semper absentium,
imperitus   66, 13, imperitis . . . harum rerum,
inimicus   As this occurs in 352, 5, 18, humanorum actuum servans fidele testimonium, praeteritorum loquax, oblivionis inimica, it is natural to take it for an adjective. Cf. Cic. Tusc. 4, 15, *animorum motus inimicissimi mentis* (Harpers').
proprius   159, 3, 30, Sed nos quorum est proprium . . . custodire,

Both genitive and dative occur with *proprius* in the Variae, genitive more frequently.

Similis takes genitive or dative without apparent distinction in meaning (passim). The use of either case is rare, the genitive occurring about six times, the dative three.

B. The genitive does not occur with the following in classical prose:

idoneus 286, 5, 25, donec suscepti operis idoneus reperitur.
    K.-Steg., II, 1, 315, and II, 1, 384, shows a classical absolute use, a use with *ad,* a use with the dative, none with the genitive, and none with *de.* In the Variae the word occurs several times absolutely, with the dative, e. g. 50, 1, 8, eight times with *ad.* These uses are classical. It occurs with *de* and the abl. in 163, 2, 12. It occurs with the gen. in the above, 286, 5, 25. These uses are non-classical.

largissimus 247, 1, 32, a domino largissimo beneficiorum.
    (Harpers' mentions *largus* with gen. occurring in Plaut., Verg., Luc., and Sil.)

loquax 352, 5, 18, praeteritorum loquax,
    Through the influence of the genitive with present participles, in Silver and Late Latin the genitive was used with verbal adjectives in *-ax. Capax* with gen. begins with Ovid and Livy (L.-Hof., 406). Harpers' cites Tert. apol. 16, *mendaciorum loquacissimus.*

C. The employment of a present participle with a genitive was fully developed as early as Plautus. Sallust and Livy were the first to use it frequently in prose (L.-Hof., 405). The use of the genitives listed below is explained by the substantival nature of the participles, as they do not come from verbs that take the genitive.

abstinens 193, 2, 11, abstinens est iugiter alieni.
    (Quint. apud Lact. inst. 6, 23, 20, *neque alieni matrimonii abstinens neque sui custos.* T. L. L., I, 198, 15.)

continens 288, 4, 31, alieni continens

potens 15, 11, 13, *armorum potentem,* and 168, 3, 31, *Erebi potentem.*
    Use of the genitive begins with Plaut.; in prose, with Livy (L.-Hof., 405).

12. The Genitive with Verbs
(L.-Hof. 406-409)

Of the various types of genitives with verbs few examples are found in the Variae. Only in a few instances is the scarcity of these genitives due to the employment of another case for the genitive. The verbs themselves which take a genitive in the earlier Latin rarely occur.

A. Verbs of Remembering and Forgetting. I have noted only *oblitus* in 123, 1, 31, oblitus pietatis. It is used in the classical sense of *completely disregarding*. The accusative occurs after infinitive forms of the verb in 34, 1, 25, qui mortuorum fidem non possumus oblivisci, and 97, 3, 16, qui impensa servitia non possumus oblivisci. The accusative is frequently found even in classical prose to denote a thing as object, though the participle *oblitus* regularly takes the genitive (K.-Steg., II, 1, 471). Cassiodorus' usage in these examples is therefore classical.

B. Verbs of Reminding. Not found with genitive. *Commonere* and *ammonere* occur with *de* and the ablative, e. g., 180, 3, 31, monetamque facis de nostris temporibus futura saecula commonere, and 194, 2, 8, ut . . . de vigore semper principis ammonerent.

C. *Misereri* occurs only once and then with a dative, 71, 8, 17, ut . . . miserantur errantibus.

D. Impersonal Verbs of Feeling. None occur with a genitive denoting the cause of the feeling. *Paenitet* is used with a personal subject, 314, 4, 13, ut tali facto eam non paeniteret mutata religio.

The personal usage of *paenitet* is in imitation of a similar usage of *pudet* in Early Latin, but came into use much later, being cited for Corippus (fl. 565) and Cassiodorus in L.-Hof., 407, 3. *Pudet* and *piget* occur with an infinitive as subject, e. g., 14, 8, 32; 25, 1, 9; 221, 1, 21; 301, 8, 5; 370, 4, 26. The usage is classical. *Taedet* does not occur.

E. *Interest* takes the genitive of the person concerned, as it does in Classical Latin. It occurs rather frequently, e. g., 61, 1, 28, in qua divinae reverentiae credimus interesse; 146, 2, 33, (and frequently) quorum interest.

Cf. use of *interest* with dative, p. 30.

F. The impersonal *refert* does not occur.

13. Genitive with *causa, gratia, instar, propter*
(L.-Hof. 496; 505)

The genitive with prepositions appears in Latin only with improper, recent prepositions of substantival origin (L.-Hof., 496, 1).

Causa and *gratia* are of this origin. So is *instar*, which was originally an infinitive used substantively. *Propter*, however, owes its origin to *prope*.

In the Variae the genitive with *causā* and *gratiā* occurs as in Classical Latin, e. g., 61, 1, 3, probitatis gratiā and 117, 1, 19, studiorum causā. The genitive may, however, follow, as in 170, 3, 16, causā misericordiae. *Causā* in this position occurs once in Ennius, once in Terence, and is more frequent in Late Latin. In 163, 2, 14, in quos contigerit a militia morbi causā suspendi, *causā* preceded by a genitive has the meaning *because of, owing to*.

Instar with the genitive occurs in 106, 7, 6, ad instar solis, and in 214, 10, proditionis instar. . . . The genitive with *instar* is classical, but the use of *ad instar* is Late Latin (L.-Hof., 496, 2).

On the analogy of *causā*, *propter* occurs with a genitive in a few instances in Late Latin, e. g., Fulg. myth. 1, praef., p. 8, 14, *itineris propter* and Marcell. chron. II, 462, p. 88, 14, *sui propter* (L.-Hof., 505, 1). It occurs in the Variae, paired with *causa misericordiae*, 170, 3, 16, si causa misericordiae susceptus est . . . si nostri propter expulsus est, etc.

The position of *propter* in this sentence, i. e., postpositive, is frequent both in Early and Late Latin.

V. *The Dative Case*

1. The Dative with Verbs
(L.-Hof. 410-412)

The dative with verbs is of frequent occurrence. Its frequency is due in some measure to the author's preference for the dative where Classical Latin requires or prefers another construction—usually a preposition with the accusative or ablative—and in some measure to his employing the dative with verbs which do not occur in classical prose, or at least in the sense in which he uses them.

A. The following is a list of prepositional compounds which take the dative where classical prose employs another construction:

			Classical Construction.
adquiescere	83, 2, 22,	si fraudatis *oblationibus* adquiescat,	*in* with abl.; abl. alone. Dative is colloquial.
applicare	105, 2, 19,	victoria equorum *meritis* non potest applicari	*ad* with acc.

Classical Construction.

arridere	81, 5, 4, quem vestris *utilitatibus* arridere cognoscitis,	Accusative classical. Dative is colloquial; in prose since Livy.
contendere	95, 2, 2, quae enim urbium audeat tuis *culminibus* contendere?	*cum* with abl.
degenerare	39, 4, 24, pudor est degenerasse *prioribus*	*ab* with abl. Dative is poetic.
illigare	71, 10, 28, se . . . *soliditati* arboris illigavit	*in* with acc. or *in* with abl.
impendere	95, 1, 7, *rei publicae* . . . curam desideremus impendere	*ad* or *in* with acc.
incidere	281, 3, 21, senatus consulta *tabulis* . . . incidi	*in* with abl.; *in* with acc. Dative is poetic and Late.
incumbere	54, 4, 30, incumbe ergo talibus *studiis.*	*in* with acc.
infundere	12, 3, 25, te nostris *sensibus* infuderunt	*in* with acc.
ingerere	310, 2, 24, quicquid . . . *sensibus* ingeramus	Dative is Silver and Late Latin. Tac., Petr., Suet., etc.
insinuare	78, 4, 19, qui *vobis* et mandata nostra sufficienter insinuent	*in, ad, inter* with acc. Dative with intransitive use.
insistere	123, 1, 22, efficaciam tuam insistere credamus *iniunctis.*	acc. or *in* with acc. Dative in Tib., Tac., etc.
interesse	340, 1, 14, nec interest *talibus* an sumere cibum an sustinere ieiunium	Genitive.
observare	136, 6, 3, *His* . . . te observare praecipimus,	Accusative classical. Dative occurs several times in Variae where the verb = *servire.* Cf. Traube, 563.
postponere	194, 3, 16, *cui* tot videntur nobiles . . . postponi,	Absolute use. Dative in poets and Late prose.
praeterfluere	103, 2, 26, *huic* Athesis inter fluvios honorus . . . praeterfluit.	Accusative.
proficere	133, 1, 10, nos . . . *quibus* universorum hominum proficiunt incrementa	Absolute use or *in* with acc.

		Classical Construction.
reponere	254, 1, 17, hoc vere *thesauris* reponimus quod famae commodis applicamus.	*in* with acc. or *in* with abl.

B. The following simple verbs take the dative, where classical prose employs another construction:

mereri	159, 1, 6, qui bene *nobis* meriti fuerint	*De* with abl. (Plaut. *erga* with acc.). Dative in one inscription. (Georges.)
misereri	71, 8, 17, ut . . . misereantur *errantibus*	Genitive is classical. Dative is Late. Hyg., Diom. etc.
sociari	151, 6, 17, *mulieribus* . . . nuptiali foedere sociari	*cum* with abl. Dative is poetic and in Livy and Late writers.

C. The following verbs used here with the dative either do not occur in Classical Prose or occur in other meanings.

		Relation to Classical Usage.
adiacere	70, 1, 4, adiacet enim *vobis* doctum eligere	Classical citations are for its use in literal sense with acc. alone or *ad* with acc.
associare	242, 1, 17, *sollicito* talis associandus fuit,	Late Latin word. Dative in Iuvenc., Claud., Dig. etc.
augmentare	276, 2, 7, subtrahimus pecuniae quod augmentetur *gloriae*	Late Latin word. Paul. Fest., Fulg., Ambrosiaster, etc.
competere	98, 1, 12, partem . . . *sibimet* legibus competentem	Late in sense of *belong to*. Dig., Iust. Inst. etc.
connasci	82, 1, 14, laus *nobilitati* connascitur	Late Latin word. Hil., Mar. Merc. etc.
copulari	35, 2, 10, pro copulatis *sibi* animas ponunt	Silver and Late.
deputare	117, 1, 31, ut hominis *vitio* deputetur	Early, Silver and Late in sense of *attribute*. Late Latin uses *ad* with Accusative. Dative also used.

			Relation to Classical Usage.
exponere	118, 19,	se *iniuriis* testantur exponi	Silver and Late in sense of *expose to.* *Ad* in Livy; dative in Tac., etc.
illidere	258, 2, 15,	ne . . . unda vestris *aedibus* illidatur	Word poetic and Silver. Dative in Verg., Hor., Ov., Suet.
immorari	104, 4, 4,	delphini . . . vadosis *litoribus* immorantur	Word Silver and Late. Dative in Col., Plin.
imputare	51, 2, 12,	*rationibus* imputari	Word Silver and Late. Dative in Sen., Tac. etc.
iniungere	83, 1, 29,	quod *ei* constat iniungi	Used thus with dat. from Livy on.
inspirare	170, 1, 7,	deo *nobis* inspirante	Poetic, Silver and Late in sense of *inspire.*
mancipare	95, 4, 31,	templa . . . *subversioni* fuisse potius mancipata	Silver and Late in sense of *give up to.* Dative in Tac., Apul., etc.
miscere	125, 1, 15,	quis *certamini* misceatur	Accusative in poets. No dative found in sense of *take part in.*
obviare	95, 4, 24,	*cui* . . . raro poterit obviari	Late Latin word. Dative in Macr., Dig. etc.
pensare	124, 3, 8,	ut quinque *senatoribus* . . . hanc causam . . . pensetis	Word chiefly Silver and Late. Dative in Luc., Tac.
permiscere	163, 2, 25,	se *causis* . . . permisceat	Late Latin in sense of *take part in.*
praeferre	86, 1, 24,	alienis *moribus* praeferaris	As synonym of *praeficere.*
praeiudicare	63, 1, 18,	Non praeiudicat *iuri* publico	Late Latin with dative in sense of *injure.*
praesentare	93, 2, 30,	praesentati a u t e m *tribunalibus*	Word is Late Latin.
praevalere	80, 3, 7,	tanto *regno* . . . praevaluerit	Word Silver and Late. Dative in Lact. *Supra* also used in eccl. Latin.
provenire	73, 2, 12,	illa *mihi* feliciter bella provenerunt	Silver and Late in sense of *result.*
reputare	162, 5, 21,	*argutiae* suae reputare poterit	Late in sense of *attribute.* Dative in Tert., Vulg., Dig. etc.

			Relation to Classical Usage.
subdere	177,	2, 17,	*alteri* subdi non pos- sumus	Word poetic and Late. Dative in Tib., Pers., Claud. etc.
subiacere	119, 25,		cuius *ordinationi* vid- d e t u r subiacere provincia	Word post-Aug. Dative in Quint., Apul. etc.
subiugare	115,	2, 27,	subiugasti . . . auda- ciam *veritati*	Word is chiefly Late Latin.
subrepere	202,	1, 10,	(obprobria) *his* sub- repunt	Not in classical prose in tropical sense. Da- tive, accusative and accusative with *sub* used.

2. The Dative of Possession
(L.-Hof. 412-413)

The dative of possession rarely occurs. Examples of its classical use:

32, 4, 26, spectandi eis, ubi delegerint, . . . sit facultas.
139, 9, 3, cui a multifaria imitatione nomen est
297, 1, 23. novis regibus mos est . . . gaudia nuntiare,

Besides its occurrence with *esse*, it is found with *existere*, where Cassiodorus employs this verb (as he does very rarely) as the equivalent of *esse*, e. g., 158, 1, 3, si . . . nullus ei aut testamento heres extitit, and with *emergere* by parallel construction with *esse* in 86, 2, 31, si quod negotium Romano cum Gothis est aut *Gotho* emersit aliquod cum Romanis.,

Habere occurs frequently where in Classical Latin the dative of possession would be a natural construction, e. g., 182, 5, 13, habes . . . tributorum non minimam quantitatem; 292, 5, 2, stirpem nos habere regalem; 350, 5, 27, habetis . . . castissimum iudicem.

3. The Dative with Adjectives

The dative with adjectives is a classical construction. I have noted here only the occurrences of datives with adjectives which either do not occur in classical prose or occur followed by another case.

				Relation to Classical Usage.
accommodus	84,	3, 18,	ornatui probatur accommodum	Word poetic, Late. Dative in Verg., Stat., Cod. Th.
aequaevus	231,	3, 14,	annis vobis paene videbatur aequaevus	Word poetic, Silver. Dative in Plin.
concolor	213,	1, 7,	nivibus concolor	Word poetic, Silver. Dative in Ov., Col., Plin.
discolor	343,	5, 24,	vitreo sint aequori discolores	Word poetic. Dative in Verg., Ov., Col.
devotus	236,	3, 12,	regno pietatis nostrae devoti sunt	Word Silver, Late. Dative in Suet., Inscr.
dignus	116,	4, 7,	dignum adepto culmini	Dative, Late Latin. Ps. Quint. etc.
dulcis	238,	6, 27,	dulcis erat iusto principi rationabilis contrarietas obsequentis	Dative in Val. Fl.
exosus	79,	1, 24,	Superbiam divinitati semper exosam	In sense *odious to* Late; Dative in Macr. Sat., Amm., Eutr., Vulg.
extraneus	96,	1, 21,	nec ei iudicari potest extraneus	Mostly Late. No dative found.
indigenus or *indigena*	154,	5, 2,	mittat Padus noster indigenas pelago naves.	Word not in Caes., Cic. No dative found.
insolens	195,	3, 12,	non permittas milites esse possessoribus insolentes	Late in sense of *insolent.* Genitive used in sense of *unaccustomed.* Cassiodorus has dative for both.
	183,	2, 1,	insolens libertati genus est rusticorum	
onerosus	152,	1, 19,	ut principis desiderium nulli existere debeat onerosum.	Word poetic, Silver. Late. Dative in Plin.
pervius	118, 19,		quorum adulescentia pervia videtur incommodis	Word poetic, Silver. Late. Dative in Ov., Luc., Plin.
praeconialis	231,	2, 7,	pietati vestrae praeconiale est	Word cited for Cassiodorus only. Dative only here.
providus	183,	8, 36,	providus nostris apparatibus	Classical with genitive.
suavis	246,	3, 16,	suavissimum vobis	Dative in Plaut., Cael. apud Cic. epist.

With the following adjectives Cassiodorus uses at times the dative and at times the genitive or another case.

conscius, e.g. 379, 7,15, sibi . . . conscius	Cf. genitive 326, 3, 15 (p. 26).
idoneus, e.g. 50, 1, 7, cui te idoneum iudicantes	Cf. genitive and other uses, p. 27.
proprius, e.g. 127, 1, 3, culmini urbano tam proprium	Cf. genitive 159, 3, 30 (p. 26).
similis, e.g. 369, 3,23, Sabino simile	Cf. genitive (p. 27).

4. The Dative with Verbal Substantives

Only one clear example has been noted, 147, 1, 19, decem milia solidorum *reliquatorem* nostris *utilitatibus* extitisse.

The dative in 237, 3, 19, habentes concordiam *regno nostro* per omnia debeant esse purissimi, appears to be directly connected with the noun *concordiam.* Silver and Late Latin use the dative after *concors,* and this use with the adjective helps to explain the dative after the noun. The dative which developed with verbal substantives was also extended to non-verbal nouns.

5. The Dative of Advantage and Disadvantage
(L.-Hof. 414)

Many examples of the dative of advantage occur in the Variae, notwithstanding the frequent use of *pro* with the ablative as the equivalent of this construction (Cf. p. 126). The dative of disadvantage is somewhat less frequent. There are no special peculiarities in Cassiodorus' use of these datives. The following examples are typical:

A. Advantage:

13, 4, 4, voces *tibi* militavere laudantium
73, 1, 7, estote *illis* remissi
88, 3,17, eum credimus *vobis* profutura decernere
90, 4,11, *cui* a nobis assurgitur
115, 1,20, facile est quemque *sibi* degere: *multis* autem electum vivere
 decet.
354, 3,11, quid semper *inferis* laboras? aliquando et *superis* milita.

B. Disadvantage:

23, 2, 4, frumenta *sibi* inimicorum subreptionibus concremata
23, 2, 5, *quibus* . . . sunt commoda deminuta

90, 26,   piaculi genus est absentem *sibi* Romam diutius facere, qui, etc.

133, 4, 22, (loca) *filiis* perire non debeant

170, 12,   1, homicidii reatus est *illis* esse tenacem

6. The Sympathetic Dative
(L.-Hof. 415-416)

A. The sympathetic dative, i. e., a dative designating the animate being whose body, soul, or possession is drawn into sympathy with the action of the verb without the ideas of advantage or disadvantage predominating, is employed in the classical manner. It serves as a substitute for a genitive of possession or a possessive adjective. The following example, where it alternates with the genitive of possession, indicates that the writer disregards any shades of difference between the two constructions and is merely seeking variety of structure: 360, 5, 9, persona tua refugium sit *oppresso*, *infirmi* defensio, praesidium aliqua calamitate *concluso*.

Other typical examples:

70, 4, 25, intellectum *obtusis* acuit

71, 10, 25, qui *nautis* . . . obstruxit auditum

126, 1, 5, maius *reatui* pondus est inopinata deceptio

168, 5, 4, pater *huic* . . . Opilio fuit (Late Latin; cf. L.-Hof., 416)

288, 3, 22, tot *consularibus* patrem

289, 6, 10, nam licet nuncupemini *omnibus* generaliter patres, *huic* etiam estis specialiter et parentes.

B. The dative designating the person from whom a thing is taken or removed is considered also as a sympathetic dative (dative of separation). The following are typical:

4, 6, 3, quod enim spatium possis publico *labori* subripere . . . ?

11, 1, 7, *cui* usum subtrahendo

24, 4, 19, ut huius modi portenta provinciae *finibus* abigantur (Cf. T. L. L., I, 98, 7, for citations of *abigere* with dative from Silver and Late writers).

35, 5, 20, *Agnello* . . . extortam constiterit fuisse pecuniam

38, 3, 32, sed in nulla se *nobis* parte dissocians. Classical prose uses a preposition with the ablative with *dissociare*. Examples in T. L. L., V, 1494, 38 ff. of use without a preposition may be either dative or ablative.

196, 26,   *cui* praesul adimitur

276, 2, 7, subtrahimus *pecuniae* quod augmentetur gloriae

367, 4, 19, ut daret quod utique nisi *habenti* non probatur emergere.

C. Ethical dative and dative of reference in the narrower sense, i. e., *dativus iudicantis,* do not occur in the Variae.

7. The Dative of Agent
(L.-Hof. 417)

With the gerundive and the passive periphrastic Cassiodorus usually expresses the agent by the dative, as is the rule in classical Latin. For the sake of clearness, even in classical Latin an ablative of agent may be used. A few examples of the ablative of agent occur in the Variae where the use of the dative would be quite as clear. These will be noted in the section on the ablative.

Occasionally the dative is used for the agent with other passive verbs, both the compounded and the simple forms, e. g., 72, 17, 30, Sed quoniam *nobis* facta est voluptuosa digressio; 287, 9, 4, cesset nunc illa satyricis *doctoribus* querulis usurpata sententia; 36, 2, 19, *illis* ingenii provectus adquiritur; 236; 1, 20, cuius *vobis* noscitur regnare progenies. These uses are classical, and their frequency is no greater than in classical prose.

The dative of agent is also used with adjectives in *-bilis,* e. g. 10, 1, 4, omni quippe regno desiderabilis debet esse tranquillitas; 78, 2, 5, Terribilis est hominibus conflictus; 149, 2, 1, paucis inexplicabile. This usage also occurs in classical prose.

One intransitive verb with passive meaning is found with a dative of agent in 237, 3, 2, quatenus et *nobis* vestra sinceritas laudabiliter innotescat. This usage is classified as " purely poetical " (L.-Hof., 417, 4).

8. The Dative of Purpose (Final Dative)
(L.-Hof. 417-418)

Final datives are rare in the Variae. The prepositions *ad* and *in* with the accusative are frequently employed where a final dative is possible (Cf. p. 92 and p. 132).

Among the adnominal uses, the final dative occurs more frequently with *locus* (always in the tropical sense) than with any other word, e. g., 127, 3, 13, non habet *veniae* locum. Parallel construction is responsible for its use with *aditus* in 13, 4, 3, excludens vel *querelis* aditum vel *derogationibus* locum.

Among adverbial uses, *cordi* is the most used word, e. g., 59, 1, 19, cui *cordi* est rerum omnium tenere mensuram.

All examples, both adnominal and adverbial, are classical.
For the use of the dative of the gerundive in a final sense, see
p. 168.

9. The Double Dative
(L.-Hof. 418-419)

The double dative, i. e., a dative of the person and a final dative,
is rare.

Several examples occur with *cordi* as the final dative e. g., 59, 1,
19, above, and 17, 1, 25, cordi nobis est.   Another typical example
of double dative is 93, 1, 11, tibimet esse terrori.

10. The Dative of Goal or Limit
(L.-Hof. 419)

This construction, almost unknown to classical prose, is found in
the poets at all periods and had a more extended use in Late Latin,
though its use by prose writers never became a frequent one.   In
many of the examples of its use another dative idea, such as advantage, is also discernible.

Cassiodorus uses it rather sparingly, generally preferring the
ordinary prose constructions, *ad* and *in* with the accusative.

The following examples have the added idea of advantage or
disadvantage:

48, 1, 2, Gaudete, patres conscripti, redisse *vobis* stipendia dignitatum
69, 8, 9, sic medicabili *substantiae* venit a sulfure quod calet
88, 5, 25, *vobis* vicarium praefecturae direximus.
152, 3, 12, *innocentibus* detrimenta non veniant.
285, 3, 16, redeat amor *omnibus* disciplinae
344, 1, 17, *quibus* dominorum clementia voluit descendere
372, 3, 31, *corpori* aquas caenosas sorbere

The following appear to be pure goal or limit:

102, 1, 23, (Jovinum) Vulcanae *insulae* perpetua relegatione damna-
        mus.
166, 3, 27, *Ori* tuo altercantium desideria convenerunt
240, 4, 3, *neci* dedit Bulgares
241, 10, 14, regnator ille vix *litori* constitutus . . . undas iterum desi-
        derabat intrare.
377, 4, 8, (vasa) sacris *liminibus* deportari . . . imperavit.

VI. *The Ablative Case*

1. The Ablative of the Point of Departure
(L.-Hof. 420-422; K.-Steg. II, 1, 361-372)

Cf. use of Preps. *ab, de, ex*

I have noted only five verbs followed by the simple ablative indicating the local point of departure, where classical prose regularly used a preposition.

effluere 11, 3, 17, quod solet vivis *corporibus* . . . effluere
  Only citation of *effluere* without a preposition is from Plin. nat. (T. L. L., V, 192, 59). May be dative.
evadere 71, 10, 25, *quibus* solus Ithacus evasit
  Cited for Verg. Aen. 9, 99; Sall. Iug. 56, 5 (K.-Steg., II, 1, 362), Liv., Curt. (Kr.-Schm., I, 528). All these examples refer to escape from a thing, such as danger. The accusative also occurs in Livy (Kr.-Schm., I, 528). Cassiodorus uses the accusative with *evadere* in 71, 10, 29. The above *quibus* is the only instance I have found where persons are meant.
labi 71, 11, 31, illo lapso *caelo* psalterio
  Labi is thus used by Verg. georg. 1, 366, *stellas Praecipites caelo labi* (Harpers'). Also Val. Fl. 5, 244; Tac. hist. 3, 29 (K.-Steg., II, 1, 361).
manare 369, 1, 10, manat . . . lac uberibus fistulosis.
  Classical prose used *ex* in this sense. Ablative alone in Lygd. and Val. Max. (K.-Steg., II, 1, 36).
removere 209, 1, 2, Quamvis artes lubricae honestis *moribus* sint remotae.
  Cited for Ov. met. 7, 256 and 13, 467; Tac. ann. 2, 50 (Harpers'); Vell. 2, 32, 5; Suet. Tib. 42, 1 (K.-Steg., II, 1, 362).

One example of a word indicating temporal point of departure has been noted, 175, 1, 9, Si antiquitatis ordinem perscrutemur *origine* dignitatum. I have found no examples or discussion of this use of the ablative, but because of the similarity of time-constructions to those of place I have listed it under this heading.

2. The Ablative of Source or Origin
(L.-Hof. 422-423)

Examples of the ablative of source without a preposition are rare and are limited to the stereotyped *gente* or *stirpe*, e. g.

165, 6, 13, quacumque gente sint editi,
238, 4, 17, qui tantorum regum fuerat stirpe procreatus,

244, 6, 27, qui contemptibili stirpe nascuntur,
299, 3, 3, Hamalorum stirpe progenitus

In figurative expressions, i. e., where the origin is not that of a
person, Cassiodorus regularly uses a preposition, e. g.

34, 4, 18, ne inopia . . . a neglegentia matre nata esse videatur
83, 1, 32, nascitur de pietate crudelitas
285, 1, 7, momenta iustitiae de iniquitatis occasione nascuntur.

3. The Ablative of Separation
(L.-Hof. 423-425; K.-Steg. II, 1, 375, 595)

Cf. *ab, de, ex*

The verbs listed here as taking the ablative of separation without
a preposition either do not occur in classical prose or are used in
classical prose with a preposition. A few verbs which may take
either of two cases are listed, e. g., *carere.*

carere 102, 2, 25, Careat proinde patrio *foco*
> *Carere* with the ablative is regular at all periods. Scattered ex-
> amples of the genitive and accusative occur both in Early and
> Late Latin (K.-Steg., II, 1, 387). Only the ablative occurs in
> the Variae.

colligere 70, 6, 33, *terris* quandam harmoniam doctissima inquisitione
collegit,
> *Ex* is classical; *ab* occurs in Rhet. Her. and in the poets and in
> Silver and Late Latin; *de* in the poets and Late. Ablative alone
> once in Cic., then Poets and Late (T. L. L., III, 1620, 69 ff.).

destitui 99, 2, 21, cum virtus corporeo fuerit robore destituta.
> Ablative in Vell., Val. Max., Sen., Col., Petron., Quint. etc. (T. L.
> L., V, 765, 41 ff.).

egere 240, 7, 23, eget enim *astipulatoribus* corpus illaesum
> In Early Latin *egere* took the genitive, though one example of the
> accusative is cited from Plautus (K.-Steg., II, 1, 468). Classical
> prose nearly always had the ablative. Then beginning with Livy
> the genitive again became more frequent (L.-Hof., 408, 1). In
> the Variae only the ablative occurs.

enudare 137, 1, 3, agrorum fructibus enudati.
> The word is cited by Harpers', Georges and Benoist-Goelzer only
> for Cassiodorus. Its use with the ablative alone seems to follow
> the use with *nudare,* which is classical. Compounding with *e-*
> would also give sufficient reason for ablative alone.

eradere 103, 2, 23, tumulus . . . silvis erasus.
> Tac. ann. 4, 42, uses *eradere* with ablative and Tac. ann. 3, 17,
> *radere.* As our example is that of a perf. pass. participle the

analogy of *nudatus,* etc. seems rather to be followed. The word
is ante-classical and in use again from the Augustan period.
exonerare 26, 3, 27, nec iustis petitionibus retentatores exoneres.
  Usage begins with Livy (K.-Steg., II, 1, 373).
indigere 193, 3, 18, *pecuniis* potest indigere mediocris
  The genitive is regular with *indigere* in Early Latin, is preferred
  to the ablative by Cicero and Sall. but not by Caes. (L.-Hof.,
  408, 1) or Liv. (K.-Steg., II, 1, 468). Cassiodorus does not use
  the genitive, but has accusative 3 times and ablative several
  times. Cf. accusative, p. 16.
inserere 242, 4, 6, insertus stirpe regia vocabulum vobiscum volui
  habere commune.
sublevare 137, 1, 3, ut . . . subleventur onere tributariae functionis.
  I have not found any example of this verb used with a person as
  subject and taking an ablative. K.-Steg., II, 1, 280 cites Caes.
  Gall. 1, 40, 5, *quos aliquid usus ac disciplina sublevaret.* This
  adverbial accusative is the nearest parallel I have found.
vacare 108, 7, 1, arithmeticam indicas, *auditoriis* vacat.
  The ablative alone and less frequently the ablative with *ab* follows
  vacare in classical Latin in the sense of *be free from* (K.-Steg.,
  II, 1, 373). Here it means rather *to lack = carere, egere.*
vacuare 290, 6, 12, vacuabat alios labore
  Word mostly post-Augustan. Ablative alone in Aur. Vict. Epit. 43.

4. The Ablative of Comparison
(L.-Hof. 425-429)

One Silver and Late Latin innovation is seen in Cassiodorus'
use of the ablative of comparison. This is his rather frequent use
of a preposition, *a* or *ab,* with this ablative. The employment of
the preposition began in the Silver Latin period, but became frequent only in very late authors. As this ablative is in origin an
ablative of the point of departure, the use of the preposition is a
virtual repetition of the ablative idea and specially emphasizes the
point of departure.

Examples:

14, 7, 28, iudicetur tamen ab omnibus plus mereri (Cited by Traube,
        510. May, however, be ablative of agent or with *mereri*).
147, 3, 7, si quis autem a modulo definito amplius fuerit habere
        repertus,
187, 7, 9, amplius aliquid a militibus ceteris promereri potuisse
        videatur
207, 3, 30, cives a suis commodis plus amabat
212, 5, 22, ne quid ab illis sciat minus

3

215, 12,   aliquid minus a consuetudine percipiat
235, 2, 21, ne quid a praesentibus minus fecisse videamini
255, 1, 2, quanto a ceteris mortalibus maiora suscipimus
273, 5, 10, tantum a communibus balneis salubrior invenitur quantum
            ab humana industria celsior est natura.
305, 3, 33, plus est amandus a domino

In other examples his usage is classical. Comparison expressed by *quam* is very rare in the circumstances where the ablative of comparison is possible.

5. The Ablative of Agent
(L.-Hof. 435)

As in classical prose, the ablative with the preposition *a* or *ab* is the reguar method of expressing the agent with a passive verb. The dative of agent with the ordinary passive verb seems to occur with no greater frequency than it does in classical prose (Cf. dative of agent, p. 37).

With the passive periphrastic, classical prose occasionally employs the ablative of agent, chiefly to avoid ambiguity resulting from the presence of another dative in the same clause, e. g., Cic. Manil., II, 6. This use of the ablative occurs rarely where no such ambiguity is possible, e. g., Cic., Manil., XII, 34. Poets and Late writers use it more freely.

A few examples of the ablative of agent with the passive periphrastic occur in the Variae. In the following the motive seems to be the avoidance of ambiguity: 282, 5, 14, non credant a nostra mansuetudine neglegendum and 349, 3, quod est a plurimis asserendum. In the following the author seems to take advantage of the Late Latin freedom in choosing the ablative construction.

290, 7, 14, quod a multis fuit proceribus sincerissime peragendum
308, 1, 9, sic est a principe gravis vincenda suspicio
349, 3, 23, honorabiles quidem a cunctis habendi sunt veterani

In one example the ablative of agent is used with an abstract noun and the verb *sum*, which results in a passive meaning, 66, 12, ab imperitis enim harum rerum statuae facilis eversio non fuisset.

In a few instances the ablative of agent occurs where an abstract concept is personified. The construction is the same as for persons.

Thus 57, 2, 13, quae ab humana condicione deseritur, and 201, 1, 6, ab ipsis legibus ferrum constet esse porrectum.

Classical prose never omitted the preposition except in instances where the ablative was also sociative or instrumental and these ideas prevailed over that of agent. The Augustan poets, Livy, and the Silver writers generally frequently omitted it. Late Latin is, in general, reactionary and omissions of the preposition are not numerous (L.-Hof., 435; Stangl, I, 272). I have noted only one certain example in the Variae, 159, 1, 24, clamat enim sibi Gudila vel Oppane incognitam suo generi condicionem servitutis imponi.

In 341, 3, 26, ne obsessa potius itinera videantur esse latronibus, and similar examples elsewhere, we should expect the ablative of agent with *ab* as the ordinary construction. In the above and similar examples we are probably dealing with a dative of agent.

6. The Instrumental Ablative of Accompaniment and Association
(L.-Hof. 429-430)

I have noted only one unusual example of this ablative without the preposition *cum*. This is in 114, 4, 22, vos tantae feminae decore copulavimus. Some of the manuscripts read *decori* (For use of the dative with *copulare* see p. 31).

Cicero uses *copulare* once with the dative and elsewhere with *cum* and the ablative. It occurs with the dative in Livy and later writers (K.-Steg., II, 1, 318).

Copulare occurs frequently in Late Latin with the accusative (or the nominative, when the verb is passive) designating one of the contracting parties in matrimony, e. g., Cod. Iust. 5, 11, 3; 5, 27, 51; Heges., 1, 28, 5; Ambrosiast. in I. Cor. 7, 14; Pelag. in Rom. 7, p. 675a. No certain example of the other contracting party in the ablative is found (T. L. L.), and most probably we have to do here with an orthographical problem.

7. The Ablative of Attendant Circumstance
(L.-Hof. 430)

Attendant circumstance is regularly expressed in classical prose by the ablative with the preposition *cum*, especially when the ablative has no attribute. Early Latin had a number of fixed expressions with which the preposition was not used. In general these survived in the later periods, though few new expressions of this nature were added at any time. The following examples from the Variae are typical of both Early and Classical usage:

16, 18, 12, prospero auspicio suscipiatur eius provectus,
126, 27,   qui contrario omine pro eius tuitione directus est,

Cassiodorus' general practice is to use *cum* or *sub*, the latter more frequently (Cf. p. 125 and 146), whether or not the noun has an attribute. In a number of instances, however, he expresses a circumstance without any preposition, e. g.

13, 8, 20, patriciatus tibi apicem iusta remuneratione conferimus
16, 16, 2, Vixit . . . honore iudicis et securitate privati
58, 1, 25, Ecdicii filios . . . votivo quidem reditu, sed acerbo casu, remeare iubeatis,
79, 1, 6, meo graviter dolore peccatis
174, 5, 20, prosperrimae condicionis eventu vos in pace ingenuitatem ceditis famulis
385, 7, 3, Pace tanti patris dixerim:

8. The Ablative of Accordance
(L.-Hof. 430)

The examples listed here differ from those above in this that they indicate the rule or custom according to which something is or is done. Leümann-Hofmann includes this type with the ablative of attendant circumstance. No preposition is used, and the examples represent classical usage.

70, 2, 9, ad aures nostras disciplinae suae lege pervenerit
174, 1, 2, Priscorum iudicio qualis sit consulatus, hinc omnino datur intellegi,
255, 6, 30, ecclesiasticis vivite constitutis

9. The Ablative of Manner
(L.-Hof. 430-431)

In classical prose, regularly an unmodified noun denoting manner, and frequently a noun with an attribute, is found in the ablative with *cum*. Certain words, such as *merito, immerito, iure, iniuria, sponte,* etc. were used in Early Latin without either preposition or attribute and continued to be so used in the classical period.

In the Variae *merito* (e. g., 15, 14, 28), (*non*) *immerito* (e. g.,

51, 1, 28), *iure* (e. g., 15, 9, 4), *sponte* (72, 12, 8), *iniuria* (175, 2, 14) etc., occur without *cum*, as they do in the classical authors. The only unusual word noted in this connection is *astu* in 247, 3, 1, astu quaedam neglegens praesumptione tui. T. L. L., II, 983, 17 shows that this word after being used in Early Latin was revived by the Augustan poets, then used by Livy and many Silver and Late writers. (E F H G I have *actu*.) Cassiodorus very frequently expresses manner by *sub* with the ablative, rarely by *cum*. Cf. p. 148.

10. The Ablative of Means
(L.-Hof. 433-439)

The ablative of means is used as in classical prose chiefly with verbs and adjectives.

A. With Verbs.

(a) The five Deponent Verbs (L.-Hof., 435-436; K.-Steg., II, 1, 382-383).

Of the five deponents, *potior, fungor, vescor, fruor,* and *utor,* which regularly take the ablative in classical prose, *vescor, fruor,* and *utor* are always found with the ablative. *Fungor* and its compound *perfungor* occur regularly with the ablative, but we find the accusative in 345, 13, dum prior *militiam* perfunctus exierit. The accusative occurs with *fungor* in Early Latin, but not in classical prose, except once in Nepos. It occurs in Tacitus, Suetonius, and later writers (Kr.-Schm., I, 616). *Perfungor* is found with the accusative in Lucretius, Apuleius, and Fronto. An example in Cicero's Letters is due to zeugma (Georges).

Potior never takes the genitive, which case sometimes followed it in classical prose. In 156, 1, 23 and 243, 1, 24, etc., it takes the ablative. The accusative occurs, e. g., 125, 2, 6, ut porticum cum areola post Turasi thermas . . . absoluta liberalitate potiaris. The accusative occurs in Early Latin and again in Silver and Late Latin, but is avoided in classical prose except by Sallust (L.-Hof., 435).

(b) Other Verbs.

Gratulari is used with the ablative in 159, 1, 6, maiore munificentia gratulentur. K.-Steg., II, 1, 261, 312, 474, mentions its use for things with the accusative, with *de* and *in* with the ablative, with the genitive, but not with the ablative alone.

Miscere in 343, 4, 22, quae misceri posse simili liquore sentitur. The usage is classical. Cf. use of this verb with dative, p. 32.

Docere, 73, 4, 24, arte sua doctum. Either the accusative or ablative is classical with *doctus* (K.-Steg., II, 1, 298). In the Variae always the ablative.

Erudire, 299, 5, 10, ecclesiasticis est litteris eruditus. *Eruditus* follows *doctus* in using either accusative or ablative, but also may take ablative with *in* or *de* (K.-Steg., II, 1, 299, 381). In the Variae always the ablative.

Epulari, 71, 7, 12, suavitatibus epulari. Poetic and Late. Found in Verg. Aen. 3, 224, and georg. 2, 537 with ablative alone. Also in Vulg., Deut., 12, 12 al (Harpers').

Pullulare, 246, 1, 6, quatenus bonis sacerdotibus ecclesiarum omnium religio pullularet. (Not in Leumann-Hofmann or Kühner-Stegmann. A similar use of the verb occurs in Verg. Aen. 7, 329, tot *pullulat atra colubris.*)

Gaudere with the ablative is classical. One example of a word designating a person occurs, 38, 2, 22, qui principe Zenone non tam benivolo quam affine gaudebat. *Gaudere* is thus used with persons by Vergil, Aen. 7, 220.

Complere and *implere* govern only the ablative in the Variae, e. g.

86, 2, 11, implens etiam *doctrina* . . . dignitatem
315, 1, 32, *inundatione* completus.
354, 5, 21, atria tua *vacuitatibus* impleantur

There is no trace of the usage with the genitive. Cf. L.-Hof., 407.

B. With Adjectives.

Plenus. Cassiodorus uses only the ablative with *plenus,* which occurs frequently, e. g., 12, 1, 19, plenus meritis aestimatur.

In Early Latin and in Cicero the genitive was the only case used with *plenus.* The use of the ablative began with Catullus and Lucretius, in prose, with Caesar. Late Latin uses the two cases indifferently (L.-Hof., 403-404). The prepositions *de* and *cum* also occur in Late Latin (L.-Hof., 438). They are not used with *plenus* in the Variae.

Dignus and *indignus.* Regularly with ablative, as in classical prose, e. g., 47, 6, 35, ut dignus genere, dignus urbe, dignus nostro iudicio, dignus trabeis aestimeris.

The use of *dignus* with the dative has been mentioned on p. 34.

C. For the use of *per* and other prepositions as a substitute for the ablative of means cf. the chapter on prepositions, especially p. 106.

In a few examples the prepositional construction is paired with the ablative in such a way as to indicate that the author regarded the two as equivalent, e. g.

31, 4, 9, ut culpa *legibus,* non *per* praesumptam coerceantur *iniuriam.*
361, 1, 26, alter *cibis* reficitur, alter *per* abstinentiae *beneficia* tenuatur.

Notwithstanding the rather frequent occurrence of *per* and other prepositions in phrases equivalent to the ablative of means, the ablative itself is proportionately much more frequent and remains the chief way of expressing means in the Variae.

Classical prose never uses the preposition *ab* with the ablative of means. Rare examples of this usage appear, however, in Early Latin and in the Silver Period, while in Late Latin the instances are somewhat more numerous (Cf. T. L. L., I, 34, 59 ff.). The following seem to be examples of this usage rather than that of the thing personified as an agent:

201, 1, 4, tua tantum dignitas a terroribus ornatur,
299, 5, 10, a quibus (i. e., *ecclesiasticis litteris*) semper quicquid est pro homine commonemur.

11. The Ablative of Price
(L.-Hof. 439)

The ablative of price occurs very rarely in the Variae. The following examples illustrate the classical usage and show the instrumental nature of this ablative:

130, 3, 18, emimus nostro dispendio prosperitatem Gothorum.
350, 4, 21, scripsimus inempti quod magnis pretiis optabatur impleri:

The ablative of price, used to indicate the penalty after *damnare,* occurs in 102, 1, 23 (Iovinum) Vulcanae insulae perpetua *relegatione* damnamus. The usage of the ablative for the penalty other than a money fine with *damnare* occurs in Livy and Silver and Late writers (T. L. L., V, 15, 75 ff.). Punishment by exile was first expressed in this way by Quint., decl. p. 194, 11. The expression *exilii relegatione damnare* occurs in Pallad. hist. mon. I, 49.

The ablative is used for the charge with *accusare* in 193, 2, 9, tu age, ne ullis cupiditatibus accuseris, and in 216, 3, 7, (ut) nullis vilitatibus accuseris. With *accusare* the ablative is classical for the charge " in re iudiciali," but no citations of this ablative are found " in re non iudiciali " (T. L. L., I, 351, 9 ff.; I, 352, 35 ff.). The above examples belong in the latter class. The ablative is used for a money penalty in 176, 3, 11, magna quantitate multat errantes.

12. The Ablative of Respect
(L.-Hof. 443-444)

The ablative of respect is used as in classical prose, as the following selected examples show.

16, 17,   6, equinis *gregibus* principes vinceret
22,   2,   7, quod . . . inferebatur *genere* tertiarum
102,   4,   9, *rebusque* omnibus reformatus
114,   3, 16, *aspectibus* iucundi, usibus gratiores:
130,   2, 28, contra Inquilinam *nomine*
149,   3, 17, *corpore* aut *qualitate* meliora
343,   5, 26, quem se peregrinis undis non videas *colore* posse miscere
        Cf. usage of *in* as ablative of respect, p. 141.

13. The Ablative Absolute
(L.-Hof. 445-449)

The ablative absolute in the Variae ordinarily conforms to classical norms. The perfect passive participle and the present participle are the only ones occurring in this construction. Examples employing the perfect passive participle occur in 12, 7, 9; 13, 4, 2; 17, 3, 18; 18, 3, 7; 22, 2, 19; 23, 1, 1; 24, 2, 11; 25, 2, 1; 25, 4, 23; 25, 4, 24, etc. Examples of the present participle in 12, 3, 27; 25, 1, 11; 27, 1, 21; 24, 2, 9; 29, 3, 18; 34, 3, 3; 120, 3, 9; 138, 6, 26, etc. Examples with substantive and adjective in 24, 2, 9; 120, 3, 9, etc.

In a few examples the person or thing in the ablative absolute is identical with the subject of the clause within which the ablative absolute occurs. This usage is avoided in classical prose, but occurs in inscriptions of the classical period in such examples as *se vivo fecit* (L.-Hof., 447).

Examples of this usage in the Variae:

145, 4, 36, pudoris enim sustinere iacturam nesciunt, qui se prius iudice corriguntur.

161, 1, 11, Gravis est Patzenis . . . conquestio. qui se in expeditione Gallica constituto in eum Brandilam prosiluisse testatur excessum, ut, etc.

216, 3, 32, facile enim sequuntur vestigia verbi alieni, qui se possunt monitore compelli.

280, 9, 25, si quis vero quae dederit aut promiserit eodem superstite timuerit publicare, ab heredibus vel proheredibus eius ecclesia repetat.

14. The Ablative of Place and the Locative
(L.-Hof. 450, 453)

In the Variae place where is usually indicated by means of the prepositions *in*, *sub*, etc. A few examples occur of stereotyped uses of the ablative without a preposition, such as 69, 12, 28, toto orbe, and 376, 3, 12, dextra laevaque.

Other examples noted without the preposition:

38, 2, 23, et quid *illa re publica* gratia non potuit obtinere parentis . . . ?

41, 10, 19, ostendit quod *caelo* volvitur

156, 2, 28, actus illos *mundo* celeberrimos

Here too belongs the ablative in the title of the letter in 136, 22, Universis Provincialibus Et Capillatis Defensoribus Et Curialibus Siscia Vel Savia Consistentibus Theodericus Rex. Mommsen in the Index Locorum, 508, informs us that Siscia and Savia are provinces, not towns. Cf. also 151, 31, In Savia Provincia.

The following combine the ideas of ablative of place and ablative of respect:

363, 5, 10, miroque modo incipit esse novum, quando *cellis omnibus* reperitur antiquum.

371, 2, 14, raro illic ab area venit *umeris* gravatus agricola

In the titles of a few letters a first declension name of a town occurs in the ablative instead of in the locative. Thus:

23, 15,   Universis Gothis Et Romanis Dertona Consistentibus Theodericus Rex.

61, 25,   Universis Iudaeis Genua Consistentibus Theodericus Rex. Cf. 128, 25.

125, 24,   Universis Massilia Constitutis Theodericus Rex.

341, 1,   Edictum De Pretiis Custodiendis Ravenna.

In the Late Latin period the locative tended to vanish entirely
(L.-Hof., 453). Cassiodorus uses it only in the following stereotyped examples:

Romae, 188, 4, 26 and 243, 7, 14.
Ephesi, 212, 4, 9.
Rhodi, 212, 4, 10.

15. The Ablative of Cause
(L.-Hof. 442)

The ablative of cause rarely occurs in the Variae, owing to the
frequent use of *ab, de,* and other prepositions. *Ob* and *propter*
are, however, extremely rare. The gerund in the ablative of cause
will be treated under the Gerund, p. 170. Examples of ablative of
cause:

23,   3, 12,   ne aliqua neglegentia reddaris obnoxius
66,   2, 19,   praesentis edicti unusquisque auctoritate cognoscat, etc.
70,   1, 3,   sola ratione . . . quod . . . noveramus
101, 3, 2,   divino favore habetote fiduciam
114, 3, 15,   magna mole celerrimi

16. The Ablative of Time
(L.-Hof. 451)

A.   The ablative of time in the Variae shows few variations from
classical usage.   Contrary to Late Latin practice and in conformity
with classical usage, Cassiodorus seldom uses the preposition *in*
where the ablative has an attribute.   Thus, e. g., 22, 2, 8, annis
singulis; 46, 2, 11, primis auspiciis; 81, 3, 18, modernis saeculis;
133, 2, 11, paschalibus diebus.   One example has *noctibus* without
the preposition, followed by *die* with *in,* viz., 210, 4, 29, Officium
tuum et milites consuetos *noctibus* potius invigilare compelle: *in
die* autem civitas se ipsa custodit:

Noctu, an ancient form equivalent to a locative (L.-Hof., 451,
4), occurs in 36, 1, 13, quod die noctuque assidua deliberatione
volvamus.

B.   Duration of time was in classical prose regularly expressed
by the accusative.   The ablative was first used by Catullus.   Of
classical prose writers Caesar alone employs it.   It becomes more
frequent in Silver and Late writers (L.-Hof., 452).   In the Variae

duration of time is regularly expressed either by *per* with the accusative or by the ablative. The accusative alone does not occur. Examples of the ablative:

11, 3, 18, cum sex paene mensibus marinae deliciae a vitali fuerint vigore separatae
15, 15, 33, praefecturam bis novennis annis gessit
26, 3, 14, longissima cupiunt aetate constare
82, 2, 18, qui tot annis continuis similis splendet claritate virtutis
90, 31, qui longa nobiscum aetate versatus es,
102, 2, 26, cum tot saeculis iugiter consumantur.
121, 3, 31, viro multis temporibus iam probato,
137, 6, 27, tot saeculis mons habetur, qui erogationibus tantis expenditur.
260, 9, 22, promittant anni parte maiore se in civitatibus manere,

A similar use of the ablative to indicate extent of space occurs in 343, 2, 7, a fronte sexaginta *milibus* dulcissimi aequoris amoenitate perfruitur.

CHAPTER III

The Adjective and the Adverb

I. *The Adjective*

1. Adjectives Replacing the Genitive
(L.-Hof. 397)

Though the practice of substituting for a noun in the genitive (especially objective or subjective genitive) an adjective derived from that noun occurs in classical authors, even Cicero, it is chiefly a development of the popular language, and the frequent use of such adjectives, especially of those derived from common nouns, belongs to Late Latin.

Cassiodorus frequently uses adjectives in this manner. Some of the examples may be regarded as replacing an appositive or a prepositional phrase, but the greater number serve as substitutes for a genitive.

The following are typical examples:

3, 6, 23, praetorianae sedis	18, 2, 14, Augustanae civitatis
3, 6, 24, exercituales . . . expensae	36, 1, 15, in Syracusana civitate
10, 2, 9, concordiam vestram	36, 1, 17, Romanam . . . civitatem
11, 6, 3, epistularis sermo	42, 2, 9, in civitate Romana
11, 3, 18, marinae deliciae	59, 12, clementia principalis
11, 3, 18, vitali . . . vigore	66, 2, 20, de Comensi civitate
13, 4, 1, sub praecinctu Martio	69, 11, 20, Antenorea terra
13, 7, 18, respectu publico	89, 2, 16, de humana morte
14, 6, 23, praetoriano culmini	108, 1, 14, de partibus Africanis
14, 8, 30, coetu Romuleo	124, 1, 34, In Spoletina civitate
17, 2, 18, munificentia principali	146, 6, 11, Vergiliano carmine
17, 1, 28, vituperationem nostram	158, 14, in Mediolanensi urbe

2. Adjectives and Participles used Substantively
(L.-Hof. 455-458)

While adjectives and certain participles are used substantively in all periods of Latin, the use was greatly extended in Late writers. Apart from the greater frequency in this construction, it should be observed that the later writers extended the substantival use to forms of the adjective and participle not so employed in the Classical period. Early and Classical Latin employed substantively only the present and the perfect participles, but Silver and Late Latin also use as substantives the future active participle and the gerundive as a future passive participle.

Cassiodorus' use is consistent with the Late Latin tendency to employ a great number of adjectives and participles substantively. In the first preface of the Variae alone (three pages of text), twenty-two adjectives and thirty-one participles are so used. Throughout the work the number of substantive uses is so large that a detailed study of all individual peculiarities is impossible here. The following paragraphs will, however, illustrate the chief peculiarities of Cassiodorus' usage.

A. ADJECTIVES

a) Masculine Adjectives Denoting Persons.

Masculine plural adjectives are frequently used as substantives, even in classical prose, when a class of persons is meant, such as *docti, indocti, probi, improbi*, etc. The singular is less commonly used as a substantive and, when it is used, is regularly in a collective sense, so that it too designates the class rather than the individual, e. g., *sapiens = the wise man,* not an individual, but any wise man (Cf. K.-Steg., II, 1, 223-224).

Cassiodorus frequently uses adjectives substantively to represent various classes in the political and social order of his time. The plural occurs regularly as in classical prose, but the singular occurs at times and designates an individual. Thus the terms *illustris, spectabilis,* and *clarissimus* are applied in the singular to members of the official hierarchy both as adjectives and as substantives, and in the singular they always designate the individual.

36, 1, 15, spectabilis . . . Philagrius in civitate Syracusana consistens
96, 1, 23, clarissimo Armentario . . . ea faciat exhiberi
186, 3, 3, quae inter illustres ingreditur
233, 9, 19, illustrem Sigismerem comitem nostrum

As these belonged to orders called *illustratus, spectabilitas,* and *clarissimatus,* we may conclude that the adjectives in these examples are not mere attributes but are used substantively.

Other examples of masculine adjectives as substantives indicating classes:

domestici	= *officials,*	e. g., 18, 2, 27, Domestici partis equitum et peditum . . . conquesti sunt
idonei	= *the well to do* ⎫	e. g., 211, 3, 15, idonei damna vix
tenues	= *the poor* ⎭	sentiunt, tenues autem levi dispendio vulnerantur,
mediocres	= *the poor,*	e. g., 60, 1, 16, quod per mediocrium damna sentimus.
praepotentes	= *the powerful,*	e. g., 60, 2, 18, cognovimus domos aliquas praepotentum suas non implere per ordinem functiones.
potiores	= *the powerful* ⎫	e. g., 18, 1, 24, si . . . per potiores
humiles	= *the lowly* ⎭	currat et humiles,

b) Masculine and Feminine Adjectives Denoting Things.

Solidus, the name of a coin used in the Empire and in the Gothic kingdom, is made a substantive by the ellipsis of *nummus.* It occurs in literature as early as Apuleius and is mentioned in the Vulgate and in Justinian's Code and Digests. The word is frequent in the Variae, e. g., 18, 2, 30, conquesti sunt . . . nec integri ponderis solidos percipere. . . .

Comitiva, the office of count, is used substantively in the Theodosian Code and thereafter in legal and other writings (T. L. L., III, 1800, 46). It is frequent in the Variae, e. g., 54, 2, 16, te . . . comitivae domesticorum vacantis honore provehimus.

c) Neuter Adjectives.

Adjectives in the neuter plural are frequently used substantively in the Variae. This use is especially found in connection with a dependent partitive genitive (Cf. partitive genitive, p. 19), e. g., 25, 2, 17, inania verborum = *inania verba* (Cf. *inania verba,* 31, 4. 8).

Many examples of this type and of other neuter plural adjectives used substantively are listed by Traube, 512-513.

One example of an adjective in the neuter singular used substantively in this connection occurs in 4, 9, 18, in obscurum silentii

(Cf. partitive genitive, p. 20, for this and examples of the plural). Traube, 512, gives a list of adjectives in the neuter singular used substantively.

In classical prose the neuter plural is frequently used substantively, the neuter singular usually only in philosophical discussions of *bonum, malum, verum,* etc. (K.-Steg., II, 1, 228-229).

B. PARTICIPLES

a) Present and Perfect Participles.

The substantive use of the present participle in the nominative singular, though occurring in Early Latin, was generally avoided by classical prose writers and by Livy. It becomes more frequent with Seneca.

A few examples occur in the Variae, e. g.

328, 7, 24, non enim aut legatus moram aut *interpellans* aliquam sustinet . . . iacturam,
338, 6, 20, iudicem me *observans* inveniet, quocumque respexerit.
383, 2, 10, accipiat minus *habens* indulgentiam principalem
385, 8, 9, votum est vendenti magis perdere, ut quaestum *comparans* debeat invenire.

The masculine singular of the perfect participle in any case is rarely used substantively in classical prose. The substantive use of this form also becomes more frequent with Seneca.

Only a few instances occur in the Variae, e. g.

12, 2, 21, quem *moderatus* ascivit,
15, 11, 14, cum *supra dicti* filio Carpilione
18, 2, 4, si nihil est quod rationabiliter a *pulsato* possit opponi,

With the exception of the forms mentioned in the preceding paragraphs the present participle and the perfect passive participle (as also the perfect participle of deponent verbs) were used substantively by writers in all periods of the language. Late Latin differs from classical prose only in the greater frequency of the substantival use. The following examples taken from two successive pages of the Variae are not at variance with classical usage, but are presented here merely to show their frequency. In other words, a classical prose author might have used any of these examples, but it is not probable that within the same number of lines he

would have furnished so many examples of the substantival use.
Examples:

22, 3, 1, insonantium manibus agitur,
22, 1, 5, vox est iusta poscentium,
22, 2, 11, importunitates competentium summovemus.
22, 1, 15, ut sequentibus . . . praestares.
22, 1, 17, nulli enim propria res a discedente committitur,
22, 2, 21, videtur occasio in delictum trahere,
22, 2, 22, non potest animum pervadentis . . . terrere.
22, 1, 27, regnantis enim facultas tunc fit ditior,
23, 1, 2, manum porrigimus oneratis,
23, 2, 8, unde constat subiectos commoda consecutos.
23, 2, 25, quae devotos maxime noscitur adiuvare.

b) Future Participles.

The use of the future active participle as a substantive is almost
unknown in classical prose. Cicero has two examples of *futurorum*
(gender undetermined), Sallust uses *profutura* (neuter plural) and
futuros. Silver and Late Latin use the future participle substantively with greater frequency.

Cassiodorus is sparing in his use of future participles as substantives, but the following classical examples occur:

futurus, e. g. 5, 14, 7, ita quae dixi de praeteritis conveniunt et futuris,
profuturus e. g. 50, 18, non est sapientiae profutura contemnere.
    Cf. also 61, 1, 4; 88, 3, 17; 91, 1, 27; 99, 1, 13; 104, 1, 17, etc.

Note also his use of *transiturus,* e. g., 336, 6, 5, si auribus tuis
transitura placeant.

The substantive use of the gerundive as a future participle passive
is mentioned on p. 165.

3. Comparison

A. STRENGTHENING OF THE COMPARATIVE
(L.-Hof. 464-465)

A few examples of the comparative of adjectives and adverbs
strengthened by *magis* occur. The usage is colloquial. The first
clear example occurs in Bell. Afr. Examples:

 30, 2, 3, magis verius
143, 1, 3, ferro magis quam auri pretio ditiores
159, 1, 20, magis miserabiliorem

169, 7, 13, magis . . . mitior
184, 3, 24, magis nescio quid amplius meriti
192, 5, 4, magis studiosior
231, 2, 11, magis affectuosius
250, 6, 26, multo magis praestantior
305, 1, 16, magis posterius

A similar use of *amplius* occurs in 273, 1, 23, tanto amplius grandiora. *Minus* with a comparative occurs in 338, 6, 19, minus locupletior. The use of *minus* with the comparative first appears in Late Latin. *Valde* with the comparative occurs once in the first preface, 4, 10, 26, valde certior. An example of a similar strengthening of the superlative by means of an adverb occurs in 108, 3, 26, minutissimarum . . . omnino muscarum.

B. COMPARISON EXPRESSED BY *Magis, Maxime,* ETC.

a) Comparative.

The comparative is occasionally formed by *magis* with the positive instead of the regular comparative form. Thus, e. g., 188, 3, 24, quanto magis grata est. Other expressions equivalent to a comparative are: *plus,* e. g., 34, 2, 32, plus fuerit onerata; *supra* with its object, e. g., 381, 5, 29, ut supra solitum hiems sicca redderetur; *ultra* with its object, e. g., 335, 5, 25, ultra omnes dementes est.

b) Superlative.

Maxime with a positive adverb occurs in 13, 2, 29, maxime desideranter. T. L. L., V, 709, 39, cites a superlative *desiderantissime* for Ven. Fort. *Nimis* and *nimium* with the positive produce the effect of a superlative, e. g., 66, 1, 16, relaxata nimis poena and 293, 12, 4, tam nimium desideratus. Traube, 524, gives the following list of " comparativi et superlativi praeter usum aut regulam ": *agrestissimus,* 203, 2, 27; *animosius,* 65, 13; *annosior,* 304, 2, 25; *dignissime,* 253, 4, 30; 301, 7, 2 cet.; *enixius,* 287, 9, 4; *fuscior,* 343, 4, 20; *gratissime* (s. v.); *proximior,* 226, 2, 10; 350, 2, 11; *purissime,* 205, 3, 29; *segnissime,* 34, 4, 11; *terrentior,* 157, 3, 6; *tutissime,* 23, 4, 33; *veracissimus,* 156, 2, 4; *vivacius* (s. v.); *utillimus,* 72, 14, 18; 165, 9, 23; 191, 1, 15; 259, 3, 4, etc. (Those indicated by s. v. are mentioned and examples given elsewhere in his Index). We may add to the list " praeter usum " the super-

lative of *albus* occurring in 270, 4, 22, argento confert albissimam
lucem. Varro, ling. 8, 75, mentions the degrees of comparison
" Album albius albissimum." This passage from the Variae is the
only other citation for a superlative of *albus* in T. L. L., I,
1502, 78.

C. INTERCHANGE OF THE DEGREES OF COMPARISON
(L.-Hof. 465-466)

That Cassiodorus did not draw sharp distinctions in the various
degrees of comparison is shown by the following examples:

11, 3, 19, nesciunt esse gravissimae	= positive
25, 1, 31, unicuique patria sua carior est	= superlative
38, 4, 10, illa, quae potiora credimus, ad conservandum melioribus damus	= superlative
66, 2, 22, metalla quam invenire possumus pretiosiora	= superlative
72, 17, 32, citharoedum ... sapientia vestra eligat praesenti tempore meliorem.	= superlative
73, 1, 3, Alamannicos populos caesis fortioribus . . . subdidistis.	= superlative
105, 2, 16, quos ipse fecerat *tristes,* laboravit iterum reddere *laetiores*	= positive
120, 2, 2, dum semper aviae cura tenerior est suorum	= superlative
120, 2, 4, ornatior cupit novis thalamis apparere	= superlative
144, 3, 8, proinde requirite nos saepius per vias.	= strong positive
149, 3, 15, si aut eorum carpenta itinere longiore quassantur	= strong positive
163, 1, 8, allegationibus tuis diutius perquisitis	= positive
165, 3, 2, *saevioribus* morbis *accelerata* remedia tribuamus	= comparative
171, 4, 17, suavius nobis fuit ista reddere quam multo grandia suscepisse.	= comparative
224, 10, fuge longius iniqua compendia.	= emphatic positive.
231, 1, 3, (pacem) quam parentes meos constat ardentius expetisse:	= strong positive
255, 1, 2, tanto divinitati *plurima* debemus, quanto a ceteris mortalibus *maiora* suscipimus	= comparative
287, 3, 25, in tanta virorum fortium multitudine solus inventus est, qui patriam plus amasset.	= superlative

4. Interchange or Joining of Adjective and Adverb

A. ADJECTIVE FOR ADVERB
(L.-Hof. 467-468)

The most striking example is *festinus* in 17, 3, 20, festinus occurre, and in 94, 3, accelera festinus adventum (Cf. incunctanter occurre, 161, 3, 8). The use of *festinus* in this manner is cited in T. L. L., VI, 621, 62, as " paene pro adverbio." It occurs once in Vergil, twice in Valerius Flaccus, in Apuleius, and in a number of later writers. This example is cited in T. L. L., VI, 621, 74. The adverb *festine* occurs in Variae, 99, 1, 12.

B. ADVERBS FOR ADJECTIVES
(L.-Hof. 468)

Quondam occurs about 14 times as an adjective, e. g. 34, 1, 22, locum te iubemus quondam Benedicti . . . suscipere. It is usually with the name of a person in the sense of *the deceased*. Harpers' and Georges cite Curt. 10, 1, 23, *Cyro quondam rege*, Cod. Iust., and inscriptions. Bonnet, 305, gives several examples from Gregory of Tours. *Retro* is met twice as an adjective, 123, 2, 17, quae retro principum constiterint humanitate deputata, and 320, 4, 5, quod temporibus retro principum laudabili opinione fundatum est. *Retro* is thus used in inscriptions and in Late Latin authors, especially Tertullian (Kr.-Schm., II, 514). It is cited once for Aug. Conf., 11, 13, by Arts, 60.

Iugiter occurs as an adjective through the use of an appositive in place of a relative clause in 53, 3, 26, ciconia redeuntis anni iugiter nuntiatrix. The word itself is Late; first cited for Apuleius (Harpers' and Georges).

Tunc as an adjective occurs in 15, 11, 12, tunc rerum dominus, and in 139, 11, 14, tunc homines.

C. ADJECTIVE AND ADVERB IN JUXTAPOSITION

A notable example of the juxtaposition of adjective and adverb is found in 149, 22, sed ne species ipsae aut corruptae aut difficile praeberentur. The author here is unusually sparing in his words; he might have repeated the verb to bring out the meaning, which is *lest the articles themselves be supplied corrupted, or be with diffi-*

culty supplied. We may note too that the adverbial use of *difficile*
is a Silver and Late Latin usage for the classical *difficulter* or the
rare but classical *difficiliter* (T. L. L., V, 1091, 1 ff.).

5. Numeral Adjectives
(L.-Hof. 492-493)

A. Cardinal Numerals.

Of the cardinal numerals only *unus* and *mille* present any peculiarities.

Unus is occasionally paired with *alius* or *alter*, as in 42, 1, 6-7,
(horologia) unum, in quo humana sollertia videtur colligi . . .
aliud, ubi solis meatus sine sole cognoscitur, and in 71, 9, 20, (duo
. . . metra) unum quod erigeret, alterum quod placaret. This
pairing of *unus* with *alius* is rare in cassical prose, more frequent
in Silver and Late writers. T. L. L., I, 1649, 76, gives examples
of *unus-alius,* two from Cic., one from Caes., then Liv., Sen.,
Plin., and several Late writers. T. L. L., I, 1742, 47 ff. gives examples of *unus-alter* from several Early writers, several from Cic.
and Caes., then many Silver and Late.

Unus is used for *alteruter* in 78, 3, 12, inter duos enim nobis
affinitate coniunctos non optamus aliquid tale fieri, unde unum
minorem contingat forsitan inveniri, and 80, 3, 27, absit ille conflictus, ubi unus ex vobis dolere poterit inclinatus (Cf. Traube,
596). Kr.-Schm., II, 695, erroneously calls this usage " neulatein-
isch," a term used ordinarily for the Latin later than 600 A. D. T.
L. L., I, 1761, 75 does not mention *unus* among the synonyms
of *alteruter*.

Unus occurs as a substitute for *singuli* in 135, 3, 24, per unum
equum centum solidos multae nomine cogatur inferre, and in 147,
2, 1, per unum equum centum statim solidos a te cogatur exsolvere (Cf. Traube, 596. I have found no discussions of this use).
Elsewhere he uses *unusquisque* or no adjective at all, e. g., 149, 2,
12, per unamquamque condamam; 149, 23, tres solidos per condamam; 151, 7, 19, per annum . . . semel accedat.

In 225, 1, the title of Formula VII, 45, is Formula, Qua Census
Relevetur Ei Qui Unam Casam Possidet Praegravatam. As the
formula itself does not emphasize the singular nature of the *casa,*

this seems to be an example (the only one in the Variae) of the use of *unus* approaching that of an indefinite article. This usage of *unus* is mostly colloquial, but occurs in Cicero, de orat. 1, 132 (Kr.-Schm., II, 694).

One peculiar usage of *milia* occurs in 147, 1, 19, comperimus Thomatem . . . decem milia solidorum reliquatorem . . . extitisse. The critical apparatus suggests the use of *ad decem*. A second citation dealing with the same subject is 148, 1, 3, usque ad decem milia solidorum . . . reliquatorem . . . extitisse, which offers no difficulty. If we take the text as it is in the Monumenta edition, it appears that *milia* is accusative after the verbal substantive *reliquatorem*. This usage occurs rarely in Early Latin, but is frequent in Late Latin (L.-Hof., 378).

Milibus with ellipsis of *passuum* has the meaning of the English word *miles* in 343, 2, 7, a fronte sexaginta milibus dulcissimi aequoris amoenitate perfruitur.

Tot is used for an indefinite number, e. g., 187, 7, 9, tot librarum auri = a fine of *so many* pounds of gold, and in 220, 2, 25, copiam tot mensuum. The use of *tot* in this manner belongs to Late Latin (L.-Hof., 485). The pronoun *ille* is frequently used in a similar manner for an indefinite ordinal numeral, e. g., 175, 4, 29, ab illa indictione = from *such and such* an indiction. Cf. p. 77.

B. Ordinal Numerals.

Quadragesimum (188, 2, 15) and *centesimum* (177, 5, 27) are used as substantives with ellipsis of *miliarium*. (See Mommsen, Neues Archiv, 15, 182; cf. Boecking ad Not. dign., Oc. c. 4; Traube s. v. *milliaria*). A similar use with *primum* is found in Gaius, inst. 4, 104 (Harpers' s. v. *miliarium*). The only similar ellipsis with *centesimum* noted in T. L. L. is in Colum., 5, 8, 5 (T. L. L., III, 818, 42).

The use of the forms *bis sena* (4, 13, 35) *quinos* (152, 4, 34) *binos aut ternos,* (153, 5, 3) *trina* (160, 1, 27) *duplices* (298, 2, 27) may be ascribed to poetical or rhetorical imitation. They substitute for cardinal numerals.

Bis seni is noted in T. L. L., II, 2009, 25 as occurring over 50 times. Authors cited are Vergil, Manilius, Germ. frg., Seneca, Martial, Commodian, Avienus.

II. *The Adverb*
(L.-Hof. 466-468)

Cassiodorus uses many adverbs which do not appear in classical prose. I mention here only adverbs (both classical and non-classical) which in the Variae are used with meanings different from their usual one or which have encroached upon the function of some other " part of speech."

absolute = *aperte, perspicue*, e. g. 21, 3, 29, hunc ergo . . . tot meritis
absolute relucentem favor vester excipiat.
    Cited for Paul., Tert., Iren., and many late authors. This passage
    cited (T. L. L., I, 180, 46). Classical in meaning of *perfecte,*
    simpliciter. Thus, e. g., 189, 4, 14, unde absolute colligitur pri-
    miceriatus meritis datum uti.

adhuc frequently used to strengthen a comparative, e. g. 242, 2, 18,
adhuc minus probatus; 243, 8, 19, adhuc meliora.
    As a temporal adverb it emphasizes the continuance or intensity
    of the action of the verb, and is used with various tenses (Cf.
    L.-Hof., 662).
    Examples: 105, 2, 13, ne adhuc ambiguum redderemus; 147, 2, 29,
    possemus enim adhuc ultra differre; 366, 2, 7, si adhuc nudare
    velis exutos; 370, 2, 14, quid adhuc . . . temptabis . . . ?

alibi 283, 1, 7, plus debuit cogitare iura publica, qui se noverat alibi
non posse sustinere vindictam.
    In this example *alibi* = *alioquin.* The only classical usage of the
    word is in reference to place. It is used in the meaning of
    alioquin in Liv., Ulp. dig., Tert. (T. L. L., I, 1555, 5; see also
    Kr.-Schm., I, 137, where this example is the only one given).

amplius = *magis*, e. g. 127, 2, 7, quid amplius esse possit incongruum
    . . . ?
    159, 1, 21, necesse est ut amplius permoveat visa quam audita
    calamitas.
= *potius*, e. g. 362, 2, 1, timeri te amplius volumus quam probari
    In classical Latin *magis* denotes a higher degree and is used with
    verbs, adjectives, and adverbs; *potius* denotes that one thing is
    chosen to the exclusion of another.
    Amplius refers to extension in space or time (K.-Steg., II, 2, 461),
    but in Late Latin is used for *magis* or *potius* (L.-Hof., 732. See
    also T. L. L., I, 2012 and Kr.-Schm., II, 45 and II, 313).

ardue = *vix*. It occurs only in 242, 3, 4, quod mihi ardue potuissem
optare.
    The adverb from *arduus* is cited only in this passage and in Hier.
    adv. Lucif. 15 (T. L. L., II, 496, 58).

bene substantively, 365, 9, 7, opto meis bene, sed quod possit esse commune.

I have found no exact parallel. T. L. L., II, 2121, 39, has *bene* with *optare, sperare,* but the use is adverbial.

With *velle,* 320, 34, ut bene velitis, quos, etc.

celerius = statim, 164, 1, 6, ut quae possunt noxie crescere, debeamus celerius amputare

The comparative can be regarded as equivalent to a positive, but *celeriter* regularly refers to speed of action, not to promptness in beginning (T. L. L., III, 753, 34 ff.).

difficile = vix, 376, 1, 2, difficile magna res geritur, quae signorum praecursione minime declaretur.

(Cf. Adj. Paired with Adv., p. 59) = *with difficulty.* As an adverb *difficile* is Silver and Late. Velleius is the first to use it (Kr.-Schm., I, 445). Cited for Fronto, Ps. Cypr., Tert., Herm. Pal. (T. L. L., V, 1093, 48).

exinde = source, origin, e. g. 150, 1, 27, aliquid exinde suis applicare compendiis (also, 160, 10; 244, 7, 29; 278, 2, 16; 278, 2, 17; 370, 1, 11, etc.). Used thus by Apul., Cod. Iust. (Harpers').

= *cause,* e. g. 32, 3, 21, ut exinde hostilis ira fervescat. (Also 104, 3, 26; 213, 1, 8; 226, 2, 11, etc.)

Causal use is late (Kr.-Schm., I, 547). *Exinde* is frequent in the classical use, *from that place,* e. g. 135, 5, 21; 138, 6, 28; 382, 3, 25; 382, 3, 27.

hinc, e. g. 384, 3, 8, quasi inde nudos, hinc stare contigisset armatos:

The use of *inde* and *hinc* to indicate *on the one side, on the other* is Silver Latin, occurring in Curt. and Plin. (Kr.-Schm., I, 652).

hinc = means, e. g. 174, 1, 2, hinc omnino datur intellegi.

The use of *hinc* to express means is Late Latin, found in Tert., Claud. Mamer., Sedulius, Lucifer, Filastrius (Kr.-Schm., I, 652).

The use of *hinc . . . quod,* etc. is chiefly Late Latin (Kr.-Schm., I, 652). This occurs very frequently in the Variae, e. g. 3, 5, 19, hinc est quod cogimur animo per cunctas ire provincias.

Hinc denoting source or cause is also very frequent in the Variae. This use is classical.

inde, for non-classical use cf. *hinc* above.

localiter, e. g. 70, 4, 22, localiter sparsit gratiam. Late Latin word. Amm., Ter., Cass. var. (Harpers').

magis = potius; occurs thus very frequently, e. g. 152, 4, 33, aut conducat eum classibus serviturum aut, si hoc ipse magis elegerit . . . publico cedat sui iura dominii.

See *amplius,* above. This use of *magis* for *potius* occurs occasionally in Cicero and Sallust (Kr.-Schm., II, 45).

modo = nunc, e. g. 164, 1, 8, ista enim quae modo facili avulsione dirimuntur, postea vix securibus icta succumbunt.

In classical prose *modo,* temporal, is not used to indicate the present or the immediate future (Kr.-Schm., II, 93).

nihilominus = *aeque, pariter, etiam, adeo.* Of this use 31 citations are
listed by Traube, 562.
In some of these the word seems to be quite superfluous. It has
little or no force, e. g. 359, 3, 14, dum tale institutum fuisse
creditur, qualia gesta nihilominus sentiuntur.

omnino = *by all means,* 109, 6, 12, huic tamen mechanicus omnino
iungendus est.
= *imprimis,* e. g. 301, 3, 22, estote ergo circa eos . . . omnino solliciti. (Other examples in Traube, 564.)
Omnino meaning *by all means* is found in Cicero followed by *sed* or
other adversative conjunctions.
Omnino as equivalent of *imprimis* does not occur in classical prose.

pariter as a mere strengthening of *et . . . et . . .* 153, 2, 22, (ut)nunc
mittamus aliis provinciis et terrorem pariter et decorem.
Pariter cum is used for accompaniment in Sall. and Liv. (Kr.-
Schm., II, 243). I have seen no examples elsewhere of such a
use of pariter . . . et . . . et.

plus = *magis,* e. g. 3, 5, 18, quae supra omnia populi plus requirunt.
See *amplius* above.
Plus regularly refers to greater quantity or number. There are
occasional examples of *plus* for *magis* in classical prose (K.-
Steg., II, 2, 461).
The same usage may explain 29, 1, 8, reverentiam plus habere.

primitus = *prius* (3 times) e. g. 55, 2, 13, nec passus est sibi regem
quaerere, nisi rectorem primitus perdidisset.
Primitus occurs in Early and in Silver Latin and in poetry in the
meaning of *for the first time.* The meaning here is *previously.*

primum = *primi,* adj. e. g. 168, 4, 34, (ludum) Athenienses primum ad
civitatis suae perduxere culturam.
The meaning is *the Athenians were the first to,* and classical prose
would employ the adj. in agreement with the subject (K.-Steg.,
II, 1, 238).
The adjective is so used, e. g. 129, 3, 18.

prius = *formerly, in times past,* e. g. 181, 2, 30, Quid enim prius
facerent inter servos iura publica, qui personam legibus non
haberent?
In classical Latin *prius* means *before, earlier,* etc. in relation to a
later point of time, i. e., the comparative idea prevails. The
usage as above is not comparative, except in comparison with the
general idea of the present. It is listed as poetic and cited for
Cat. 51, 13, and 4, 25, and Prop. 1, 1, 18 (Harpers').

procul dubio = *sine dubio,* e. g. 92, 1, 18, (ut) procul dubio nostris
aerariis inferatur:
Procul with the ablative is found in Horace; with *dubio,* in Liv.,
Plin., Suet., etc. (Harpers'; Kr.-Schm., II, 389).

quam = potius quam, e. g. 32, 4, 4, ut tonos possit quilibet credere quam
clamores.

Similar examples are found in Early, Classical, and Silver Latin,
but the greatest frequency is in Late Latin, especially among
the archaists and the jurists. Vulgar Latin also shows examples
(L.-Hof., 730).

quam with positive = superlative, 327, 9, 14, Thesaurus ipse quam
facile profunditur.

The origin of this usage is in exclamatory sentences. Later it was
extended to non-exclamatory types. It is found in Cicero and
becomes frequent from Apuleius on (L.-Hof., 462-463).

quamvis as an adverb modifying chiefly adjectives is classical. It
occurs very frequently in the Variae.

The example in 149, 3, 17, quamvis parvis sanis animalibus
adquiescant, seems to bring out clearly its relation to the conjunction *quamvis,* used in concessive clauses. The author appears
here to be striving for brevity. The meaning is *quamvis parva
sint.*

saepe = bis, 126, 5, 20, saepe dictus saio; the *saio* has been mentioned
only twice.

singulariter = singillatim or *a singulis* (agent). 154, 1, 15, laudis
occasio est, si in causa communi aliquid singulariter videatur
impleri.

Word is Early, Silver, and Late. In prose it means *exceedingly.*
or, *in the singular number.* It is used as above by Lucretius
(Harpers'; Kr.-Schm., II, 582).

ulterius = ultra, e. g. 212, 5, 15, Sed quis illa ulterius praecipua puta-
bit . . . ?

Word is mostly poetic and in post-Augustan prose. It is used in a
local sense in Prop. and Ovid in the meaning of *ultra.*

In the Variae it occurs with a verb in the future or with a future
significance, e. g. *purpose, command.*

ultra = plus, 147, 3, 3, non ultra quam centum libras iubemus imponi.

Ultra quam is mentioned in L.-Hof., 732, 2, for authors from Rhet.
Her. to Lact., including Cicero. Here it is in a substantive use.
All examples in Harpers' appear to be adverbial.

unde = cur, e. g. 29, 5, 27, unde ergo irasci volunt . . . ?

= *quamobrem* 22, 1, 15, unde fit ut bona vobis crescat opinio.

= *de* with ablative, e. g. 314, 3, 11, De Ranildae quoque causa, unde
vestra serenitas me commonere dignata est,

314, 4, 14, Earum siquidem rerum iudicium non praesumimus, unde
mandatum specialiter non habemus.

The uses of *unde* in the sense of *quamobrem* and in the sense of *de*
with the ablative are Late Latin (L.-Hof., 492, 1).

CHAPTER IV

The Pronoun

I. *Personal Pronouns*
(L.-Hof. 468-469)

1. Non-agreement

Instances of the non-agreement in number of possessive adjectives and relative pronouns with the personal pronouns with which they are used in the plural of majesty and the plural of reverence have been mentioned, pp. 8-9.

2. Personal Pronoun Subject Expressed

The occasional omission of a personal pronoun subject where the expression of it would be an aid to clearness has been mentioned on page 11.

The opposite tendency, namely, to express a personal pronoun subject unnecessarily, is not to any great degree in evidence in the Variae. Colloquial speech at all times showed a tendency to express such pronoun subjects, even in commands and in statements where the subject was not emphatic. Late Latin usage in general favored the expression of the subject. Cassiodorus seems, however, to adhere rather closely to classical standards in this respect.

It is true that the word *nos* appears often as subject. This is due chiefly to the fact that very many sentences are in the first person plural, owing to the frequent use of the plural of majesty. The first person singular is rare. But even in the plural of majesty the subject is more frequently omitted than expressed, and the rather large number of times that it is expressed is chiefly a consequence of the author's using it as the antecedent of a relative limiting its meaning.

Examples of the following type are very frequent:

93, 2, 12, Sed nos, qui donatas dignitates iustitiae parere cupimus, . . . nostra te tuitione vallamus
120, 3, 5, Ideoque nos, qui desideria supplicantum consuevimus remittere . . . hanc causam legibus committimus audiendam,

66

Where *nos* is expressed as subject without the relative, the reason
is usually one of emphasis. Often a transition to the first person
from the second, and more frequently from the third, is marked
by the expression of *nos* at or near the beginning of the sentence.
Thus, e. g., following a third person, 161, 1, 1, hanc nos, si tamen
vera est, in femina quam maxime mirantes audaciam, transire non
patimur impunitam, and 161, 1, 14, haec nos, si vera sunt, transire
nequaquam patimur impunita. The transition itself requires, or
at least justifies, the expression of the subject, i. e., it brings out
the idea, *Now we, for our part, etc.*

Ego occurs much less frequently. Its use regularly indicates
emphasis or contrast. In fact, the mere employment of the first
person singular in the Variae is usually emphatic in itself, even
where the pronoun is not expressed. Cf. p. 8. An excellent example of the use of *ego* in a contrast is in 373, 7, 24, alii dicant
insulas, ego habitationes tuas appellem potius Fortunatas.

Vos as subject occurs less frequently than *nos*. This is due in
part to the fact that most of the documents are written to indi-
viduals and, notwithstanding a rather frequent use of the plural
of reverence, the second person singular is frequently employed.
Vos as subject with a following relative is much less frequent than
is *nos* in a similar usage. Examples, however, occur, such as
365, 2, 20, vos tamen, quos ad publicas amministrationes pervenire
nostra fecit electio, de actionum honestate confidite, and 380, 1, 1,
sed vos, qui numerosa navigia in eius confinio possidetis, pari
devotionis gratia providete, ut quod illa parata est tradere, vos
studeatis sub celeritate portare. Both these examples have their
main verbs in the imperative. It is not because of the imperative,
however, that the subject is expressed, for the author's general
practice is to omit a subject with the imperative, but because of
the transition and the use of the relative following the pronoun.
In the second example the *ut*-clause has its subject *vos* expressed
because of the contrast with the preceding *illa*.

Tu occurs much less frequently than *vos*. Many sentences which
are logically in the second person are grammatically in the third
because of the use of third person titles of honor as subjects. Where
the second person is used, the subject is not often expressed and,
where it is expressed, its presence is regularly due to the same

reasons which occasion the expressing of *nos* and *vos*. Thus, e. g., in a letter to Boethius, after some extravagant praises of the latter, the author continues, 40, 5, 17, Tu artem praedictam ex disciplinis nobilibus notam per quadrifarias mathesis ianuas introisti. tu illam in naturae penetralibus considentem, auctorum libris invitantibus, cordis lumine cognovisti, cui ardua nosse usus, miracula monstrare propositum est. Desire to emphasize the subject is a sufficient explanation of the *tu*; cf. also, e. g., 186, 5, 9; 377, 3, 27.

Apart from the possessive uses (see following paragraph), the syntax of the personal pronouns conforms to that of classical prose.

3. Personal Pronoun for Possessive Adjective

In rare instances Cassiodorus uses the personal pronoun in the genitive in place of the corresponding possessive adjective. This usage in classical prose is confined to the use of the reflexive *sui* in one example in Nepos and doubtful examples in Caesar and Cicero (Cf. K.-Steg., II, 1, 598-599).

In Silver and Late Latin authors not only is *sui* thus used, but also *nostri*, etc. Examples from the Variae:

89, 1, 26, *cordi nostri* est levamen humilium
119, 2, 12, hoc hactenus fieri *nostri ignorantia* fortasse pertulerit: nunc necesse est remedium de legibus habeat, quod nostram potuit intrare notitiam.
158, 1, 23, multo tamen acceptiora credimus quae *nostri praesentia* conferuntur,
272, 1, 17, metuens ne per *absentiam tui* . . . fructus videatur auferri
335, 3, 17, *actus* enim *tui* iudicis opinio est

There are textual variants in some of these examples. Traube, 567, also adds 207, 3, 1, *actus tui* venatio nocturna est. Mommsen's text has *actus tuus*.

In two examples the form *vestrorum* occurs as a partitive genitive in place of *vestrum.* These are 167, 3, 28, quis enim vestrorum a Cypriani devotione summotus est? and 319, 1, 19, ut . . . sic videamur pacem vestram quaerere, tamquam nos nemo vestrorum putetur ante laesisse. This form, of which the genitive *vestrum* is a contraction, is in use among the early dramatists (L.-Hof. 284, 1).

With these examples of vestrorum, cf. 359, 2, 9, quod nulli accidit vestrum. In 319, 4, 6, Mommsen's text reads additur, quod unicuique virorum vestrorum testis assisto. Manuscript B omits the word *virorum*; the reading without the word *virorum* would necessitate classifying this example with the two above mentioned.

Vestrorum appears to be used as a possessive genitive in 319, 2, 27, eius debet filia cogitari, quam *nisus vestrorum omnium* perducere decuisset ad regnum. If we assume that *vestrorum* is for *vestrum*, this example is to be paired with 241, 1, 22, quod ad agendas optimo regi gratias *omnium vestrum studia* debent concitari, a usage of the possessive genitive which is classical (Cf. K.-Steg., II, 1, 246). However *nisus vestrorum omnium* may mean *the efforts of all your men*. Several other examples employ *nostrorum* and *vestrorum* apparently as adjectives with an omitted substantive. Thus:

143, 2, 28, hanc levissimam substantiam, sicut et vestrorum relatio continebat, exportat:

215, 18, si et populos peregrinos prudenter excipias et nostrorum commercia moderata aequalitate componas.

239, 8, 7, atque ideo eum nostrorum fama concelebrat:

282, 1, 32, facilius quippe inimicorum acies cadunt, si nostrorum delicta subducimus.

Possessive adjectives would seem to be the natural words to use here if the author intended to convey the meanings, *your reports, our commerce,* etc. As Cassiodorus regularly uses the possessive adjectives *noster* and *vester* in the classical manner, it seems safe to conclude that here he means *the report of your men, the commerce of our people,* etc.

II. *Demonstrative Pronouns*

The following table shows the relative frequency of the various demonstrative pronouns in the Variae, arranged according to gender, number, and case. Discussion of various features of the table will be included in the treatment of the individual demonstratives.

SINGULAR

	Is M.	Is F.	Is N.	Hic M.	Hic F.	Hic N.	Ille M.	Ille F.	Ille N.	Ipse M.	Ipse F.	Ipse N.	Iste M.	Iste F.	Iste N.	Idem M.	Idem F.	Idem N.
Nom.	15	2	5	21	57	70	114	50	33	59	31	3	27	13	0	0	0	3
Gen.	85	30	12	12	18	8	17	9	2	10	8	4	0	1	1	0	0	1
Dat.	21	4	2	15	10	3	37	11	2	5	0	1	2	1	0	1	0	0
Acc.	69	19	6	22	52	118	98	63	61	6	11	3	0	0	3	0	2	0
Abl.	14	23	10	8	60	15	43	54	10	14	23	11	2	3	0	3	7	1
	204	78	35	78	197	214	309	187	108	94	73	22	31	18	4	4	9	5

PLURAL

	Is M.	Is F.	Is N.	Hic M.	Hic F.	Hic N.	Ille M.	Ille F.	Ille N.	Ipse M.	Ipse F.	Ipse N.	Iste M.	Iste F.	Iste N.	Idem M.	Idem F.	Idem N.
Nom.	1	0	1	4	0	22	37	1	17	16	9	10	4	0	11	0	0	0
Gen.	32	5	1	0	19	2	11	0	2	2	1	0	1	0	0	0	0	0
Dat.	23	1	1	9	5	10	47	0	3	6	2	0	3	0	0	0	0	0
Acc.	70	2	14	9	9	48	34	14	40	7	4	11	1	0	14	0	1	2
Abl.	15	1	4	14	9	24	20	8	5	12	4	11	0	0	0	2	0	1
	141	9	21	36	42	106	149	23	67	43	20	32	9	0	25	2	1	3

	Is	Hic	Ille	Ipse	Iste	Idem
Total	488	673	843	284	87	24
Pct. of total	20¼%	28%	35¼%	12%	3½%	1% *

* For purposes of comparison with other prose writers the reader is referred to the tables in Meader, 30-32 and Hrdlicka, 254. Meader's percentages for Caesar and the continuators, as representing in some degree classical usage, and his percentage for Boethius, De Consolatione, as representing the usage of a contemporary of Cassiodorus, may be of special interest. They are as follows:

	Is	Hic	Ille	Ipse	Iste	Idem
Caes. etc....	50½%	20½%	9½%	14%	⅛%	6%
Boeth.	23½%	35½%	20½%	13%	1½%	3½%

1. *Is*

(L.-Hof. 478)

The pronoun *is* tends gradually to disappear from the Latin language. The poets used most of its forms rather sparingly, and the popular language of the Empire made frequent use of *hic, ille, iste,* and *ipse* in its place. By the Late Latin period the nominative masculine and feminine forms, both singular and plural, had been almost driven out of existence, and the neuter nominative, especially in the singular, was rarely used. Other forms, while still in use, became less frequent than the corresponding forms of *hic* and *ille*.

In general, Cassiodorus' usage is that which prevailed in Late Latin. The nominative plural is represented by only two examples, one masculine and one neuter. The masculine example is 162, 7, 28, ii enim, qui portanda susceperant, morarum taedia non ferentes destinatum frumentum in Africae partibus pro suo dicuntur vendidisse compendio. As the critical apparatus gives " hii plerique hi DAe," it is at least very probable that the phonetic falling together of these forms with *ii* is responsible for the occurrence of this unusual form. The form *hi*, however, occurs only four times. The neuter example is 222, 2, 31, ut in competenti foro ea quae in his causis reverenda legum dictat antiquitas, sollemniter actitentur. Manuscripts T and U omit *ea*; the omission would be in conformity with a very frequent practice of the author in omitting unemphatic antecedents.

Of the nominative singular forms the masculine occurs 15 times. In 8 of these occurrences it is followed by a relative, i. e., in the stereotyped phrase *is qui*. Where *is* occurs without the relative there are usually variant manuscript readings, chiefly an ablative *his* in place of *is*. One example, for which there are several variant readings, involves a violent transition in the structure of the sentence if we accept Mommsen's reading *isque*, since the clause *isque . . . subtraxit* occurs between a relative clause and the main clause as a parenthetical or anacolouthic insertion. The sentence is 87, 14, ideoque illum, quem dudum ad viri illustris Sonae iudicium decrevimus convenire *isque* se inveterata calliditate subtraxit, examini vestro committimus audiendum, ut finem detis iurgio plectibili machinatione dilatato.

The disproportion between masculine and feminine forms in the nominative and in other cases is due in part to the fact that this pronoun is used chiefly for persons, and the persons spoken of by Cassiodorus are chiefly males. Feminine nominatives occur in 28, 29, and 349, 5.

Of the five occurrences of *id* in the nominative, all are in the stereotyped phrase *id est*. Thus, 70, 5, 32; 71, 9, 20; 124, 3, 8; 131, 3, 30; 154, 6, 6.

Perhaps the most frequent use of this pronoun, all forms being considered except *eius*—which serves as a genitive of other demonstratives—is that in which it serves as antecedent for a relative, in which capacity the forms of the oblique cases occur quite frequently, though the nominative form, as has been shown, is rare. In some instances the antecedent is a definite person who has been previously mentioned, e. g., 17, 1, 10, ut eum, quem sumptu proprio iuvare debuisses, dispendio proprietatis affligeres.

More frequent is its use as a weak or unemphatic antecedent, in sentences of the type of 17, 3, 20, ut inter vos ea quae iustitiae conveniunt ordinemus, where *ea* has no definite meaning until it is explained by the relative.

Cassiodorus' *most frequent practice,* however, is to omit such an antecedent altogether. Sentences of the following type are very numerous, 16, 17, 8, quod a parentibus accepit hereditaria largitate custodit; 17, 2, 16, perire enim pupillo non patimur quod . . . dederamus. Omissions of antecedents in all cases are noted, though omissions of the nominative are the most consistent. Omissions of the antecedent in sentences of the type of 24, 1, 7, ne fiat exemplum pravum qui electus ad laudabile cognoscitur institutum, are regular.

Classical prose did not always express the antecedent. Antecedents, which, if expressed, would be a form of *is* in the nominative or accusative, could usually be omitted with no sacrifice of clearness, and omissions of the forms of *is* as antecedents in the other cases are by no means unknown among classical authors. Cassiodorus, however, is much more inclined than were classical authors to omit the forms of *is,* and this feature of his style no less than the encroachments of the other demonstratives is responsible for the low percentage of occurrences of *is* in most forms shown in the table on page 70.

The following are a few selected examples of the omission of *is* in various cases where its form has to be determined from the context and is not immediately obvious:

23, 2, 7, quorum non possumus accusare desidiam, relevandam aestimemus esse fortunam.

24, 1, 6, non licet delinquere, qui alios creditur . . . continere

32, 1, 9, nam a quo melius moderatio debet sperari, quam cui potuit Roma committi?

33, 1, 11, debet primum prodesse cui nascitur,

70, 4, 18, ad quod vult deducit,

123, 2, 6, si manus non incursarint exigentum, quos frequenter plus affligunt damna, quam solent nudare naufragia.

149, 26,   tale sit iter vestrum, quale decet esse qui laborant pro salute cunctorum.

205, 1, 16, interesse arbitramur, quod utilitas necessaria gratificat et
   quod pulchritudinis tantum causa commendat.
300, 4, 16, exploravit conscientiam, cui erat regni traditura censuram,
328, 4, 8, huic gloriosum praestat obsequium cui omnia serviunt.
   The antecedent of *cui* is not *huic,* but *is,* the understood
   subject of *praestat.*

Traube, 533, mentions the almost constant omission of the demonstrative antecedent of the relative. A few examples of the same
usage from one of the scriptural studies of Cassiodorus, viz., ad
Corinthios prima, are given by Stangl, *Cassiodoriana I,* 268.

Uses of *hic, ille, ipse,* and *iste* in place of *is* are considered under
the treatment of each of those demonstratives.

2. *Hic*
(L.-Hof. 474-475)

Most of the 673 occurrences of the pronoun *hic* in the *Variae*
conform to classical standards. The chief deviations are (A) the
employment of *hic* for *is* in the combination *hic qui = is qui,* (B)
the use of *hoc* for *id* in the phrases *hoc est, ad hoc, ob hoc,* examples of all these, however, being rare, (C) the use of *hic* in the
sense of *idem.*

(A) *Hic qui* occurs in classical prose regularly only when reference is made to something near the speaker, that is, *hic* has the
force of a " pronoun of the first person." In Silver Latin the distinction between *hic qui* and *is qui* began to be disregarded, and in
Late Latin *hic qui* for *is qui* is frequent.

Hic qui is found in many examples where *hic* is used in its primary meaning, indicating something near the speaker in time,
place, or thought. Examples of *hic qui* used for *is qui* are not especially numerous in the *Variae.* I have not made a complete list
of such occurrences, but the following are typical:

62, 4, 27, nec quicquam in his debes metuere, quae forsitan novella
   usurpatione temptantur.
191, 7, 8, interdum et hoc loquitur, quod a nemine perpetratur.
253, 2, 21, hos etiam intrare in vestram curiam decet, qui ad primos
   honores non expendunt meritum suum,
310, 4, 15, pietatem vestram hoc studere cognoscimus, quod nobis per
   omnia prodesse sentimus.
315, 3, 18, ut hi, quibus commissum est exercere singulos apparatus, de
   iniusto gravamine non querantur.
   4

339, 2, 16, aptum est enim ab his iussa cognosci, quos decrevimus
    ammoneri.

349, 2, 23, honorabiles quidem a cunctis habendi sunt veterani, sed ab
    his maxime, qui militiae labore detinentur.

(B) The explanatory *hoc est* occurs twice, in 252, 5, 24, contulit
etiam dignitatem sacrarum largitionum, hoc est laborum tuorum
aptissimum munus, quam sic casta, sic moderata mente peregisti,
ut, etc., and 271, 1, 5, ut . . . indulgentiae praeconia reperirent,
hoc est, ubi dominus adversum sua iudicia amabili concertatione
dissentit.[1]

Another usage of *hoc est* which occurs several times is that in
which *hoc* is used as a superfluous appositive after an infinitive or
clause as subject, as in 69, 8, 10, talia posteris non tradere hoc est
graviter in longa aetate peccare. Cf. 205, 1, 18; 213 1, 20; 290,
10, 31.

Since in many authors of the Silver and Late period the phrases
ob hoc and *ad hoc* contribute a large number of examples to the
total of the uses of *hic* for *is* (Cf. Meader, 71-79; Hrdlicka, 231-
232), it seems well to call attention here to the infrequency of
these phrases in the Variae.

Ob hoc occurs only twice, viz. in 20, 2, 9, and 102, 1, 20. *Ad hoc*
in a final sense occurs in 32 3, 21; 59, 1, 15; 245, 4, 22; 314, 2, 26.
The usage of *ad hoc* after *idoneus* in 37, 8, is sufficiently like this
usage to deserve to be mentioned here.

(C) Various forms of *hic* occur in the sense of *idem*. Usually
the form is *hoc quod,* but other forms, even without the relatives,
are in use. Examples of *hic = idem*:

38, 4, 8, Numquid hoc est palatia regere et domos proprias ordinare?
94, 1, 7, hoc sunt enim regia dona, quod semina:
277, 3, 21, quia hoc est propria delicta corrigere quod et non facere.
288, 5, 1, hos habetis iudices quos parentes.
327, 2, 31, ut hoc putemus utile quod honestum,
366, 2, 21, quia hoc est bona desideria suspendere quod illicita perpe-
    trare.

---

[1] Meader, 59, states that Cassiodorus uses the explantory *hoc est* once. In
the example in 252, 5, 24, Manuscript A omits *est*; the Monumenta edition
does not place a comma after the *est,* but the insertion of *hoc est laborum
tuorum aptissimum munus* between *dignitatem* and *quam* can be only to
explain that *munus* is an appositive of *dignitatem*.

In at least one example, viz. 289, 4, 3, agnoscat se praeconem habere quem dominum, the relative alone with ellipsis of the demonstrative produces the effect of expressing identity.

3. *Ille*
(L.-Hof. 477)

The table on page 70 shows that of all the demonstratives *ille* occurs most frequently in the Variae. Its 843 occurrences represent approximately 35¼% of the total number of demonstrative forms.

Three chief causes contribute to the unusual frequency of this pronoun, (A) its use in place of *is,* (B) its use in place of *hic,* (C) its use in an indefinite sense, that is, where the author is unwilling, or unable to give the proper name of a person or place or to state precisely a number or a date, and uses the pronoun to fill the vacancy.

A. *Ille* Used for *Is*

The use of *ille* in place of *is* began in Early Latin and increased steadily. In the Silver Age the numerical increase of *ille* and corresponding decrease of *is* became quite pronounced. (Cf. Meader, 194-195 and his tables, 30-31). It is particularly in the phrase *ille qui* in place of *is qui* that the change in the relative frequency of the two pronouns took place.

In the Variae *ille qui* occurs very frequently as a substitute for *is qui.* The following examples are typical:

10,1, 3, quando ille moribus iam tenetur obnoxius, qui ad iusta deprehenditur imparatus.
16,3,25, illud appetitur quod a salutis iudice gravare posse sentitur.
20,1,19, ut illud magis aestimemur elegisse, quod cunctos dignum est approbare.
22,1,26, Illud amplius nostris utilitatibus applicamus, quod misericordi humanitate concedimus.
26,3,27, illa enim lucra vera iudicamus, quae integritate suffragante percipimus.
36,2,23, illi prudentiores sunt semper habiti, qui multorum hominum conversationibus probantur eruditi.
61,2,10, nimis enim iniquum est, ut ille patiatur dispendium, qui imperium fecit alienum.

73, 2, 12, illa mihi feliciter bella provenerunt, quae moderato fine
peracta sunt.
88, 5, 27, intellegite . . . illos merito crescere qui possunt aliis iusta
praestare.
99, 2, 4, cognoscat illa sibi vestris temporibus fuisse subtracta, quae
mos priscus indulserat,
103, 1, 17, quando illud, quod vos debuistis expetere, nos videtis offerre.
164, 2, 34, pro illius voluntate dare, qui ad suum commodum amplius
festinat exigere.
271, 1, 3, si cognoscant illum aliis misertum, quem et sibi optant esse
propitium.
310, 4, 14, illud desideramus efficere, quod vestro nequeat iudicio
displicere:
313, 1, 30, illa nos hortamini facere, quae ad mercedem nostram possint
omnimodis pertinere.
316, 4, 21, illis maxime, qui armorum exercitatione floruerunt,
326, 3, 15, neque enim semper iin illis valemus, quae interdum posse
iudicamur.
333, 1, 14, crescit enim in illo meritum, cui maius datur officium,
337, 6, 7, remuneratorem enim illi me esse promitto, quem se aliqua
honestate tractasse cognovero.

B. *Ille* Used for *Hic*

While *ille* is not found as a substitute for *hic* indicating things
that are physically near the speaker, it frequently indicates the
thing that is near to him in thought. This usage is especially in
evidence in those sentences where *ille* is explained by a clause or
infinitive phrase immediately following the pronoun. Cf. K.-Steg.,
II, 1, 622. While *ille* is so used even in classical prose, its greater
frequency in the Variae is worthy of notice. In the examples
given below there has been no previous reference to the thing indicated by *ille:*

13, 2, 29, Illud tamen maxime desideranter appetimus, ut collegium
vestrum ornent lumina dignitatum,
25, 1, 11, illud enim . . . labores nostros asserit, quod se otiosam gener-
alitas esse cognoscit.
32, 4, 24, Illud etiam, quod crebras inter eos seditiones exagitat,
34, 2, 26, Illud etiam . . . commonemur, ut . . . filios . . . civili facias
tuitione vallari,
42, 1, 3, ad illud tantum tenditur, ut cupientis animus expleatur
92, 3, 3, Illud praeterea vos credidimus ammonendos, ut non in vos,
sed in hostem saevire cupiatis.

101, 2, 31, illud etiam . . . adiciens defensorum tibi patrocinia saepius postulanti fuisse subtracta,

151, 3, 6, illud quoque praecipimus inquirendum, ut . . . ratio vestigetur

231, 4, 20, illud mihi est supra dominatum tantum ac talem rectorem habere propitium.

310, 3, 4, sed illud est omnimodis singulare in extranea gente laudes proprias invenire,

319, 3, 29, Illud etenim vos debuit permovere, quod . . . vos divinitas nostram fecit habere notitiam,

338, 4, 3, illud solum nobis iudicamus esse commodum, si vos iuvante domino servemus illaesos.

C. *Ille* in Indefinite Sense

When Cassiodorus is unwilling, or possibly unable, to give the proper name of a person or place, or to name a precise number or date, he uses the pronoun *ille* to fill the vacancy. Thus the pronoun is used under circumstances where in English we would say, *Mr. X and Mr. Y, so many pounds, on such and such a day*, etc. This usage of *ille* is mentioned in Leumann-Hofmann, 476, as chiefly Late Latin and is discussed at length in Salonius, 232-235. It occurs, e. g., in Cicero, S. Rosc. 21, 59, *quaesisse, num ille aut ille defensurus esset*, where the two uses of *ille* connected by *aut* refer to two or more unnamed persons. Suetonius uses *illum et illum* (and also the single *ille*) precisely as Cassiodorus uses it, in Iul. 41, quoting a letter of Julius Caesar, *Caesar dictator illi tribui. Commendo vobis illum et illum ut vestro suffragio dignitatem suam teneant.*

This usage of *ille* contributes to the total number of forms of *ille* in the Variae a considerable number of singular forms, very few in the plural. It is found in all three genders, but chiefly in the masculine, where the accusative singular form is very frequent. Many royal commissions are entrusted to two envoys, whose identity is unknown to us. Thus *illum et illum* are frequently brought into the text, e. g., 10, 4, 18; 42, 1, 5; 73, 3, 18; 78, 4, 17; 80, 4, 31; 115 4, 13; 143, 3, 13; 170, 4, 21, etc.

That Cassiodorus uses the words *illum et illum* to indicate two persons, not one, is indicated by his use of plural appositives and plural relative pronouns in agreement with this pair of demonstratives. Moreover, a single *ille*, or *illa*, or *illud*, occurs consist-

ently where a single person or thing is meant.[2] Examples of the
use of a single form of *ille* are found in 18, 2, 29, ab illo arcario
praefectorum; 184, 4, 25, ab *illa* indictione *illud* tibi . . . defende;
193, 4, 24, per *illam* indictionem in *illa* provincia. Many similar
examples, passim. *Illum* also occurs in one instance three times in
succession, indicating three " unknowns," 267, 3, 21, illum et illum
atque illum tradite, per quos res facto debeat elucere.

4. *Ipse*
(L.-Hof. 479-480)

In the majority of its occurrences in the Variae *ipse* performs
its original function as an intensive pronoun. The prevalence of
nominative forms, as shown in the table on page 70, is an indica-
tion of its use for emphasis or contrast, for it is usually the subject which needs to be emphasized or which marks a contrast with
another subject. *Ipse* occurs as an emphatic nominative, either
alone or supporting the grammatical subject.

Evidences of the weakening of *ipse* to a mere demonstrative or
determinative pronoun are not lacking, however. It is particularly
in the oblique cases that we see it substituting for *ille* or *is*, but
nominative forms occur also, in which the element of emphasis or
contrast is weakened or totally absent. The use of *ipse* in the
meaning of *ille* or *is* begins with Cicero and is frequent from
Curtius on (Cf. L.-Hof., 480; Meader, 184-188).

A. *Ipse* Used Instead of *Ille* (or *Is*)

In the following examples little, if any, emphasis is evident, and
ipse may be regarded as the equivalent of *ille*, or possibly of *is*.

37, 2, 21, ornatus enim ipsorum est, si, quae solent illi deligere, nos
 iubemus.
57, 1, 27, reddat Ravenna copiam Liguriae, quam ex ipsa consuevit
 accipere.
68, 5, 21, Sed inter alia loci ipsius bona illud quoque stupendum esse
 didicimus,
70, 1, 5, qui disciplinam *ipsam* . . . potuistis attingere. Quid enim
 illa praestantius . . . ?

---

[2] The only difficulty is in reconciling his use of both singular and plural
in the instance mentioned on page 7.

108, 1, 15, ubi ars ipsa pro locorum siccitate magno studio semper excolitur,

114, 3, 17, quiescitur in ipsis potius quam laboretur.

145, 2, 24, Aestimate, quid de *illo* debeat iudicari . . . Ab *ipso* legum peritia postulatur

145, 2, 25, penes ipsum civilitatis nostrae fama reponitur.

186, 2, 23, quod a iudicibus breviter dicitur, ab ipsis efficacia famulante completur.

189, 2, 4, quando ab ipsis aliqua instructio quaeritur, tunc loquantur:

189, 1, 23, per eum interpellantium vota cognoscimus et ipsis responsa reddimus,

191, 1, 17, ipsa enim morbo periclitantibus . . . assistit, ipsa contra dolores . . . confligit.

212, 3, 5, moles *illas* . . . excavatas, ut magis *ipsas* aestimes fuisse transfusas,

218, 2, 20, partem iudicis habent priores, quando ab ipsis requiritur, si quid a vobis insolentius excedatur

334, 1, 3, nam ipsius quodammodo res agitur, cuius in alterum vota complentur.

B. *Ipse* Used Instead of *Is* (or *Ille*)

In the following example *haec* and *ipsa* are used referring to the same previously mentioned thing (divinitatis). *Ipsa* seems to be used as the equivalent of *ea*.

72, 16, 29, *haec* veraciter perennitatem praestat, *haec* iucunditates accumulat: et sicut praeter *ipsam* creatura non extat, ita sine *ipsa* incommutabilem laetitiam habere non praevalet.

Other examples of *ipse* in the sense of *is* (or possibly of *ille*).

58, 3, 11, si eorum opera vel labore turpis dessicaretur illuvies, ipsis liberata rura proficerent.

108, 8, 5, forum ipsius agri deserti sunt.

125, 2, 31, ipsa est enim perfecta pietas, quae antequam flectatur precibus, novit considerare fatigatos.

201, 4, 23, ipsa est enim recta amministratio, quae et sine potestate defenditur,

210, 2, 7, moderata pretia ab ipsis quorum interest facias custodiri.

268, 2, 25, decem librarum auri dispendio feriatur, ipsi qui aliquid tale pertulit nihilominus profuturarum,

275, 1, 10, ipsa est enim vera securitas, quae de nulla iudicis iniquitate formidat.

300, 5, 19, in ipsa est enim decus regnorum omnium, in ipsa nostrae originis flos bonorum.

317, 3, 22, ad ipsius arbitrium gressus movet, ipsius voluntate cibos capit,

C. *Ipse* Used as Reflexive

Ipse is at times made to perform the functions of a reflexive pronoun. Classical examples of *ipse* used in this manner have an element of emphasis. Clear examples of *ipse* as a non-emphatic reflexive are first found in Curtius (K.-Steg., II, 1, 630-631). Examples from the Variae:

70, 3, 12, operosa delectatio haec cum . . . ornata processerit, reliquae cogitationes exiliunt omniaque facit eici, ut ipsam solummodo delectet audiri.

107, 7, 33, videant artis huius periti, quid de ipsis publica sentit auctoritas.

160, 8, onera sibi servilia a vobis causantur iniungi, quae nec ipsos deceat perpeti

177, 2, 15, ut optent se legibus teneri, quae ab ipsis sciuntur potuisse constitui.

180, 5, 1, subdidit eius arbitrio aliena iudicia, ut ad ipsum rediret quod alter visus est praestitisse.

D. *Ipse* Used Instead of *Idem*

Ipse occurs several times under circumstances where Late Latin writers were inclined to use *idem*, namely, to refer a second time to something which had just been mentioned, e. g., 37, 4, animos subito ad arma non erigunt nisi qui se ad ipsa idoneos praemissa exercitatione confidunt (Cf. Hrdlicka, 252). However, this is the proper sphere of the pronouns *is* and *ille*. The only examples I have observed where *ipse* is used as the equivalent of *idem* expressing identity are 19, 7, 32, aut integra tribuis aut non ipsa quae dicuntur exsolvis, and 168, 3, 30, hanc triplicem deam falsa imaginatione finxerunt, *ipsam* in caelo Lunam, *ipsam* in silvis dominam, *ipsam* apud inferos Proserpinam esse firmantes.

5. *Iste*
(L.-Hof. 476-477)

The pronoun *iste* is rare in the Variae. Of the 87 forms occurring, 40 are in the nominative singular, while the nominative and accusative plural neuter forms are the only others occurring with any degree of frequency (11 and 14 respectively).

A. *Iste* in Connection with the Second Person

Casiodorus' usage of *iste* is such as to leave the reader in doubt as to whether he felt this pronoun to have any connection with the second person. It is true that in a large number of examples a connection with the second person can be established, but this connection is usually remote, and the use of *iste* to refer to the subject that has been under discussion or is to be discussed immediately often has no connection with the second person. This makes it appear probable that the uses of *iste* which occur in reference to the second person are more by accident than by design.

Perhaps the most frequent usage of *iste* where the idea of the second person is prominent is in the formulae of appointments to office in Books VI and VII and in similar documents among the letters. In these *iste* frequently refers to things pertaining to the office of the person to whom the document is being addressed. Even here, however, the office or honor, as the chief point of discussion, may be regarded as the thing present to the mind of the writer and as having as close connection with the first person as with the second. The following are examples of this type:

176, 6, 30, licet aliae dignitates habeant titulos praefinitos, ab ista paene totum geritur,
178, 7, 6, nam si isti dignitati par fueris, nihil est quod a nobis minime consequaris.
207, 3, 30, merito tibi gloriosum nomen praefecti prudens antiquitas deputavit, quia istud facere non poterat, nisi qui cives a suis commodis plus amabat.

The following examples illustrate other uses of *iste* in connection with the second person:

12, 5, 1, tanta te istius nominis praesumptione defendis,
201, 2, 10, arma ista iuris sunt, non furoris.
201, 2, 13, civilis est pavor iste, non bellicus, quem tu sic facies esse gloriosum, si, etc.
208, 4, 25, Xenia sunt enim ista, non debita.
210, 2, 21, quem inter ista deceat esse neglegentem?
278, 1, 14, ut nec isti aliquid de futuro metuant nec tu per ignorantiam quae dicuntur incurras.
(*Isti* means *people under your charge*.)

B. *Iste* in Meaning of *Hic*

The use of *iste* in the sense of *hic* seems to have begun in literature with Catullus, in prose with Valerius Maximus.   Subsequently the usage steadily increases (Cf. Meader 111-161; Hrdlicka 235-236).

In the Variae it is found in this meaning in the correlations *ille-iste* and *iste-ille* (to be discussed below, p. 83). This usage sometimes gives occasion for the writer again to refer to the *iste* of the *ille-iste* correlation by this pronoun, as in 109, 6, 12, huic tamen mechanicus omnino iungendus est, ut undas quas *iste* repperit, *ille* levet. . . . The next sentence, in which the correlation is not continued, also refers to this person (first referred to as *huic*) by the word *iste,* viz., habeatur ergo et iste inter reliquarum artium magistros.

Other uses of *iste* in the sense of *hic* are usually those in which *iste* is made to refer to the thing that has just been mentioned or is just about to be mentioned.   Proximity in place or time is also indicated by *iste* in some examples.   The following instances illustrate this usage:

32, 4, 4, numquid inter ista rixae decent aut inflammata contentio?
   (*Ista* means *your amusements* which *we* have been discussing.
   Would be translated by *these.*)
55, 5, 30, nam cum homines soleant de vicinitate collidere, istis praediorum communio causam videtur praestitisse concordiae:
   (*Istis* refers to Goths and Romans, who have just been mentioned and who are, moreover, the writer's people.)
69, 2, 27, Sed quis ista conservare neglegat . . . ?
   (Things just spoken of.)
164, 1, 9, ista enim quae modo facili avulsione dirimuntur, postea vix securibus icta succumbunt.
   (Things present in time.)
168, 6, 8, Vicit iste maiores suos felicitate saeculorum
   (Person near in time.)
171, 3, 12, eat nunc actus iste per gentes
171, 4, 17, recipite igitur munera sensibus suscepta, non manibus. suavius nobis fuit ista reddere quam multo grandia suscepisse.
192, 6, 11, sed credimus iam ista sufficere,
   (The admonitions which have just been given.)
217, 1, 14, relativa ista intellectui sunt nomina: si praesulem ademeris, militem non relinquis:
   (Terms about to be mentioned.)
241, 9, 12, tunc iste nautis pereuntibus cum caro pignore evasit.
   (Person who has been the subject of discussion.)

251, 5, 27, vestris iam moribus peccatis, si post ista delinquitis.
258, 1, 23, cuius ista salubritas continetur, si quod ore quis suscipit, alia parte corporis relaxatus effuderit.
263, 8, 16, proponantur ista quae diximus,
271, 1, 7, nam et iste rationabilis ordo est militia tandem solvere, qui impares laboribus probantur existere.
(*Iste ordo* explained by *solvere.*)
303, 2, 28, decet enim ut et orbis iste Romanus iuvamine vestro resplendeat,
(*Orbis iste* present in place and thought.)
353, 4, 13, nam si antiqui eorum fuerunt ad dispendia devoti, cur isti non sint ad compendia solvenda munifici?
(*Isti,* those of the present time.)

C. *Iste* in Meaning of *Ille*
(Cf. Meader 159-161)

In the following examples *iste* refers to what is remote from both the writer and the recipient of the letter and appears to be used in the meaning of *ille*:

130, 2, 12, (exercitus) praeteriens tamen istorum culta vastavit.
189, 3, 29, non tantum interpellator formidat negotii sui casum quantum sustinet iste in relatione periculum.
262, 3, 9, Est enim conventus iste et nimia celebritate festivus, et, etc.
263, 8, 11, Fiat omnium sermone venerabilis fons iste caelestis:
291, 4, 34, iste reges Gothorum longa oblivione celatos latibulo vetustatis eduxit. iste Hamalos cum generis sui claritate restituit,

D. *Iste* in Meaning of *Is*

114, 2, 9, ut non minus patria vestra istius splendeat moribus quam suis triumphis.
179, 4, 35, per *eum* nominis nostri destinatur evectio et *isti* principaliter creditur, quod tam necessarium esse sentitur.
374, 1, 5, diligenda sunt ista, unde res publica videtur esse firmissima.

E. Correlations of the Demonstratives

Classical prose usually expresses a contrast by the use of *hic* for the nearer of the two things, *ille* for the more remote. However, as early as Valerius Maximus the combination *iste-ille* had made considerable headway (Meader, 132). In the Variae, while *hic-ille* is occasionally used, the regular correlation is *iste-ille*, e. g.

169, 10, 26, sic haec machina ... istos spe refovet, illos timore discruciat:
246, 2, 25, melius agnoscitur elegisse nobilem quam fecisse felicem:
        quia iste commonitus per veterum se facta custodit, ille
        exemplum non habet nisi quod fecerit.
        (*Iste* = the former, *ille* = the latter.)
248, 4, 12, Amicitiis ille praestat fidem: sed magnam promissis debet
        iste constantiam.
252, 2, 7, nam sicut ille fluendo non expenditur, sic nec ista celebri
        sermone siccatur.
364, 3, 4, quoniam et illis dare et istis sumere pro temporis qualitate
        necesse est,
364, 5, 19, cum illi videantur praedictas regiones protegere, isti non
        desinant patrioticas possessiones excolere.

In these last two examples *illi* is used for the one just previously
mentioned; *isti* for the more remote.   No other considerations of
nearness and remoteness can be observed, for the *illi* of the first
example denotes the same persons as the *isti* of the second and
vice versa.

In 363, 6, 23, *istud-illud* indicates the same things that have
previously been paired as *illud-hoc* in 363, 6, 20.   Thus:

363, 6, 20, ut illud de rosis, hoc credatur natum esse de liliis.
363, 6, 23, istud intueris rubore laetum, illud conspicis candore festivum.

The discussion which intervenes between the two examples is
not of a nature to reverse the positions of the two objects.   This
would indicate that the writer is quite arbitrary in his choice of
demonstratives used to express a contrast.   In referring to things
in a series the choice of demonstratives seems to be quite free.
Three things are indicated by *illa, ista, haec media* in 72, 13, 10,
illa acuta nimia tensione, ista gravis aliqua laxitate, haec media
tergo blandissime temperato.

In other examples, as in the previously mentioned 109, 6, 12,
(see p. 82), *hic* and *iste* refer to the same thing and are contrasted
with *ille*.   Thus in 354, 6, 28, *altera* and *illa* denote one thing,
while *haec* and *ista* denote the other; altera contulit teterrimum
carcerem, haec novit splendidam tribuere libertatem: ista prae-
stabit ut velis vivere, illa dedit ut eligeres iam perire.   Another
example where *hic* and *iste* are identical and are contrasted with
ille is 385, 10, 22, hic autem cunctis large vendidit, functionem

debitam reliquit et plus iste generaliter contulit tributariis quam ille solis visus est praestitisse germanis.

6. *Idem*
(L.-Hof. 479)

Idem is the least frequent of the demonstratives in the Variae, occurring only 24 times (See table, p. 70). It may be noted that the seven occurrences of the ablative singular feminine are not in stereotyped phrases, but occur with a variety of words.

Uno eodemque occurs in 189, 4, 14, ut in uno eodemque titulo dispar esset dignitas aequaliter adquisita. The usage of *unus idemque* occurs from the time of Lucretius (L.-Hof., 479).

The following examples show a weakening of the concept of identity, and *idem* is used merely to refer to something which has been previously mentioned. *Idem* may here be regarded as the equivalent of *is*. The weakening began in the classical period, and in many Late Latin authors *idem* is a mere substitute for *is*.

90, 21,   ad provinciam quattuor mensium indutias pietas nostra largitur: ita ut expletis eisdem ad penates proprios redire festines,

91, 2, 31, atque ideo parientiam vestram saepius approbatam nunc quoque eidem praesenti monstrate,

102, 5, 15, quos utpote nescientes in eadem causa quolibet loco vel tempore interfuisse constiterit.

169, 10, 25, Alter labenti rota feris offertur: eadem alter erigitur,

212, 2, 33, eodem commonente peragite,

216, 2, 31, necesse est enim, ut, quod a natura conceditur, summonente iterum eadem suaviter audiatur.

222, 3, 17, legitimam tibi fieri censemus uxorem et filios ex eadem coniuge . . . heredum volumus iura sortiri,

258, 2, 15, quas debuit abluere, easdem vobis cogatur inferre.

280, 9, 25, si quis vero quae dederit aut promiserit eodem superstite timuerit publicare, ab heredibus vel proheredibus eius ecclesia repetat.

Elsewhere *idem* expresses identity, e. g., 82, 1, 14, idem vobis est dignitas quod vitae principium.

The small number of occurrences of *idem* in the Variae can be accounted for in some measure by the use of *hic* and *ipse* for expressions of identity (cf. pp. 74 and 80). The use of *talis-qualis* is also a near approach to an expression of identity. In such an expression as 38, 4, 9, nec tale est cellam vinariam tuendam suscipere, quale pretiosa diademata custodire, where it follows close upon identity expressed by *hoc,* the *tale-quale* correlation may be regarded as the equivalent of *idem quod.*

III. *Reflexive Pronouns*
(L.-Hof. 469-470)

1. Non-classical Use of *Sui*

The chief departure from classical usage in Cassiodorus' employment of the reflexive pronouns is his occasional use of the genitive *sui* in place of the possessive adjective *suus.* This has been mentioned in connection with a similar use of the personal pronouns, p. 68. Examples:

5, 18, 27, quod propter nobilitatem sui est in editiore constitutum,
103, 1, 21, quod a positione sui congruum nomen accepit.
115, 2, 30, usus es sub exceptionis officio eloquentis ingenio: favebat
        ipse sui delectatus auditor, dum meliora faceres, cum recitare coepisses.
143, 2, 11, enses, qui pulchritudine sui putentur esse Vulcani,
246, 1, 24, qui similia nequeunt in sui genere reperire.
270, 3, 17, rivosque de flamma venientes tanto igne depurgant, quousque pulchritudinem sui prodant,
312, 3, 32, si quid est quod difficultate sui nobis non oportet imponi,
319, 1, 21, et ne pro parvitate sui neglegi potuisset,
368, 1, 16, quando puritatem sui illa sola custodiunt,

The example given above, 115, 2, 30, presents the special difficulty of having the word with which *sui* belongs omitted. I interpret it to mean, favebat ipse *suo ingenio* delectatus auditor.

In a few examples the reflexive occurs where classical prose employed a personal pronoun. The most striking example is 15, 11, 12, quem tunc rerum dominus propter sapientiam sui et gloriosos in re publica labores in omni consilii parte sequebatur. *Sui* refers to the person denoted by *quem.*

Similar uses of the reflexive referring to a word which is not a grammatical subject of either the main clause or the subordinate clause in which the reflexive is found are 131, 2, 13, Proinde illustris magnitudo tua Gravassianos atque Pontonates nobis supplicasse cognoscat a Ianuario, sed et Probo discussoribus iniquis *se* oneribus ingravatos, cum sterilitas ieiuna locorum nulla *sibi* fieri augmenta

patiatur, and 133, 2, 33, Viri illustris itaque comitis Arigerni suggestione comperimus Iudaeorum querela se fuisse pulsatum, etc.
In these examples the person indicated by the reflexive may be
regarded as the logical subject. Classical prose sometimes used a
reflexive under such circumstances, but Late Latin was more free
in the use of the reflexive (Cf. L.-Hof., 470).

In 161, 1, 11, Gravis est Patzenis clementiae nostrae sensibus
intimata conquestio. qui *se* in expeditione Gallica *constituto* in eum
Brandilam prosiluisse testatur excessum, ut uxorem *eius* Reginam
proprio sociandam duceret esse coniugio, the reflexive *se* is used in
the ablative absolute to refer to the subject (*qui*) of the relative
clause in which the ablative absolute occurs. Later in the same
sentence *eius* is used instead of the reflexive possessive adjective
suam. Classical prose sometimes used the reflexive in the ablative
absolute under similar circumstances.

2. Extended Use of the Reflexive Adjective *suus*
(L.-Hof. 470)

Classical prose regularly uses *suus* only when the possessor is the
subject. Colloquial speech, however, in all periods made some use
of this word when the possessor was the object or related to the
object. This free use of *suus* occurs frequently in Nepos and Livy
and especially in Late Latin.

In the Variae *suus* occurs frequently without relation to the subject of the sentence or clause, e. g.

17, 2, 29, comperimus Neoterium fratrem suum, affectum germanitatis
   oblitum, bona parvuli hostili furore lacerasse.
42, 1, 6, horologia cum suis dispositoribus credidimus destinanda:
55, 2, 6, Venantium, tam suis quam paternis meritis elucentem, . . .
   subveximus.
56, 3, 29, eos ad curiam suam remeare permittat,
65, 2, 9, ut unicuique proficiat labor suus
126, 3, 11, impugnavit hominem auxilium suum
131, 3, 1, finitum iure negotium in sua manere facite firmitate,
159, 1, 21, magis miserabiliorem reddidit virum luminis sui ademptus
   ornatus,
165, 6, 15, ne cuiquam labor suus videatur ingratus,
203, 1, 4, ut unicuique sua iura serventur
243, 7, 12, Romanum denique eloquium non suis regionibus invenisti,
366, 2, 9, invictas securitates illis dedit calamitas sua:

3. *Proprius* Used for *Suus*, etc.

Proprius is frequently used in the sense of *suus, meus, tuus*, etc. in Late Latin (Cf. L.-Hof., 473; Kr-Schm., II, 408; Svennung, 65). This usage is rather frequent in the Variae. As in the case of *suus*, the possessor is not always the subject. Typical examples:

4, 7, 7, illa tibi de aliis honoribus principes videntur imponere, quae proprii iudices nequeunt explicare.

12, 6, 4, (= *tuae*) si salutis propriae tangit affectus

26, 3, 12, Aves ipsae per aera vagantes proprios nidos amant:

108, 9, 11, quibus est necessarium rebus propriis adhibere culturam.

123, 1, 11, (= nostra) qui propria cupimus sponte largiri,

145, 3, 28, Unicuique propria iura custodit,

252, 1, 2, Licet propriis frequenter honoribus et germani tui fueris dignitate laudatus,

IV. *Reciprocal Expressions*
(L.-Hof. 471-473)

Cassiodorus' usual method of expressing the reciprocal relation is by the reflexive alone (or a personal pronoun used as a reflexive). This usage is found in Cicero's Letters, but becomes common only with Vergil, and is not common in prose until Apuleius. In the Variae the reciprocal relation is occasionally made clear by the use of such a word as *mutuus* in some syntactical relation in the sentence but the reflexive alone occurs in most of the examples. The following illustrate the usage:

15, 11, 10, Sed ut se pares animi solent semper eligere,

31, 5, 14, sed pugnis se quamlibet fervida lacessebat intentio,

55, 5, 29, cum se homines soleant de vicinitate collidere,

70, 5, 30, sine se esse non possunt quae alterna sibi vicissitudine referuntur,

71, 6, 6, omnia sibi adversa crediderunt, i. e., *all opposites trusted one another.*

92, 3, 3, ut non in vos, sed in hostem saevire cupiatis.

106, 7, 3, dum se praepropere conantur elidere,

115, 3, 12, gentes autem sibi olim virtutum pignora praestiterunt.

169, 6, 9, pari in se cursu festinant

205, 1, 14, Romuleae fabricae collatae sibi

257, 3, 7, ita enim duo mutua se amplexatione consociant

314, 3, 31, quam homines in se exercuisse cognoscit.

360, 1, 16, habemus utrimque quod in nobis diligere debeamus:

Invicem is also used rather frequently both with and without forms of the reflexive. The reciprocal use of this expression begins with Livy. Examples from the Variae:

138, 8, 36, invicem sicut virtutes necessariae sibi esse videantur.
143, 3, 18, invicem solliciti mutuis possimus utilitatibus obligari.
192, 5, 3, ut cum vobis non vultis cedere, inventa vestra invicem
videamini dissipare.
272, 3, 8, quia vobis debetis invicem in hac parte consulere,
362, 3, 26, cunctae dignitates invicem sibi debent necessaria ministrare,

Other reciprocal expressions used are classical, such as *inter se,* *unus-alter* etc., e. g.

10, 5, 23, Quas non solum oportet inter se otiosa dilectione coniungi,
verum etiam decet mutuis viribus adiuvari.
68, 3, 14, inter se contraria intelliguntur varietate pugnare.
185, 2, 14, nam utraque sibi coniuncta sunt: unum pendet ex altero:

V. *Indefinite Pronouns*
(L.-Hof. 482 ff.)

Several minor irregularities with respect to number in indefinite pronouns have been mentioned on p. 6.

The only notable departure from classical norms is in various uses of *aliquis.*

(1) After *si, nisi, num,* and *ne,* classical prose employs *quis,* using *aliquis* only when the pronoun is to be emphasized. In Late Latin many authors use *aliquis* without emphasis (Cf. L.-Hof., 482).

Num does not occur in the Variae. After *si, nisi,* and *ne* Cassiodorus usually employs *quis,* e. g., 32, 1, 12; 61, 3, 14; 65, 2, 11; 86, 2, 30, but examples of *aliquis* without emphasis are also found, e. g., 23, 3, 11, ne aliqua neglegentia reddaris obnoxius; 134, 4, 10, si aliquid sibi contra Iudaeos . . . crediderit suffragari; 318, 5, 4, quod si aliquis praebere contempserit postulata.

(2) Classical prose uses *quisquam* in general negative sentences, *aliquis* only in a qualifying sense (Cf. K.-Steg., II, 1, 640). Many Late Latin writers use *aliquis* in any kind of negative sentence. In general negative sentences Cassiodorus uses either *quisquam* or *aliquis,* more frequently the latter. *Quisquam* occurs in 33, 1, 3; 63, 2, 13; 338, 4, 5; 360, 1, 15; 374, 3, 14, etc.

Selected examples of aliquis:

53, 1, 13, nec aliquis nititur quod parum est vindicare
63, 1, 7, Quamvis nullos velimus gravamen aliquod sustinere,
63, 3, 30, quatenus . . . nec aurariae aliquid pensionis impendat
64, 4, 31, ut . . . nec quisquam inde aliquid praesumat attingere,
98, 2, 27, nec aliquid illos a nostris sinatis pati,
103, 2, 26, ubi nec adversarius *quicquam* praesumat nec inclusus *aliquid* expavescat.
115, 1, 3, ut prius se velint mori quam aliquid asperum patribus videatur infligi.
120, 3, 12, non decet per vim eos aliquid agere.

(3) For the use of *aliquis* in place of *ullus* after *sine,* cf. p. 122.

(4) The Variae present a single example of *aliquis* used in place of the indefinite second person singular, 55, 4, 22, credita sibi tanta integritate disposuit, ut miraretur aliquis sic simpliciter devotum. Elsewhere, under similar circumstances the author uses the indefinite second person.

CHAPTER V

The Preposition
(L.-Hof. 494-542)

I. *Prepositions Governing the Accusative*
1. *Ad*
(L.-Hof. 496-498)

A. *Ad* Expressing Limit or Direction of Motion

The most frequent use of *ad* in the Variae is its employment to denote limit or direction of motion, either in a literal sense, as in 50, 1, 7, legationem nos ad Orientem deliberasse transmittere; 54, 5, 5, ad vestrum facite venire iudicium; 54, 4, 1, ad campos exeunt; 73, 3, 18, illum et illum legatos nostros ad excellentiam vestram . . . direximus, or in a transferred sense, as in 52, 1, 1, error matris transit ad filios; 37, 4, animos subito ad arma non erigunt; 47, 1, 3, nos provocant ad frequens praemium; 46, 2, 14, ad honorem rei publicae meruit pervenire. Beyond a greater relative frequency of occurrence I have noted no deviations from classical usage.

B. *Ad* Used Instead of the Dative

In the following examples *ad* with the accusative is used with verbs with which classical Latin usually employs the dative. The substitution of *ad* with the accusative for the dative belongs largely to colloquial language and becomes frequent in the Late period (Cf. L.-Hof. 410).

dare, e. g. 31, 3, 30, ad praefectum urbis data praeceptio
    33, 1, 2, ad Albinum atque Avienum . . . praecepta nos dedisse.
    Dare ad aliquem occurs in Plaut., Ter., Cato, Nep., Ov. *et al.* (T. L. L., I, 475, 15).
exhibere, e. g. 36, 1, 17, studiorum causa fratris filios ad Romanam exhibuit civitatem.
patere 52, 2, 6, dum sexus ille femineus ad mutabilitatis vitia patet.
    Patere in this sense is used with dative in Cic., Cels., Vulg. (Harpers'). No use of *ad* noted.
praebere responsum 24, 1, 7, ad interrogationem vestram curavimus praebere responsum.
    Cic. uses *respondere* with *ad* (T. L. L., I, 554, 44).

subicere 59, 1, 17, ad omnes iustitiae partes subiectos libenter parere
docuistis.
Aug., Conf. 8, 2, 3 (Cf. Hrdlicka, 121).
vacare 133, 2, 15, cum vacatur ad planctus.
Occurs with *ad* in Ov., Sen. (Harpers').

C. *Ad* with the Accusative Instead of the Accusative Alone

respicere, e. g. 154, 1, 13, ad conservationem respicit omnium.
This verb occurs with the accusative alone in Caesar, Cicero, *et al.*
in sense of *have care for, have regard for.* Quintilian uses *ad*
(Harpers').

D. *Ad* in the Sense of Reference after Adjectives

In classical prose *ad* occurs after many adjectives. The usage
was widely extended by Silver and Late writers (L.-Hof., 497).
I have observed the following examples of *ad* with adjectives
where classical prose rarely or never employed it.

avarus 276, 2, 7, avari ad laudes
cautus 171, 4, 18, ad similia cauti
circumspectus ⎫
instabilis　⎬207, 3, 6, circumspectus ad omnia, instabilis ad ventura,
trepidus　⎭　　　　　trepidus ad insidias
copiosus 332, 3, 21, donet quieta tempora et ad laudem sui nominis
copiosa
delicatus 343, 6, 28, omnia amoena delicata sunt ad labores
devotus 59, 2, 26, devotus ad propria
deses 303, 1, 32, ad quae si essemus desides
dignus 116, 3, 20, nunc ad colloquia dignus
facilis 13, 4, 5, facilis ad querelas
idoneus 90, 3, 4, ut ad ea quae iussa sunt idoneus nequeat reperiri
(Cf. genitive with adjs. p. 27.)
imparatus 10, 1, 3, qui ad iusta deprehenditur imparatus
paratus 178, 3, 22, paratus semper ad subitum
proclivis 35, 1, 3, proclivior ad misericordiam via . . . patet
promptus 380, 1, 4, estote ergo promptissimi ad vicina
rigidus 289, 3, 31, te in dictationibus amoenum, te ad iustitiam rigidum
(Note contrast of *in* with abl. and *ad* with acc.)
sollicitus 171, 4, 18, ad ventura solliciti
sufficiens 292, 7, 9, ad universa sufficiens

E. *Ad* in Final Expressions

a. WITH NOUNS

Ad with the accusative expressing purpose is classical, but the usage was widely extended in Late Latin (L.-Hof., 497; K.-Steg., II, 1, 522). It occurs frequently in the Variae. I have not observed any examples of its use in place of the final dative in double dative expressions or of its use directly with nouns.

The following examples are classical:

30, 1,13, qui ad continuos excursus constituti sunt,
30, 1,15, quod ad celeritatem constat inventum,
50,17,   quod potest ad decorem crescere civitatis.
51, 1, 6, benigni quippe principis est ad clementiae commodum transilire terminos aequitatum,

b. WITH THE GERUNDIVE AND THE GERUND

Ad is used with the gerundive and the gerund to express purpose, as it is in classical prose. For examples with gerundive cf. p. 168; with gerund, p. 169.

The freer use of abstract nouns in Late Latin makes this usage of *ad* with the gerundive and the gerund slightly less frequent in the Variae than in classical prose.

The following examples illustrate this use of *ad* with abstract nouns. It will be observed that a gerund or gerundive could be substituted for the abstract noun in each example:

25, 1,30 Provocandi sumus . . . ad *augmenta* civitatis
28, 3, 1, cogunt pullos teneros ad *volatum*
51, 2,25, nec scelerati ad *irrisionem* iustitiae fraudum suarum valeant compendia vindicare.
66, 1,16, ad *proditionem* sceleris relaxata nimis poena sufficiat
67, 4,   cognoscat Spoletinis civibus ad *exhibitionem* thermarum . . . aliam millenam esse deputandam
72,14,17, hanc igitur ad *imitationem* variae testudinis Mercurius dicitur invenisse,
107, 4,22, Hanc . . . ad *dimensionem* terrae et *rucuperandas formas* finium transtulerunt,
          (Note juxtaposition of abstract noun and gerundive.)
134, 3, 5, non autem iustum fuit . . . ad fabricarum *incendia* festinari.
381, 5,26, ad *considerationem* revertere naturalium rerum

F. Consecutive Use of *Ad*

I have observed only one example of the use of *ad* to indicate the result of an action, 4, 11, 27, Dixisti etiam ad commendationem universitatis, *etc.* The usage of *ad* in this manner appears to have begun with Cicero and to have been rare at all periods (T. L. L., I, 544, 32; K.-Steg., II, 1, 522).

G. Adverbial Uses of *Ad*

Ad occurs in many phrases which are the equivalent of an adverb, or an ablative of manner, circumstance, or specification. Examples:

5, 14, 4, ad subitum	= *manner*
28, 3, 13, ad statutam praestationem	= *according to*
59, 1, 15, ad hoc	= *moreover*
70, 5, 30, ad medium	= *with reference to*
72, 14, 17, ad imitationem	= *according to*
88, 4, 22, ad libitum	= *manner*
89, 2, 16, ad pretium	= *with reference to*
166, 13, 4, ad hunc modum	= *according to*
175, 3, 19, ad similitudinem	= *according to*
273, 3, 29, Sed hoc quantum est ad tuarum notitiam litterarum?	= *compared to*
383, 2, 8, ad viginti quinque modios per solidum	= *at the rate of*
385, 8, 6, ad denos	= *at the rate of*

H. Temporal Use of *Ad*

The expression *ad diem,* usually with a modifier, to denote *time when* is classical. Cassiodorus uses it in such phrases as 148, 3, 14, *ad supradictum diem.* He appears to have deliberately sought the effect of the repetition of *ad* in different senses in the following, 220, 2, 5, Et ideo otii delectatione postposita ad illam diem ad urbem illam venire depropera, for he disregards the possibility of the reader construing *postposita* with *ad illum diem.*

Usque ad occurs several times as a mere strengthening of *ad.* All examples appear to follow classical usage.

2. *Apud*
(L.-Hof. 499)

In the Variae *apud* adheres to its usual meaning of *rest in a place* (K.-Steg., II, 1, 523-524). It is not used for direction or limit with verbs of motion.

I have noted only two examples of its use with things. It occurs with the name of a town in 105, 3, 22, hoc apud Elidem Asiae civitatem Oenomanus ferter edidisse. One example of *apud* with the name of a town occurs in Plautus, but no other author until Tacitus is known to have used it in this manner (L.-Hof., 499). It occurs with *conscientiam* in 99, 1, 13, apud conscientiam nostram laesionis genus est profutura tardare. *Apud* is not found with *conscientiam* until Tertullian (T. L. L., II, 339, 38), but a similar usage with *animum* occurs in Cicero and Sallust (T. L. L., II, 339, 10; Kr.-Schm., I, 191). This example therefore follows classical usage.

In all other examples observed *apud* is joined with words indicating persons. The primary idea of place, i. e., *in the presence of the person,* is still foremost in some examples, e. g., 135, 8, apud arbitros . . . causa legibus audiatur. This usage is classical (T. L. L., II, 341, 41 ff.).

But in many examples the presence of the person, while implied, is obscured, and *apud* is made to perform many duties other than that of indicating place. Classical prose authors made many extensions of the use of *apud* to ideas other than mere location. Silver and Late authors extended the usage still further. I cite the following examples, which appear to be rather wide extensions of the original sense of *apud:*

= *in the possession of, under the control of*
26, 2, 7, si apud aliquem constet residere pecuniam
37, 1, 26, in tutum apud nos reponit omnis devotio quod meretur
128, 2, 16, comperimus res Tufae apud Johannem . . . fuisse depositas

= *from* with *mereri* and similar verbs.
16, 18, 10, apud nos laudes posse reparare
37, 2, 29, apud amantem provectus tui causam tardius impetrasti,
38, 3, 30, apud nos mereretur aulicas dignitates.

= by, i. e., *agent.*
21, 4, 5, meministi, quotiens apud nos laudati sint innocentes.

The use of *apud* as an expression of agency is developed by Anders Gagner in his exhaustive study, " *Studien zur Bedeutung der Präposition Apud,*" in Uppsala Universitets Årsskrift, Uppsala, 1931, especially page 140.

3. *Ante*
(L.-Hof. 499-500)

Ante occurs several times in the classical manner, both for time,

e. g., 24, 2, 12, ante designatum tempus, and for place, e. g., 85, 3, 18, ante ipsum Libertatis gremium.

It is used to express superiority in 144, 2, 1 (substantiam) quam ante omnes homines patria vestra offerente suscipitis. This usage is not found in Caesar or Cicero, but occurs in Sallust and in both earlier and later writers (L.-Hof., 500, 2; K.-Steg., II, 1, 533).

The temporal use is extended in one example to denote the exclusion of the object, i. e., *ante* is used as the equivalent of *sine,* in 57, 3, 1, convenit sacerdotalibus institutis, ut ante controversiam iustitiam magis ipse cognoscas, quam de iudicio victus abscedas. The full force of *ante* is best understood if we realize that in this sentence *magis* is used as the equivalent of *potius* (Cf. p. 63).

The duration of time since an event (i. e., *so long ago*) is expressed by *ante* with the accusative in the following: 103, 5, 9, Memorant autem aevi pristini servatores hanc insulam ante aliquot annos . . . erupisse, and 134, 1, 20 (the second *ante*), Stephanus . . . conquestus est casam iuris sui ante decessorem prodecessoremque vestrum longa aetate possessam ante hos fere novem menses . . . fuisse pervasam. This construction occurs once in Cicero (K.-Steg., II, 1, 406 " wo man vielfach hat ändern wollen." T. L. L., II, 133, 30 does not use this example) and increases in frequency from Livy on. The first ante in this sentence illustrates a usage which became common from Cicero's time, that of using *ante* in a temporal sense with a word indicating a person (L.-Hof., 500; T. L. L., II, 134, 66). It is explained as being due to an ellipsis of a participle indicating time (Landgratf-Weyman, *Archiv,* 11 (1898), 246).

4. *Post*
(L.-Hof. 499-500)

Post with the accusative occurs as in classical prose, both in its temporal sense, e. g., 66, 11, post diem venerabilem, and in its local sense, e. g., 68, 3, 7, post recurva spatia, and 125, 2, 6, post Turasi thermas.

The unusual examples of this preposition are analogous to those of *ante* (Cf., above), Thus 88, 1, 8, post longa tempora. This usage, a substitute for the classical *longis post temporibus,* occurs in classical prose but, like *ante,* becomes common only with Livy (K.-Steg., II, 1, 406; Kr.-Schm., II, 333, and lexica).

The elliptical temporal use, mentioned in connection with *ante* (p. 96) occurs several times, e. g., 37, 20, post regale iudicium, 48, 2, 10, bona norunt durare post hominem; 50, 21, ornent aliquid saxa iacentia post ruinas. This usage was more common in classical prose than was the similar use of *ante,* but it became frequent only in Silver and Late Latin (L.-Hof., 501; K.-Steg., II, 1, 534).

The example in 108, 9, 9, talem eligite, post quem partes erubescant impudenti fronte litigare, illustrates the same usage and has the additional peculiarity of indicating lapse of time after the beginning of an event or state. The meaning is *after he begins to serve as judge.*

5. *Penes*
(L. Hof. 502)

Penes occurs three times, always in the classical manner, i. e., with a pronoun, and denoting possession or control. Examples: 145, 2, 25, penes ipsum civilitatis nostrae fama reponitur; 224, 8, penes quem officii est digna reverentia; 300, 3, 9, penes quem est scientiae magnitudo.

6. *Iuxta*
(L.-Hof. 502-503)

Iuxta occurs five times in the classical meaning of *near* or *by the side of.* Examples: 23, 1, 18, castrum iuxta vos positum; 69, 8, 3, iuxta caput fontis . . . meatum provida natura formavit; 71, 6, 5, iuxta praedonem suum praeda gaudebat; 127, 2, 18, porticus, quae iuxta domum Palmatam posita forum . . . includit; 374, 1, 28, iuxta montem Caprarium.

It occurs four times in the Late Latin sense of *according to.* Examples: 120, 1, 18, iuxta consuetudinem veterem victualia praebeantur; 212, 1, 26, unusquisque iuxta voluntatem suam cogitat vivere; 345, 2, 10, unusquisque iuxta matriculae seriem . . . vulgetur; 345, 18, iuxta consuetudinem praesentatus spectabilitatis decoretur insignibus.

7. *Propter*
(L.-Hof. 504-505)

Propter occurs very rarely. A few examples occur in the causal sense, which is classical, e. g., 15, 11, 12, quem tunc rerum dominus propter sapientiam sui . . . sequebatur, and 131, 1, 25 (avaritiam) quam propter vicinitatem generis nostri sic in animis vestris coalescere nolumus, ut, *etc.*

Two examples occur which appear to have a secondary final sense, with ellipsis of the word denoting the actual purpose, 28, 2, 9, propter Romanae moenia civitatis . . .portum Licini deputatis reditibus reparari iussio nostra constituit, and 94, 1, 25, illustris sublimitas tua spectabilem virum Johannem nos direxisse cognoscat propter splendidas Romanae cloacas civitatis. We should expect to see a word indicating limit of motion with *direxisse,* but *propter* seems to be used in a causal-final sense, i. e., *propter curam* or *propter reparationem cloacarum.* In two other examples the final usage is more in evidence, viz., 269, 1, 26, cur non ipsa diligenter exquirimus, propter quae alia poscere videbamur, and 378, 1, 17, reliqua vero propter sollemnes expensas relinquimus devotae provinciae.

The final use of *propter,* which is closely related to the causal, or even includes it, is rare in classical prose, but is more frequent in Late Latin (L.-Hof., 504; K.-Steg., II, 1, 530).

8. *Ob*
(L.-Hof. 505)

Ob occurs but four times. Each time it is causal, and always it is in the stereotyped phrases, *ob hoc, ob id,* or *ob aliud.* Examples: 20, 2, 9, civilitatem premere dicuntur armati et ob hoc iustitiae parere despiciunt; 102, 1, 20, sanguinis effusione pollutum (ob hoc cum . . . rixam verborum usque ad nefarium collegae deduxit interitum . . .) ; 152, 1, 17, ob id omnibus possint esse gratissima; 271, 1, 4, neque enim ob aliud curiales leges sacratissimae ligaverunt.

9. *Contra*
(L.-Hof. 506-507)

Contra with the accusative occurs rather frequently, while its synonym *adversus* is extremely rare. (Cf. relative frequency of these two prepositions in the Confessions of St. Augustine as discussed by Hrdlicka, 138-139, with remarks on classical usage.) It occurs at times after verbs of motion and after verbs of saying, but as the sense is always that of hostility or opposition, Cassiodorus' use of this preposition is entirely classical. Examples: 50, 2, 11, qui possit contra subtilissimos disputare; 55, 2, 10, contra quos multa fecisse videbatur inimicus; 61, 3, 14, si quis contra haec saluberrima constituta ausu temerario venire temptaverit; 71, 10, 26, contra noxiam dulcedinem cogitavit vir prudentissimus felicissimam surditatem; 238, 6, 26, resistebas contra vota principis.

10. *Ultra*
(L.-Hof. 507)

I have not observed any occurrence of *ultra* in its literal, i. e., local sense, nor in the temporal sense in which it occurs in Silver and Late Latin. It occurs several times in the figurative sense, in which it is rare in classical prose but more common in poetry and in Silver and Late Latin (K.-Steg., II, 1, 547). The idea of *excess* is present in these examples, and in some the phrase formed with *ultra* may be regarded as the equivalent of a comparative. Examples: 95, 3, 18, non possumus admissi qualitatem ultra iura corrigere; 108, 2, 22, arborum genera quae tamen ultra naturam suam felici proceritate luxuriant; 118, 3, 6, crudelitatis enim genus est ultra naufragium velle desaevire; 166, 1, 16, ultra desideria supplicum frequenter nos praestitisse beneficia gaudeamus; 251, 3, 16, ultra omnes impietates est nocere laesos; 335, 5, 25, ultra omnes dementes est, qui ulcisci non appetit; 370, 4, 27, ultra omnes crudelitates est divitem velle fieri de exiguitate mendici.

11. *Extra*
(L.-Hof. 509-510)

I have recorded only one example of *extra* with the accusative, 138, 2, 7, ut . . . aspectum suum extra urbem esse non sentiat. The usage is classical.

12. *Inter*
(L.-Hof. 510-511)

Inter occurs frequently in various classical uses, e. g., 10, 4, 22, inter utrasque res publicas . . . aliquid discordiae permanere; 15, 9, 7, inter fortes viros eximii; 17, 3, 20, ut inter vos ea quae iustitiae conveniunt ordinemus; 31, 4, 4, Intersit igitur inter splendorem vestrum moresque mediocres; 48, 5, 27, vixit enim inter vos; 70, 4, 20, hoc totum inter homines quinque tonis agitur; 80, 3, 2, inter initia (temporal).

The following examples illustrate extensions:

   3, 5, 16, inter haec cur requiritis dictationis eloquium . . . ?
> *Inter haec* in the meaning of *interea* begins in Livy and is regular in Late Latin (L.-Hof., 511, 4; K.-Steg., II, 1, 552).

  69, 10, 16, spatium, quod inter aedem publicam et caput igniti fontis interiacet.
> The use of *inter* together with its compound *interiacere* is first found in Plin. nat. (K.-Steg., II, 1, 271).

143, 1, 25, inter tot gentes viam praesumere non est aliquid facile concupisse.

226, 1, 1, Moyses . . . inter alia definivit, ut, *etc.*
> *Inter alios* is used for persons with verbs of excelling, etc., but the use of *inter alia* in a partitive sense appears to be Silver and Late. Cf. K.-Steg., II, 1, 551.

243, 2, 27, inter gymnasia litterarum adscitus
> The use of *inter* with a verb of motion (literal or figurative) begins with Vergil and increases in Late Latin (L.-Hof., 510, 4).

A contrast is expressed with *inter* and a substantive as the first member and a dative as the second member in 146, 6, 15, *inter bene moratos* enim asseruisse iusta facillimum fuit: *provincialibus* autem se vaga libertate tractantibus nimis arduum.

13. *Intra*
(L.-Hof. 511-512)

The following examples illustrate the classical usage of *intra* in its local terminal, and temporal meanings, and in the transferred sense. In all these the sense is *within the bounds of.*

local 63, 2, 12, ut praediis vel hominibus huius ecclesiae intra Siciliam constitutis tuitionem studeas . . . praestare,

terminal 102, 1, 22, intra ecclesiae saepta refugiens declinare se credidit ultionem.

temporal 129, 3, 31, si petitio vestra a veritate non deviat et intra annorum spatia deget, quibus, *etc.*

transferred 14, 7, 26, dum intra modestiae terminos magna cohibuit
63, 1, 19, nec intra regulas constituti potest munificentia regalis artari.

The following are non-classical uses:
Local, as the equivalent of *in* with the ablative.

242, 2, 20, nam ita intra te fuit quamvis ampla professio litterarum.
Late Latin use. Vell. Quint. etc. (K.-Steg., II, 1, 549).

Temporal, as the equivalent of *ante*.

12, 6, 4, intra illum diem . . . venire festina.
147, 2, 27, si : . . . solvere intra praefinitum tempus fortasse potuerit,
214, 18 (214, 26; 215, 10), intra kal. Martiarum diem.
        Juridical expression (L.-Hof., 512, 3).

Various uses, almost as the equivalent of *citra* (L.-Hof., 512-3).

273, 1, 20, nullius adquiescit ingenium iacere intra aestimationem su-
        orum.
280, 6, 10, suggerentes nobis intra tria milia solidorum cum collectione
        chartarum censemus accipere.
280, 7, 14, intra duo milia solidorum iubemus expendere.

14. *Supra*
(L.-Hof. 513-514)

Supra occurs in the local meaning, both with verbs of rest and
with verbs of motion. The following examples illustrate the classical usage:

47, 6, 34, respice te supra omnium umeros atque ora volitare
106, 8, 11, supra dorsa hostium ambulantes
177, 3, 20, consides supra omnes scilicet consulares
194, 1, 4, cum supra cervices suas districtionem cognoverit imminere

The most frequent usage of *supra* is that in which a comparison
is implied. A large number of examples are given by Traube, 588.
The following are selected to illustrate various phases of this usage:

= *altius* 68, 2, 4, supra terminos suos aquarum dorsa turgescunt
quam 81, 4, 22, crescens supra privatos publicus amor
= *melius* 231, 4, 20, illud mihi est supra dominatum
quam
= *diutius* 317, 1, 7, qui solent in carnali substantia supra millenos
quam annos vivere
= *magis* 78, 4, 21, ut supra vos iniquitas illa praevaleat
quam 106, 11, 26, illic supra cetera spectacula fervor animorum . . .
rapiatur
175, 8, 5, si supra vires aliquid inponeremus invitis

All the above examples are classical. But in 3, 5, 18, quae supra omnia populi plus requirunt, there is in effect a double comparative in the use of *supra omnia* and *plus*. This usage is cited as a peculiarity of Cassiodorus in L.-Hof., 428, 1.

Supra also occurs in several examples in the meaning of *in addition to*. Thus,

67, 4,   supra consuetudinem aliam millenam esse deputandam
215, 13,   nec possessor supra modum professionis exsolvat
271, 1, 26, supra temporis necessitatem . . . sustinere saevitiam

This usage is extremely rare. The lexica cite Liv. 2, 18, 3, and also Plin. nat. 21, 3, 9. Hrdlicka, 142, notes Aug. Conf. 1, 16, 26.

15. *Circa*
(L.-Hof. 515)

Nearly all examples of *circa* in the Variae represent Silver and Late Latin usage. It occurs twice in the local sense, which is rare but classical, 103, 15, Universis Gothis et Romanis circa Veruccas castellum consistentibus, and 343, 3, 11, Circâ quem conveniunt in coronae speciem . . . summitates. It does not occur at all in the sense of *approximately* with expressions of number and quantity, which sense occurs frequently from the time of Horace.

Its most frequent use is with persons and things toward which feelings, emotions, etc., are directed (T. L. L., III, 1090, 17 ff.; K.-Steg., II, 1, 543). This usage also begins with Horace. In classical prose one would expect *erga* or *de* instead of *circa* in the following examples:

62, 2, 15, permutatio iudicum numquam circa te variavit affectum
64, 1, 11, Grata nobis est . . . circa utilitates publicas impensa devotio
64, 2, 15, glorioso circa rem publicam amore devinctus
81, 4, 22, Pendebant quin immo circa eos anxia vota civitatis
81, 4, 24, firmum circa eos custodiebat arbitrium voluntas vaga populorum
96, 1, 19, Gratum nobis est vota nostra circa sacri ordinis augmenta proficere
124, 1, 20, ut circa te augeat gratiam custodita iustitia
125, 1, 25, antiqua circa vos beneficia custodimus
132, 1, 9, circa minores fortunas clementiora sunt nostri pectoris instituta
233, 9, 18, primordia . . . circa vos benignitatis

236, 3, 13, animos nostros circa se minores non desiderant effici,
301, 3, 22, Estote ergo circa eos . . . omnino solliciti:
307, 5, 26, nostrum circa vos in omni parte animum propitium sentientes (Dative is regular after *propitius* in classical prose).
312, 3. 33, affectum, quem circa regnum vestrum habere coepimus
339, 2, 16, excitetur nunc amor omnium circa dominos felices.

In the following examples the feeling is one of hostility, so that *circa* becomes almost the equivalent of *contra*:

59, 10,   cessabit ergo circa vos improborum nefanda praesumptio
206, 2, 26, circa fures esto sollicitus.
268, 3, 31, circa saionum et militantum molestias iudicum protegantur auxilio.

Circa occurs more rarely with verbs of saying or expressions of judging, as the equivalent of *de*. Thus:

37, 18,   quae circa referendos curiae priscus ordo dictavit.
82, 6, 6, nec nostrum circa te errare posse iudicium.

Traube, 521, notes the following parallels for the use of *circa*: The example above in 37, 18, is contrasted with 222, 2, 32, quae *in* his causis reverenda legum dictat antiquitas; 129, 2, 2, quaecumque legum statuta moverunt, *circa* vos illibata serventur, is contrasted with 222, 2, 33, ut *alienandis rusticis vel urbanis praediis* constitutionum servetur auctoritas, and with 61, 5, 20, in aurariis denique priscus ordo servetur. He adds " similia passim." Several other constructions are indeed employed by Cassiodorus as the equivalent of this usage of *circa*. The sense of all is essentially that of reference or specification.

16. *Praeter*
(L.-Hof. 516-517)

Praeter occurs very rarely. The local and comparative uses, which are classical, are not found in the Variae. It is found in a classical usage in the meaning *exclusive of* in 224, 16, illum locum proprietario iure concedimus, praeter aes aut plumbum vel marmora, si tamen ibi fuerint latere comperta (Cf. Hodgkin, 344).

It is used as the equivalent of *sine* in 41, 10, 17, ubi praeter solis radios hora dinoscitur, and 47, 3, 20, conservasti divitias, cum ad eas praeter laboris studia pervenisses. This usage is only Late Latin.

In 72, 16, 29, sicut *praeter ipsam* creatura non extat, ita *sine ipsa* incommutabilem laetitiam habere non praevalet, *praeter* is apparently contrasted with *sine*. The meaning, however, seems to be a near approach to that of *sine*; it can perhaps be rendered by *independently of*. (Hodgkin, 194, translates " and as *outside of Him* no creature can exist, so *without Him* changeless happiness cannot be." He takes a previous *divinitatis* as the antecedent. *Harmonia* is, however, the general subject of discussion and seems to be meant here also).

17. Secundum
(L. Hof. 517-518)

Secundum occurs only in the meaning of *according to*. In classical prose this usage is largely confined to the phrase *secundum naturam*. Silver and Late Latin used it in this sense with a great variety of words (Hrdlicka, 137; K.-Steg. II, 1, 536).

Cassiodorus has the following phrases:

```
17,  2,  2, secundum brevem subter annexum
35,  5, 22, secundum leges
84,  2,  3, secundum morem veterem
84,  2,  4, secundum . . . fidem
106, 7,  5, secundum zodiacos decanos
122, 2,  6, secundum . . . praecepta
125, 3, 21, secundum priscam consuetudinem
126, 5, 20, secundum edictorum seriem
130, 3,  2, secundum iustitiam legesque
154, 30,    secundum priora praecepta
155, 1,  7, secundum ordinationem
203, 1,  1, secundum edicta nostra
257, 2, 21, secundum facti aestimationem
309, 2, 13, secundum forum rerum venalium
344, 2,  6, secundum modum
373, 6, 18, secundum evectiones concessas
385, 10, 27, secundum tenorem iussionis
```

18. Adversus
(L.-Hof. 518-519)

The preposition *adversus* occurs very rarely. Cf. *contra,* p. 98. I have noted it only in 222, 2, 1, praesentis beneficii iussione, ad-

versus Gothos illa, adversus Romanos illa, facile te fides et diligentia custodivit. The sentence offers difficulty on account of the
indefinite nature of the pronoun *illa* (Cf. p. 77). I take it to
mean *Our protection and diligence has guaranteed you these
(rights?) against the Goths and these against the Romans.* This
usage of *adversus* is classical.

The same preposition in its older form *adversum* occurs in 271,
1, 5, ubi dominus adversum sua iudicia amabili concertatione dissentit. The usage is classical.

19. *Erga*
(L.-Hof. 520)

I have noted only one occurrence of *erga*, 61, 5, 22, beneficia
nostra erga negotiatores. The usage is classical.

20. *Per*
(L.-Hof. 520-522)
A. Local Use

The local use of *per* denoting motion through, both literal and
figurative, occurs very frequently. No striking deviations from
classical usage are noted. Examples:

15, 9, 5, quod vocabulum etsi per alios videatur currere
26, 3, 12, Aves ipsae per aera vagantes
26, 3, 26, per medium iustitiae tramitem moderatus incede,
47, 2, 10, currat quin immo honorum gratia per parentes
64, 6, excursus . . . per alveum Padi solito more faciatis

It also occurs in the local meaning of *throughout,* both with verbs
of rest and with verbs of motion. Examples of the classical usage:

20, 1, 5, ut per provinciam . . . nulla fieri violenta patiaris,
33, 2, 15, per loca singula . . . faciat commoneri
120, 1, 27, Gothi per Picenum sive Tuscias utrasque residentes
275, 1, 7, Per provincias . . . tales viros cupimus destinare

B. Temporal Use

The use of *per* with the accusative to denote duration is found
first in Quadrigarius. It occurs rarely in classical prose, but is
frequent in Livy and succeeding writers (K.-Steg., II, 1, 555).

5

The simple accusative of duration does not occur in the Variae (Cf. ablative of time, p. 50). Examples:

67, 2, 14, per hoc iuge biennium
101, 1, 9, per annorum longa curricula
147, 2, 30, per tam longum temporis spatium
285, 3, 13, per triginta dies
298, 3, 11, per longa saecula

Duration seems also to be the sense of the frequent phrase *per indictionem*. Some of the verbs used with this phrase suggest rather a point of time. We may assume an ellipsis of this nature, *Assume this office (and hold it) throughout this indiction.* Examples:

38, 3, 4, te per indictionem . . . tertiam ad praefecturae urbanae culmen erigimus.
47, 5, 31, sume itaque per indictionem quartam consulatus insignia.
    96, 1, 9,
Also 115, 2, 20, and many other similar examples.
    148, 1, 1,

C. *Per* with Persons Used as Means

When a person is used as a means or a secondary agent classical prose regularly employs *per* with the accusative. This usage is very frequent in the Variae. Examples:

11, 6, 2, cetera vero per praesentium latores . . . suggerenda commisimus
27, 2, 25, per Nandum saionem nostrum ammonendum curavimus, *etc.*
50, 1, 9, nostris iussionibus per te procuretur effectus
73, 3, 19, per quos . . . consequamur effectum
359, 1, 5, per milites suos intellegitur iudex

D. *Per* as Equivalent of the Ablative of Means

Cassiodorus very frequently uses *per* with the accusative instead of an ablative of means in speaking of things. This usage existed in classical prose, but was rare; it became more frequent in Silver and Late Latin (Cf. K.-Steg., II, 1, 556). While this usage is rather frequent in the Variae, still the ablative of means predominates. Examples:

29, 1, 9, ut per moderationis exemplum luceat gratia dignitatum
41, 8, 10, diei index per umbram exiguam horas consuevit ostendere
268, 2, 26, per fustuaria supplicia laceretur

270, 5, 28, Aurum si quidem per bella quaerere nefas est, per maria
periculum, per falsitates opprobrium,
360, 5, 7, per dulcedinem superat

Several examples of the juxtaposition of *per* and the ablative of means are found, e. g.

31, 4, 10, ut culpa *legibus,* non *per* praesumptam coerceatur iniuriam
36, 2, 25, sicut duris *laboribus* instruitur, ita *per* otia . . . fatuatur
82, 3, 24, *per* formae gratiam, mentis *pulchritudine* plus placentem

E. *Per* in Causal Sense

Per occurs frequently instead of the ablative of cause. Cf. abl. of cause, p. 50. The usage is rare in classical prose (K.-Steg., II, 1, 557). Examples:

20, 3, 13, ne per dilationis incommoda eorum videatur supplex odisse victoriam.
24, 1, 8, ne per dubitationem possitis errare
32, 4, 3, theatrum per vos resonat
36, 2, 28, ne . . . per tarditatis vitium incurrat obstaculum
42, 2, 11, per vos propositum gentile deponit
56, 5, 2, amicitiae populis per damna creverunt
61, 1, 27, per nostra beneficia fraudes fieri legibus non amamus,

The causal usage of *per* with neuter demonstrative and relative pronouns is found only in Silver and Late Latin (L.-Hof., 521, 4; K.-Steg., II, 1, 557). I have observed only one example, 354, 7, 31, Illa iuste refugitis, per quae tristia pertulistis.

F. *Per* in Modal Phrases

In several examples *per* expresses manner, especially in such phrases as those listed below. *Per iniuriam* is found thus in Cicero (K.-Steg., II, 1, 557). The other phrases are used in a similar manner.

3, 3, 10, per moram
17, 2, 17, per calumniam
31, 4, 11, per excessum
60, 2, 18, per ordinem   Cf. *ordine,* 60, 2, 20.
232, 2, 19, per quietem
278, 3, 23, per iniuriam

G. *Per* in Limiting Phrases

Per occurs in the limiting phrases *per cuncta,* etc., in the following and similar examples:

13, 5, 10, egisti per cuncta iudicem totius erroris expertem
62, 2, 13, per tot . . . casus fixum tenuisti militiae probatae vestigium

The usage of *per omnia* as a limiting phrase (cf. abl. of respect) begins with Livy (L.-Hof., 379, 3; K.-Steg., II, 1, 558). The above examples appear to be extensions of the use of *per omnia*.

H. *Per* in Distributive Sense

A distinctly Late Latin usage is that of *per* in a distributive sense. Leumann-Hofmann, 522, 1, mentions it only for Cassidorus and the rule of St. Benedict. Meyer-Lübke, Grammaire des langues Romaines, vol. III, par. 473, discusses the survival of this use in a temporal sense in Romance. English has adopted *per diem, per centum,* etc. Examples:

51. 2, 11, ut alterum solidum per mensem . . . accipiat
135, 3, 24, per unum equum centum solidos multae nomine cogatur
        inferre
147, 2, 1, per unum equum centum statim solidos a te cogatur exsol-
        vere
149, 2, 12, per unamquamque condamam ·sumptus eis tres solidos
        largitas nostra direxit
149, 23,   tres solidos per condamam elegimus destinare
151, 7, 19, per annum in unumquodque municipium semel accedat
341, 2, 7, per singulos excessus sex solidorum multam a se noverit
        exigendam

II. *Prepositions with the Ablative*

Ab, De, and *Ex* Denoting Departure or Separation
(L.-Hof. 523-530)

The three prepositions, *ab, de,* and *ex,* denoting separation or departure are used in Classical prose largely as follows: *Ab* indicates external departure or separation, *ex* departure or separation from the interior of a place or thing, *de* separation of an object from something essentially united with it. Even in classical prose, however, these distinctions were frequently disregarded, and Silver and Late Latin to a much greater degree lost sight of the distinctions. *De* steadily increased in use in colloquial language, and in the Late Latin period encroached notably upon the functions of the other two prepositions. Of the three, it alone survives in Romance.

The Variae reflect the changes mentioned. The finer distinctions of the three prepositions are to a considerable extent disregarded. *Ab* is used with words where *ex* was employed in Classical prose, and *de* occurs for both *ab* and *ex*. Thus the increase in the use of *de* tended more to the elimination of *ex* than to that of *ab*. Occasionally, however, *ab* occurs where *de* was used in Classical prose.

1. *Ab*

A. *Ab* with Compounds of *Ex*

a. CLASSICAL USE

Ab occurs frequently with compounds of *ex* where it was also used thus in Classical prose. The following are a few selected examples of this usage:

50, 2, 1, a quadam porta provinciae gentiles introitus probatur excludere
61, 4, 18, nullam ab eis exigat pensionem
70, 1, 2, a nobis citharoedum . . . expetisset

b. NON-CLASSICAL USE

With the following compounds of *ex* Cassiodorus uses *ab*. Classical prose regularly repeated the preposition *ex*.

eicere 19, 2, 1, falsitatem a consortio veritatis eiciat,
    Ab occurs in Accius, Varro, Lucan (T. L. L., I, 6, 22).
emanare 132, 2, 19, velut a iustitiae fontibus emanarent
    Cassiodorus also uses *de*, 157, 3, 3. Cf. p. 112.
excidere 106, 12, 30, ab honestis moribus sic constat excidi
    Ex and *de* in Cic.; *ab* in Prop. (Harpers').
eximere 351, 1, 28, a damnis exemit
    Only *de* and *ex* are Classical (K.-Steg., II, 1, 331). *Ab* is Late (Kr.-Schm., I, 547).
exire 138, 7, 30, ut paene ab homine non credatur exire
    Ex and *de* in Cic.; *ab* in Liv., Plin. (Georges). Cassiodorus uses *de*, 67, 1, 26.
exprimere 363, 4, 3, ut . . . liquores eius a purpura credantur expressi.
    Ex in Plin. and Curt.
exulare 270, 3, 9, exulant a sole
    Ab in Plaut. Cf. K.-Steg., II, 1, 363.

B. *Ab* occurs with the following simple verbs with which *ex* was regular in classical prose:

carpere 327, 9, 17, si a matre lectione carpatur
    Macr. sat. is the only previous citation in T. L. L., III, 494, 24. *Ex* and *de* are cited for Cicero.

colligere 18, 1, 11, fidem siquidem rerum a ratione colligimus
 Ov., Plin., Val. Max., etc. (T. L. L., III, 1621, 9).
nominare 31, 5, 15, Belus . . . a quo et bellum placuit nominari
 Cf. Liv. 38, 18, 4, *ab re nomen habet*
 Cf. 116, 5, 30, de clementia nominati

C. *Ab* occurs with the following verbs expressing separation or departure with which it was not regularly used in classical prose. The ablative alone is the usual construction.

deviare 12, 3, 29, mentes ab obstinatione praecipiti deviasti.
 Word is Late. Abl. alone and *ab* with abl. are regular in intransitive use. Serv. and Cass. first citations for active use with *ab* (T. L. L., V, 864, 1 ff.).
dimovere 19, 4, 15, a tali non potest condicione dimoveri
 One citation from Sall. with *ab* in this sense. Regular in Late authors (T. L. L., V, 1218, 53 ff.).
excipere 364, 7, 31, a praesenti devotione . . . excepta
exuere ⎫
nudare⎭ 188, 2, 13, exuendus a crimine non nudetur ab innoxia facultate
 The simple ablative is classical with both verbs (Kr.-Schm., s. v.).
liberare 163, 2, 13, a diversorum insidiis . . . liberatus
 Ab is rare in classical prose (K.-Steg., II, 1, 372).
relinquere = *to release* 15, 13, 26, tristis ab obsequio suo reliquit, quem, etc.
 I have not found this meaning of *ab* elsewhere or its use with this verb.

D. *Ab* = *Contra*

Ab appears to be used as the equivalent of *contra* in 62, 4, 27, ab omni ergo damno oneribusque sordidis ius te munivit antiquum. Citations for this use in T. L. L., I, 31, 81, include one from Caesar and one from Sallust. Other citations are poetic, Silver and Late.

E. *Ab* with Adjectives

Ab occurs with the following adjectives with which it was not used or was used very rarely in classical prose.

alienus 50, 2, 30, ut nullus a nostra munificentia reddatur alienus
 Rare with things, though frequent with persons in this sense (K.-Steg., II, 1, 372).
dissimilis 361, 4, 2, dissimilis ab accusato debet esse qui iudicat.
 Caecil. (T. L. L., I, 12, 7). Cledon., Iren., Porph., Sol., Claud. Don., Lact., Aug., etc. (T. L. L., V, 1475, 35).
extraneus 306, 4, 22, Amovete suspiciones ab ordine vestro semper extraneas.

ieiunus 5, 15, 11, a litterarum sapore ieiunis
   Hier. epist. (T. L. L., I, 12, 14).
longinquus 83, 1, 16, dum a terrena fuerint cupiditate longinqui.
   Diom. (T. L. L., I, 11, 79).
peregrinus 368, 3, 28, ne . . . a gratia nostra peregrinus reddaris
   Ennod. (T. L. L., I, 11, 79).
quietus 136, 28, quietosque vos ab sceleratis ausibus reddat,
   Liv. (T. L. L., I, 12, 35).
securus 147, 1, 33, qui nos a dispendiis fecere securos.
   Planc. in Cic. epist., Liv. (K.-Steg., II, 1, 437).

F. *Ab* in Temporal Use

The phrases *a tempore* and *a temporibus* denoting temporal point
of departure occur several times, e. g., 28, 2, 28, usque a . . . temporibus, and 28, 2, 29, a tempore. Other phrases employing words
that are not of themselves temporal are used in a similar way, so
that in their context they also denote temporal point of departure.
Several of these are stereotyped phrases; others are extensions of
the same usage.

26, 1, 1, ab ipsis cunabulis
31, 3, 32, ab antiquis
48, 5, 28, ab ipsis quippe primordiis
53, 2, 20, a parvulis
54, 1, 12, ab exordio
292, 6, 5, ab antiquitate
353, 5, 18, ab avis atavisque

The regular use of *ab* with the ablative of agent and its occasional
use with the ablative of comparison have been mentioned, p. 42.

2. *De*

A. With Verbs of Separation and Departure

a. WITH COMPOUNDS OF *Ab* AND *Ex*

With many compounds of *ab* and *ex* denoting separation or
departure Cassiodorus uses *de*. A brief note on the usage of the
various prepositions is given with each example.

abducere 52, 2, 5, de propriis penatibus . . . abductam
   De occurs in Plaut., Sen. (Guillemin 22).
abradere 225, 2, 14, de vasariis publicis diligenter abradi
   Cf. 281, 1, 12, ab splendore suo cupiens maculam . . . abradere
   De occurs in Cassian. and Cassiod. (T. L. L., I, 128, 41).

abscedere 57, 3, 2, de iudicio victus abscedas
   Ab occurs in Early Latin, in Bell. Afr., Liv., Silver, Late. *De* in
   Aug., Ennod., Eugipp. (T. L. L., I, 145, 41 ff.).
auferre 202, 3, 22, quae qualitatem famae suae de ore hominum possit
   auferre
   Ab, de, and, *ex* in Cicero (T. L. L., II, 1329, 38). *De* most frequent
   (Guillemin, 20).
ebullire 137, 6, 28, glebas . . . de tam profundis hiatibus ebullisse
   Literal use very late. No prepositions until Salonius and Cassio-
   dorus, who use *de* (T. L. L., V, 2, 16, 62 ff.).
educere 128, 2, 6, de saxi sterilitate copiosos latices eduxit
   Ex in Cic. etc. *De* in Itala, Vulg., Amm. (T. L. L., V, 2, 120, 74).
eligere 48, 5, 32, de magnis raro eligi potest
   De in Cicero (Guillemin, 22).
emanare 157, 3, 3, qualem de pura conscientia decet emanare.
   Ex in Cic., Pacian., Ruf., Cod. Iust. etc. *De* in Lact., Cassiod.
   (T. L. L., V, 2, 446, 70 ff.). Cf. Cassiodorus' use of *ab,* 132, 2, 19.
emergere 79, 1, 3, ut de uno aliquid dolendum possit emergere.
   Ex frequent in Cic. *De* rare in Classical and Silver Latin (Guillemin, 27-28).
exigere 277, 1, 1, de quarta indictione non exigant,
   Ab in Cic., Quint., etc. *De* in Ov., Flor. (Georges).
exire 67, 1, 26, quod de memoria nostra nescit exire.
   Both *ex* and *de* in Cicero (Guillemin, 13).
exudare 11, 3, 16, cruorem de se . . . exudare
   Ab in Claud. (Georges).

b. WITH OTHER COMPOUNDS AND SIMPLE VERBS

A brief note on the use of *de* is given with each verb with which
I have found it used by other authors.

advenire 181, 7, 14, qui de extremis mundi partibus advenerunt.
   Ab in Plaut., Lucr., Liv., Vitr., Mart.
   De in Stat., Tert., Filast. (T. L. L., I, 831, 21 ff.).
amputare 164, 2, 12, silvam . . . de Ravennati forma . . . amputari
   Dative classical. *Ab* in Col.
   De in Aug. (T. L. L., I, 2024, 24).
assumere 20, 3, 12, quae de praesumptione potest virtutis assumi.
   Ex in Varro, Cic., Cels., etc.
   De in Verg., Aug., Hier., etc. (T. L. L., II, 931, 47 ff.).
destinare 33, 2, 22, quae de Calabro atque Apulo litoribus . . . con-
   suerant destinari.
   (Cf. *destinare ex,* 100, 2, 8)
   Late Latin use of word. *De* in Canon. (T. L. L., V, 760, 7).
devehere 118, 13, de locis vestris ad Alfuanum trabes . . . devehatis.
   Ex in Liv.; *de* in Cassiod. (T. L. L., V, 848, 59).

discedere 89, 1, 14, de mundi conversatione discedant.
  Ab Classical. Ablative alone in Ov. (K.-Steg., II, 1, 371).
fugare 103, 4, 5, de quo alterum crudeliter fugavit exitio,
  Ab in Cic., Eutr. (Georges).
furari 191, 7, 7, non licet aliquid furari de populo:
  Ex in Cic., Quint., Suet., etc. *De* in Apul., Coll. Mos., Vulg., Aug.,
  etc. (T. L. L., VI, 1640, 43 ff.).
legere 49, 7, 6, Legit . . . fasces de moenibus Gallicanis
  Ex in Eutr. *De* in Verg. (Georges).
perire 66, 7, de Comensi civitate aeneam statuam quae perisse suggeritur.
  Ex in Plaut. in this sense (Georges).
postulare 368, 3, 5, quae de provinciis sollemniter postulantur.
  (Cf. *postulare ab,* 39, 2, 31) *Ab* in Cic., Tac. (Georges).
procedere 70, 3, 11, de secreto naturae . . . processerit
  Ex in Cic. *De* in Sall. (Georges).
rapere 66, 2, 20, qui statuam de Comensi civitate rapuerunt.
  Abl. alone in Verg., Val. Flacc. *Ab* and *de* in Ov. (Georges).
relevare 56, 16, de tertiarum illationibus vobis noveritis esse relevandos.
  Ex in Cic. Abl. alone in Ov. (Georges).
reddere 21, 4, 3, honores ergo quos sumis ex chartis, redde de meritis.
subducere 19, 2, 2, aliquid de illa integritate subducere
  (Cf. *subducere ab,* 131, 1, 7) *Ex* in Verg. (Georges).
subtrahere 116, 5, 29, nihil de genio vestro subtrahitur.
  Dative in Cic. etc. *Ex* and *ab* in Liv. (Georges).
sumere 48, 5, 31, sumeret de publica auctoritate constantiam.
  (Cf. *sumere ex,* 21, 4, 3) *Ab* in Ter., Ov. (Georges).
suspendere 79, 2, 30, ut aut se de Wisigotharum conflictu . . . suspendat
  Used in sense of *se abstineat.*
venire 195, 1, 2, non enim querelas de Sicilia volumus venire, sed laudes.
  Ex in Plaut. *Ab* in Cels. *De* in Apul. (Georges).

c. *De* INSTEAD OF THE SIMPLE ABLATIVE

De occurs in the Variae with the following verbs with which
Classical prose regularly employs no preposition.

confidere 88, 3, 19, quid enim potest esse felicius quam homines de solis
  legibus confidere . . . ?
fraudare 26, 2, 10, nullum enim de largitate nostra fraudari
gloriari 334, 6, 32, ipsi autem in domino de promerita ubertate glori-
  entur.
gravare 339, 1, 10, ne . . . de ipsa sollicitudine gravaremus.
laetari 80, 2, 20, ut . . . de vestra concertatione laetentur.
liberare 385, 9, 19, de famis periculo cognosceris esse liberatus.
ornare 93, 2, 28, ornasti de conscientiae integritate palatia:

The adjective *contentus* is also followed by *de* in 291, 11, 4, non sumus tantummodo de tuorum temporum laude contenti. Elsewhere it occurs in the Classical manner without a preposition, 291, 3, 30, creditis his tantum fuisse contentum.

B. Other Uses Instead of *Ab* and *Ex*

Besides its use with verbs of separation and departure *de* occurs instead of *ab* or *ex* with the following verbs. (Uses unclassified.)

aestimare 21, 1, 14, qui de gloriosis virtutibus aestimatur.
agnoscere 335, 3, 19, sic mens praesulis de te probatur agnosci:
cognoscere 135, 3, provinciam se deseruisse ieiunam de copiae inventione
  cognoscant
esse 53, 1, 1, reatus sit inoxiis de contemptibus alienis.
  138, 3, 15, moles ipsa sic tota de cautibus fuit
facere 97, 3, 1, ars est facere de irato benivolum
  Ex is Classical (K.-Steg., II, 1, 505).
laborare 318, 2, 30, ut de eius fama laboraret,
  (Cf. simple abl., 137, 2, 9.)
metiri 20, 1, 19, voluntatem nostram de ratione metimur
nominare 116, 5, 30, parentes publici de clementia nominati,
  Ab is regular. *Ex* also Classical.
  De is not Classical (K.-Steg., II, 1, 506).
pensare 338, 7, 23, qui minime de pravitatum actione pensatur
praesumere 318, 2, 31, quamvis de propria virtute praesumeret
sentire 100, 2, 10, auxilium provinciae de tam magna congregatione
  sentirent
terrere 22, 2, 22, animum pervadentis de resultatione terrere
vocitare 25, 2, 13, populi de colore vocitentur
  Cf. note on *nominare* above.

C. *De* with the Ablative instead of an Accusative

Sapere takes the accusative once in Cicero and more frequently in poets and later writers. We find *de* used in 331, 3, 15, quod de vera sapientia sapit.

D. *De* in Partitive Sense

De occurs several times in a partitive sense. In some examples it occurs with a verb of separation indicating that a part is taken away from the whole. I have listed these as partitive.

Examples of this kind are found in Early Latin, and Late authors greatly extended the usage. It should be observed that Cassiodorus does not employ the elliptical mode of expression by which many

Late authors omit the substantive denoting the part (Cf. L.-Hof., 392). Examples:

25, 2, 1, ne tenuis de proprio cogatur exsolvere,
25, 4, 23, de Helladio et Thorodon qui . . . aptior fuerit aestimatus
. . . constituatur a vobis prasini pantomimus,
37, 19, nihil imminuimus sacro ordini de solita auctoritate
39, 4, 3, fas est de cunctis optimos quaerere
54, 3, 25, ut de plurimis pauca sufficiant
67, 3, 17, ne . . . quicquam de credita summa existiment postulandum
118, 2, 3, nec quicquam miseris de aquarum nimietate nisi solas lacri-
mas restitisse.
126, 4, 16, quicquid . . . de causis memorati supplicantis accepit
155, 2, 15, aliquid de alienis facultatibus violenter abscidi
166, 12, 1, habeant liberum unum tantum de duobus expetere
271, 1, 12, paucos perdidisse de plurimis
283, 1, 4, nec aliquid de eius districtione detestabili volumus tempera-
tione mitigari

E. *De* = *concerning*

De occurs in the Classical manner with many verbs of saying, thinking, etc. to indicate the subject of speech or thought, e. g., 38, 4, 34, sed quid ultra de eius moribus est dicendum; 49, 2, 32, cogitare de militis transactione. The only unusual examples seem to be one with a verb of promising and one with a verb of supplication, 51, 2, 21, promitterent de nece mariti, and 73, 2, 9, de vitae munere supplicare. It should be observed that in these two examples the verbs are used absolutely.

F. *De* with the Ablative of Origin

De occurs instead of the simple ablative with several verbs denoting birth, descent, etc. It is frequent with *nasci*, referring to the origin of things, e. g., 136, 7, 9, nascitur de adversitate prosperitas. The word usually refers to the origin of persons, and the simple ablative is the most common construction in Classical prose, though *ex* occurs quite frequently, *ab* and *de* less frequently (K.-Steg., II, 1, 375-376; cf. T. L. L., V, 54, 23).

Examples with other verbs are:

4, 10, 27, quod de arcano pectoris gignitur
31, 1, 24, convicia . . . nec de laetitia procreantur
49, 6, 5, qui (person) de speciosa stirpe descendit.

G. *De* for the Ablative of Cause, Means or Agent

a. CAUSE

The use of *de* to denote cause is frequent in Classical prose only with *causa* in a few fixed expressions, as Cic., Att. 7, 3, 3, *gravi de causa*. Silver and Late Latin writers frequently use *de* with other words to denote cause (K.-Steg., II, 1, 499-500).

Besides the examples mentioned on page 114, some of which are causal, many more examples of *de* denoting cause are found in the Variae. The following is only a partial list illustrating the usage.

13, 4, 6, ut . . . possint iudices etiam de suspicionibus accusare.
28, 3, 1, de quibus possit pietas materna praesumere
28, 1, 7, de initiis praedicatio debetur invento, de custoditis adquiritur laudata perfectio.
48, 1, 3, de tali auspicio maiora promittite.
55, 5, 29, cum se homines soleant de vicinitate collidere
56, 5, 1, gratia dominorum de cespitis divisione coniuncta est; (Cf. *per damna*, 56, 5, 2.)
115, 1, 2, gratiam non de natura, sed de solis meritis habent,
152, 1, 21, de voluntate simul et actione laudatur.
161, 3, 8, exceptura de iniqua praesumptione vindictam aut de mulieris improbitate victoriam.
201, 1, 7, ut . . . de optata ultione gauderent.
250, 1, 2, senatum volumus etiam de numerositate praedicari
277, 1, 27, de domesticorum excessibus . . . provinciales damnis plurimis ingravatos
310, 2, 26, de causarum nostrarum aequitate praesumpsimus
328, 7, 24, non . . . sustinet de mediatoris tarditate iacturam
355, 9, 16, sustine de omnium securitate iacturam, qui habuisti de multorum afflictione laetitiam.
361, 1, 24, tanta est in re publica de morum varietate diversitas,
369, 1, 7, diversae provinciae de suis deliciis laudarentur
380, 5, 25, nesciunt de penatibus invidere

b. MEANS

No clear-cut example of *de* as the equivalent of an ablative of means is cited for Classical prose. The usage appears to begin with the Augustan poets. It was used rather sparingly in Silver Latin, but became more common in Late Latin (L.-Hof., 437, 526; K.-Steg., II, 1, 501; T. L. L., V, 62, 18). It is frequent in the Variae. The following illustrate the usage:

47, 1, 6, firmatur omnis indubitata de repetitione sententia.
47, 4, 25, quod ille assumere non valuit, de eius opibus efficisti.
50, 1, 8, (paired with *per*) ut et tibi de aestimatione nostra crescat
     ornatus et nostris iussionibus per te procuretur effectus.
82, 4, 30, de avita laude primordia teneri pectoris erudire.
101, 3, 2, de nostra promissione recreati
115, 1, 17, de claritate servientium crescit fama dominorum.
124, 1, 21, de integritate placuisti
127, 2, 6, de mora quaeritis commoda,
225, 1, 3, Cum de agri utilitate vivatur
318, 5, 6, contemptum vindicans de fetore.
335, 3, 18, sicut penetrale domus de foribus potest congruenter intelligi,
     sic mens praesulis de te probatur agnosci:
337, 5, 3, de aequitate potius quam de rapacitate proficitur.

C. AGENT

One clear example of *de* with an ablative of agent occurs in 115, 3, 10, adoptat te talis, de cuius gente tu potius formideris. This construction is quite unusual. It is mentioned as a forerunner of the Romance use of *de* for agent in L.-Hof., 527, 4. Examples cited are Iren. 1, 7, 3, and Heges, 5, 42, 5 (This one is cited in T. L. L., V, 64, 32), in both of which it serves as a translation of the Greek. Traube, 531, adds to this example the following: 123, 2, 12, quod de fisco . . . praestatur; 342, 2, 5, de vestra concordia videbamur accepti; 99, 2, 18, de illis (cultis) exercituales iuventur expensae; 377, 1, 17, de fide publica . . . reparatur quicquid a privatis amittitur; cf. 47, 6; 56, 1; 84, 20; 336, 16; 337, 3; 342, 7; 377, 27. To explain any of these as agent requires that we consider an inanimate thing as personified. I believe that all these examples should be listed under other uses of *de,* origin, causal and instrumental, found in the Variae and discussed above.

H. *De* Dependent on Nouns

In several examples the noun with *de* is directly attached to another noun without intervening verb, e. g.

88, 3, 3, de calamitate tristitia
327, 6, 2, libellos . . . de praefecturae actione
341, 3, 25, lucra de civibus
352, 5, 15, continuitas de minutiis
361, 1, 24, de morum varietate diversitas.

Various uses of *de* occur in the above examples. Beyond greater frequency in the Variae, the usage itself is not un-Classical.

One example calls for special comment, viz., 31, 4, 11, ultio de cive. We might expect an objective genitive, but *de* with the ablative can be explained either by the ellipsis of the participle *sumpta* or by the analogy of *ulcisci de*. With the verb *sumere*, *de* is used with the person from whom a penalty is exacted, e. g., Cic. Verr., 6, 64, *de quo supplicium sumi oportet* (Cf. T. L. L., V, 62, 6). *Ulcisci de aliquo* occurs in Spart. Sev. 11, 3, and Vulg. Iud. 6, 32 and 16, 28 (Cf. Zucker, 68).

3. *Ex*

A. Ex with Verbs of Separation and Departure

Examples of *ex* denoting separation or departure are not numerous in the Variae. The large number of instances where *ab*, and especially *de*, is used in place of *ex* is partially responsible for this fact, though it appears also that Cassiodorus has little occasion to use *ex* in its original sense of departure or separation from the interior of a place or thing. The example in 136, 2, 19, cum te egredi ex urbe divino favore contigerit, illustrates this original usage.

A few examples occur where *ex* is used instead of *ab* or *de*. *Ex* occurs with a compound of *ab* in 124, 1, 1, abscedat ritus e medio iam profanus. *Abscedere ab* is found in Early Latin, in the Bell. Afr., and in Silver and Late Latin (T. L. L., I, 145, 41). *Abscedere ex* is found in one example in Plautus, one in Livy, then Ammianus (*e medio prospectu*) Vulg., Cod. Th. (T. L. L., I, 145, 60). *Abscedere de* is found in Aug., Ennod., Eugipp. (T. L. L., I, 145, 64). *Ex* occurs with a compound of *de* in 144, 2, 3, ex arboris suco defluens. An example of *ex* with this verb in connection with the flowing of water appears in Cicero, one with *de* in Cato and one in Tertullian, with *ab* in Pliny the Elder (T. L. L., V, 362, 55). In the case of other liquids, as in our example, T. L. L., V, 363, 10, cites Cic., Prop., and Lucan with the preposition *a*; no examples of *ex* or *de*.

Ex is rarely used to indicate temporal point of departure. It occurs thus with *tempore* in 136, 2, 18, ut ex illo tempore supputentur. This usage is classical. The use of *ex quo* to indicate temporal point of departure begins with Livy. I have noted 24, 2, 9, ex quo . . . Sonti fluenta transmisimus.

Ex occurs in Classical prose indicating transition from one state or condition to another (K.-Steg., II, 1, 505). It occurs thus in 273, 3, 31, quae etiam ex obscuro nobilem facit.

B. *Ex* Denoting Source or Origin

At all periods of Latin the prepositions *ab* and *ex*, and more rarely *de*, had some employment in place of the simple ablative with verbs denoting source or origin. Late Latin used these prepositions very freely and employed all three for source or origin without discrimination (Cf. L.-Hof., 422). When Cassiodorus uses a preposition it is regularly *ex*. His use of *ab* and *de* is mentioned on p. 115. Examples of *ex* for source or origin:

20, 3, 30, nati sunt fasces ex fascibus
30, 1, 21, orta quidem ex causis levibus
71, 9, 21, ex quibus . . . progenita sunt
144, 2, 21, venturarum rerum cursus ex alto est imperio divinitatis,
146, 5, 7, ex huius fecunda . . . stirpe
222, 2, 12, ut ex ea liberi nati nomen nanciscantur heredum
231, 3, 17, ex filio vestro genitus
232, 3, 25, ex vobis qui nascitur
232, 3, 25, qui ex hac familia progreditur
248, 7, 28, ex senatore natus est

C. *Ex* Denoting Cause, Material, Means, Agent

a. CAUSE

In Classical prose *ex* is rare in a causal sense. In the greater number of examples in Classical authors *ex* indicates an external cause, while *ex* indicating an internal cause, closely allied to the final meaning, is very rare (Cf. K.-Steg., II, 1, 504-505).

Cassiodorus uses *ex* rather freely for both external and internal causes. Examples:

4, 12, 32, cum me viderem ex affectione culpari
18, 2, 28, quod ex magnis fieri doloribus solet
63, 3, 31, nec . . . quodlibet gravamen ex permissa nundinatione sustineat
84, 2, 16, dolorem monstrare ex memoria praecedentium saeculorum

95, 5, 32, ne concessa videatur ex taciturnitate licentia.
145, 4, 8, tu Decoratus ex illo es, ille Honoratus ex te est.
163, 2, 15, ex prioribus factis habendi sunt iure reverendi.
248, 3, 12, ut hoc potius sit incertum, qui magis praedicetur ex altero.
363, 4, 8, rugescit, non liquescit ex senio:

b. MATERIAL

Ex is used at times in Classical prose to denote the material of which a thing consists (K.-Steg., II, 1, 505). Cassiodorus uses this construction to describe the complex nature of man, 331, 4, 24, homo constat ex dualitate. There is a close parallel in Cic. nat. deor., 1, 98, *qui ex animo constet et corpore.*

c. MEANS

No certain examples of *ex* used instead of the simple ablative of means are found in Classical prose. The usage is cited for Propertius, and in prose for Pliny the Elder. *Ex* used in this manner remained rare in Silver Latin, but became more common in the Late Latin period (K.-Steg., II, 1, 505).

Several examples occur in the Variae, e. g.

19, 4, 10, ex modicis praevalet maiora complecti.
38, 4, 9, plerumque honor ex commendatis adquiritur
39, 1, 9, Caritatem . . . ex ipsa cura potestis agnoscere
42, 3, 14, beluarum quippe ritus est ex ventris esurie horas sentire
54, 1, 11, ex parentum virtutibus prolis iudicare successus
256, 3, 17, fruere iuvante deo rebus propriis ex nostra quoque auctori-
           tate solidatis.

d. AGENT

Ex instead of *ab* denoting personal agent with a passive verb is found only in Late Latin, and even there the examples are not numerous (Cf. L.-Hof., 530). I have observed one such example of *ex* in the Variae, 305, 5, 8, erectus ex nobis sustinendo potius quam vindicando laudaberis. The examples in 145, 4, 8, and 248, 3, 12 (see, above), may possibly be regarded as agent. I have considered them as causal.

D. *Ex* in Partitive Sense

The use of *ex* instead of the partitive genitive is regular in Classical prose when the part is indicated by a cardinal numeral.

Examples of this usage are 63, 2, 23, unum . . . ex negotiatoribus, and 64, 4, 28, duos ex vestro corpore.

Late Latin made a freer use of *ex* in a partitive sense, as also of *de* (L.-Hof., 391-392). Cf., e. g., such a use of *ex* in 14, 8, 30, Sensit tunc res publica ex illo coetu Romuleo innocentiae virum.

E. *Ex* Meaning *according to*

The use of *ex* with the ablative to denote the rule or standard according to which something is done is Classical, but restricted to certain phrases, as *ex edicto, ex decreto,* etc. (Cf. K.-Steg., II, 1, 505).

The only extensions which I have noted are *ex iussione*, which is frequent, e. g., 126, 5, 22, tuitionem . . . ex nostra iussione . . . praestabis; *ex legibus* in 100, 1, 17, nisi vivatur ex legibus; *ex auctoritate* in 128, 1, 3, quae . . . ex nostra auctoritate suscepit.

F. *Ex* in Adverbial Phrases

Examples of the Classical usage of *ex parte* with a modifier are found in 73, 2, 17, nec sitis solliciti ex illa parte, quam ad nos cognoscitis pertinere, and in 271, 3, 20, nam et ex ea parte bonis moribus vixisse probandi sunt, quando, *etc.*

ex contrariis 41, 10, 22, quod illam ex contrariis appetit imitari.

The phrase *e(x) contrario* is Classical, occurring in various authors from Rhet. Her. down to the Cod. Iust (T. L. L., IV, 769, 39). *Ex contrariis* seems to be used in the meaning of this common phrase. I have found no occurrence of it elsewhere.

ex ordine 13, 6, 16, quicquid ex ordine tribuitur, dispendium non putatur.

This phrase is Classical (K.-Steg., II, 1, 506; examples of both *ordine* and *ex ordine* in Cicero appear in the lexica).

ex toto, e. g. 284, 9, 26, turpis actus ex toto sit a iudicibus alienus.

Ex toto meaning *totally* is first found in Ovid; in prose, in Seneca the Elder (K.-Steg., II, 1, 506; Wölfflin, Archiv 4 (1887) 144 ff.).

G. *Ex* in the Phrase *Ex Principe*

In 62, 6, we find as the title of Letter 28 in Book II, Stephano

V. S. Comiti Primi Ordinis et Ex Principe Officii Nostri Theodericus Rex. A similar example occurs in 62, 4, 25, privilegia quoque, quae tribui scholae tuae exprincipibus divalia constituta voluerunt, simili munificentia condonamus. In this phrase the preposition *ex* keeps its ablative, instead of entering into composition with the noun. Examples of this use of the ablative in such phrases in Classical authors are doubtful, but it is found in late inscriptions and in some very late authors, e. g., Cod. Iust. and Ammianus (Harpers').

4. *Sine*
(L.-Hof. 530)

The chief peculiarity in Cassiodorus' use of *sine* is its frequency with a form of *aliquis* instead of *ullus*, particularly in the frequently recurring *sine aliqua dilatione*, e. g., 36, 1, 2, and *sine aliqua dubitatione*, e. g., 49, 1, 30 (Cf. use of *aliquis*, p. 89). In clauses containing a negative, *sine* is found in phrases similar to these in Classical prose (T. L. L., I, 1613, 12), but the use of *aliquis* for *ullus* after *sine* in affirmative clauses is a rare Late Latin development. T. L. L., I, 1613, 22, cites examples only from Corp. VI and IX and from the Variae. Leumann-Hofmann, 530, mentions Filastrius, 104, 3.

The Classical *ullus* with *sine* occurs in the Variae only once, viz., 51, 2, 24, sine ulla facies dilatione restitui. Frequently, however, in phrases conveying the same idea as those mentioned above, *sine* occurs with the noun without a modifier, e. g., 18, 2, 5, sine dilatione, and 27, 3, 16, sine dubitatione.

The stereotyped Classical expression *sine dubio* occurs a few times, e. g., 29, 5, 27, quod sine dubio se optasse cognoscunt. *Sine fine*, another fixed expression from the time of Livy, occurs, e. g., 63, 1, 21, quem decet sine fine laudari and 72, 16, 27, ubi veraciter sine fine gaudium est.

5. *Absque*
(L.-Hof. 531)

Absque occurs very rarely in the Variae, e. g., 241, 8, 3, adquisivit rei publicae Romanae aliis contendentibus absque ulla fatigatione provinciam; 270, 3, 13, soli sunt hominum qui absque ulla nundinatione pretia videantur adquirere; 367, 1, 4, hereditas quae est sine proximis, absque parentela successio. It serves as a mere substitute for *sine*, a usage of the word which prevailed from the time of Fronto (Cf. K.-Steg., II, 1, 510-511; T. L. L., I, 186, 10).

The juxtaposition of *sine* and *absque* in 367, 1, 4, seems to be a mere seeking of variety of expression and shows that the author regarded the two prepositions as synonyms.

It is noteworthy that, while *sine* is consistently (with the exception of 51, 2, 24) employed with *aliquis* instead of *ullus*, *absque* is in 241, 8, 3, and 270, 3, 13, used with *ullus*. Traube, 514, informs us that the same usage of *sine* with *aliquis* and *absque* with *ullus* prevails in the Acta Synhodorum Habitarum Romae, with one exception, S 421, 1, *sine ulla de prolixo itineris cura,* where the reading *ulla* is doubtful. He has not noted the exception in 51, 2, 24, sine ulla . . . dilatione (for which no variants are given in the Monumenta edition), but says "constanter 'aliquis' ponitur post 'sine' (contra 'absque ulla fatigatione' 241, 3, 'absque ulla nundinatione' 270, 13)." T. L. L., I, 187, 7, 3, calls attention to these uses of *sine* and *absque* in the Variae and mentions Traube's obesrvations.

6. *Cum*
(L.-Hof. 531-532)

A. *Cum* Expressing Accompaniment

Cum with the ablative of accompaniment presents no special pecularities. The most frequent examples are those of the association of one person with another person, e. g., 15, 11, 14, cum . . . Carpilione . . . destinatus; 19, 5, 16, delectat nos . . . cum scientibus loqui, though examples of persons with things, things with persons, and things with other things, also occur, e. g.

12, 6, 5, cum blatta venire festina.
42, 1, 5, horologia cum suis dispositoribus credidimus destinanda.
125, 2, 6, porticum cum areola.

In 284, 7, 13, iugo servitutis cum filiis suis . . . addicatur uxori, the subject with the addition of the *cum*-phrase constitutes a logical plural. The *filii* are, however, thought of in a subordinate relation, and the syntax is that of simple accompaniment.

An example with ellipsis of the verb and the predicate adjective *commune* occurs in 273, 6, 13, quid mihi cum pretiis, si animus non fruatur optatis?   The thing accompanying the person is the equivalent of an appositive in 289, 2, 23, Nam quem ille virum aut exercitibus praeficiens cum victoria (= victorem) non recepit aut iudicem cingens non iustissimum comprobavit?

The verbs *iungere* and *miscere,* which generally occur in the Variae with the dative (cf. p. 32), are also found with *cum* and the ablative, e. g., 14, 7, 29, iunxit bene cum universorum gaudiis nostra compendia; 19, 6, 28, si integritas cum fraudibus misceatur. The use of *cum* with these verbs, as well as the use of the dative, is classical (K.-Steg., II, 1, 318).

One use with a verb of hostile association occurs, 73, 2, 11, si cum reliquis confligis (Cf. T. L. L., IV, 238, 81 ff.).

All the above uses are Classical.

B. *Cum* Expressing Likeness or Equality

In a few expressions *cum* has the sense of likeness or equality. This usage is very rare in Classical prose (Cf. K.-Steg., II, 1, 509). Examples:

19, 3, 3, quam cum caelestibus aequaliter novimus
29, 3, 1, commune cum universis possessoribus onus solutionis
    agnoscat
68, 6, 28, collega est cum viriditate gemmarum

C. *Cum* Meaning *among*

A few examples from Classical prose and from Silver Latin of *cum* in the sense of *in, inter, apud* are given in T. L. L., IV, 1348, 33.   I have noted one example of this usage, 15, 9, 7, cum togatis clari.

D. Temporal Use of *Cum*

Cum occurs in several examples indicating time, i. e., that one thing occurs simultaneously with another.   The usage is rare in Classical prose, but is more common in Silver and Late authors (K.-Steg., II, 1, 509; T. L. L., IV, 1361 ff.).   Examples:

46, 2, 13, crevit cum libertate provectibus
47, 2, 16, mutatur enim fortuna cum dominis
48, 2, 7, Romam recepere cum gloria,
    i. e., simultaneously they have retaken Rome and recovered
    their glory.   It is possible, however, to consider *cum gloria*
    as a modal ablative.

54, 4, 31, ut nostra quoque iudicia cum tuis provectibus tendas
268, 1, 21, tunc libertatem suam cum fortunis videtur amittere.
286, 6, 31, residua vero anni tempora cum annonarum debita redhibitione claudantur:

E. Instrumental Use of *Cum*

Cum with the ablative expressing means does not occur in Classical prose. Rare examples are found in Early and in Silver Latin, while in Late Latin the usage is frequent (K.-Steg., II, 1, 510; T. L. L., IV, 1369, 40 ff.). The clause in 214, 26, cum eorum solacio . . . quantitas deferatur, is cited in T. L. L., IV, 1370, 5, thus: "cum eorum (scrinariorum) solacio (i. illorum auxilio) . . . quantitas exactionis deferatur." Traube, 529, also notes this example and adds five similar ones from the Acta Synhodorum and Cassiodori Orationum Reliquiae. The author of the T. L. L. article states that many of his examples listed under means may be modal. I believe that a clearer example of *cum* as means is found in 361, 5, 6, te officiumque tuum cum dei iuvamine possessorem praecipimus ammonere, *etc.* This expresses the same thought which Cassiodorus frequently expresses by the ablative absolute *deo iuvante*, e. g., 115, 3, 11; 274, 1, 25. If the aid of the *scrinarii* can be regarded as a means and not a mere accompanying circumstance, the help of God can be regarded as a means also.

F. Modal Use of *Cum*

The modal use of *cum*, which is frequent in Classical prose, is very rare in the Variae. This is due largely to the author's frequent use of *sub* in circumstances where *cum* was used by Classical authors. See use of *sub*, p. 148. Where it does occur, it is used precisely as in Classical prose, e. g.

129, 3, 20, ne sicut latentia cum laude sunt prodita, ita inventa cum vituperatione videantur esse neglecta.
206, 1, 24, audis proceres cum ammiratione laudare.
232, 4, 30, cum magno gaudio secuti sunt
278, 4, 30, commodum debet esse cum modo.

7. *Prae*
(L.-Hof. 532-533)

Prae with the ablative occurs only twice in a local sense, 157, 3,

7, quem prae foribus haesitantem videras, and 319, 2, 26, si commendatio divae memoriae Amalasuinthae reginae prae oculis habetur. The local use of *prae* is rare in Classical prose, where its use is restricted to such phrases as *prae se ferre, prae se mittere,* etc., with verbs of motion. With verbs of rest, its use begins with Livy.

It occurs twice in a comparative sense, in the meaning of *above, in preference to,* each time in the phrase *prae omnibus.* Examples: 301, 2, 33, ita te custodire iustitiam prae omnibus sentiamus, and 362, 3, 3, Cogitetur prae omnibus pecuniae publicae fidelis exactio. The usage of *prae* as the equivalent of a comparative is very rare in Classical prose, but is somewhat more frequent in Late Latin (K.-Steg., II, 1, 513).

8. *Pro*
(L.-Hof. 533-534)

A. *Pro* Meaning *in behalf of*

Pro does not occur in the original local sense, meaning *in front of,* but is frequent in the figurative sense which developed from the local, i e., in the meaning of *for, in behalf of, for the benefit of.* The following examples are typical of the use of *pro* in this sense in the Variae.

17, 1, 27, et metum nostri pro parvulis insolentibus opponamus
18, 3, 5, si quid est quod pro suis partibus intentio retentatoris
        obiciat,
35, 2, 9, arietes pro suis ovibus capitaliter insaevire
35, 2, 10, ita pro copulatis sibi animas ponunt
38, 2, 24, ut nos ipsi, pro quibus haec fecisse cognoscitur, merito
        stupere videamur,
39, 1, 9, pro quibus ita videmur esse solliciti
39, 1, 30, sit ergo pro re publica et cum ludere videmur.
53, 2, 21, pro altera potius aetate peccatur.
53, 2, 22, pro quibus subire non recusamus exitium
130, 3, 17, dicat pro illis noster animus.

The example in 130, 3, 17, combines with the thought of *in behalf of* the additional idea of substitution, i. e., *in their place.* This usage of *pro,* as also the usages in the meaning *in behalf of,* etc., is Classical.

B. *Pro* Instead of an Appositive

In several examples *pro* with the ablative is used as the equivalent of a noun in apposition, showing that for which a thing serves. The usage is Classical. Examples:

13, 8, 23, haec pro remuneratione tribuimus
14, 3, 5, patriciatus dedimus pro remuneratione suggestum:
17, 3, 18, quae pro iugalis tuae assereris portione . . . divisisse
18, 2, 29, pro emolumentis sollemnibus nec integri ponderis solidos
            percipere

C. *Pro* Expressing Relation

Pro is used in Classical prose to express the ideas of *in relation to, in proportion to, according to,* but is restricted almost entirely to fixed expressions, such as *pro copia, pro re, pro viribus, pro parte,* etc. (L.-Hof., 534; K.-Steg., II, 1, 516). Wide extensions of this usage are found in Late Latin authors, who employed *pro* with almost any word with which they wished to express relations such as accordance or proportion. Examples of *pro* in the meaning of *according to* (Cf. abl. of accordance, p. 44):

18, 3, 7, pro consuetudine nostrae iudicemus aequitatis
27, 2, 8, quibus pro legum ratione susceptis
30, 3, 7, cum necessario pro temporis qualitate largitur
31, 2, 27, ut pro facti qualitate discussa excipiat promulgatam iure
            sententiam
37, 2,   pro nostra iussione arma necessaria procurabit
56, 2, 27, prudentia vestra pro integritatis suae proposito . . .
            discutiat
59, 2, 27, quod pro sua quisque voluntate aliquid exigentibus dignetur
            abicere
151, 3, 4, pro libito suo quorundam onera in alios proiecerunt,

In the meaning of *in proportion to.*

65, 2, 12, habeat iuris proprii spatia pro parte quam suscipit,
107, 6, 30, possessio . . . quam pro tributorum susceperat quantitate
            solvenda

This last example with the gerundive may have the meaning of *in proportion to the amount of tribute to be paid* or *in return for paying a (specified) amount of tribute.* If we take the latter meaning, the usage is more definitely a causal one. Elsewhere *pro* with the gerundive occurs in a final sense. Cf. p. 129.

D. *Pro* in Causal Sense

The causal use of *pro* is a development from its use in relations such as those mentioned in the preceding paragraph, especially from that of proportion. An example of this use is found as early as Plautus, one is noted in the Monumentum Ancyranum, but the usage is not frequent until the Late Latin period.

Few, if any, examples of *pro* in the Variae are definitely causal to the exclusion of other relations, but many examples which express the thought of *in proportion to* imply the additional thought *because of*. Another argument for classifying certain examples of *pro* as causal is that the final usage, which developed from the causal (L.-Hof., 534, 3), is quite definitely marked in the Variae. Cf. the following paragraph.

Examples of *pro* with causal significance:

17, 2, 30, quod nos pro rerum suarum acerbitate commovit
20, 3, 28, pro labore honoris tui honorem alterum accipere meruisti.
23, 2, 6, pro ingenita humanitate considerandum esse iudicamus
25, 1, 8, pro amore rei publicae Romanae non pigebit has quoque cogitationes intrare
28, 3, 14, nostra iussa pro sua reverentia in nullo violanda sunt,
30, 1, 22, pro spectaculorum voluptate ad discriminis se ultima pervenisse
35, 3, 15, pro amore pudicitiae porrigere ferrum maritis non est leges calcare,
51, 1, 5, nec pro affectu pietatis fines potest iustitiae custodire.
58, 1, 2, cui debet pro sedulitate conferri praemium,
108, 1, 15, ubi ars ipsa pro locorum siccitate magno studio semper excolitur,
122, 2, 25, quod nos pro sacerdotali honore relinquimus impunitum,
281, 2, 33, illum atque illum Romanos pro sola suspicione seditionis tam longae custodiae poena maceratos,

E. *Pro* in Final Sense

From the use of *pro* to denote relation there developed in connection with the causal use that of *pro* in expressions of purpose. This is not a clear-cut usage distinct from other relations in Classical prose, but in Late Latin *pro* becomes a definite final preposition (Cf. L.-Hof., 534; K.-Steg., II, 1, 516). Its use with a gerundive seems to be in precisely the same meaning as *ad* with the accusative of the gerundive. Svennung, 41, mentions the following Late authors who use *pro* with the gerundive for purpose, Orosius, Optat., Mileuit., Cassian., Vict. Vit. In addition to the use with the gerundive, *pro* with the ablative of nouns is also used to express purpose.

Examples of the use of *pro* with gerundive in final sense:

3, 1, 2, dicta mea, quae . . . pro explicanda negotiorum qualitate profuderam,

15, 11, 11, patricio Aetio pro iuvanda re publica magna fuit caritate sociatus:

49, 19, amminicula saionis, quae pro vindicandis titulis antefatis nostra tibi sollemniter deputavit auctoritas

56, 2, 28, pro implendis muniis eos ad curiam suam remeare permittat.

159, 1, 5, pro accipiendo donativo ad comitatum faciat incunctanter occurrere,

179, 5, 2, pro aequitate servanda et nobis patimur contradici

182, 2, 34, Patrimonium siquidem nostrum pro sublevandis privatorum fortunis tibi credimus,

256, 2, 31, quae ordinavit pro disciplina servanda,

351, 3, 11, quicquid pro continendis omnibus gratificationis accipimus, eorum iuste provisionibus applicamus.

Examples of *pro* with nouns in final sense:

11, 6, 4, nec aliquid pro utilitatibus nostris praetermisisse videremur

25, 3, 22, pro illorum utilitate delecti sunt,

25, 4, 25, sumptum, quem pro spectaculo civitatis impendimus,

27, 1, 21, pro communi utilitate exercitum ad Gallias constituimus destinare,

49, 2, 32, qui pro generali quiete finalibus locis noscitur insudare

63, 5, 4, cultus competens pro nostrorum temporum laude servetur.

63, 2, 22, pro expensis pauperum . . . unum sibi ex negotiatoribus urbis suae desiderant oportere praestari

73, 3, 20, quae ad nos pro vestris utilitatibus pervenerunt,

83, 2, 25, qui non soletis pro rebus magnis excedere,

162, 1, 29, frumentum in Africae partibus pro suo dicuntur vendidisse compendio.

F. *Pro* Used for Duration of Time

Duration of time is the evident signification of *pro* in 4, 8, 10, Regum quin etiam gloriosa colloquia pro magna diei parte in bonum publicum te occupare noverunt. This usage, for which I have found no parallel in Cassiodorus or elsewhere, seems to be a development from the use of *pro* meaning *in proportion to*. It is noted by Traube, 574, as a temporal use.

III. *Prepositions with the Accusative and the Ablative.*

1. *In*

A. *In* with the Accusative

(L.-Hof. 537, 538)

a. LITERAL LOCAL USE

In with the accusative is used in Classical prose literally in a local sense for physical motion into or among. Cassiodorus uses it in the literal sense in many examples, of which the following are typical:

52, 2, 8, cum in sacrosanctae ecclesiae saepta refugisset

68, 6, 30, in undam, qua viri recreantur, si mulier descendat, incenditur,

125, 1, 14, in stadium luctaturus introeat

270, 2, 4, intretur beneficio artis in penetrale telluris

The following examples are unusual:

47, 2, 13, cum . . . in antiquam patriam commeasses.
    Commeare ad is classical and more frequent at all times than *commeare in*. Examples of *commeare in* are found in Livy and Tacitus (T. L. L., III, 1868, 75).

68, 7, 35, imitus in auras erumpere excocti fontis inriguam puritatem.
    Erumpere in with the accusative in a hostile sense is frequent in classical prose in figurative expressions. It does not seem to occur in a literal sense.

85, 4, 21, locatus in medium cunctorum ad se trahit aspectum
    In with the accusative with *locare* is classical only in the expression *locare in matrimonium*.

108, 3, 23, lana sicca in terram ponitur iam provisam
    Ponere with *in* and the accusative is not found in classical prose. It occurs at times in Early Latin, in poetry, and in Silver and Late Latin to denote the act of placing (K.-Steg., II, 1, 590). *In* and the ablative takes account of the consequent rest and would be more natural here.

Other Classical usages are represented by the following examples:

41, 10, 17, noctes in partes dividens:
    (Distributive; cf. K.-Steg., II, 1, 569)

114, 3, 13, costae in quandam latitudinem porriguntur;
    (with *patere* and similar verbs in Caesar.)

b. FIGURATIVE LOCAL USE

In the case of a large number of the verbs of motion occurring with *in* and the accusative in the Variae the motion itself is a figurative one. In general the usage in the Variae is Classical. In the following examples *in* appears to be used for *ad*:

14, 6, 23, evectus in celsum inde magis despexerit vitia prosperorum.
  Ad is found with *evehere* in Curt., Tac., Amm. *In* occurs in Vell.
14, 6, 25, in cothurnum se magnae potestatis erexit,
  Both *ad* and *in* occur with *erigere* in Livy.
31, 4, 9, in praefecti urbis notitiam deferatur,
59, 1, 19, in vestram notitiam credidit perferendum,
60, 5, 8, hoc etiam nos . . . in cunctorum noveritis provincialium notitiam pertulisse,
  Ad is more common than *in* with *deferre* and *perferre*. (Cf. K.-Steg., II, 1, 330). *In notitiam alicuius perferre aliquid* occurs in Plin. epist. 10, 18, 2.
157, 4, 9, memoria . . . tanta in eum firmitate consedit,
  The usual local construction with *considere* is *in* with the ablative. *In* with the accusative occurs in Curt. 7, 4, 23.
234, 3, 8, ut Gothorum Romanorumque suavissimus consensus in regnum nostrum accederet,
  In figurative expressions *ad* is chiefly used with *accedere* (K.-Steg., II, 1, 326).
240, 5, 11, in tantam se similitudinem eius cogitationis adiunxerat, ut, *etc.*
  Dative or *ad* is the usual construction with *adiungere; in* occurs rarely, as in Livy 27, 15, 6, *in societatem adiungere* (K.-Steg., II, 1, 330).

This figurative usage of *in* with the accusative occurs with verbs of changing from one thing or condition to another. *Convertere,* which occurs, e. g., 30, 1, 25, is regular in classical prose (T. L. L., IV, 866, 22). *Mutare* occurs very rarely in this use in classical authors. It is used with *in* in the Variae, e. g., 58, 3, 10, in melius cuncta mutare, and 126, 3, 14, qui benigna iussa in truculenta ministeria mutaverunt.

In with the accusative is found in the meaning of *in exchange for* in 162, 2, 33, quia naucleri ducentos octoginta solidos in triticum . . . accepisse perhibentur.

The previous context refers to the *naucleri* having sold the grain, so this passage can scarcely refer to their having received so much money *in wheat.* Cf. also the use of the ablative *in naulis* immediately following and referring to their receiving money in the form of fares, passage-money. *In* with the accusative also occurs in 378, 1, 16, et ideo memoratae species in tot solidos datae pro tributaria functione vobis de praesenti prima indictione reputentur. The reference is to the collection of taxes in the form of wine, oil, and wheat *to the amount of so many solidi.*

The same transaction is ordered later in these words, 379, 1, 22, ut in tot solidos vini, olei vel tritici species de tributario solido debeas procurare, in aliis vero tot solidis, quos a nostro arcario percepisti, tam a negotiatoribus quam a possessoribus emere maturabis. *In* with the accusative is used as in the previous example. *In* with the ablative apparently occurs in a similar use, such an inconsistency not being unknown in the Variae (Cf. p. 138). It also appears possible to explain the ablative as the equivalent of an ablative of price.

c. TEMPORAL USE

In with the accusative of certain nouns, or adjectives used substantively, is used to express duration of time, the phrase being equivalent to an adverb., e. g.

in inmensum 16, 1, 16, In inmensum trahi non decet finita litigia
> *In inmensum* is found in a local meaning in Sall. Iug. 92, 5, and in Ov. met. 2, 220.

in aevum 85, 1, 3, quia in aevum vivit quod munificentia principalis indulserit.
> The usage of *in aevum* begins with Hor. carm. 4, 14, 3, *virtutes in aevum . . . aeternet.* Also in Prop., Luc., Plin. nat., Tert., Itala, Vulg., etc. (T. L. L., I, 1169, 81 ff.).

in perpetuum 28, 1, 22, quae semel annuimus rescindi in perpetuum non merentur,
> *In perpetuum* is Classical.

d. FINAL USE

In with the accusative denoting purpose occurs in rare instances in Classical prose, but becomes frequent from the time of Livy (K.-Steg., II, 1, 566-567). It occurs frequently in the Variae, e. g.

4, 8, 10, colloquia . . . in bonum publicum te occupare noverunt,
38, 1 19, hoc certe in praemium damus,
52, 1, 23, in usus nostros propitia divinitate servetur,
70, 2, 7, quicquid enim in conceptum alicuius modificationis existit,
125, 2, 7, in licentiam reparationis accipiuntur potius praemia quam donantur.

128, 1, 13, nequaquam detestabilis calumnia in invidiam regnantes affligat.

174, 1, 7, reperta *in* libertatis ornatum, inventa *ad* generale gaudium. (Note the juxtaposition of *in* and *ad*.)

340, 1, 13, escas enim in auxilium humani corporis contributas . . . reddit inutiles.

e. CONSECUTIVE USE

In with the accusative denoting the result of an action is rare in classical prose, but is used more freely in Silver and Late Latin (K.-Steg., II, 1, 567-568). The two following examples, listed by Traube, 548, under the final uses, appear to be examples of the consecutive use: 4, 12, 31, Victus sum, fateor, in verecundiam meam, and 71, 10, 22, Sirenas in miraculum cantasse curiosa prodit antiquitas. The phrase *in miraculum* may, however, be taken instead as modal in the meaning of *wonderfully, marvelously.* (Cf. Leumann-Hofmann, 790, citing Cypr. *cum miraculo = mirifice.*) Unless we accept this as a modal use, it must be considered as consecutive, not as final. The Sirens did not sing to achieve a marvel, but sang so well that the result was one. Similarly, *Victus sum, fateor, in verecundiam meam* certainly means: *I have been vanquished, I confess, to my shame.* His shame results from his being vanquished, but was not an end to be achieved.

f. USE OF *In* IN ADVERBIAL PHRASES
(Cf. also temporal phrases, p. 132)

Many adverbial phrases consisting of *in* and an adjective used substantively or of *in* and a simple noun in the accusative occur. Since they represent a wide variety of uses and their introduction into Latin literature occurred at various times, they are listed below with one example of each from the Variae and a comment as to their usage in authors earlier than Cassiodorus.

In with the Accusative of Adjectives Used Substantively

in cassum 5, 16, 14, neque enim tria genera dicendi in cassum prudens definivit antiquitas.

> The only citation from classical prose in T. L. L., III, 522, 30, is Sall. or. Macri, 11; it occurs in Plautus and Lucretius and is frequent in Silver and Late Latin; frequently written as one word.

in commune 17, 1, 25, Cordi nobis est cunctos in commune protegere,
   Occurs in Plaut., Ter., Liv., and in Silver and Late Latin (T.
   L. L., III, 1976, 63 ff.; cf. K.-Steg., II, 1, 569).

in contrarium 127, 2, 6, in contrarium foedo ambitu de mora quaeritis
   commoda,
   In contrarium occurs frequently from Cicero on with verbs of
   motion, striving, etc. (T. L. L., IV, 768, 69). As a phrase equivalent to *e contra* or *e contrario,* as in the above example, it is not
   cited.

in duplum 119, 3, 17, in duplum cui vim fecit direpta restituat,
   Cic., Tac., Suet., Dig. (Georges).

in integrum 130, 3, 1, patronum vestrum . . . in integrum restitui
   nostra quoque permittit auctoritas,
   In integrum restituere is found both in Cicero and in Caesar
   (Harpers').

in medium I have listed above (p. 130) as a local use the example in
   85, 4, 21, This example is cited by Traube, 549, among the *adverbialiter
   dicta.* The phrase *in medium* noted in L.-Hof., 538 as beginning
   with Sallust is used in a sense similar to that of *in commune.*

in quadruplum 278, 6, 35, in quadruplum iubemus ablata restitui,
   Used thus in Cic., Verr. 2, 3, 13; Dig. 48, 13, 13 (Harpers').

in solum 65, 1, 5, ut . . . possideas in solum rura revocata.
   Refers to sole possession. I have not found it in other authors.

in totum 190, 5, 34, sed ut actionis ipsius in totum merita perscrutemur
   Usage begins with Celsus, then Col., Sen., Plin. Used frequently in
   Late Latin, especially by the Jurists. Also in Min. Fel., Tert.,
   etc. (Cf. K.-Steg., II, 1, 569 and Wölfflin, Archiv 4, 146).

in tutum 37, 1, 26, in tutum apud nos reponit omnis devotio quod
   meretur
   There are variant readings for *in tutum.* It can be explained as
   an adverbial expression meaning *safely* or *in safe-keeping.* I
   have not found the phrase elsewhere.

In with the Accusative of Nouns in Adverbial Phrases

in abolitum 133, 2, 1, in abolitum missa sententia . . . patriae te rebusque omnibus nostra reddit auctoritas,
   The phrase *in abolitum* and, in fact, the noun *abolitus* is known
   only from this passage. It is cited as a fourth declension noun
   in T. L. L., I, 120, 31. The usage here is that of limit of motion,
   figuratively.

in caudam 355, 8, 6, Scarus . . . in caudam labitur, paulatim se ab
   angusto subducens.
   Listed by Traube, 549, as adverbial phrase equivalent to *retrorsum.*
   T. L. L. shows no example of *in caudam* in this sense. As it is
   with the verb *labitur,* it may be classified with the local uses of *in.*

in formam 67, 2, 26, Caerulum fontem vidimus in formam dolii
> *In formam* with a dependent genitive occurs in Tac., Suet., Paul., Prob. (T. L. L., VI, 1087, 57; cf. K.-Steg., II, 1, 568).

in latitudinem 114, 3, 13, costae in quandam latitudinem porriguntur:
> The phrase *in latitudinem* is classical, occurring in Caesar with *patere* and similar verbs. (Cf. Kr.-Schm., I, 703.)

in locum 220, 1, 2, quae in locum muneris solent postulata conferri,
> Classical usages in this meaning are *in loco* and more frequently *loco* (Harpers'; cf. K.-Steg., II, 1, 349).

in modum 64, 2, 16, paludem Decemnovii in hostis modum vicina vastantem
> This usage is classical, occurring in both Cicero and Caesar; also Livy, etc. (K.-Steg., II, 1, 538).

in morem 261, 2, 3, ut in morem stagni non tam currere quam stare videantur.
> The meaning is the same as that of *in modum*. The ablative *more* with a dependent genitive occurs in Cic., Verg., Hor., etc. *In morem* is found in Verg. georg. 1, 245, Hor. sat. 2, 1, 63.

in partem 129, 1, 6, et illis in nullam partem profutura linquuntur.
> There are various classical phrases consisting of *in partem* with a modifier, such as *eam, utramque, optimam, neutram*; also *neque in ullam partem* meaning *on neither side*.

in pretium 17, 2, 5, quia illud est semper in pretium, quod ad decorem fuerit exquisitum.
> *In pretio esse* occurs in Ov., Liv., Sen. (Harpers'). *In* with accusative is used here for *in* with the ablative.

in similitudinem 106, 7, 5, septem metis certamen omne peragitur in similitudinem hebdomadis reciprocae.
> *Ad similitudinem* is classical. *In* occurs in Tac. (Harpers'). Cf. *in similitudine*, 68, 2, 3.

in speciem 108, 3, 27, addunt etiam in columnae speciem conspici quendam tenuissimum fumum,
> Meaning similar to that of *in formam*. Cited for Dig. 43, 11, 1, par. 2 (Harpers').

in species 165, 12, 33, suggeritur intolerabilis esse causa damnorum, quando et in species exigitur
> This phrase refers to payment *in kind* and is an example of the use of *in* with the accusative instead of *in* with the ablative. Cf. p. 136.

in usum 384, 6, 25, in usum est viris fortibus feliciter egisse pugnas.
> *In usu* is classical, occurring in Cicero to denote what is habitual. *In* with the accusative is used here for *in* with the ablative. Cf. *in usu tuo*, 385, 9, 17.

in vicem 190, 4, 3, in vicem cotis ingenia splendida reddimus,
> *Vicem* alone is used in this meaning (Cf. L.-Hof., 385). *In vicem*

usually means *instead of* (Harpers'). Cf. also Hor. ars 304, *fungar vice cotis.*

g. *In* WITH THE ACCUSATIVE INSTEAD OF *In* WITH THE ABLATIVE

In addition to its occurrence in the phrases mentioned above (p. 135), *in* with the accusative occurs in place of *in* with the ablative in the following examples: (I have noted only those appearing *as accusative* in Mommsen's text).

48, 5, 26, ut paternarum laudum in hunc recognoscatis esse vestigium,
52, 1, 4, ut crimen sit magnum conscientiae alienos affectus in reverentiam non habere.
90, 16,   quamvis in usum habeantur eximia,
145, 4, 6, nemo perdidisse se sentit quod in alterum invenisse cognoscit.
194, 4, 19, esto in te continens, ut possis in alios esse iudex.
204, 3, 18, ut et antiqua in nitorem pristinum contineas
308, 2, 16, nam quicquid in subiectos pietatis efficimus, illum nobis repensare sine dubio iudicamus.
320, 3, 1, non est difficile illum in affectum retinere, qui gratiam constat desideranter expetere.
330, 19, 18, tamquam in speculum purissimum sua praeconia mox videret.
333, 7, 9, ut in mentem vestram dulciora remaneant,
       (Perhaps as a result of contamination. Cf. *venire in mentem.* See L.-Hof., 538.)
333, 1, 15, habendus est in iudicum partem, qui meruit aulicis potestatibus assidere.
334, 1, 3, ipsius quodammodo res agitur, cuius in alterum vota complentur.
359, 2, 10, sustinemus tales casus, quales nos in alios iudicare non possumus.

In the two examples listed above, 194, 4, 19, and 359, 2, 10, *in* may perhaps have a limiting sense, i. e., it may indicate the persons with reference to whom one acts as judge or is a judge. There is a usage, chiefly Late Latin, of *in* with the accusative in the sense of reference (K.-Steg., II, 1, 569).

The Late Latin use of *in* with the accusative instead of *in* with the ablative with the verb *esse* is mentioned in L.-Hof., 538, 3. Examples of the use with other verbs are found in Orosius (Cf. Svennung, 45-46).

B. *In* with the Ablative
(L.-Hof. 536-537)

a. LOCAL USE

The local use of *in* with the ablative occurs frequently in the Variae. In general the usage is classical. There is, however, a local use of *in* with the ablative for *in* with the accusative. See p. 138.

Several examples occur where *in* is used with *urbe* or *civitate* and the name of a town in the form of an adjective or appositive, as 117, 1, 18, in Syracusana civitate, and 135, 2, 19, in urbe Roma. Classical authors used the preposition also in expressions similar to these (Cf. K.-Steg., II, 1, 480). A non-classical use occurs in 98, 2, 25, in Avinione. Classical usage is the locative ablative alone for a noun of this type when it is not accompanied by *urbe* or a similar word. The earliest use of *in* with the name of a city is in Liv., 42, 26, 7, *Antiochum in Syria, Ptolemaeum in Alexandria,* where the influence of the phrase *in Syria* was a contributing factor to the use of the preposition with the name of the city. *In* with the name of a city occurs in Pliny the Elder and in later writers (Cf. K.-Steg., II, 1, 479).

In occurs with *loco* and an attribute in 64, 4, in Hostiliensi loco. Classical prose occasionally used *in,* but preferred the ablative alone in such expressions (K.-Steg., II, 1, 348-349).

The Variae show numerous examples of *in* with the ablative indicating persons, especially where there is a reference to the existence of qualities in persons. Cassiodorus seems to prefer this form of expression to the use of *habere* or the dative with *esse.* Examples illustrating this usage:

10, 2, 11, in vobis singulare aliquid inesse cognoscunt,
24, 1, 26, perniciosa res est in imperante tenuitas.
59, 2, 1, in his personis mutua sunt officia pietatis,
60, 3, 31, in vobis erit huius summa consilii,

The same construction is used at times referring to animals or inanimate objects, e. g.

16, 3, 25, voluntas recta in gravibus passionibus non est,
57, 2, 13, pietas in avibus invenitur,
69, 11, 24, in his aquis non solum sensum, sed etiam verum constat
    esse iudicium

6

Various classical phrases which employ *in* with the ablative in a figurative sense occur, such as, *in ore, in oculis, in formidine, in honore* and the use of *ponere in,* meaning *consider* or *attribute to,* e. g.

14, 6, 20, excessus tunc sunt in formidine, cum creduntur iudicibus displicere.

48, 2, 9, in ore quippe rumoris est

48, 3, 11, est adhuc in oculis omnium

51, 1, 29, in honore esse meretur,

72, 16, 26, si causam caelestis beatitudinis non in sonis, sed in creatore posuissent,

One such phrase is especially to be noted, viz., 27, 2, 25, ut ad expeditionem in dei nomine . . . moveatis. The phrase *in dei nomine* occurs only once in the Variae. It is obviously a Scriptural echo, as *in nomine Dei* occurs in Ps. 19, 6, and *in nomine Domini* is frequent in the Bible, e. g., Mich. 4, 5; Soph. 3, 9.

b. *In* WITH THE ABLATIVE INSTEAD OF *In* WITH THE ACCUSATIVE

The use of the accusative instead of the ablative has already been mentioned, p. 136. The confusion in Cassiodorus' use of the two cases with the preposition *in* becomes even more evident when we discover in some of his uses of *in* with the ablative the sense of *in* with the accusative. The chief divergences from classical prose usage are noted in his use of *in* with the ablative with verbs of motion, both literal and figurative, and in his use of *in* with the ablative in a final sense. A similar interchange in the functions of the two cases is found in several Late Latin authors. It had its beginning in a phonetic falling together of accusative and ablative singular endings and resulted in a complete confusion in the use of the two cases in colloquial speech as early as the second century, A. D. (L.-Hof., 538).

Examples of *in* with the ablative instead of *in* with the accusative with verbs of motion:

68, 4, 17, unda descendens . . . tactu fit habilis, cum recepta fuerit in lavacris:

93, 2, 14, furor animorum in suis cautibus elidatur

134, 2, 1, in quibus cum fuisset pro districtione publica resecatum,

138, 2, 6, quanta laude in suburbanis suis Romam traxeris,

178, 1, 13, ille qui est in cogitationum nostrarum participatione
    susceptus.
    (Cf. 170, 2, 12, Gesalecum . . . in vestram defensionem sic
    fuisse susceptum.)
272, 4, 32, in visceribus aequoris terra promota est!
309, 1, 11, summa non mittuntur in casu,
340, 3, 27, lac autem tam pingue, ut haereat digitis, cum exprimatur in
    vasis.
359, 3, 17, ulciscitur poenis quod misistis in fabulis
378, 3, 30, fruitur in septentrione progressa caeli admiranda temperie
381, 5, 30, hinc aer nivibus nimio rigore densatus ardore solis in nulla
    raritate perductus est.

In these three examples note that *in* with the ablative is used in a consecutive sense:

103, 2, 22, tumulus saxeus in rotunditate consurgens,
125, 2, 19, qui etiam in spe erigimus vota marcentia,
133, 2, 33, quod in dominorum caede proruperit servilis audacia:

In with the Ablative in a Final Sense

The use of *in* with the ablative to express purpose is not found in classical prose. It occurs occasionally in Ecclesiastical writers (Cf. Hrdlicka, 221). We may reasonably attribute Cassiodorus' final use of *in* with the ablative to the influences mentioned above in connection with the local use. Examples of final *in* with the ablative:

  38, 2, 25, stupere videamur in unius gratia tot desiderabilia fuisse
      contempta
  47, 2, 16, in laude regnantis proficit, quod subiectus adquirit.
  49, 7, 6, ne . . . in damno suo praecipua contemneret
  49, 1, 26, quanto magis in utilitate rei publicae delectatur expendere,
  95, 1, 11, plura in praeiudicio urbis Romanae detestabiles praesump-
      tores assumere,
168, 2, 26, spectaculum . . . in honore Scythicae Dianae repertum,
171, 4, 18, instructus redditur animus in futuris, quando praeteritorum
      commonetur exemplis.
      This example, which is given by Traube as final, may be an
      example of *in* as the equivalent of an ablative of respect.
191, 7, 7, quod in civitatis damno committitur, silentio non celatur.

c. *In* WITH THE ABLATIVE WITH VERBS

In with the ablative occurs with several verbs in the figurative

local, causal, instrumental, sense, etc., with which classical prose
employed the ablative without a preposition.

confidere 312, 3, 15, confidimus enim in virtute divina,
    Dative and ablative are both classical. *In* used in Late Latin (K.-
    Steg., II, 1, 400). *In* occurs in Hil., Amb., Hier., Aug., Itala,
    Vulg. (T. L. L., IV, 208, 39).
gaudere 334, 1, 2, Gaudere vos quidem in eis credo, quae, *etc.*
    Abl. is classical. Use of *in* is poetic, Silver, Late. Cf. T. L. L.,
    VI, 1706, 47.
gravare 60, 3, 27, gravatum se sentit in aliena calculi functione,
    Sense is causal or instrumental.
implicare 278, 3, 3, ut . . . in damnis provincialium aut praeiudiciis
    implicetur
    Abl. is classical; *in* occurs in Livy (K.-Steg., II, 1, 381-382).
miscere 257, 2, 20, in direptionibus possessorum se miscuisse
    Cf. accusative 267, 1, 9, in eius vos interitum misceretis.
    Dative also occurs; see p. 32. This meaning of *miscere se* is not
    classical.
praesumere 333, 6, 6, qui minus in humana potestate praesumimus.
    In this use of *praesumere = presume*, *de* is more frequent than *in*
    in the Variae. Abl. alone also occurs. Cf. Traube, 572.

A causal use of *in* with the ablative without close connection
with a verb appears in 60, 4, 3, ne necesse sit curiali . . . in
exiguis vestris illationibus sua potius damna suscipere. The use
of *in* to replace an ablative of cause is found as early as Propertius
(Cf. L.-Hof., 438), but the usage is not frequent until the ecclesiastical writers.

d. TEMPORAL USE OF *In*

In with the ablative occurs in some examples with *tempore* and
other expressions of time where classical prose uses the ablative
alone (K.-Steg., II, 1, 355). The use of the preposition is common in Late Latin (L.-Hof., 452; K.-Steg., II, 1, 357-359).
Examples:

    5, 14, 6, in angusto tempore
    47, 3, 18, in prima aetate
    54, 1, 11, in tenera aetate
        (A similar expression, 69, 8, 10, *in longa aetate* implies the
        idea of duration, as does Cic. Cato 66, *in tam longa
        aetate.*)
    59, 1, 15, in illo principio

67, 3, 16, in hoc biennii spatio
133, 2, 12, in ipso laetitiae tempore
204, 3, 22, ut in hora commonito famuletur tibi copiosa notitia.

Cassiodorus' use of *in* with unmodified nouns which do not of themselves denote time but are used as temporal expressions is classical, e. g.

23, 1, 19, res proeliorum bene disponitur, quotiens in pace tractatur.
33, 1, 21, maiori nunc studio quaerenda sunt quae etiam in abundantia
             expeti consuerunt.
37, 3,   discat miles in otio, quod perficere possit in bello.
68, 3, 9, quod in origine dare poterat mortem,

Where such a noun has an attribute Cassiodorus sometimes uses *in*. Classical prose usually omitted the preposition, though there are some instances of its use. Examples:

12, 3, 27, in ipso quippe imperii nostri . . . exordio
46, 3, 15, in ipso pueritiae flore
55, 2, 9, in adversitate nostra

e. *In* WITH THE ABLATIVE EXPRESSING VARIOUS RELATIONS

While Cassiodorus at times uses the simple ablative of respect in the classical manner, he frequently employs the preposition *in* to denote respect or limitation. Classical prose used *in* with the ablative to denote various relations of one thing or person with another, such relations as we express in English by *in relation to, with reference to, in the case of* (Cf. K.-Steg., II, 1, 562-563).

Examples of this usage are frequent in the Variae. In the following *in* takes the place of an ablative of respect:

18, 2, 30, conquesti sunt . . . in numero gravia se dispendia sustinere.
328, 6, 20, excellit cunctos in propriis,
367, 4, 20, ceteris dominis in hac tantum sorte deterior,
371, 2, 11, ager . . . qui in solo aridissimus approbatur

In the following examples relation with persons is expressed. Classical prose also frequently used *in* with the ablative in this connection.

62, 2, 14, quod raro in serviente provenit,
63, 3, 28, salva in aliis negotiatoribus commoditate publica,
203, 2, 6, unam nobis in omnibus aequabiliter esse caritatem:
269, 6, 19, habetis per leges potestatem in civibus vestris.

Relations with things are expressed in a similar manner, e. g.

11, 5, 27, dum sacrilegus sit reatus neglegentiae in tali veste peccare
28, 3, 14, nostra iussa . . . in nullo violanda sunt,
48, 4, 15, Vehemens disputator in libris,
62, 2, 17, silentium in secretis, in actionibus efficaciam, in observationis
              labore frequentiam:
66, 1, 18, delectat nos munificos esse in amore vindictae.

One example of the use of *in* with a person, where this preposition is the equivalent of *de, concerning,* has been noted, 308, 1, 27, nec liceat falsis suspicionibus errare, dum manifeste teneatur quod credatis in principe.

An example of the use of *in* with the ablative in the meaning of *with reference to,* or in a final sense, is found with the adjective *aptus,* while both *in* with the accusative and *ad* with the accusative follow the same adjective in the same sentence, 107, 3, 16 ff., Geometriam . . . Chaldaei primum invenisse memorantur, qui rationem ipsius disciplinae generaliter colligentes *et in astronomicis rebus et in musicis et in mechanicis et in architectis et in medicinam et ad artem* logisticam . . . aptam esse docuerunt, ut sine ea nihil horum possit ad agnitionem verissimam pervenire. The three constructions with *aptus* are used as equivalent by Cassiodorus. *Ad* with the accusative is classical and regular (T. L. L., II, 331, 59). *In* with the accusative occurs in Pliny the Elder and Quintilian (T. L. L., II, 332, 72). *In* with the ablative does not occur with *aptus,* but the use of the ablative of respect with *aptus* is Ciceronian (T. L. L., II, 334, 17).

f. ADVERBIAL PHRASES WITH *In*

In with the ablative is used in various adverbial phrases. The interchange of accusative and ablative mentioned above, p. 138, appears here also. Examples:

in absoluto 291, 3, 27, in absoluto datur probare quod dicimus.
    The phrase *in absoluto* is used as the equivalent of *certe.* It occurs
    also in Hil. trin., e. g. 2, 34, and in Cod. Iust. 11, 59, 13, *in abso-
    luto est, ut,* etc. (T. L. L., I, 178, 60).
in auro 149, 22, in auro vobis tres solidos per condamam elegimus
    destinare
    Refers to payment *in gold.* Cf. acc. with *in, in species,* p. 135.

in duplo 126, 4, 17, a te constrictus in duplo ei cogatur exsolvere:
    Cf. *in duplum*, p. 134. Use seems to be modal or instrumental.
in modo 103, 2, 24, in mollissimi fungi modo
    Cf. *in modum*, p. 135.
in procinctu = *in readiness* 50, 2, 1, in procinctu semper erit, qui bar-
    baros prohibere contendit,
    The modal expression *in procinctu* occurs in Cic., Sen., Tac., Quint.
    (Harpers').
in toto 210, 4, 32, statuae nec in toto mutae sunt.
    Cf. *in totum*, p. 134.

Other Unusual Uses of *In*

in = *in exchange for* 66, 2, 22, damus in aeneo compendio aureum
    munus:
    Cf. acc., *in triticum*, p. 131.
in = *in the form of, as a result of* 162, 2, 33, in naulis septingentos
    quinquaginta octo solidos accepisse perhibentur
in = *to the extent of* 53, 1, 3, debitorem publicum in quadringentis
    solidis
    28, 2, 28, onera titulorum praefata ecclesia in ea summa non sentiat,
in = *represented in,* equivalent to an adjective, 40, 6, 27, Diomedes in
    aere gravius bucinat.
A bronze Diomedes is the meaning. Cf. L.-Hof., 537.

2. *Sub*
(L.-Hof. 539)
A. *Sub* with the Ablative Instead of the Accusative

Sub is not used with the accusative in the Variae. One example occurs where the ablative is used with a transitive verb indicating *to bring under,* and this ablative may be regarded as employed in place of an accusative, 150, 19, ignorat modum servare prae-sumptio nec potest *sub modo redigi,* cui licentia fuerit visa concedi.

Sub with the accusative with *redigere* is found in Caesar, Gall., 5, 29, 4, though the usual classical construction is *in* with the accusative. Cf. the similar use of *in* with the ablative for *in* with the accusative, p. 138.

Another example occurs with a verb of motion, where the most natural interpretation of the sentence seems to be a similar use of the ablative in place of the accusative, 58, 2, 8, tellus . . . sub utroque iactata dispendio nec aquarum puros liquores meruerat et decus terrenae soliditatis amiserat. The meaning of *iactata sub* seems to be *placed under*. The meaning of *iactata* may, however, be that of *oppressed,* and *sub* with the ablative will then be attendant circumstance, bordering closely on the sense of an ablative of means.

B. *Sub* with the Ablative

a. LOCAL USE

The local use of *sub,* both in its literal sense and in figurative expressions, is very rare in the Variae, but otherwise does not deviate from classical usage.

b. TEMPORAL USE

Except where a temporal force is implied in expressions of subordination (see modal uses), the temporal use of *sub,* in the meaning of *during, at,* or *in,* is rare in the Variae. This temporal usage is rare in classical prose, but is frequent in Livy, Celsus, and later writers (Cf. K.-Steg., II, 1, 570). Examples:

48, 2, 5, Iacebat nobilis origo sub Gallicano iustitio
67, 3,17, quatenus sub induciis supradictis et datam possint reparare
      pecuniam et, *etc.*
99, 2, 8, nec licet negari, quod te cognoscis sub antiquitate largiri.
159, 2, 8, decet etiam nos sub hac occasione singulorum facta
      perquirere
164, 3,36, ut sub ordinationis vestrae novitate inveteratae possit con-
      suetudini nil licere.
349, 1,29, ut quod erat sub vitae termino positum praemium, non
      haberet incertum.

c. MODAL USE

While the local and the temporal examples of *sub* in the Variae are rare, the modal uses are so numerous that *sub* is one of the most frequently occurring prepositions in the work. All examples of *sub* except the local and the temporal uses can, in a broad sense, be called modal. However, as the examples are numerous and there is considerable variety in their use, I have classified the various usages I have observed, as follows: Subordination, Condition, etc., Attendant Circumstance, Manner. All these, especially attendant circumstance, can be subdivided, but, since in the subdivisions, and even in the main groups, the lines of demarcation can not be clearly drawn, this division seems to be adequate. A number of examples showing traces of cause, means, and agent will be discussed under Attendant Circumstance.

Subordination.

The preposition *sub* frequently indicates that one person or thing occupies an inferior or subordinate position in relation to another person or thing. This usage of *sub* was rare in classical prose, but became much more frequent with the Augustan poets and Livy (K.-Steg., II, 1, 570). Examples:

27, 3, 29, sub vobis videant, quod posteris referre contendant.
42, 2, 10, discat sub vobis Burgundia res subtilissimas inspicere
67, 1, 23, augmenta regalis gloriae sunt, cum sub nobis nulla decrescunt,
133, 1, 8, sub parente publico genitoris minime sentiri debet amissio.
162, 1, 25, ut antiquum vectigal sub nobis felicior Roma reciperet.
203, 1, 5, sub diversitate iudicum una iustitia complectatur universos.
244, 2, 6, haec cum tu sub tanto iudice laudata perageres, gratiam quoque loci alterius invenisti.

Expressions of subordination frequently have also a temporal connotation. This results from the reference to acts performed *under* a certain ruler, i. e., at his command or by his authority. From this usage there developed in Tacitus and later writers a usage of *sub* in the meaning of *during the reign of*, which is purely temporal (K.-Steg., II, 1, 570). In some of the examples given above the temporal element is present. In the following list it is more in evidence, though none of these examples can be classified as purely temporal. Examples:

10, 4, 22, utrasque res publicas, quarum semper unum corpus sub antiquis principibus fuisse declaratur,
14, 6, 21, His itaque sub praecedenti rege gymnasiis exercitatus emeritis laudibus ad palatia nostra pervenit.
15, 10, 8, sub Valentiniano principe gessit tribuni et notarii laudabiliter dignitatem:
138, 3, 12, ut . . . non videatur sub melioribus posteris imminutum.
235, 3, 30, qui sub nostris parentibus copiosa virtutum laude floruistis.
247, 7, 25, quando sub ingrato successore palatinum officium praeconia eius tacere non potuit.

Condition, etc.

The use of *sub* to express a condition, a pretext, a claim to possession, etc., begins with Ovid, in prose, with Livy, and is frequent in subsequent Latin (K.-Steg., II, 1, 570-571). Examples of this usage are very frequent in the Variae. The following examples are selected from a large number:

17, 3, 19, si tamen appellanda divisio est, quam sub unius celebratam constat arbitrio—,
19, 4, 14, auctori quippe suo omnis creatura sub numero est
21, 4, 8, pio principi sub quodam sacerdotio serviatur.
24, 1, 6, qui alios creditur sub aequitatis regula continere,
35, 3, 14, nec sub praetextu cruentae mentis causam pudoris intendis,
99, 1, 2, quocirca sub opinione munifici parcum non decet inveniri,
102, 4, 7, ut nulli post constituta nostra sub qualibet interpretatione tibi liceat obicere crimen infamiae,
115, 3, 29, usus es sub exceptionis officio eloquentis ingenio:
123, 1, 12, quod de fisco sub antiqua sollemnitate praestatur!
126, 4, 18, quia sub poena restitui dignum est, quod improba temeritate constat extortum.
147, 2, 23, ut universam substantiam supradicti Thomatis sub hac condicione fixis titulis publico debeas applicare,
148, 1, 6, sub hac ratione satisfacere te velle testaris, si, *etc.*
150, 18,   Commodius enim sub expensarum lege tenetur exercitus, quam si, *etc.*
209, 1, 4, amministranda   est   sub   quadam   disciplina   exhibitio voluptatum.
236, 2, 10, ita ut sub iurisiurandi religione promitterent
277, 1, 29, sub quadam excusatione peccare creditur, cui necessaria non praebentur.
368, 2, 1, sub indulgentia laedit, qui consuetis temporibus exigere tributa distulerit.

Attendant Circumstance.

Sub with the ablative denoting the circumstances attendant upon an action or situation is found as early as Lucretius; in prose it begins with Celsus and becomes very frequent in Late Latin (K.-Steg., II, 1, 571).

Examples are very numerous in the Variae. The following list is representative of the usage:

17, 2, 16, perire enim pupillo non patimur quod parentibus sub nostra laude dederamus.
35, 5, 24, Candacis tibi tuitionem sub aequabili defensione praestamus,
55, 4, 23, sub   generalitatis   gratia   publica   videtur   procurasse compendia,

101, 1, 24, praestandum est sub iustitiae laude moderamen,
120, 1, 16, quae omnes rei publicae partes sub caelesti favore
circumspicit,
121, 3, 32, qui se hactenus sub vestra omnium laude tractavit
128, 2, 16, comperimus res . . . sub emissione chirographi fuisse
depositas.
145, 3, 31, locum . . . qui sub nostra potuit expedire praesentia, nonne
vobis dignus est collega?
158, 1, 25, qui . . . nec sub aliquo honore vivit,
207, 4, 10, licet haec sub profunda caligine videantur geri,
246, 3, 30, Nam militiae ordinem sub fraterna laude didicisti,
364, 7, 29, Rectoribus autem exercitus a rerum dominis sub mea praesentia cognoscite delegatum,

This circumstantial usage of *sub* at times approaches closely to
the meaning of an ablative of means, and in Late Latin *sub* became
one of the ways of expressing means (Cf. L.-Hof., 539; K.-Steg.,
II, 1, 571). While scarcely any of the examples in the Variae can
be regarded as an outright substitute for the ablative of means,
there is in many of the circumstantial occurrences a near approach
to such a usage. *Sub* in the following examples, may be regarded
rather as a means than as a circumstance (Cf. Goelzer, *Le Latin
de Saint Avit,* 219).

32, 4, 3, profertis voces organo dulciores et ita sub quadam harmonia
citharae concavum theatrum per vos resonat,
64, 2, 16, ultro postulavit voto mirabili, quod vix potuisset sub consilio nostrae potestatis imponi.

The instrumental sense may also be perceived as implied in many
of the examples given under the modal usage of subordination and
under the temporal usage. Reasonable grounds might be alleged
for listing such an example as 47, 2, 10, sub imperio boni principis
omnium fortuna proficiat, under temporal usage, under subordination, under circumstantial usage, or for calling it an instrumental
usage equivalent to an ablative of means.

Likewise the use of *sub* with persons in the temporal and the
subordination groups frequently borders on the use of the ablative
of agent. Where the verb is passive, as in 60, 2, 24, cum alienis
debitis sub truculentis compulsoribus urgerentur, possessionum
quoque suarum amissione privati sunt, we see in the persons to
whom others are subordinated not only those in the superior position
but also those who are the authors of the act.

A causal usage can also be observed as implied in several of the circumstantial examples; in some it is the prevailing idea, e. g.

12, 4, 31, lucratus es damna provinciae, quae meruit sub devotione nescire:
    Causal or instrumental. We might expect Cassiodorus to use *per*.

114, 3, 15, hi sunt sub pinguedine nimia mansueti.
    Horses are being described. They are gentle *because* they are very fat.

118, 3, 4, modiationem tritici quam sub hac sorte perisse probaverint,
    A quantity of grain has been lost *because of* a storm.

164, 2, 32, sic mala pace quasi ludo corruunt, quanti vix potuissent cadere sub necessitate bellorum.
    Meaning *because of* the exigencies of war.

204, 4, 2, ut nec gentiles . . . suscipias nec nostros ad gentes sub incuriositate transmittas.
    The recipient of the letter is warned against allowing *through his carelessness* Gothic subjects to transfer their allegiance, and perhaps their residence, to other nations.

Manner.

Another usage of *sub* related to the circumstantial is that in which *sub* serves in place of *cum* with the ablative of manner or as the equivalent of an adverb. This usage of *sub* does not receive a formal treatment in Leumann-Hofmann or Kühner-Stegmann, but examples in the Variae are very numerous., *Cum* is almost entirely supplanted by *sub* in this usage. The following are representative phrases:

5, 17, 22, sub festinatione
13, 6, 16, sub aequitate
26, 2, 24, sub integritate
42, 3, 14, sub veritate
51, 1,   sub confusione
51, 2,   sub ratione
60, 3, 30, sub silentio
60, 3, 30, sub iustitia
67, 2, 11, sub laetitia
72, 12, 6, sub diversitate
81, 2, 13, sub lenitate
95, 3, 21, sub largitate
99, 1, 23, sub communione
132, 5, 6, sub moderata civilitate
149, 2, 11, sub omni . . . moderatione
158, 2, 30, sub omni continentia

159, 1, 25, sub libertate
165, 10, 26, sub consueta . . . aequitate
177, 6, 34, sub nulla venalitate
202, 1, 10, sub velocitate
202, 2, 20, sub ammiratione
205, 1, 17, sub assiduitate
205, 3, 26, sub delectatione
206, 5, 9, sub magna deliberatione
222, 2, 4, sub incivilitate
222, 3, 18, sub dubietate
246, 2, 9, sub puritate
274, 6, 18, sub raritate
321, 5,   sub celeritate
328, 8, 29, sub quiete

3. *Super*
(L.-Hof. 540-541)

The preposition *super* is rare in the Variae. With the accusative in the local sense, which is classical (Cf. K.-Steg., II, 1, 573) it occurs only once, 343, 3, 14, super hunc frondosae vineae latus montis ascendunt.

Super with the accusative occurs a few times as the equivalent of *praeter* in the meaning *in addition to*. *Praeter* is not so used by Cassiodorus. This usage of *super* is found as early as Plautus in expressions which repeat the noun, as in Pseud., 948, *savia super savia*; in expressions without the repetition it begins with Vergil, in prose, with Livy. Examples in the Variae:

38, 3, 26, Qui super hanc eximiam fidem solatia nobis suae confabulationis adiecit,
151, 3, 7, quicquid . . . super tributarium solidum se possessor probaverit intulisse

The use of *super* to denote a preference (cf. *supra*, p. 101) began with Livy (Cf. K.-Steg., II, 1, 573). The following example illustrates this usage:

186, 4, 5, super omnia bona concitare nescit invidiam.

With the ablative *super* occurs only in the meaning of *de, concerning*. This colloquial usage occurs in Early Latin, in Cicero's Letters, in Livy, but becomes common only in Late Latin (Cf. K.-Steg., II, 1, 572).

In the Variae the usage is confined to the stereotyped phrases *super qua re,* 124, 2, 5, and *super hac parte,* which latter occurs several times, e. g., 22, 2, 8.

CHAPTER VI

The Nominal Forms of the Verb
I. *The Infinitive*
1. Substantive Use of the Infinitive
(L.-Hof. 577-578)

Cassiodorus presents several examples of infinitives used substantively accompanied by an attributive adjective or a dependent genitive. Possessive adjectives were used in this manner by Plautus, but are not found in classical prose, except in Cicero's Letters; they are frequent in Petronius, Persius and Martial. The use of other attributes begins with Pliny and is more frequent in Late Latin. The use of a substantive in the genitive dependent on an infinitive is Late Latin (Noted in L.-Hof., 578, for Mar. Victor, Cassiod., Greg. M.).

Examples of infinitives with adjective or dependent genitive:

10, 5, 25, Romani regni unum velle, una semper opinio sit.
55, 5, 31, ut utraque natio . . . ad unum velle convenerit.
133, 1, 30, ambire propriae civitatis incendium non est velle Romanum.
138, 8, 36, ostendens homines posse et sine oris affatu suum velle declarare.
143, 3, 18, gentium nostrarum velle iungamus
178, 2, 18, mentis nostrae velle suscipit,
183, 3, 10, pensabit loqui tuum dominantis examen,
188, 2, 25, dum ad suum velle festinat
190, 5, 5, sit velle vestrum quale videtis nostrum esse propositum.
201, 3, 19, nemo redemptionibus tuum velle deflectat:
278, 3, 5, nostrum dare nobilitas est:
303, 5, 11, Velle nostrum antiquorum principum est voluntas,

The substantive use of an infinitive with a preposition begins with Cicero's use of infinitives after *inter*. In Late Latin any preposition could be used in this manner. One example occurs in the Variae, 91, 3, 16, non sit coniunctum negotium perdere *cum perire*.

Substantive uses of the same infinitives without modifiers occur in 3, 3, 11, loqui . . . datum est; 98, 2, 2, dum velle creditur quod

150

posse iudicatur; 144, 2, 22, loqui datur; 183, 2, 3, temperamentum simul damus, cui posse concedimus.

Cassiodorus uses the infinitive as subject of *est* with a predicate adjective or a predicate noun in the classical manner. The use of the infinitive as subject of impersonal verbs or of verbs in the passive voice will be discussed below, p. 154.

2. The Infinitive With Adjectives

In only a few instances in the Variae does an infinitive occur in direct connection with an adjective.

Dignus with a passive infinitive occurs several times, e. g., 46, 4, 23, dignus est eligi; also 114, 1, 26; 146, 7, 22; 163, 2, 15; 255, 5, 28; 347, 5, etc. *Dignus* with the infinitive is found first in Lucretius and Catullus, in prose, first in Seneca the philosopher (L.-Hof., 578; Cf. T. L. L., V, 1152, 32 ff.).

Nescius and *promptus* occur in 145, 3, 28, nescius decipere, promptissimus subvenire (*nescius* also in 162, 1, 2). *Nescius* with the infinitive occurs in Vergil, Horace, Ovid, etc. (K.-Steg., II, 1, 685). *Promptus* with the infinitive occurs in Lucan (K.-Steg., II, 1, 686).

In Silver and Late Latin an infinitive occasionally depends upon a single substantive (L.-Hof., 579). I have noted the following example: 144, 1, 17, novam in te fecimus legem parentes in amministratione succedere.

3. The Infinitive Expressing Purpose
(L.-Hof. 580)

The use of the infinitive to express purpose is strictly avoided in classical prose, but occurs, chiefly with verbs of motion, in Early prose and in the poetry of all periods. Its revival in prose begins with Valerius Maximus. I have observed the following examples in the Variae:

166, 15, 14, non enim decet ab ingenuis famulatum quaerere, quos misi-
    mus pro libertate *pugnare*.
242, 2, 22, quamvis traheret te eloquentia pro defensione *dicere*, suade-
    bat tamen aequitas iudicanda proferre.
242, 3, 31, cum finem faceres, adhuc *dicere* quaerebaris:
269, 4, 3, date studium *recuperare* quae vos male cognoscitis amisisse.

319, 3, 1, parentum periculis evocatus adveneram communem cum
omnibus *subire* fortunam:

4. The Complementary Infinitive
(L.-Hof. 581; K.-Steg. II, 1, 667-676)

The infinitive occurs as the complement of the following verbs
with which it is not used in classical prose. I am citing only one
example of each verb to illustrate the usage.

adquiescere 308, 2, 30, libenter adquievimus facere, quod generalitatem
probamus optasse.
> Heges., Oros., Cassian., Leo M., Avell., Paul. Petr., etc. Cassiod.,
> var. (T. L. L., I, 424, 79 ff.; cf. L.-Hof., 581).

affectare 222, 1, 29, quisquis habere liberos contractus constanter
affectat.
> Quintilian is first prose citation. Ovid and later poets (T. L. L.,
> I, 1183, 33 ff.; cf. K.-Steg., II, 1, 674). Cassiod. var. is cited.

amare 47, 1, 2, Amamus beneficia nostra geminare
> Hor., Calp., Tac., Apul., Tert., etc., Cassiod. var. (T. L. L., I,
> 1956, 35 ff.; cf. L.-Hof., 581; K.-Steg., II, 1, 674).

ambigere 4, 11, 30, quid ambigis et haec publico dare . . . ?
> Liv., Tac., Apul., Ulp., etc., chiefly with subject accusative, Cas-
> siod. var. (T. L. L., I, 1839, 51 ff.).

ambire 259, 3, 18, ambiunt enim aliquid soli agere,
> Stat., Tac., Heges., etc. Cassiod. not cited (T. L. L., I, 1850, 75 ff.;
> cf. L.-Hof., 581).

amplecti 49, 14, sequi regulas constitutas libenter amplectimur,
> Lucif., Amm., Gaudent., Avel. Cassiod. not cited (T. L. L., I,
> 1994, 76 ff.).

assumere 4, 9, 19, tu enim illos assumpsisti vera laude describere
> Drac., Ennod., Cassiod. var., Vita Caes. Arel. (T. L. L., II, 931,
> 10 ff.).

callere 49, 6, 3, quam societas bonorum morum callet infundere
> Pacuv., Lucr., Hor., Pers.; Curtius first prose writer; Cassiod.
> var. cited (T. L. L., III, 160, 70 ff.).

contemnere 318, 5, 4, si aliquis praebere contempserit postulata
> T. L. L., IV, 642, 31 ff. cites only Late authors in this sense. Ulp.,
> Spart., Hermog., Ps. Amb., Vulg., etc. Cassiod. hist. cited. Cf.
> K.-Steg., II, 1, 674, Hor., Sen., Apul.

deligere 65, 2, 11, si quis hunc laborem iuncta tecum societate subire
delegerit,
> Tert., Lucif., Rufin., Aug., etc., Cassiod. in psalm. (T. L. L., V,
> 455, 73 ff.).

deproperare 220, 2, 6, ad illam urbem venire depropera,
> Plaut., Symm., Ambr., Mart. Cap., etc. Cassiod. var. (T. L. L., V,
> 617, 4 ff.; cf. L.-Hof., 581).

despicere 20, 2, 10, iustitiae parere despiciunt,
    Carm. de Sod., Vulg., Cassian., Salv., etc., Cassiod. var. (T. L. L.,
        V, 747, 33 ff.).
detrectare 24, 2, 29, Gothorum fiscum detrectat implere,
    Ulp., Arnob., Paul., Iul. Val., Lact., etc., Cassiod. var. (T. L. L.,
        V, 835, 73 ff.; cf. K.-Steg., II, 1, 675).
differre 297, 1, 2, distulimus hactenus indicare filii nostri . . . occasum,
    Hor., Liv., Curt., Petron., etc., Cassiod. var. (T. L. L., V, 1074, 65).
dignari 305, 3, 33, qui parentis nomen dignatus est praestare subiecto.
    Lucr., Cat., Verg., Hor., Ov., Sen., Curt., etc. Cassiod. not cited
        (T. L. L., V, 1141, 1 ff.; cf. K.-Steg., II, 1, 674).
disponere 256, 1, 28, Quidilanem Sibiae filium priorem vobis quidem
    facere disponebat:
    Vopisc., Iul. Val., Arnob., Pallad., etc., Cassiod. var. (T. L. L.,
        V, 1428, 58 ff.).
eligere 203, 2, 10, cur eligant quaerere violenta . . . ?
    Itala, Lucif. (T. L. L., V, 383, 47 ff.).
erubescere 108, 9, 10, erubescant impudenti fronte litigare,
    In prose from Livy (L.-Hof., 582).
evalescere 97, 3, 3, qui flectere animum iudicantis evaluit
    Since Vergil (L.-Hof., 582).
ferre 35, 1, 6, quis enim ferat hominem ad leges trahere . . . ?
    This passage cited in T. L. L., VI, 538, 17, under inf. with acc.
    Cf. K.-Steg., II, 1, 675: Inf. in Ov., Prop.
formidare 290, 7, 18, formidat contra manifesta bona aliquid profiteri,
    Plaut., Cic. (once), Hor., Apul., Tert., Itala, Vulg., etc. Cassiod.
        inst. (T. L. L., VI, 1096, 4 ff.; cf. K.-Steg., II, 1, 673).
gratulari 99, 2, 17, non gratulamur exigere, quod tristis noscitur solutor
    offerre.
    Acc. with inf. is classical. I have not found infinitive alone.
ignorare 292, 11, 29, ignorans nisi graviter lacessitus irasci.
    Hor., Claud. (K.-Steg., II, 1, 675).
indigere 274, 2, 29, et non indiges ammoneri.
    Gellius (K.-Steg., II, 1, 675).
instituere 193, 5, 28, instituе pecunias non quaerere
    Vergil (L.-Hof., 580).
merere 12, 4, 31, quae meruit sub devotione nescire
mereri 51, 1, 29, in honore esse meretur
    Ov., Vell., Tac., Val. Max., and later prose writers (K.-Steg., II,
        1, 675).
metuere 329, 12, 14, metuerunt cum nostris inire certamen
    In prose from Rhet. Her. (L.-Hof., 581).
nosse 48, 2, 10, quia bona norunt durare.
    Early, poetic, Late. Ennius, Cato, Verg., Gell. (K.-Steg., II, 1,
        674).

pati 128, 1, 13, patimur enim superari salva aequitate per leges,
  Vergil (K.-Steg., II, 1, 674).
perferre 384, 6, 27, dimidiam relaxare pertulit fiscalis calculi functionem,
  Ovid (K.-Steg., II, 1, 675).
perquirere 41, 10, 21, naturae potentiam, ut tantum possint, nosse
  perquirunt:
    No mention of infinitive in lexica or grammars, but inf. with
    quaerere is poetic and Silver.
persuadere 150, 1, 23, Iustitiae ratio persuadet excedentes reprimere,
  Nepos, Sen., Iustin., Val. Max. (K.-Steg., II, 1, 682).
praesumere 39, 2, 16, quis . . . praesumat excedere.
    Word used in Late sense. Inf. in Ruf., Fest. brev. (Harpers',
    Georges).
praevalere 109, 6, 13, quod ascendere non praevalet per naturam.
    Word used in Late sense. Inf. in Vulg. 1 Par. 21, 30. Infinitive
    with *valere* in prose since Curtius (L.-Hof., 582).
promerere 16, 15, 2, quae in utroque orbe clara esse promeruit.
    Word used in Late sense. Inf. with *merere* since Ov.; in prose since
    Val. Max. (K.-Steg., II, 1, 675).
promittere 64, 2, 17, paludem Decemnovii . . . promisit absorbere,
    Plaut., Plin., Amm. (Harpers', Georges).
renuere 16, 3, 24, qui suo vitio renuit esse pacificus.
    Infinitive used in Late Latin (L.-Hof., 582).
retractare 348, 27, si beneficia sua vendere non retractet,
    No mention of inf. in lexica or grammars.
trepidare 177, 1, 14, qui apud te trepidant dicere proprias causas.
    Verg., Hor., Stat. (K.-Steg., II, 1, 674).

5. The Simple Infinitive as Subject of Impersonal Verbs

The infinitive alone occurs as subject of the following impersonal
verbs and verbs used impersonally in the passive, with which it is
not found in classical prose.

adiacet 70, 1, 4, adiacet enim vobis doctum eligere
    Vulg. Rom., Aug. epist., Ennod., Cassiod. var. (T. L. L., I, 665,
    1 ff.).
datur 117, 1, 32, unde raro datur evadere,
    Lucr., Verg., Prop., Ov., Manil., Vitr., etc. (T. L. L., V, 1689,
    48 ff.).
delectat 32, 4, 2, quod ipsas quoque beluas delectat audire:
    Cic. epist. (once), Cassiod. var. (T. L. L., V, 426, 38 ff.).
imponitur 192, 6, 8, quibus . . . animas imponitur obligare.
    Use of inf. with active *imponere* begins with Vergil (L.-Hof., 580;
    K.-Steg., II, 1, 683).

incumbit 326, 2, 13, cui iugiter incumbit responsum reddere
  Incumbere in sense of *be incumbent upon* is Late. Cf. lexica.
inseritur 35, 2, 7, Feris insitum est copulam suam extrema concertatione
    defendere,
  Ut-clause occurs in Cic. Sull. 30, 83. I have found no inf.
oblectat 13, 6, 13, oblectat igitur nos actus praefecturae recolere,
  I have found no precedent. Inf. with *aliquem delectat* is classical.
vacat 210, 2, 19, quae si vacet eripere,
    Cass. in Cic. epist., Verg., and later poetry and prose (K.-Steg.,
    II, 1, 669).

6. The Accusative With the Infinitive

A. WITH VERBS IN THE PERSONAL CONSTRUCTION

(L.-Hof. 583-587; K.-Steg. II, 1, 687-721)

The accusative with the infinitive occurs with the following
verbs with which it is not used in classical prose.

a. Verbs of Thinking and Saying

Note. The verbs *adicere* and *iungere* become the equivalent of
verbs of saying when they follow such a verb and add an additional
statement.

adicere 101, 2, 31, adiciens defensorum tibi patrocinia saepius postulanti
    fuisse subtracta,
    Varro, Liv., Sen., Vell., Val. Max., Plin. nat., Plin., Quint., etc.
    (T. L. L., I, 672, 25 ff.; cf. K.-Steg., II, 1, 692).
aestimare 23, 2, 7, relevandam aestimamus esse fortunam.
    Phaedr., Plin. nat., Plin., Quint., and many Late, especially eccl.
    writers (T. L. L., I, 1106, 62 ff.).
allegare 101, 2, 28, allegasti . . . te . . . in confessionem . . . fuisse
    compulsum,
    Suet., Afric., Papin., Tert., etc., Cassiod. var. (T. L. L., I, 1669,
    7 ff.).
non ambigere 90, 30, quos tibi non ambigimus esse gratissimos,
    Liv., Tac., Apul., Ulp., Hil., Symm., etc., Cassiod. var. (T. L. L.,
    I, 1839, 33 ff.). Citations from Liv., Tac., and Apul. are with
    passive. With active voice of *ambigere* Ulp., Hil., Symm., etc.
asserere 67, 2, 12, hostium se asserunt depopulatione vastatos:
    All citations Late. Apul., Ps. Cypr., Spart., Lampr., etc., Cassiod.
    gramm. (T. L. L., II, 867, 34 ff.).
causari 163, 1, 5, attritum corpus debilitatem tibi causaris attulisse
    membrorum,
    Vulg. Rom. 3, 9, Salv., Paul. Petric. (T. L. L., III, 706, 59 ff.).

clamare = *conqueri* 159, 1, 24, clamat enim sibi Gudila vel Oppane incognitam suo generi condicionem servitutis imponi
  Cic., Hor., Prop., Liv., etc. in sense of *exclaim* (T. L. L., III,
  1252, 38 ff.; some examples from Cicero seem to mean *complain*).
congemiscere acc. to Traube ⎰ 384, 2, 2, expugnatum se hostis sua prae-
congemere   acc. to T. L. L. ⎱   sumptione congemuit
  Hil., Cassiod. var. (T. L. L., IV, 275, 4 ff.).
conqueri 101, 1, 9, conquesti sunt . . . Simplicium domum in sacratissima Urbe positam . . . comparasse
  Plaut. (doubtful), Lucr., Ov., Liv., Sen., Curt., etc., Cassiod. var.
  (T. L. L., IV, 351, 40).
deplorare 30, 1, 22, deplorat . . . ad discriminis se ultima pervenisse,
  Cod. Th., Sulp. Sev., Avell., Boeth., Cassiod. var (T. L. L., V,
  575, 13 ff.).
designare 62, 1, 9, athletam populis palma designat esse victorem.
  Lucif., Comm. (T. L. L., V, 716, 65 ff.).
diiudicare 195, 3, 31, ut dulcissimam vitam te ibidem invenisse diiudices,
  Cf. *ut*-clause, 298, 2, 7. Plaut., Cic. epist. (once), Plin. nat., Fulg.,
  Macedon., Cassiod. var. (T. L. L., V, 1156, 65 ff.).
inspicere 202, 1, 6, inspexit antiquitas provinciarum dignitates annua
  successione reparari,
intimare 124, 2, 23, quos elapsos intimat mentis alienatione custodum.
  Gall. apud Treb. Claud. 17 (Harpers').
intueri 65, 3, 16, intuere quippe omnium ora, atque oculos in te esse
  conversos:
iungere 119, 2, 7, his multo acerbiora iungentes: alienis debitis ad solu-
  tionem alios trahi
  Acc. with inf. is in apposition with *acerbiora*.
nosse 4, 8, 11, colloquia . . . te occupare noverunt.
  Late Latin use of this verb for *scire*. Acc. with inf. occurs in Rhet.
  Her. and in poetry (K.-Steg., II, 1, 690).
percipere 328, 9, 33, Placidiam . . . purpurato filio studuisse percepimus
  Classical usage avoids acc. with inf. (L.-Hof., 586), Plaut., Vitr.
  (K.-Steg., II, 1, 690).
praesumere 309, 1, 29, qui se per vos praesumpsit augeri.
  Apul. met. 7, 27 (Harpers').
recognoscere 48, 5, 26, ut . . . in hunc recognoscatis esse vestigium
respicere 47, 6, 34, respice te supra omnium umeros atque ora volitare
  Ov. (K.-Steg., II, 1, 690).
retinere 33, 1, 4, praecepta nos dedisse retinemus
  In Late Latin = *memoria retinere*. Inf. occurs in Dig. 35, 1, 92
  (Harpers').
suggerere 101, 1, 10, quam . . . ecclesiam Romanam quieto iure suggerunt
  possedisse
  Suggerere in this sense is Late Latin.

suspirare 344, 3, 26, gravia vobis inferri dispendia suspirastis,
Lucr. 2, 1164 (Harpers').

b. Verbs of Emotion

adquiescere 137, 1, 4, quod fieri debere nostra merito pietas adquiescit.
Aug., Prosp., Marc., Cassiod. var. (T. L. L., I, 425, 1 ff.).
amare 61, 1, 28, fraudes fieri legibus non amamus
Sall. (once), Hor., Ov., Apul., Tert., etc. (T. L. L., I, 1956, 20 ff.;
cf. K.-Steg., II, 1, 693).
amplecti 31, 3, 2, quae vos reserari libenter amplectimur,
T. L. L., I, 1994, 76 ff. cites use of inf. alone, not acc. with inf.
delectari 100, 1, 15, Delectamur iure Romano vivere (eos) quos armis
cupimus vindicare,
Plin., Fronto. (K.-Steg., II, 1, 691).
detestari 50, 23, privatis compendiis calumniam detestamur inferri.
Cassiod. var., Greg. Tur., Greg. M. (T. L. L., V, 810, 66 ff.).
erubescere 29, 5, 27, cum se superatos turpiter erubescunt.
ferre 57, 1, 8, quis enim ferat in domesticis praesidiis locum fuisse periculis . . . ?
Cic. (with *non ferendum*), Lucr., Ciris, Hor., Tib., Prop., Ov.,
Liv., etc., Cassiod. var. (T. L. L., VI, 538, 1 ff.; cf. K.-Steg.,
II, 1, 694).
gratulari 163, 3, 31, ut . . . ab illicitis se liberatam gratuletur incommodis.
ingemiscere 278, 4, 23, conventionibus se gravari omnimodis ingemiscunt,
Begins with Cic. (L.-Hof., 587). Poetic (K.-Steg., II, 1, 691).
obstupescere 40, 5, 20, quod obstupescant homines evenisse
Transitive use of this verb is Late.
optare 10, 3, 17, quem non optatis a vestris moribus discrepare.
Early, rare classical, Silver (Cf. K.-Steg., II, 1, 693).
perferre 37, 1, 29, differri te pertulit noster affectus:
Plaut., Prop., Mela, Tac. (K.-Steg., II, 1, 694).
permoveri 33, 2, 22, frumenta publica . . . nec autumno venisse . . .
permovemur,
stupere 38, 2, 25, stupere videamur in unius gratia tot desiderabilia
fuisse contempta.
Vergil (L.-Hof., 587; K.-Steg., II, 1, 691).
stupescere 261, 2, 7, ut stupescas sic subito perturbatam, quam nullus
tactus exagitat.
vereri 59, 9, nec vereamini ad alias actiones posse traduci (eos) a
quibus, *etc.*
Plaut.; then not till Curtius. (L.-Hof., 587).

c. Verbs of Command and Exhortation

persuadere 83, 1, 29, ratio persuadet ab unoquoque postulari quod ei
constat iniungi
Apuleius (L.-Hof., 585).

praecipere 23, 1, 18, castrum . . . praecipimus communiri,
124, 2, 24, eos te praecipimus . . . ducere,
Acc. with passive inf. from Curt. and Plin. nat. Acc. with active
inf. from Apuleius (L.-Hof., 585).

d. Verbs of Petition

deposcere 128, 2, 32, Oblata itaque supplicatione deposcitis privilegia
vobis debere servari,
Liv., Iul. Val., Auson., Symm., etc., Cassiod. hist. (T. L. L., V,
590, 42 ff.).
depromere 222, 2, 11, depromis mulierem . . . iugali honestate debere
sociari,
Cod. Iust., Cassiod. var. (T. L. L., V, 616, 72 ff.).
supplicare 117, 1, 18, reverti se ad lares proprios supplicavit,
Supplicare with the infinitive is Late.
petere 49, 23, quem tibi petis prodesse,
Plaut., Lucr., Suet., Gell., and later authors (K.-Steg., II, 1, 693).
adire 99, 2, 4, nos aditos esse cognoscat illa sibi vestris temporibus
fuisse subtracta,
Word used in similar sense in examples in T. L. L., I, 617, 43 ff.
No infinitives in examples.

e. Verbs of Permission

permittere 27, 3, 17, hoc imitari reliquos sine dubitatione permittit.
Accusative with a passive infinitive used from time of Tacitus.
Frequent in Late Latin (L.-Hof., 585).

f. Verbs of Causing and Other Verbs

compellere 210, 4, 29, Officium tuum . . . invigilare compelle:
Tert., Ulp., Arnob., Auson., Symm., etc (T. L. L., III, 2035, 45 ff.;
cf. K.-Steg., II, 1, 683).
curare 125, 3, 22, Petrum . . . in album sacri ordinis . . . curet referri,
Plaut., Lucil., Cic. (twice), Suet., Apul., etc. (T. L. L., IV, 1500,
5 ff.).
facere 41, 10, 23, haec enim fecisse dinoscitur Daedalum volare: haec
. . . Cupidinem . . . pendere: haec hodie facit muta cantare,
insensata vivere, immobilia moveri.
Enn., Plaut., Lucil., Cic. (once), Verg., and in Silver and Late
authors; Cassiod. var. (T. L. L., VI, 115, 37 ff.; cf. L.-Hof.,
584—rare in Early Latin, more frequent in poetry and in Silver
and Late Latin.
festinare 299, 1, 33, ut illud mihi festinaretis . . . evenire,
Avell., Cassiod. var. (this sentence) (T. L. L., VI, 619, 84 ff.).
invitare 216, 1, 12, Invitat nos consuetudo sollemnis . . . ornatum
officii dirigere
Vergil. (K.-Steg., II, 1, 683). Since Afranius (L.-Hof., 580).

niti 98, 2, 27, quos ab hostili nitimur oppressione liberari.
  Arnob. nat. 2, 24.
sancire 147, 4, 13, nec quicquid eos potestatis habere reverenda sanxit
    antiquitas,
  Liv., Suet. (Harpers').

Cassiodorus rather frequently omits the subject accusative when this is a pronoun which can be supplied from the context. The construction is not otherwise altered by the omission. This usage is classed as colloquial (L.-Hof., 592; K.-Steg., II, 1, 700-701), but occurs at times in classical prose. It is employed frequently by the poets and by Late Latin prose writers. Notable examples from the Variae are:

133, 2, 10, Clarissimorum igitur adultorum Marciani atque Maximi nos
    querela pulsavit . . . (eos) utilitatem suam pio neglexisse
    contemptu,
148, 1, 1, tua igitur suggestione comperimus per illam indictionem
    patrimonii nostri praedia in Apulia provincia constituta,
    id est illud atque illud, honesto viro Thomati libellario
    titulo (nos) commisisse,

B. WITH IMPERSONAL VERBS
(L.-Hof. 587-588; K.-Steg. II, 1, 675)

The accusative with the infinitive is found with some impersonal verbs, and verbs used impersonally in the passive, with which it does not occur in classical prose. Examples:

agnoscitur 246, 2, 25, melius agnoscitur (esse) elegisse nobilem quam
    fecisse felicem:
  Acc. with inf. with active *agnoscere*, T. L. L., I, 1358, 21. No
    examples with passive.
ambigitur 41, 11, 27, ut quod compositum (esse) non ambigitur veritas
    aestimetur.
  Liv., Tac., Apul., and Late authors (T. L. L., II, 867, 34 ff.).
claret 79, 4, 18, nisi omnino claret . . . nostra potius esse certamina.
  Spart., Ambr., Heges., Pelag., etc (T. L. L., III, 1263, 73 ff.; cf.
    L.-Hof., 588).
congruit 90, 28, Congruit comitatum nostrum viris nos decorare nobilibus,
  Apul., Tert., Frg. Mur., Lact., Leo M. (T. L. L., IV, 301, 61; this
    sentence cited under use of infinitive alone, 301, 60).
contingit 4, 10, 25, contingit enim dissimilem filium plerumque generari:
  Gaius, Ps. Apul., Tert., Hil., Avien., Amm., etc, Cassiod. hist.
    (T. L. L., IV, 719, 75; cf. L.-Hof., 588).

datur 69, 11, 26, (id) quod humana nequit altercatione dissolvi, fontium
    datum est aequitate definiri.
    Tert., Ennod., Verec. (T. L. L., V, 1690, 33 ff.).
delectat 31, 1, 23, Romana sit vox plebis, quam delectet audiri.
    Cic. (once), Epist. Vesp., Quint., Plin., Fronto, Prisc., Fulg. Rusp.
    (T. L. L., V, 428, 51 ff.).
invenitur 70, 5, 31, utiliter inventum est artificialem musicam . . . modis
    quindecim contineri.
    Nom. with inf. is classical (L.-Hof., 589).
legitur 261, 3, 11, legitur quidem nonnullos fontium variis scaturrire
    miraculis,
    Nom. with inf. in use since Propertius (L.-Hof., 589; K.-Steg., II,
    1, 706). I have not found acc. with inf.
occurritur 100, 1, 3, Non occuritur sub principe benigno remedia postu-
    lare subiectos,
pervenit 122, 1, 18, ad nos multorum suggestione pervenit Laurentium
    . . . divitias inter hominum cadavera perscrutatum (esse)
    Context with *suggestione* makes *pervenire* equivalent to a verb of
    saying.
proficit 67, 3, 19, quid enim proficit creditorem se urgere . . . ?
    Inf. alone is classical (K.-Steg., II, 1, 670).
provenit 144, 1, 13, Usu quidem provenit bene meritos dona nostra
    suscipere:
sufficit 48, 4, 24, cetera de illo meminisse vos sufficit,
    Usage begins with Quintilian (L.-Hof., 588).
suggeritur 29, 2, 11, suggeritur . . . se truculentas insidias . . . pertulisse
    As a verb of saying *suggerere* is Late Latin.

7. The Nominative With the Infinitive
(L.-Hof. 589; K.-Steg. II, 1, 705 ff.)

The nominative with the infinitive occurs with many verbs in
the passive, chiefly verbs of saying and thinking, with which it is
not used in classical prose. Classical prose used this construction
chiefly with verbs in the uncompounded forms and in the third
person. In these respects the usage in the Variae is the same.
Examples:

adverti 359, 1, 7, avarus paruisse non advertitur continenti:
    Cic. (once), Cassiod. gramm. (T. L. L., I, 863, 66 ff.). *Anim-
    adverti* is so used in Varro and Gellius (K.-Steg., II, 1, 705).
aestimari 20, 1, 19, ut illud aestimemur elegisse,
    Tert., Filastr., Amm., Ambr., Heges., Macr., Physiogn. (T. L. L.,
    I, 1107, 26 ff.).
asseri 17, 3, 18, quae pro iugalis tuae assereris portione . . . divisisse
    Ps. Cypr., Pallad., Veg., Ambr., Aug., etc. (T. L. L., II, 867, 34 ff.).

cerni 130, 1, 7, cernitur iacere prostratus.
   Edict. Diocl., Aug., Sed., Alc., Avit., Cassiod. in psal., Ven Fort., Greg. M. (T. L. L., III, 873, 53 ff.).
declarari 10, 4, 23, unum corpus sub antiquis principibus fuisse declaratur,
   Usage not given in T. L. L.; acc. with inf., III, 187, 61 ff.
delectari 49, 1, 27, in utilitate rei publicae delectatur expendere,
   Cic. (once), Hor., Phaedr., Tert., Ambr., Ruf., Aug., etc (T. L. L., V, 428, 39 ff.).
deprehendi 161, 2, 19, moribus studere deprehenditur quod, *etc.*
   Sol., Ps. Aug., Cod. Th., Chron. Gall., Faust. Rei., Boeth., Cassiod. var. (T. L. L., V, 609, 71 ff.).
desiderari 189, 1, 2, quanto amplius desiderantur agnosci.
   (No exs. in T. L. L., V, 707, 9 ff.)
dinosci 41, 10, 23, haec (i. e., ars) enim fecisse dinoscitur Daedalum volare:
   Mod. dig., Prob., Ps. Apul., Tert., Fr. Mur., Mar. Victorin., etc. Cassiod. in psalm (T. L. L., V, 1221, 50 ff.).
doceri 327, 9, 18, unde docetur et natum (esse)
   Amm., Veg., Claud. Don., Ambr., Aug., etc. (T. L. L., V, 1708, 59 ff.).
dubitari 380, 4, 21, marino fluctui tam fragilis munitio non dubitatur opponi,
   Tacitus and later writers in sense of *doubt* (T. L. L., V, 2092, 14 ff.).
formidari 222, 2, 3, dominus fieri formidatur ingratus.
   (No exs. in T. L. L., VI, 1096, 3 ff.)
insinuari 314, 2, 3, quod vobis insinuatum est tributorum gravi sorte laborare,
   Insinuare in sense of *inform* is Late.
intimari 165, 7, 18, fraus fieri utilitatibus publicis intimatur,
   Verb *intimari* is Late.
legi 138, 5, 21, libet repetere, cur antiquitas rudis legatur haec moenia condidisse.
   Since Propertius (L.-Hof., 589).
monstrari 93, 3, 20, qui sub illo esse monstraris,
   Plaut., Ov., Arnob. (K.-Steg., II, 1, 706).
nosci 19, 3, 7, quia sub modo eius esse noscuntur.
   Amm., Edict. Licin., Lact. (K.-Steg., II, 1, 706).
optari 376, 3, 11, optetur quin immo longior fuisse,
permitti 80, 1, 15, quod nulla permittitur commotione violari.
   Late Latin usage (L.-Hof., 589).
praecipi 174, 2, 12, fasces atque secures tantae potestati praeceptae sunt inligari,
   Late Latin usage (L.-Hof., 589).

praecipitari 385, 8, 11, emptor plurima praecipitatur offerre.
  Active with inf. in Val. Flacc. (K.-Steg., II, 1, 693). No usage of
  passive with inf. found.
praeponi 368, 1, 11, principalia beneficia praeponitur erogare,
probari 5, 17, 24, ista regulis accepisse probamur antiquis,
  Begins with Augustan poets (L.-Hof., 589; K.-Steg., II, 1, 706).
quaeri 60, 2, 19, quantitas procurari quaeritur,
  Active use with inf. begins with Verg. (K.-Steg., II, 1, 674). No
  usage of passive with inf. found.
referri 95, 4, 27, de ornatu moenium referuntur esse sublata,
  Active use with inf. is classical (K.-Steg., II, 1, 692). No usage
  of passive with inf. found.
sentiri 181, 2, 35, disceptare posse sentitur.
  Usage begins with Augustan poets (L.-Hof., 589).
suggeri 28, 2, 12, qui nunc diversorum usurpatione suggeruntur invasi
  (esse).
  Suggerere as a verb of saying is Late.
urgeri 378, 2, 20, dum extraneis urgemini vendere, soletis damna sentire,
  Active use with inf. is found in Cicero (L.-Hof., 585).

One example of this construction seems to merit special attention because of the use of the perfect infinitive with the verb
laudari, the infinitive giving the cause or reason for the act of
praising. The example from the Variae is 251, 2, 10, vel a malis
abstinuisse laudandus es. Juret, 121, gives a similar example from
Filastrius, 42, *plus a quibusdam . . . intellegisse laudantur.* He
mentions also Verg. Aen. 2, 585, *extinxisse nefas . . . laudabor,*
and Aug. civ., 1, 6, *se abstinuisse laudatur.* The similarity of all
the examples would suggest that the later writers all imitated the
Vergilian construction.

8. The Perfect Infinitive Instead of the Present
(L.-Hof. 591-592)

The poets of all periods employed at times the perfect active
infinitive in place of the present, partly for metrical reasons. The
usage in prose begins with Livy. Many Silver and Late prose
authors used the perfect quite freely in place of the present, chiefly
in striving for prose rhythm.

This usage is rather frequent in the Variae. The following are
typical examples which seem to have aoristic force:

  14, 8, 32, pudet enim eum peccare, qui laudatis videtur potuisse
  succedere.

85, 3, 15, Quid erit suavius quam in illa turba summorum nobile pro-
           tulisse iudicium. . . . ?
105, 1, 8, carum enim est homini repperisse, ubi aliquid se laudabile
           non putaverat invenire.
125, 2, 17, Praeconiorum ergo professio est collegium desiderasse sum-
           morum
143, 1, 25, nam inter tot gentes viam praesumere non est aliquid facile
           concupisse.
146, 6, 15, inter bene moratos enim asseruisse iusta facillimum fuit:
147, 1, 20, et nunc decem milia solidorum reliquatorem nostris utilita-
           tibus extitisse (Cf. 148, 1, 4).
154, 6, 10, ne . . . utilitati publicae voluptas privata obstitisse videatur.
186, 3, 28, aliud est enim tantum dicere legitima, aliud ad terminum
           deduxisse iustitiam.
205, 1, 18, Capitolia celsa conscendere hoc est humana ingenia superata
           vidisse.
303, 3, 5, contendisse siquidem, non litigasse repertus est.

The perfect infinitive passive occurs for the present in Early
and Classical Latin with certain stereotyped phrases such as *aequom
fuit, decuit, oportuit.* Cassiodorus seems to use the perfect for
the present in a few examples. Thus *fieri* and *factum esse* (60, 2,
18) (60, 2, 22) both seem to have the meaning of *fieri.* Cf. also
259, 4, 23, patiantur se a rusticis divisos (esse), and 308, 1, 12,
bene imperaturo non est difficile persuasum (esse).

9. The Present Infinitive Instead of the Future
(L.-Hof. 586-587)

In classical prose examples of the present infinitive after the
verbs *promittere* and *polliceri* are rare. The present infinitive was
commonly used in Early Latin and was revived in the Late Period.

Cassiodorus uses the present infinitive (or forms like *odisse*)
after *promittere* in 192, 5, 7, doctoribus enim vestris promittitis
odisse nequitiam et amare puritatem. Also 223, 2, 16, and 337,
6, 7. But in 236, 2, 10, he has the future, promitterent fidem se
regno . . . servaturos. After *polliceri* the present occurs in 234,
4, 14, portitores . . . fecimus polliceri iustitiam . . . custodire.
But in 64, 3, 23, he uses the future, hunc ergo audacem laborem
adgressurum se . . . pollicitus est.

In 105, 1, 9, the present infinitive is used for the future after
the verb *putare* in the clause, ubi aliquid se laudabile non putaverat
invenire.

10. The Present Infinitive Passive Instead of the Passive Periphrastic

The present infinitive passive is used in the sense of the passive periphrastic in 18, 2, 3, dubium non est in repetitione minoris maxime submoveri dispendia tarditatis, and in 102, 4, 5, negando credi contra fidem publicam fallaciter supplicanti.

As the supine in -*um* is totally lacking in the Variae, the future infinitive passive formed with this supine and *iri* does not occur. The chief substitute is the gerundive with *esse*. See page 166.

The infinitive is not employed anywhere in the Variae to express indignation, or command, or in the historical infinitive.

II. *The Gerundive*
1. Attributive Use
(L.-Hof. 595)

The attributive use of the gerundive is rather frequent in the Variae. The verbs occurring in this gerundive usage are usually verbs of emotion, synonyms of those occurring in classical prose, though the classical list is widely extended. The following are typical examples:

10,   3, 17, veneranda Romanae urbis affectio,
        Late, e. g., Cyprian (L.-Hof., 595).
11,   1, 8, abominandam . . . tarditatem.
11,   1, 10, adorandi muricis pretiosissimam qualitatem
        Late, e. g., Cyprian (L.-Hof., 595).
30,   1, 25, audacia plectenda
37, 12,   reverendo coetui
41,   8, 9, talium rerum praedicanda notitia
41,   8, 11, miranda solis magnitudo
        Classical (L.-Hof., 595).
68,   6, 30, stupenda quadam continentiae disciplina
79,   1, 3, ut de uno aliquid dolendum possit emergere.
97,   1, 25, miserandis fletibus audientiam non negare,
        Classical (L.-Hof., 595).
150,   2, 4, culpandae surreptionis vitium
170, 12, 2, error dolendus
195,   1, 18, obstupenda praeconia
218,   2, 31, rubigo otii fugienda
221,   1, 21, exsecranda temeritas
        Late, e. g., Cyprian (L.-Hof., 595).
288,   3, 23, liberos nulla discretione laudandos,
        Classical (L.-Hof., 595).

In several instances the gerundive occurs as a predicate adjective. The usage here is not that of the passive periphrastic, but differs from the above attributive use only in this, that the gerundive is employed as a predicate, not as an attributive, adjective, e. g.

14, 8, 33, fuit . . . militibus verendus (= venerable)
38, 3, 7, quem reverendum humano generi esse cognoscis (= venerable).
68, 5, 22, illud quoque stupendum esse dicimus, (= remarkable)
70, 4, 23, omnia sua fecit valde esse laudanda (= laudable).
281, 11, 1, qui emendum credidit totius largitatis auctorem (= venal, capable of being bought).

2. Substantive Use
(L.-Hof. 458; cf. Odelstierna 8-10)

The employment of a gerundive as a substantive begins with Horace and is frequent in Livy and in Silver and Late Latin. In the Late period the gerundive frequently has a future sense.

The following are examples of the substantive usage:

3, 5, 20, non sufficit agenda militibus imperare,
4, 8, 13, si . . . valueris legenda proferre :
18, 1, 11, a quo debent non mutanda constitui.
22, 3, 23, erigat humiles, eripiat opprimendos,
62, 2, 17, diligenda custodis
82, 6, 5, te novimus fecisse praedicanda.
87, 14,   si sacrae iussionis reverenda contemnat.
91, 1, 5, Iuvat probatis ordinanda mandare
92, 2, 1, rationabiliter agenda praeceperit
100, 3, 11, ut eorum praebendae . . . ibi debuissent . . . comparari,
121, 3, 31, cui necesse est praedicanda sequi,
126, 25,   cui iudicanda committimus,
126, 26,   dignus est inter alios sequenda decernere,
145, 4, 35, sapienter alleganda tractavit.
263, 6, 2, longa sunt illius fontis memoranda describere.
278, 1, 13, observanda iugiter praesenti iussione decernimus,
279, 7, 7, mavis a te sequenda constitui :
337, 2, 22, formidanda nescitis.

In the following the future sense is prominent, i. e., the context makes it apparent that the idea of obligation or necessity is not stressed.

3, 2, 9, creditis me impaenitenda proferre?
37, 12,   *admittendos* reverendo coetui examinare cogit

37, 18,   quae circa referendos curiae priscus ordo dictavit.
191, 6, 4, qui decenter edenda humanis usibus applicavit.
278, 4, 24, ut ad iudicium deducendi paene tanta videantur amittere.
300, 6, 27, nescit enim paenitenda loqui, qui proferenda prius suo tradit
examini.

Note especially the substantive use of the gerundive in 240, 5, 9,
ad invenienda subtilis, ad implenda robustus, ad celanda cautissimus. Here through the ellipsis of a substantive the gerundives
are used substantively where classical prose would employ a gerund.
The effect of a plural of the gerund appears to be produced by this
usage.

3. Predicate Use
(L.-Hof. 595-597)

Cassiodorus uses the gerundive with *esse* in the classical manner
to denote necessity or obligation, i. e., in the passive periphrastic
construction. Note the ellipsis of *est* in 186, 1, 18, considerandum,
quali labore servitum est, et sic de remuneratione cogitandum. For
occasional uses of the ablative of agent instead of the dative with
this construction, see p. 42.

Frequently, however, in the use of the infinitive construction, the
gerundive with *esse* loses the idea of obligation or necessity and
expresses mere futurity. Thus it serves as a future infinitive passive, and, as the author does not employ the supine with *iri*, this
is his regular method of expressing the idea of the future infinitive
passive. This usage is found only in Late Latin (L.-Hof., 556).

This infinitive usage occurs chiefly with the expression *noverit
se*, sometimes in connection with a future active infinitive, in such
a manner as to show that the gerundive is merely used in forming
a future infinitive passive, e. g., in 30, 2, 32, noverit se decem
librarum auri dispendio vulnerandum et nostrae ingratitudinis . . .
pericula subiturum . . . (also in 31, 2, 27; 35, 4, 17; 61, 3, 15;
66, 3, 27. etc.). Among other examples note:

12, 6, 7, si aliqua credideris ludificatione tardandum,
70, 1, 3, complendum esse promisimus
87, 4,   maxime a vobis confidimus exsecrandum quod matrimonii
genialis impugnat affectum.
104, 4, 8, scopulos petunt, quos fluctibus vexandos esse non credunt,
207, 1, 21, ut . . . bellum pacatum gereres, si quem civium laedendum
esse sentires,

262, 6, 32, tamquam se noverint non esse capiendos:
282, 5, 14, non credant (id) a nostra mansuetudine neglegendum,

Apart from the infinitive construction the gerundive as a future participle is rare. Cf. the following examples:

57, 1, 29, ad beneficia praestanda curritur.
            One person gives the favors; others run to receive them.
136, 2, 20, ad Romanas sedes venire festina, conventui nobilium . . .
            reddendus.
187, 5, 4, utere . . . quicquid veteranis munifica iura tribuerunt, nulli
            sordido subiciendus oneri,
315, 4, 24, poenam luat . . . poena etiam inurendus infamiae, (= Let
            him suffer the penalty. Let him also be branded with the
            penalty of infamy.)

In classical prose the gerundive in agreement with an object accusative to express purpose occurs after a limited number of verbs (Cf. L.-Hof., 595). Cassiodorus uses the gerundive thus in the classical manner after *dare* (e. g., 39, 2, 13), *suscipere* (e. g., 38, 4, 9), *curare* (e. g., 27, 2, 25), *committere* (e. g., 11, 6, 3), *concedere* (e. g., 368, 3, 26), *redimere* (e. g., 58, 2, 30), *sumere* (e. g., 26, 3, 25).

Non-classical uses of the same construction are:

18, 3, 20, cuncta transmisimus ordinanda,
            Begins with Vergil (L.-Hof., 595).
27, 3, 16, qui . . . litem neglegit abolendam,
63, 2, 27, quod pietatis exemplum ad suum quoque commodum sup-
            plicant transferendum.
81, 5, 2, vobis aliqua dicenda mandamus,
            Begins with Livy (L.-Hof., 595).
81, 1, 7, conferendas forsitan dignitates dilatione probabili librare-
            mus,
84, 3, 19, columnas . . . contradat . . . devehendas
152, 2, 24, decrevimus mille interim dromones fabricandos assumere
158, 14,   curam . . . peragendam ad te decernimus pertinere
255, 4, 20, causam deleget aequitatis studio terminandam
285, 2, 12, necessaria quaedam . . . servanda conscripsimus
287, 2, 20, in eo corrigendum aliquid inveniret.
293, 12, 2, regendam tribuimus dignitatem,
            Begins with Livy (K.-Steg., II, 1, 731).
298, 4, 16, aliqua pietati vestrae delegavimus intimanda,

Where the main verb is passive or intransitive, the gerundive is in the nominative in agreement with the subject. This usage

begins with Afranius, but is rare in classical prose (L.-Hof., 595).
In the Variae this usage rarely occurs. Examples of the classical
usage:

50, 2,11, cui . . . regni status committitur vindicandus
115, 1,19, debet esse conspicuus, qui datur imitandus

Non-classical examples:

108, 2,18, quatenus industria illa . . . venerit approbanda
        Plautus, Livy (L.-Hof., 595).
128, 3,21, ad consularem Campaniae veniant legibus audiendi,
255, 4,18, ad beatissimi papae iudicium prius conveniat audiendus,

4. The Gerundive in the Oblique Cases
(Cf. L.-Hof. 597-600)

In the genitive and in the ablative without a preposition the
gerundive rarely occurs in the Variae. The gerund of transitive
verbs is also rare in these cases.

The dative occurs in a few expressions of purpose, e. g., 106, 9,
14, ille mappam, qua tergendis manibus utebatur, iussit abici per
fenestram; 127, 2, 19, testatus es . . . superimponendis fabricis
licentiam condonari. Also with *interesse,* 58, 2, 28, qui humandis
non sinitur corporibus interesse. It also occurs with *aptus,* e. g.,
154, 3, 21, ligna fabricandis apta dromonibus. In classical prose
the gerundive occurs in the dative of purpose but is always rare.
Late Latin first extended the usage, but ultimately allowed the
dative of both gerund and gerundive to fall into disuse (L.-Hof.,
598).

The accusative of the gerundive after *ad* occurs in the classical
manner to express purpose. The following are typical examples:

53, 2, 28, ad proprios cibos quaerendos
155, 2, 12, ad laedendum possessorem

The most frequent preposition with the ablative of the gerundive
is the preposition *in,* e. g., 28, 1, 7, maior in conservandis rebus
quam in inveniendis adhibenda cautela est. (Also in 26, 3, 25;
61, 1, 32; 62, 2, 1, etc.) The usage is classical.

Pro with the gerundive to express purpose occurs at least 16
times. For discussion and examples cf. p. 128.

De in the meaning of *concerning* occurs with a gerundive chiefly in the titles of the Formulae in Book VII, but occasionally also in the text. Examples:

211, 18, Formula Ad Praefectum Urbis De Architecto Faciendo In Urbe Roma.
217, 24, Formula De Custodiendis Portis Civitatum.
222, 6, Formula De Matrimonio Confirmando Et Liberis Legitimis Faciendis.
242, 1, 13, de sociando ei litterarum peritissimo consulamus.
279, 3, 33, de talibus prohibendis suffragiis patres conscripti senatus consulta . . . condiderunt.
286, 5, 26, neque de transferendis neque de imminuendis annonis . . . patiatur improbam quaestionem
The usage is classical (L.-Hof., 600).

III. *The Gerund*
(L.-Hof. 593-600)

The usage of the gerund in the Variae is in most instances classical. The greater number of examples are confined to the genitive and the ablative without a preposition. The dative, which is rare in classical prose, does not occur at all. The accusative occurs only after the preposition *ad* to express purpose, e. g., 38, 4, 11, illa, quae potiora credimus, ad conservandum melioribus damus, and 283, 1, 6, si quis ingenuorum ad satisfaciendum legi superius definitae idoneus non habetur. This usage is classical and occurs rather frequently in the Variae.

1. The Genitive of the Gerund

The genitive with *causa* occurs in 35, 1, 29, quod res patris eius non meliorandi causa, sed deteriorandi voto, detineas. This usage is classical.

The greater number of examples of the genitive of the gerund are those of intransitive verbs, or of transitive verbs used absolutely, and are classical, e. g., 53, 2, 10, peccandi licentia non praebetur; 54, 4, 1, mox ut nati fiduciam habere coeperint ambulandi; 59, 1, 14, constat senatum populis vivendi regulam praestitisse; 201, 2, 10, scito puniendi remedium datum tibi pro salute multorum.

A few examples of transitive verbs occur. Thus 206, 2, 27, eos indagandi licentiam non tulerunt — Classical prose usually preferred the gerundive but permitted the use of a transitive gerund

7

to avoid the repetition of the *-orum* sound in the genitive plural of the gerundive construction. Thus also 238, 3, 13, crescebat visendi studium eois populis heroam nostrum. The gerund is perhaps preferred to the gerundive here in the interest of clearness on account of the Greek loan-word *heros*.

The genitive occurs after a few adjectives, e. g.

14, 8, 33, dandi avidus, accipiendi fastidiosus,
>   The gerund with *avidus* occurs in Sallust (L.-Hof., 598).
>   T. L. L., VI, 312, 14, shows no gerund use with *fastidiosus*.
>   Parallel structure probably accounts for its use here.

16, 3, 24, medendi peritus
>   The use of the genitive of the gerund with *peritus* dates
>   from Cato (L.-Hof., 597).

An unusual gerund construction, where we should expect the gerundive, occurs in 99, 3, 28, iubemus ut studium devehendi supradictae speciei commune subeatur. The gerund in this type of construction is explained as an appositive. Such a usage of the gerund occurred in Early Latin, but was generally avoided in the classical and Silver periods, though there are a few occurrences in the early writings of Cicero. The archaists Fronto and Gellius revived the usage, and it had considerable vogue among later writers (L.-Hof., 597).

2. The Ablative of the Gerund

a. WITHOUT A PREPOSITION

The gerund occurs as an ablative of respect in 222, 1, 24, minor *nascendo* grandaevus cupis esse *consilio*. Plautus in some examples combines the idea of an ablative of respect with that of the ablative of means (L.-Hof., 599), but this example appears to be purely an ablative of respect, as is evident from its being contrasted with the ablative of respect, *consilio,* and from its use as a substitute for the familiar *minor natu*.

Several examples of the gerund used as an ablative of cause occur, e. g.

16, 17, 6, ut . . . donando saepius invidiam non haberet
40, 2, 3, quatenus impetratis delectationibus perfruendo, quod nobis
>   cottidianum, illis videatur esse miraculum.
>   (Note that the gerundive could have been used.)
48, 4, 19, qui abstinendo vitiis alios formaret exemplis.
193, 2, 9, nominis tui auctor multa conferendo praedicatur.

The use of the gerund as an ablative of cause is scarcely a separate category from that of the ablative of means. L.-Hof., 599, speaks of the causal usage as implied in the instrumental. K.-Steg., II, 1, 752, cites one example from Terence and one from Cicero as causal.

All other gerunds in the ablative are either instrumental or modal, uses which occur in classical prose. However, the usage of the ablative of the gerund, chiefly in a modal or circumstantial sense, as the equivalent of a present participle in the nominative, though it has its beginnings in classical or even in Early Latin, is largely a Silver and Late Latin development. (L.-Hof., 600; cf. K.-Steg., II, 1, 752-753; Odelstierna, 22; Skerlj, 1-75). Examples are frequent in the Variae, e. g.

4, 7, 9, sic petentibus praestando gratis sub continentiae munere cuncta mercaris.
13, 5, 9, at tu consuetudinem devotionis *impendens* eo nos obligasti munere, quo tibi nos putamus omnia reddidisse: inde *amplificando* debitum, unde credi poterat absolutum.
(Note the contrast of *impendens* and *amplificando*.)
19, 4. 9. crescit nova condicione per se redeundo
Causal 30, 1, 26, ne paulatim sinendo graviorem vindicare cogamur offensam.
Causal 30, 1, 28, ne aut acriter vindicando aestimetur nimius aut leniter agendo putetur improvidus.
102, 3, 5, occurrit Bruttiorum praesulis missa relatio . . . negando credi contra fidem publicam fallaciter supplicanti.
139, 9, 7, non scribendo facit quod scriptura declaravit
145, 5, 13, age nunc inhaerendo iustitiae,
Causal 193, 1, 35, ne possit ad nos veniendo mediocritas ingravari.
234, 5, 17, inclinando nostrum eveximus principatum
269, 5, 15, voluntarie serviendo liberae sunt et invicem se diligendo muniuntur.
317, 4, 30, temptando solum cautus semper incedit,
330, 20, 27, agendo pro me communibus dominis gratias debitum meum vestra satisfactione persolvite:
381, 3, 21, mutaverunt se tempora non mutando

It will be observed that in a few of the above examples the gerunds are those of transitive verbs and take the accusative. Gerunds with the accusative are rare in classical prose but much more frequent in Late Latin (L.-Hof. 596-597).

b. WITH A PREPOSITION

The most frequent preposition occurring with the ablative of the gerund is the preposition *in.* This preposition is so used by classical authors. Examples:

52, 1, 21, cum nulla in parendo probetur sentire detrimenta.
52, 1, 30, ut quibus non fuerunt in exigendo compendia, gravem subeant in reddendo iacturam.

The preposition *a* occurs with a gerund in 174, 3, 14, consul dictus est a consulendo. The usage of *a* or *ab* with a gerund or gerundive is avoided by Caesar, but is used by other classical authors (L.-Hof., 600).

IV. *The Supine*
(L.-Hof. 600-602)

The supine in *-um,* which gradually disappeared from the Latin language, does not occur in the Variae.

The supine in *-u* occurs chiefly in the clause *quod dictu nefas est* (56, 17; 58, 1, 26; 119, 3, 17; 279, 2, 28, etc.). The infinitive passive takes its place in the phrase *quod dici nefas est* (149, 1, 6; 154, 6, 9, etc.). The accusative with the infinitive also occurs several times with *nefas,* e. g., 281, 1, 30. *Fas* is never found with the supine, but is frequent with the infinitive, e. g., 60, 2, 23, si dici fas est.

In 68, 4, 16, unda . . . tactu fit habilis, and 259, 2, 1, palus enim nec visu grata, the words *tactu* and *visu* appear to be stereotyped supine forms, but may be fourth declension nouns in the ablative of respect or even in the dative.

V. *The Participle*
(L.-Hof. 602-610)

For the substantival use of participles, cf. p. 55.

1. The Present Participle

The attributive use of the present participle presents no deviations from classical usage.

Among the predicate uses the following are noteworthy:

A. A circumstantial present participle in some instances denotes an action which takes place prior to the action of the main verb. Early Latin examples of this use are usually explained as action continuing to the time of the main verb (Cf. K.-Steg., II, 1, 756). More frequent examples are found in Sallust and in Livy, and in Late Latin the present participle often becomes a definite substitute for the missing perfect active participle. (L.-Hof., 604-605. The views of various scholars as to the nature of this usage and examples from early, Classical, Silver, and Late Latin are set forth by S. Lyer, Le Participe Présent Exprimant L'Antériorité, in *Revue des Études Latines*, VII (1929), 322).

Examples from the Variae:

12, 7, 11, talia exempla meditantes fecerunt principibus decus nobile dare rem, quae substantiam noscitur habere mediocrem.
105, 1, 10, Thomati aurigae ex Orientis partibus advenienti annonas rationabiles consideratio nostra largita est,
139, 12, 17, Hos ritus Romani . . . ad suam rem publicam inutiliter trahentes aedificium . . . condiderunt.
144, 2, 3, legitur in interioribus insulis Oceani ex arboris suco defluens . . . paulatim solis ardore coalescere.
306, 1, 8, venientes ad nos aliqui retulerunt civitatem Romanam adhuc inepta sollicitudine laborare.
382, 1, 16, veniens itaque vir venerabilis . . . declaravit, *etc.*

The following seem to be clear-cut examples of the use of the present participle for the missing perfect active participle:

57, 2, 11, qui Stephanum . . . trucidantes inhumatam quoque reverentiam eius funeris abiecerunt,
102, 1, 22, intra ecclesiae saepta refugiens declinare se credidit . . . ultionem
244, 2, 3, quem tu suscipiens patrocinium meritorum . . . auxisti
273, 2, 25, comitivae siquidem largitionum praesidens, functus etiam vicibus praefectorum, praetorianam egit integerrime dignitatem,

B. A present participle sometimes indicates an action subsequent to that of the main verb. This occurs after verbs of saying, where an additional statement is added by the use of the participles, *adiciens, iungens,* etc. The temporal relation of the participle and the main verb in this case is the opposite of that discussed in the preceding paragraph. This particular usage differs from that of the present participle to denote subsequent action mentioned in

Leumann-Hofmann, 605, in that here there is no implication of
the final idea, but the participle merely serves as the equivalent of
a second finite verb subsequent in time to the preceding main verb.
The same inexactness which, especially in the Late Latin, permitted
the present participle to wander in one direction from the earlier
and stricter idea of simultaneity may well be held responsible for
the departure in the opposite direction also.

Examples:

119, 2, 7, Provincialium . . . suggestione comperimus, *etc.* his multo
    acerbiora iungentes:
    Iungentes illustrates an anacolouthic use of the participle
    (See p. 179). It should agree with *provincialium.* Its
    time, however, is subsequent to the other action. We may
    paraphrase the thought thus: *Provinciales suggesserunt
    et iunxerunt.*
159, 1, 24, *clamat* . . . condicionem servitutis imponi . . . *adiciens* enim
    huiusmodi calumnias Pitziae comitis celebratae opinionis
    viri sibi examinatione summotas, nunc autem infirmitatis
    suae mole compressum manu vindicare non posse,
257, 1, 28, agellum . . . *causantur* ablatum *adicientes,* ne rerum suarum
    repetitionibus imminerent, liberis sibi condicionem ultimae
    servitutis imponi.

C. The present participle implying purpose occurs in 29, 2, 12,
dum ad nostrum disponerent venire comitatum remedia consueta
poscentes. This usage does not exist in Early Latin, is almost
totally absent from classical prose, but becomes frequent in Livy.
(L.-Hof., 605; cf. K.-Steg., II, 1, 757, and the discussion by S.
Lyer, Le Participe Présent à Sens Futur in *Revue des Études Latines,* IX (1931), 122).

2. The Perfect Passive Participle

The perfect passive participle usually occurs both in the attributive and in the predicate use in the classical manner.

a. IN PLACE OF *Esse*

One predicate usage, which is non-classical, is the employment of
constitutus and of *positus* to supply the missing present participle
of *esse,* e. g., 129, 2, 27, suggeritis patronum vestrum in annis
minoribus constitutum facultatibus suis potius aggregasse dispen-

dia; 101, 1, 8, domum in sacratissima Urbe positam. (A list of similar occurrences of *constitutus* in the titles and documents of the Variae is given by Traube, p. 527, of *positus*, p. 569, s. v. *ponere*.) No certain examples of this usage of *constitutus* appear prior to the Silver Age. Sen. nat. 3, 10, 3, seems to be the earliest certain example. All other citations in T. L. L., IV, 523, 45 ff. are from Late Latin.

b. IN PLACE OF A VERBAL NOUN

Cassiodorus makes frequent use of the perfect passive participle in place of a verbal noun. His most frequent employment of this construction is not its use in prepositional phrases, as is the case in most examples in Early and classical Latin, but rather as the logical subject of a clause. This use of a participle as the logical subject of a clause is rarely found in classical prose, but is frequent in Livy, Tacitus, and later authors (L.-Hof., 609).

Examples from the Variae, chiefly of the use of the participle in agreement with the subject:

67, 6,   laudes sunt nostrorum temporum celebrata gaudia populorum.
72, 12, 7,   ut vicina chorda pulsata alteram faciat sponte contremiscere,
78, 3, 13,   non vos parentum fusus sanguis inflammat, non graviter urit occupata provincia:
84, 1, 11,   non minorem laudem de inventis quam de rebus possumus adquirere custoditis.
87, 11,   Iniuria quidem nostra est laesa iustitia,
119, 1, 32, semper auget principes observata iustitia
124, 1, 20, ut circa te augeat gratiam custodita iustitia
159, 1, 21, magis miserabiliorem reddidit virum luminis sui ademptus ornatus,
285, 2, 12, quae custodita residuum ius non debilitare, sed potius corroborare videantur.
300, 2, 1,   magna ergo gratia (id) completum debet accipi, quod, *etc.*
314, 3, 13, ut tali facto eam non paeniteret mutata religio.
343, 1, 32, Regale munus impetratum gaudium debet esse cunctorum,
353, 5, 23, ut exultarent gaudiorum crementis de oneribus imminutis.
375, 2, 19, res una subtracta cuncta deformat
384, 4, 13, His additur Alamannorum nuper fugata subreptio,

A similar usage of the gerundive occurs in 360, 3, 26, Nullum repudiat sequenda iustitia: omnes clarificat, quos sui participatione sublimat:

The usage of the gerundive in this construction in the nominative case begins with Livy. It is used freely in Late Latin (L.-Hof., 609).

C. IN PLACE OF A RELATIVE CLAUSE

Cassiodorus frequently uses the perfect passive participle instead of a relative clause to refer to a person or thing already mentioned or to be mentioned. Classical authors regularly used the relative. Livy uses the participle in this manner, though his regular practice is to employ the relative. Silver and Late writers frequently use the participle (Cf. K.-Steg., II, 1, 771). Examples:

   34, 4, 11, praedictarum navium, i. e., of the above mentioned ships.
   34, 2, 27, antefati Benedicti
   36, 2, 18, in supra dicta urbe
   49, 20,   titulis antefatis
   51, 2, 11, supra memoratus equorum moderator
   52, 3, 14, supra scriptam rem
   58, 4, 16, praefatum Domitium
   90, 4, 7, saepe memoratum Castorium
  123, 1, 24, infra scriptis brevibus
  126, 5, 20, saepe dictus saio
  160, 1, 18, brevis subter adnexus
           Similar examples *passim*.

3. The Future Active Participle
(L.-Hof. 606-607)

a. ATTRIBUTIVE USE

The attributive use of the future participle is rare in the Variae and is usually limited to *futurus* (e. g., 33, 2, 26; 106, 9, 16), which is Ciceronian, and *venturus* (e. g., 4, 10, 24; 144, 2, 20), which is found once in Cicero. I have noted also *valiturus* in 30, 2, 31, iure valitura sententia; *casurus* in 69, 9, 15, unde se compago casura disrumpat; and *securus* in 376, 1, 1, serena secutura favens ventus ostendit.

b. PREDICATE USE

The predicate usage occurs rarely in Early Latin, is employed by Cicero and Sallust, and becomes more frequent in the Bell. Afr., Livy, and the poets (L.-Hof., 607). Among the predicate uses, a very frequent type in the Variae is that in which the participle follows an imperative or other expression of command or prohibition, so that the participle becomes the expression of a second command or prohibition. This usage occurs at times in classical prose. Except for its greater relative frequency in the Variae its use by Cassiodorus is entirely classical. The following are typical examples:

26, 3, 25, Sume igitur fisci nostri tuenda negotia, in utendis officii tui privilegiis decessorum exempla secuturus.

60, 3, 28, ad nostrae serenitatis audientiam venire deproperet, sciturus' nobis priores excessus omnino displicuisse,

175, 4, 30, patriciatus culmen ascende . . . facturus omnia quae tantam reverentiam decent.

Purpose is implied in several of the examples of the future participle, not only after verbs of motion, but also after verbs of rest and condition. The earlier examples of this participle used with an implication of purpose are after verbs of motion, but in the Bellum Africanum and in Livy it occurs with verbs of rest. The usage with verbs of rest is frequent in Tacitus and later writers (L.-Hof., 607).

Examples from the Variae are chiefly with verbs of motion, e. g.

32, 3, 22, Helladius de medio, voluptatem populi praestaturus, introeat,

33, 2, 17, ut non . . . naves frumentis oneret ad aliena litora transituras

125, 1, 14, quis enim palaestricae artis ignarus in stadium luctaturus introeat?

132, 3, 22, vestris intentionibus responsurus occurrat.

152, 4, 33, conducat eum classibus serviturum,

255, 2, 7, ad . . . antistitem negotium suum dicturus occurreret,

255, 4, 22, ad saecularia fora iurgaturus occurrat.

346, 2, purpuram adoraturus accede,

The following illustrate the usage with verbs of rest:

26, 4, 29, Aequitatem nobis placiturus intende:

72, 17, 32, sapientia vestra eligat praesenti tempore meliorem, facturus aliquid Orphei, cum dulci sono gentilium fera corda domuerit.

(Note also the unrelated participle. Cf. p. 179.)

4. Participles Lacking Grammatical Agreement

In the Variae there are rather frequent examples of the participle, usually the present and the future active, used without grammatical agreement with any substantive. From the general context the reader can determine the person or thing with which the " dangling " participle logically agrees, but the strict grammatical agreement which generally prevails in classical authors is not always observed in the language of Cassiodorus.

Among the absolute uses of the participle in the Variae listed by Traube, 566, is the following, 59, 1, 15, nam quod ornat nomen Romanum, a vobis legitur institutum. ad hoc patres in illo principio nominati, ut quasi filiorum per vos possit vita componi. It seems reasonable, however, to consider *nominati* the equivalent of a finite verb through the ellipsis of *sunt*. While it is true that Cassiodorus does not regularly employ such an ellipsis, the usage occurs frequently in Livy, Tacitus, and other historians (Cf. K.-Steg., II, 1, 13).

Nominati may possibly be a vocative. A similar use of the same word, where the context makes it appear to be vocative, occurs in 116, 5, 30. Cf. p. 10.

A similar ellipsis of *sumus* can be presumed in 177, 2, 17, sed hac sola ratione discreti (sumus), quod alteri subdi non possumus. . . .

In many examples a previous sentence furnishes the substantive with which the participle, which appears unrelated, is in grammatical agreement. An illustration of this type of agreement is 185, 2, 13 ff., quapropter nos dedimus delectabilem honorem, *tu* conversationis associa dignitatem, nam utraque sibi coniuncta sunt: unum pendet ex altero: non coalescunt sparsa semina, nisi et terrae qualitas fuerit operata: *habiturus* messem de nostra gratia copiosam, si, *etc.* Here, if we disregard or consider as parenthetical the intervening clauses *nam . . . operata*, we find *habiturus* in agreement with *tu*.

A similar explanation can be advanced for the following:

21, 3, 27, *aestimandus* in agreement with the subject of *conscenderet*, 21, 3, 26.

101, 2, 30, *adiciens* in agreement with the subject of *allegasti*, 101, 2, 25.

126, 3, 12, *subiungens* in agreement with *Petrus*, 126, 2, 6.

132, 2, 17, *addentes* in agreement with the subject of *allegatis*, 132, 2, 13.

159, 2, 27, *adiciens* in agreement with the subject of *clamat*, 159, 1, 24. 302, 2, 28, *ostentans* in agreement with *Patricius*, 302, 2, 26.

A few examples admit of explanation as the nominative absolute construction. I have listed on page 14 four examples in which substantive and participle are both expressed in what is clearly a nominative absolute usage.

In other examples the participle alone is expressed in the absolute construction, e. g., 49, 16 ff., definimus, ut quicquid ad Antiochum, siliquatici vel monopolii titulos exercentem, nostra iussione pertinuit, ad te ratione simili transferatur, contra omnium calumnantium insidias salva aequitate praesenti auctoritate *munitus*: *habiturus* etiam amminicula saionis, *etc.*   Here it is obvious that *munitus* and *habiturus* logically agree with *tu*, which word, however, does not occur, but is merely implied in the phrase *ad te*.

A similar example is 59, 2, 21 ff., Igitur provinciarum iudicum relatione ad magnificum virum praefectum praetorii directa comperimus sic primae transmissionis tempus exemptum, ut nihil aut parum a senatoriis domibus constet illatum: *allegantes* per hanc difficultatem tenues deprimi, quos decuerat sublevari . . . , praeterea multo acerbiora *iungentes,* etc. Here the participles *allegantes* and *iungentes* belong logically with *iudices*, but the only occurrence of that word is the genitive *iudicum*.

Other examples where the participle can not agree with any expressed substantive, though the substantive with which it logically should agree can always be determined, are the following:

60,	5,	9,	*relaturi*	158, 2, 30,	*properantes*
72, 17, 32,			*facturus*	163, 2, 27,	*concedentes*
102,	4,	9,	*reformatus*	163, 3, 31,	*muniti*
105,	4, 28,		*docentes*	312, 1, 21,	*Suscipientes*
109,	5,	8,	*accepturus*	320, 1, 10,	*dirigentes*
114,	3, 14,		*imitantes*	346, 22,	*exhibiturus*
119,	2,	7,	*iungentes*	366, 2, 4,	*commendantes*

CHAPTER VII

The Syntax of Coordination

I. *Person*

1. Agreement According to Sense

The agreement in person of a verb with its subject is in the Variae sometimes according to sense rather than according to strict grammatical agreement. This usage is in general in conformity with the practice of classical authors, but some of the examples are rather striking, e. g.

256, 3, 10, serenitas nostra vel inchoatae voluntatis desiderium vel Tuluin plenissimae donationis effectum . . . corroboramus
301, 2, 16, Si quis habuerit cum altero forte negotium, ad communia iura descendite:
314, 2, 26, illustris magnitudo vestra . . . censitote . . .
366, 3, 21, Qua de re spectabilitas tua . . . exactionem facies sub hac condicione removeri

2. Impersonal Verbs Used Personally

The following verbs, ordinarily impersonal, occur at times in the personal construction in the Variae.

constare, e. g. 94, 1, 23, eius reparationem exigere, quae ornatum constat nostrae rei publicae continere.
    Constare occurs thus in two doubtful passages in Cicero. First certain examples are Late Latin; Rufin., Epiphan., Oribas., Novell., Greg. M. (T. L. L., IV, 535, 49 ff.).
decere, e. g. 16, 1, 28, decet principem cura
    32, 4, 4, numquid inter ista rixae decent . . . ?
    The personal use is rare in classical prose except with a neuter pronoun as subject. It is more frequent in poetry and in Silver and Late Latin (Cf. T. L. L., V, 131, 42 ff.).
oportere, e. g. 170, 3, 17, si nostri propter expulsus est, non oportuerat cum divitiis ad aliena regna transmitti.
    The personal construction occurs first in Caelius and is frequent in Late Latin (L.-Hof., 622).
paenitere, e. g. 314, 3, 13, ut tali facto eam non paeniteret mutata religio.
    The usage of *paenitere* with a personal subject occurs in an inter-

180

polated passage in Plautus. It does not occur again until
Corippus and Cassiodorus (L.-Hof., 407).

II. Voice
(L.-Hof. 542-547)
1. Intransitive Verbs Used Transitively

A number of verbs which are ordinarily intransitive but which
occur in the Variae with the accusative have been mentioned under
the accusative, p. 15.

2. Transitive Verbs Used Absolutely

The following verbs which regularly take the accusative occur at
times absolutely in the Variae:

praestare = give, e. g. 4, 7, 9, sic petentibus praestando gratis sub
continentiae munere cuncta mercaris. Cf. also 255, 3, 15.

trahere = endure, continue, 331, 1, 7, per sanctos viros acceleratum
est, ne traheret diutius quod gravabat.

vehere = travel, 373, 7, 21, praesulibus annonas praeberi secundum
vetera constituta decernimus, suis expensis facta tarditate vecturis.
(Absolute use " rare and perh. only in the part. pres. and in the
gerund "—Harpers'.)

Note also the absolute use of *perfrui*, 284, 6, 10, libido est, et
recte perfrui non sinitur, and *indigere*, 383, 1, 24, nam si nullum
penitus indigere contingeret, locum proinde largitas non haberet.

3. Intransitive Verbs Used Impersonally in the Passive

Cassiodorus frequently uses intransitive verbs impersonally in
the passive. Except for greater relative frequency in the occurrence of this construction, the usage is classical. The following
are typical examples:

3, 4, 14, mox ut coepero, clamoribus imminetur.

18, 1, 10, Tuta est condicio subiectorum, ubi vivitur sub aequitate
regnantium:

82, 1, 16, ad quem vix maturis aetatibus pervenitur

114, 3, 17, quiescitur in ipsis potius quam laboretur

121, 3, 31, pareatur ergo, patres conscripti, viro multis temporibus iam
probato,

132, 1, 30, conquereris . . . eo usque perventum, ut indefensus . . .
damnareris:

169, 5, 7, Itur ergo ad talia, quae refugere deberet humanitas.
186, 1, 18, considerandum, quali labore servitum est
204, 4, 3, ad necessitatem siquidem rarius venitur armorum
227, 3, 14, quoniam illi volumus subveniri qui duris necessitatibus
  probatur astringi:

4. Ellipsis of the Infinitive After *Posse*

The ellipsis of the infinitive after *posse,* so that in effect this verb itself becomes transitive, is cited by the lexica only for Livy and Silver writers. Cassiodorus employs it thus in 308, 1, 6, nam cum deo praestante possimus omnia, sola nobis credimus licere laudanda.

5. The Passive Used As Middle

The following seems to be an example of the use of the passive in the sense of a middle voice:

94, 2, 1, pretiosior factus cunctis, quia nullo praemio vendebaris.

6. Deponents Used as Passive

Occasionally a deponent verb is used as a passive. Classical prose at times used the perfect participle of deponents in a passive sense, as in the following example from the Variae, 338, 9, 33, adepta securitate gaudentes.

The following infinitives of deponents occur in a passive meaning:

ammirari, 362, 1, 20, in principali convivio hoc profecto decet exquiri, quod visum debeat ammirari.
  The use of this verb in the passive is cited only for Hemina Prisc. gramm., Canut. Prisc. gramm., Greg. M., and Cassiodorus, this passage (T. L. L., I, 740, 47 ff.).
hortari, 303, 1, 32, a vestra potius clementia deberemur hortari.
  The perfect participle occurs in a passive meaning in the Bell. Hisp. *Hortaretur* as a passive occurs in Varro as quoted by Priscian; cf. Gell. 15, 13, 1 (Harpers').

7. Assimilation in Voice of Auxiliary Verb

The use of the passive form *deberemur* in the above example is an illustration of the assimilation of the voice of the auxiliary verb to that of the infinitive. This construction was used in the case of other auxiliary verbs in Early Latin, is found as an archaism

in poetry and in Sallust, and is revived in certain Late authors
(L.-Hof., 543). A passive form of *debere* as an auxiliary verb is
cited only for Greg. M. and Corp. VI 8520 in T. L. L., V, 95, 41;
and in a weakened sense, where apparently the idea of obligation has been lost, only for Greg. Tur. in T. L. L., V, 101, 55.

III. *Tense*
(L.-Hof. 552-565)
1. Shifting of Tenses

While in general the various tenses of the indicative are used in
the Variae just as they are in classical prose, some examples occur
in which it is evident that the author pays less attention to exactness in the use of the tenses than was the rule in classical Latin.
Late Latin in general was affected by the phonetic falling together
of various tense forms, and the analogy of such forms as had
fallen together sufficed to weaken the distinction of tenses in such
forms as were not affected by this phenomenon of phonetics (Cf.
L.-Hof., 553; 562; 572).

Various employments of one tense for another in the infinitive,
participle, and subjunctive in the Variae have already been mentioned. The indicative is also affected in several ways. A few of
the more striking examples will be mentioned here.

a. PRESENT INDICATIVE FOR FUTURE

78, 4, 23, nam ille me iure sustinebit adversum, qui vobis *nititur* esse
    contrarius.
193, 5, 28, institue pecunias non quaerere et *agnoscis* munera tibi
    copiosa provenire.
202, 3, 25, horre vitium et principis *mereris* affectum
213, 1, 19, Considera quid suscipis, et *intellegis* locum te dare non
    debere peccatis.
337, 2, 22, studete cuncti actibus bonis et formidanda nescitis.
365, 2, 20, ubi iam, male capientes, spem habebitis, quando vobis et
    rerum domini et vestri iudices *comminantur*?
379, 7, 12, Pretia vero vobis moderata sequenti occasione *declaramus*,
    cum nobis praesentium gerulus nativitatis modum missa
    relatione suggesserit.

The historical present does not occur in the Variae. The work
contains few narrative passages, and the author uses chiefly the

perfect indicative for whatever narrative he presents.   It should
be observed also that he does not employ the imperfect as an aorist,
as is frequently done in Late Latin (Cf. L.-Hof., 560).

b. FUTURE INDICATIVE FOR PRESENT

All of Cassiodorus' uses of the future as the equivalent of a
present appear to be examples of the gnomic future, which is classical (Cf. L.-Hof., 555).   Thus, examples of the following type,
though the present could be used, are not at variance with classical
syntax:

50, 2, 2, in procinctu semper *erit*, qui barbaros prohibere contendit,
123, 1, 32, quem enim *sperabit* veniae locum, qui reverendum con-
tempsit auctorem?

A future indicative of this kind is preceded and followed by the
present indicative in 53, 1, 15, inimicum trucem ratio ipsa professionis *ostendit:* iratum plerumque *poteris* invenire collegam: in-
obedientem vero filium declinare poenas non *permittit* humanitas.

Another example of gnomic future is *debebunt* in 54, 5, 4, Quid
ergo homines facere debebunt, quando hanc pietatem et in avibus
inesse cognoscunt?   *Debebunt facere* seems here to have its proper
force, i. e., obligation, and is not a mere periphrasis for *facient*
(Cf. L.-Hof. 558; Salonius, 283, for discussion of such a periphrastic use of *debere*.   See also p. 200 for the use of the present
of *debere* in a similar usage in the Variae).

c. PAST TENSE FOR FUTURE

Traube, 590, gives two examples of the use of a past tense for
the future, 4, 9, 21, quos si celebrandos posteris tradas, *abstulisti*,
consuetudine maiorum, morientibus decenter interitum, and 41,
11, 30, praedicta nobis horologia quantocius transmittere maturabis, ut te notum in illa mundi parte facias, ubi aliter pervenire
non *poteras*.

I have cited the first of these examples among the conditional
sentences, p. 247.   The perfect *abstulisti* appears to be used to
give greater emphasis to the conclusion by representing it as an
already established fact.   This is a stereotyped usage of the perfect;
even Cicero has a few examples (Cf. L.-Hof., 773).

With regard to the second example Traube notes that the use of *poteras* is *propter consonantiam,* which is perhaps the best explanation of its use.

d. PERFECT FOR IMPERFECT

The perfect indicative occurs in some examples where the imperfect would appear to be the natural tense. Thus the perfect with such words as *frequenter, saepius, semper,* is sometimes used for repeated action, e. g.

4, 11, 27, *Dixisti* etiam ad commendationem universitatis frequenter reginis ac regibus laudes:

30, 1, 21, Animum nostrum . . . *pulsavit* saepius querela populorum

Note the perfect followed by the imperfect where both seem to denote habitual action,

174, 2, 8, Per illam nimirum status imperii iugitur *crevit,* illam semper felix Roma *suscepit.* merito pridem genus *habebatur* imperii: merito supra omnes cives *poterat,* qui ab hoste patriam *vindicabat.*

e. PLUPERFECT FOR PERFECT

Traube, 590, notes the use of the pluperfect for the perfect in the following sentence *item consonantiae necessitate,*

23, 1, 3, manum porrigimus oneratis, ut pietatis nostrae remedio *surgant* qui fortunae suae acerbitate *corruerant.*

His brief statement confined to one example is likely to be misleading. The fact is that the use of the pluperfect is rather frequent, and in most of the examples similarity of ending plays no part. The following are additional examples of this usage:

17, 1, 9, cognovimus in ea te, qua non *decuerat,* actione versatum . . .

17, 1, 11, affinitatem quippe tuam solacia *debuerant* impensa testari.

17, 2, 16, perire enim pupillo non patimur quod parentibus sub nostra laude *dederamus.*

48, 4, 16, *aequiperaverat* prorsus meritis quos lectitarat auctores. commendavit etiam studiorum bona per benignitatis insignia:

51, 2, 9, Dudum siquidem aestimatis meritis Sabino aurigae unum solidum menstruum *feceramus*: nunc autem quamvis histrio honesta nos supplicatione permovit

52, 3, 13, hinc etiam prius praecepta *dederamus* et nunc iterata iussione repetimus

57, 1, 9, quis enim ferat in domesticis praesidiis locum fuisse periculis et ibi inventum dulcis vitae exitum, unde nasci
debuerat defensionis auxilium?

58, 2, 6, loca . . . inutiliter occupata largitas nostra *concesserat,*
ubi aquarum vasta profunditas terrenam gratiam in nullos
usus profuturos absorbuerat.

92, 1, 16, titulum, quem fidae dominicatus iure *dederamus* . . . ordinatio tibi nostra committit.

125, 1, 2, beneficio tuo rediviva *consurgant,* quae annositate inclinata
corruerant.
(Note the similarity of endings—*consurgant-corruerant.*)

144, 2, 22, loqui datur, quod nos sensisse nescimus, sed post casum
reminiscimur quod ignorantes veraciter *dixeramus.*

316, 4, 14, *Desederat* quidem dolor, sed dimittit reliquias fortiores . . .

338, 6, 19, nemo a nobis quam *venerat* minus locupletior redit.

Similar displacement of the perfect by the pluperfect occurs in
individual instances in all periods of Latin prose, even the classical.
Various causes contribute to the process, such as similarity of ending, assimilation to another pluperfect form, even independently of
similar sound, and the fact that in many verbs a phonetic falling
together of present and perfect active occurred, while the pluperfect form, on the contrary, showed a past form which could not be
doubted. A still greater influence was exerted in the passive voice
by the tendency to represent the tense of the compounded verb by
the same tense of *esse* for greater clearness, and the analogy of the
passive forms also affected the active. All these influences tended,
especially in Latin Latin, toward substitution of the pluperfect for
the perfect even in main clauses (Cf. L.-Hof., 562).

2. Epistolary Tenses

In epistolary correspondence the Romans regularly took the view-
point of the receiver of the letter with regard to the tenses used.
This, however, is not a hard and fast rule, and inconsistencies sometimes occur. Cicero occasionally adapts his tenses to his own view-
point and writes *scribo* and *respondeo* instead of the corresponding
perfect forms. Pliny and later writers are much less exact than
Cicero (Cf. K.-Steg., II, 1, 156-159).

Cassiodorus generally uses the epistolary tenses, but many inconsistencies occur. Thus, e. g., following shortly after the perfect in
80, 4, 32, quapropter ad excellentiam vestram illum et illum legatos

nostros magnopere *credidimus* dirigendos, per quos etiam ad fratrem vestrum, filium nostrum regem Alaricum scripta nostra *direximus,* we find the present in 81, 4, 2, Per eos etiam et verbo vobis aliqua dicenda *mandamus.* . . .

A similar use of *mandamus* occurs in 115, 4, 13, reliqua per illum et illum legatos nostros patrio sermone *mandamus.* Contrast with this present the use of the perfect of *mandare,* followed, however, by the present of *declarare* in 144, 3, 10, aliqua vobis etiam per legatos vestros verbo *mandavimus,* per quos, quae grata esse debeant, nos destinasse *declaramus.*

Declarare occurs elsewhere in the present also, e. g., 143, 3, 15, Proinde per illum et illum legatos vestros . . . arma vestra libenter nos accepisse declaramus. . . .

In 143, 2, 26, *indicamus* sucina, quae a vobis per harum portitores directa sunt, grato animo fuisse suscepta. quae ad vos Oceani unda descendens hanc levissimam substantiam, sicut et vestrorum relatio *continebat,* exportat, the tense of *indicamus* is adapted to the time of the writer, not that of the reader, while *continebat* has reference to the message, written or oral, which the writer is answering and which might have been regarded as present before him.

IV. *Interrogative Particles*
(L.-Hof. 648-649)

Interrogative particles rarely occur in direct questions in the *Variae. Nonne,* the most frequent, occurs about fifteen times. Its place is taken by *non* in 53, 2, 22, pro dolor! non merebimur eorum affectum, pro quibus subire non recusamus exitium? The use of *non* for *nonne* is rare in all periods, but is not unknown even in Cicero.

Num does not occur. Its functions began to be assumed by *numquid* even in Early Latin. It had faded from popular speech in the Early Empire, and is totally lacking in many Late authors. *Numquid* itself is extremely rare in the Variae, occurring in place of *num* e. g., in 205, 1, 18, sed numquid per ea vivitur . . . ? and 292, 11, 25, num quid tali actione praesumens aliqua se elatione iactavit . . . ?

The enclitic -*ne,* which becomes rare in Late Latin, occurs only in 136, 5, 1, hoc imitarine queunt, qui se ad publicas necessitates electos esse cognoscunt? Its unusual position in this sentence, i. e., attached to the infinitive, shows the artificial nature of its usage here.

V. *Co-ordinating Conjunctions*

(L.-Hof. 656-686)

The enclitic -que, which began in the Early Empire to vanish from popular speech and is totally lacking in certain Late authors, occurs very rarely in the Variae, e. g., 27, 2, 26, armis equis rebusque omnibus necessariis sufficienter instructi. It adds an accusative of inner object to several adverbs in 72, 13, 14, quicquid excellenter, quicquid ponderatim, quicquid rauce, quicquid purissime *aliasque distantias* sonat.

Ideoque is rather frequent in place of *ideo*, e. g., 18, 2, 2, ideoque devotio tua . . . postulatas res praedicto tutori faciat sine dilatione restitui. The use of *ideoque* for *ideo* begins with Tertullian (L.-Hof., 657).

Atque and *ac* are used frequently to join things of equal rank or importance, e. g., 147, 1, 19, illud atque illud. This usage as the exact equivalent of *et* occurs rarely in all periods (Cf. T. L. L., II, 1058, 55 ff.). *Atque* occurs in a list of names with no connectives preceding it and is itself followed by *nec non,* in 124, 3, 8, patriciis viris Symmacho Decio Volusiano atque Caeliano nec non illustri viro Maximiano. *Atque* is frequently used at the beginning of a sentence as a transitional particle, e. g., 163, 1, 20, atque ideo discant rerum bonarum suavissimum saporem. . . . The usage is classical, but somewhat rare (Cf. T. L. L., II, 1076, 18 ff.). Moreover, the combination of *atque* with *ideo,* as in the above example, is not found until Columella.

Et occurs in its customary meaning of *and*; also as an emphatic particle, = *etiam*. In some instances it gives way to *atque, sive,* or *vel*. Note its use after asyndeton and its use in juxtaposition with other conjunctions in the following:

115, 2, 6, equos enses clipeos et reliqua instrumenta bellorum
160, 1, 14, indictionum octavae nonae undecimae primae secundae et
    quintae decimae
160, 1, 17, suscipiens Marcum presbyterum, Andream et Simeonium
    vel reliquos,

Nec occurs frequently as the equivalent of *ne . . . quidem*, e. g.,

3, 4, 13, mihi nec horarum momenta praestantur;
364, 7, 32, ut . . . nec divina domus videatur excepta.
(Cf. Traube, 562)

The use of *nec* for *ne . . . quidem* occurs in Silver Latin and is especially frequent in the Late period (L.-Hof., 641).

Sive occurs frequently as the equivalent of *et*, e. g., 275, 5, Universis Gothis Sive Romanis (Cf. Traube, 585). The usage is frequent in Late Latin.

Sive . . . sive also occurs rather frequently for *et . . . et*, e. g., 310, 3, 33, ut sive beatissimus papa sive senatus amplissimus sine aliqua dilatione respondeant. . . . Both these usages of *sive* are frequent in very late Latin (L.-Hof., 677).

Vel is frequent as the equivalent of *et*, e. g., 63, 2, 12, ut praediis vel hominibus huius ecclesiae intra Siciliam constitutis tuitionem studeas salva civilitate praestare. . . . Also *vel . . . vel* = *et . . . et*, e. g., 52, 1, 2, ideo enim iura vel divina vel publica nexum coniugii tanta cautela praecipiunt custodiri, ut, *etc.* (Cf. Traube, 593). The use of *vel* for *et* and of *vel . . . vel* for *et . . . et* begins in Late Latin (L.-Hof., 676).

VI. *Rhetorical and Exclamatory Questions*
(L.-Hof. 574; 591; 645; 647; 652)

The so-called rhetorical question and the exclamatory question occur rather frequently in the Variae. No notable divergences from classical usage occur in the use of the indicative and subjunctive. Questions of an exclamatory nature are regularly in the indicative. The infinitive is not used for exclamation.

1. Examples of the indicative use in indignant questions or in questions suggesting their own answer:

31, 4, 10, quid enim discrepat a peccante, qui se per excessum nititur vindicare?
32, 4, 4, numquid inter ista rixae decent aut inflammata contentio?
38, 2, 23, et quid illa re publica gratia non potuit obtinere parentis, quae sic facillime favet extraneis?
53, 2, 18, propago vitis propriae servit origini: et discrepat homo a suo fusus initio?

2. Examples of the deliberate subjunctive:

29, 5, 22, Mores autem graves in spectaculis quis requirat?
35, 1, 6, quis enim ferat hominem ad leges trahere, qui matrimonii
            nisus est iura violare?
53, 2, 19, quid dicamus illa beneficia, quae vel extraneam possint
            obligare personam?
63, 3, 31, cur enim illud tardemus annuere, unde nulla possumus
            damna sentire?
167, 4, 2, cur tardaret negotii finis, cum tu suggestionem lucida bre-
            vitate concluderes?
285, 1, 28, nam quis eligeret tam longe petere, quod in suis videret
            sedibus advenisse?

3. Examples of exclamatory question:

12, 7, 7, Verum talis tantaque res quam facili legitur inventa com-
            pendio!
20, 2, 22, quid enim advocationis officio, si pure impendatur, orna-
            tius . . . ?
41, 8, 7, Quale est hoc homini etiam facere, quod vel intellexisse
            potest esse mirabile?
41, 12, 31, quotiens non sunt credituri quae viderint? quotiens hanc
            veritatem lusoria somnia putabunt?

VII. *The Optative Subjunctive*
(L.-Hof. 568-571)

Cassiodorus uses the optative subjunctive in the classical manner
as a rule. His usual manner of expressing a wish is without *utinam*
or any other introductory particle, e. g.

34, 2, 29, prosit ergo generi, quod potuit unius devotione praestari,
46, 1, 4, Felix a consule sumat annus auspicium portamque dierum
            tali nomine dicatum tempus introeat faveatque reliquae
            parti fortuna principii.
78, 4, 21, avertant enim divina, ut supra vos iniquitas illa praevaleat.
86, 2, 5, quod felicibus sanciatur auspiciis

Utinam, however, occurs in a few instances, e. g.

5, 17, 24, sed utinam, sicut ista regulis accepisse probamur antiquis,
            ita eadem promissae resignent merita dictionis.
304, 2, 24, atque utinam nobis Marios vel Corvinos annosior vita ser-
            vasset!
366, 2, 29, atque utinam possessor ultroneus et nobis necessitatem
            morarum tolleret et sibi damna competentibus illationibus
            abrogaret!

I have observed one example with *o si,* viz., 354, 2, 4, o si tecum liceret longis habitare temporibus! The usage of *o si* with the optative begins with Vergil and continues to be used in rare examples in Silver and Late Latin (L.-Hof., 569).

Absit ut occurs in 78, 2, 7, absit ut vobis aliquid indignatio caeca subripiat. The usage occurs in Lucan, Apuleius, Tertullian, and is frequent throughout ecclesiastical Latin (T. L. L., II, 210, 74; 211, 6 ff. Cf. K.-Steg., II, 2, 238).

A more frequent use in the Variae is *absit* with a personal subject, or with the relative *quod* referring to the thing just mentioned, e. g.

24, 1, 9, nisi, quod absit, velitis excedere.
83, 2, 26, ut . . . nunc non videamini, quod absit, in parvitate peccare.
       T. L. L., II, 210, 84 ff. cites this usage for Quintilian and
       Apuleius.

The use of *absit* with a noun subject occurs from Cicero on (Cf. T. L. L., II, 210, 37 ff.). Cassiodorus has several examples, e. g.

80, 3, 27, absit ille conflictus, ubi unus ex vobis dolere possit inclinatus.

It will be observed that in all the examples so far cited the tenses of the subjunctive are used precisely as they are in classical prose. In one type of example, which occurs several times, the perfect subjunctive is used, e. g., 88, 2, 13, quod feliciter dictum sit; 234, 3, 7, quod auspice deo dictum sit. Cf. also 235, 2, 5; 274, 4, 6; 275, 1, 11; 287, 4, 28. Early Latin at times used the perfect subjunctive in such wishes as *di melius faxint* without distinction in meaning from the present. Occasionally, too, the perfect occurs with a reference to the past, one such example occurring in Cicero rep. 4, 8 (L.-Hof., 569). The position of the wish in Cassiodorus' examples, i. e., preceding the thing said, makes it appear to be used in the first of these two ways = *May it be said happily!* If it is to be interpreted thus, it should be classed as an archaism. Similar expressions occur in Fronto and in Ammianus (T. L. L., V, 969, 57 and 975, 18).

VIII. *The Potential Subjunctive*
(L.-Hof. 571-572)

1. Without Introductory Particle

Cassiodorus uses the potential subjunctive in the present and the perfect in conformity with classical usage. The following are typical examples:

165, 6, 13, quacumque gente sint editi,
299, 5, 13, viderim quae lectio acuat ingenium: divina semper efficere
       nititur pium.
373, 7, 24, alii dicant insulas, ego habitationes tuas appellem potius
       Fortunatas.
385, 7, 3, pace tanti patris dixerim: quanto praestantius est, *etc.*

I have noted a combining of the potential and the final sub-junctives in 4, 10, 24, celas etiam, ut ita dixerim, speculum mentis tuae. . . . The combining of these two uses of the subjunctive occurs first in Cicero and later increases in frequency (L.-Hof., 571). The perfect subjunctive occurs in examples identical with or very similar to the above *ut ita dixerim* in Pliny, Quintilian, Minucius Felix, Tertullian, Macrobius, and Cassianus (Cf. T. L. L., V, 973, 37). An example of a similar combining of the final and potential ideas after *forsitan* occurs in 29, 4, 19, Sed ne forsitan magnificos viros loquacitas popularis offenderit, praesumptionis huius habenda discretio est.

Note the use of the perfect subjunctive, *offenderit.*

The use of the imperfect subjunctive as a potential had vanished from popular speech in the Late Latin period, but continued to be used at times in literature. It occurs very rarely in the Variae, e. g., 65, 2, 28, Deberemus itaque celatores deputatae pecuniae in-modica poena percellere. . . .

In classical prose, the pluperfect subjunctive does not occur in the potential use except with *forsitan, fortasse,* etc. (L.-Hof., 572). Subordinate clauses in the subjunctive are in general, how-ever, affected by a tense-shift, which, beginning with Cicero and increasing in frequency of occurrence in Silver and Late Latin, substituted the pluperfect subjunctive for the imperfect. In Late Latin all types of subordinate clauses were thus affected (L.-Hof., 562). This shifting of tenses seems to account for Cassiodorus' use of the pluperfect subjunctive in subordinate clauses of a poten-tial nature, e. g.

119, 28,   non enim decet post audientiam vestram negotium trahi, a
       quo post alios iudices debuisset audiri.

122, 1, 22, aurum exsecrabili quaesisse fertur affectu, quem suam decuisset egentibus dare substantiam
134, 1, 23, decet enim a vobis corrigi, quod a vestris familiaribus non
debuisset admitti.

2. *Forsitan, Fortasse, Fortassis, Forte*
(L.-Hof. 572)

A. *Forsitan* occurs frequently in the Variae, especially with the
potential subjunctive, and in conditions, in which uses it is classical. It occurs also in *ne-* final clauses. *Ne forsitan* is cited first
for Tertullian in T. L. L., VI, 1139, 17.

Examples with the potential subjunctive:

78, 3, 12, non optamus aliquid tale fieri, unde unum minorem contingat forsitan inveniri.
123, 2, 7, sit hoc forsitan sub quiete tolerandum: nunc autem . . ..
mercium dominis interim consulamus.
300, 3, 6, arduum sibi hoc forsitan aestiment impares mores.
314, 1, 22, ad misericordiam forsitan pascantur otiosi:
330, 20, 24, quaeratis forsitan sequestratim principis bona:

Examples with *ne* in final clauses:

161, 1, 33, ne forsitan, ut assolet, eum non veritas, sed infamaret
invidia.
256, 4, 19, Sed ne quis forsitan tam egregiae voluntatis nostrae invidus
temerator existat, iubemus, *etc.*
277, 4, 21, Et ne forsitan credatis longinquitatis difficultate latere quae
gesta sunt, Siculis fiduciam vos dedimus subsequendi.

In the following example it occurs in a condition of the less
vivid type:

130, 1, 25, proavorum forsitan oblitterentur exempla, si longi generis
minus facta recolantur.
Cf. p. 245.

It is used also in the contrary to fact condition, e. g.

81, 1, 8, Si te aut nobilitas sola decoraret aut meritorum tantum
laude polleres, conferendas forsitan dignitates dilatione
probabili libraremus

Forsitan also occurs with the indicative. This usage begins with
Lucretius and is not found in classical prose, but occurs occasionally
in the Augustan poets and is more frequent in Silver and Late
Latin.

The following are typical examples:

62, 4, 26, nec quicquam in his debes metuere, quae forsitan novella
        usurpatione temptantur.
168, 3, 31, sed solum Erebi potentem non improbe forsitan aestimarunt
212, 3, 2, credet forsitan cursus appetere
232, 5, 6, aliquid forsitan et amplius mereor sinceritatis
240, 7, 26, unius forsitan ictus sollerter eluditur:

It occurs with the indicative in the conclusion of a contrary to
fact condition, but with a modal verb, e. g.,

233, 1, 28, Si vos externus heres imperii suscepisset, dubitare forsitan
        poteratis,

It occurs in a subordinate clause with *dum* in 291, 3, 32, a quibus
dum vicissitudo praemiorum forsitan quaeritur, laboris taedia non
vitantur.

T. L. L. does not mention a use of *forsitan* with *dum*, though
cum forsitan is cited for Livy (T. L. L., VI, 1139, 35).

Forsitan occurs with a perfect participle in 119, 3, 16, nec liceat
cuiquam sua sponte nisi obligatum forsitan pignus auferre.   The
use of *forsitan* with adjectives and participles is rare and occurs
chiefly in Silver and Late Latin (Cf. T. L. L., VI, 1139, 83).

B. *Fortasse* occurs in classical prose regularly with the indicative.   The subjunctive occurs occasionally in the same type of
clauses in which *forsitan* with the subjunctive is employed, and increases in frequency in Silver and Late Latin (Cf. T. L. L., VI,
1141, 53 ff.).

Cassiodorus uses it much less frequently than *forsitan*, chiefly
with the future perfect (unless the form in -*erit* is a perfect subjunctive) in conditions, e. g.

86, 1, 5, nostram invidiam tangit, si quid vobis fortasse defuerit
147, 2, 27, quod si . . . solvere intra praefinitum tempus fortasse
        potuerit, universa ei quae sublata sunt illibata reddantur,
203, 2, 2, si quod etiam inter Gothum et Romanum natum fuerit for-
        tasse negotium, . . . certamen possit aequabili ratione
        discingere.

It also occurs with the perfect subjunctive in a potential usage,
e. g.

119, 2, 12, hoc hactenus fieri nostri ignorantia fortasse pertulerit:
        nunc necesse est remedium de legibus habeat

C. Fortassis, equivalent in function to *fortasse* (Cf. T. L. L., VI, 1143, 23), occurs very rarely, e. g., with the subjunctive, 256, 3, 15; with the indicative, 307, 3, 15.

D. *Forte* in the meaning of *fortasse* is classical only after *si*, *nisi*, *ne*. No certain example of its use in this sense without these participles occurs before Horace. The usage is rare in Silver, but more frequent in Late Latin (Cf. T. L. L., VI, 1131, 71 ff.; K.-Steg., II, 1, 812).

Cassiodorus uses it alone rather frequently, both with the indicative e. g., 34, 4, 11; 100, 3, 22; 223, 2, 14; 250, 5, 19, and the subjunctive e. g., 37, 1, 14; 183, 5, 20; 251, 1, 28.

3. The Indefinite Second Person
(L.-Hof. 623; cf. 571)

The indefinite second person singular occurs in the Variae in stereotyped phrases with the verb in the present or imperfect subjunctive, e. g., 94, 2, 26 (and frequently), *videas*; 138, 4, 18, *crederes*; 139, 9, 9 (and frequently), *credas*; 157, 4, 9, *putes*. Also 137, 5, 19, *stupeas*, following closely after *videas*. In some instances the indefinite second person occurs in a consecutive clause or other subordinate clause requiring the subjunctive. However, in the greater number of examples the subjunctive is potential or used as an apodosis of an omitted condition.

In all uses of the indefinite second person, the context is the guide as to whether or not the subject is indefinite. In the examples given below any person, or at least any one of an indefinite number of persons, would serve equally well as the logical subject.

Cassiodorus also uses the indicative in this construction, though less frequently. In several examples both moods occur. The use of the indicative belongs largely to the lower type of colloquial speech, but occurs even in Cicero. Horace, Martial, and Juvenal are other writers cited for its use. Doubtful passages occur in Silver prose writers (Cf. Nutting, VIII, 241-250; 263-265).

Cassiodorus' usage of the indicative conforms to that of the other authors mentioned, in that the indefinite use is not restricted to stereotyped verbs, as is generally the case in the use of the subjunctive. Cf. the following examples:

82, 2, 23, quamvis fulgeant communione meritorum, invenies tamen
quem possis laudare de propriis.

83, 1, 32, nascitur de pietate crudelitas, si quem neglegis ammonere,
postea cogaris exigere.

108, 7, 1, arithmeticam indicas, auditoriis vacat.

108, 8, 5, fanaticum credis, quem tortuosis semitibus ambulare
conspexeris.

157, 3, 7, ut quem prae foribus haesitantem videras, eloquentem in
certaminibus obstupescas.

262, 5, 28, ut vacuum putes lacum, quem non dubitas esse plenissimum.

373, 5, 13, hoc quia modo non habet muros, civitatem credis ruralem,
villam iudicare possis urbanam

Note that in this last example the indicative *credis* and the subjunctive *possis* are used alike. Manuscript variants for *credis* are
credit, credas, and its total omission.

IX. *The Hortatory Subjunctive*
(L.-Hof. 572)

The hortatory subjunctive is rare in the Variae. The examples
which occur are classical, e. g.

26, 1, 2, quapropter votis paribus invitemur ad dona,

78, 3, 15, obiciamus quamvis cognato cum nostris coniuratis eximias
gentes iustitiamque

299, 6, 14, Veniamus ad illam privatae vitae largissimam frugalitatem

X. *Commands and Prohibitions*
(Cf. L.-Hof. 572-576)

It is natural that in such a work as the Variae commands and
prohibitions should be frequent. Many of the documents are letters written for an absolute ruler accustomed to giving orders to
his subjects. Books VI and VII, formulae of appointments to
office, necessitate the use of some jussive construction in nearly
every document. Even in the letters written in his own name,
Cassiodorus speaks as praetorian prefect to the two peoples who
recognize his word as law.

1. Affirmative Commands

For the affirmative command the imperative naturally is frequent in occurrence, chiefly the present imperative.

The future imperatives which occur are largely of the stereotyped class, as will be seen from the following list:

habetote,	42,	2,	8; 101, 3, 3; 237, 3, 4
facito,	63,	2,	2,
deligito	156,	3, 11,	
agito	162,	5, 18,	
caveto	162,	5, 18,	
adhibeto,	189,	4, 36,	
habeto,	192,	9, 23,	
scitote,	203,	2,	6,
exhibeto,	223,	2,	2,
censitote,	314,	2, 29,	
celebrato,	367,	3, 14,	(third person)

esto and *estote* (passim).

These are the only future imperatives which occur with any degree of frequency. Their total occurrences number about thirty.

The distinction in meaning between the present and the future imperative scarcely survived the classical period (L.-Hof., 576). In the Variae we find the future imperative paired with the present imperative or with a subjunctive, e. g.

192, 9, 23, *Indulge* te quoque nostro palatio: *habeto* fiduciam ingrediendi.

367, 3, 14, Quocirca experientia tua preces illius diligenti examinatione *discutiat* et si re vera ille . . . filios non reliquit . . . introductionem memoratae rei officium vestrum *celebrato* ex more.

The use of the future indicative in the sense of an imperative, while it occurs at all periods of the language, is largely colloquial. Late Latin uses the future freely for commands, often in conjunction with an imperative (L.-Hof., 555).

This usage is quite frequent in the Variae, e. g.

28, 3, 13, Cuncta ergo ad statutam praestationem facies sine dilatione revocari:

37, 1, 2, illustris sublimitas tua Salonitanis militibus . . . pro nostra iussione arma necessaria procurabit

41, 11, 29, praedicta nobis horologia quantocius transmittere maturabis,

Many commands are given by means of the jussive subjunctive. Cassiodorus uses this subjunctive in the classical manner (Cf. L.-Hof., 572-573). Thus the present subjunctive is in regular use;

the perfect is rare except in the case of the verb *nosse,* which occurs frequently, e. g., 39, 3, 17, noveritis; 133, 4, 25, noverit. This usage is classical. *Meminisse,* of course, occurs in the perfect form when it is used, e. g., 32, 3, 19, meminerint. The jussive use of the second person is very rare, as it was in classical prose except in Cicero's Letters. The third person, which was frequent at all times, is frequent in the Variae. Moreover, here as elsewhere, what is logically a sentence in the second person is often transformed into one which is grammatically in the third by the use of a title as subject, e. g., 19, 2, 1, Quapropter prudentia vestra . . . scelestam falsitatem a consortio veritatis eiciat; 22, 3, 23, celsitudo vestra . . . erigat humiles, eripiat opprimendos et . . . proficiat cunctis.

A good example of the alternate use of subjunctive and imperative occurs in 69, 9, 11 ff., Quapropter antiqua illic aedificiorum soliditas *innovetur,* ut sive in cuniculis sive in thermis fuerit aliquid reparandum, te debeat imminente reconstrui. virgulta quoque noxia importunitate nascentia evulsis cespitibus *auferantur,* ne radicum quidam capilli paulatim turgentes fabricarum visceribus inserantur et more vipereo prolem sibi fecunditate contraria nutriant, unde se compago casura disrumpat. Palatium quoque longa senectute quassatum assidua reparatione *corrobora.* spatium, quod inter aedem publicam et caput igniti fontis interiacet, silvestri asperitate *depurga. rideat* florenti gramine facies decora campestris: quin etiam ardentis aquae fertilitate laetatur miroque modo dum proxime salem generet sterilem, *nutriat* pariter et virores.

2. Prohibitions

Prohibitions or negative commands are usually expressed by the subjunctive in the Variae. Occasionally the classical *noli(-te)* with the infinitive is used, e. g., 31, 4, 8, nolite truculenter insequi inania verba populorum; 31, 1, 24, nolite modo vitia turbulenta contrahere; 255, 6, 31, nolite ad mortalium errores et humilia vota descendere.

The use of *cave (cavete, caveto)* with *ne* and the present subjunctive is also infrequent. It occurs, e. g., 52, 2, 24; 155, 2; 162, 5, 18; 305, 5, 9; 337, 6, 11; 368, 3, 28. The usage is classical. Cf. T. L. L., III, 634, 29 ff. *Cavete* with the infinitive occurs in 78,

1, 4, cavete subito in aleam mittere quos constat tantis temporibus exercitia non habere. This usage, though classical, is infrequent. Cf. T. L. L., III, 635, 68 ff.

The use of *ne* with the present subjunctive in prohibitions occurs in Early Latin; in the classical period it is found only in Cicero's Letters. In the subsequent periods it rarely occurs (L.-Hof., 573). Only a few examples occur in the Variae, e. g., 305, 1, 15, Ne quis nos, patres conscripti, in honoribus dandis non aestimet habuisse rationem, quod post insignia consulatus minora magis posterius conferamus. The nature of the sentence which follows is such that it would be impossible to explain the *ne*-clause as dependent upon it. Moreover the *ne* and *non* are not to be regarded as the equivalent of a mere *ut*. The meaning is: *Let no one* think that we have *not* a system, *etc.*

The following examples occur under circumstances where the *ne*-clause may possibly be a dependent final clause. They appear, however, to be prohibitive.

17, 3, 6, His sumptus subvectionesque praestabis: *ne* quemquam nostrum *gravet* imperium, quod ad utilitatem volumus respicere singulorum.
91, 3, 16, abiurator alieni furtum, non animam reddat: *ne* plus intentio civilis *rapiat* quam bella consumant:

By far the most frequent method of expressing prohibition in the Variae is by use of *non* or *nec* with the present subjunctive. This use of *non* in place of the more common *ne* is found rarely in Early Latin, occurs once in Cicero, but is more frequent in Livy, in poetry, and in Silver prose. It becomes much more frequent in Late Latin (L.-Hof., 573-574). The use of *nec* to introduce a prohibition following an affirmative command is classical (L.-Hof., 574).

Typical examples of *non* and *nec* in prohibitions:

26, 4, 29, non quaeras de potestate nostra . . . victorias
31, 5, 18, non permittatis ergo . . . fieri
36, 2, 18, Quos illustris magnificentia tua . . . in supra dicta urbe constituat: nec illis liceat ante discedere
80, 2, 22, virtus vestra patriae non fiat inopinata calamitas
106, 10, 20, (following an indicative) nec illud putetur irritum,
123, 2, 5, portus nostros navis veniens non pavescat,

135, 2,   navis eis usum . . . praeparate nec aliquid eis necessarium deesse faciatis,

The alternation of imperative, jussive, and prohibitive uses is well illustrated in 87, 3, 27 ff., *Age* igitur mandata, si cupis in te proficere nostra iudicia. turbulenta *non ames*: *avara declina,* ut talem te iudicem provincia fessa suscipiat, qualem Romanum principem transmisisse cognoscat. desiderat viros egregios coacta cladibus suis. *effice* ut victam fuisse delectet. *nihil* tale *sentiat* quale patiebatur, cum Romam quaereret.

XI. *Periphrasis*

(L.-Hof. 557-558 on *debere, posse,* and *velle*; Traube, 531, 569, 593)

Cassiodorus uses many verbs as auxiliaries. In some instances, as often in the case of *debere, posse,* and *velle,* the use of the auxiliary appears to be a circumlocution for the future; in other examples, the use of these and other verbs appears to be quite redundant. In still others, notably in the case of *credere* and *videri,* it appears that the author simply makes a cautious assertion, that is, rather than make an absolute statement he compromises by saying, e. g., that the thing appears to be so. The use of *probare, cognoscere,* and other verbs of this meaning in the passive voice seems, on the contrary, to give definiteness and precision to the statement, that is, that it not only is true, but that it is known or proved to be a fact.

However, Cassiodorus is a wordy writer who is interested no less in the rhythm of a well-rounded period than he is in expressing a precise thought, and it may be that his desire for rhythm is itself a sufficient explanation for his use of such circumlocutions. (Cf. Traube, s. v. *debere, posse*). I have included in the list such verbs as *constare, nescire,* etc., which, though classical, are nevertheless often circumlocutions for a simple statement which might have been expressed by *est* or *non est* or other verbs used in a similar manner.

It is impossible in many instances to determine the precise meaning or shade of meaning to be attributed to the auxiliary, and in some, notably in the case of *cognoscere,* it is impossible to determine whether the verb is used as an auxiliary at all or in its own proper sense as a main verb. The vagueness of many of the documents of the Variae, sometimes a studied vagueness, and the paucity of other historical sources which might throw light upon obscure situations are contributing causes to the difficulty of rendering a decision as to the precise meaning of these verbs in their varied uses.

In the greater number of instances the auxiliary is in the passive voice, but the active also occurs.

The following is a list of the verbs occurring in this manner both in the active and the passive voice in the Variae. Some occur very frequently, but the examples quoted will suffice to illustrate the usage:

cognosci, 11, 1, 7, cui usum subtrahendo sollemnem abominandam potius inferre cognosceris tarditatem.

    35, 3, 12, Homo autem quemadmodum patiatur adulterium inultum relinquere, quod ad aeternum suum dedecus cognoscitur omisisse?

    Cognoscor with the nominative and the infinitive occurs in Cicero's Letters; then not till Late Latin (T. L. L., III, 1509, 28). Examples from Cod. Th., Aug., *etc.,* appear to illustrate the use as an auxiliary.

cognoscere, 124, 1, 20, in eis maxime studiosior esse debes, quae nostra tibi auctoritate delegata cognoscis . . .

comprobari, 107, 2, 13, Quid isti facerent, si . . . indiscreta terrae facies redditur, ubi omnia limus tegere comprobatur?

    Nominative with infinitive occurs with *comprobari* only in Late Latin. (Cf. T. L. L., III, 2166, 21 ff.) Most examples are not of mere auxiliary use. An example from Cassiod. hist. is cited of *comprobatur (fere i. q. est).*

constare, 97, 21, ut quicquid ex nostra ordinatione patricium Liberium tibi matrique tuae per pittacium constiterit deputasse, in suo robore debeat permanere. . . . The accusative with the infinitive after impersonal uses of *constare* is classical. Cf. T. L. L., IV, 534, 72 ff. Classical authors appear to use it in the definite meaning, *it is certain.* In Cassiodorus it appears at times to be a mere auxiliary.

credere, 78, 4, 18, legatos nostros illum atque illum ad vos credidimus esse dirigendos

    The syntax is regular, but the context shows that he has sent the envoys, and *credidimus* seems to have only auxiliary force.

debere 40, 2, 2, postulavit, ut horologium . . . cum magistris rerum ei transmittere deberemus:

    8

56, 3, 31, instructam personam modis omnibus destinate, quae adversariorum debeat intentionibus obviare.

64, 5, nostra praecepit auctoritas ut in Hostiliensi loco constitui debeatis

78, 3, 10, Quapropter sustinete, donec ad Francorum regem legatos nostros dirigere debeamus, ut litem vestram amicorum debeant amputare iudicia.

90, 18,   indutias tibi postulas debere concedi

100, 3, 12, ut eorum praebendae . . . ibi debuissent sine alicuius dispendio comparari

152, 1, 19, tractandum tamen est, ut principis desiderium nulli existere debeat onerosum.

As a circumlocution for the future, the use of *debere* begins with Petronius. It is frequent in Chiron, less frequent later (L.-Hof., 558). Occasionally in classical prose, but more frequently in Silver and Late Latin, it occurs in a weakened sense, almost as the equivalent of *posse* or *licere* (Cf. T. L. L., V, 100, 8 ff.). Its use as a mere auxiliary, as in the above examples appears as yet to have been given little formal treatment by investigators of Late Latin.

doceri, 54, 5, 9, genus pietatis est in illos distringere, qui contra naturae ordinem sceleratis se docentur actionibus miscuisse.

201, 1, 3, Quamvis . . . civilibus vestibus videantur induti qui districtionem publicam docentur operari,

Nominative with infinitive occurs with *doceri* from Cicero on. (L.-Hof., 589; cf. T. L. L., V, 1718, 30, for uses similar to the above in Prisc., Veg., Sacr., Cassiod. var., and perhaps Boeth.).

ignorare, 125, 1, 26, servare quippe terminos ignorat humanitas

iudicari, 65, 3, 18, ut dignus tanta re emersisse iudiceris, qui iam nunc omnium admiratione laudaris.

monstrari, 93, 3, 20, praefectos praetorio remotos esse cognoscis, qui sub illo esse monstraris,

nescire, 11, 3, 20, nescit ante subtrahi quam vestis possit absumi.

82, 2, 20, nescit inde aliquid nasci mediocre:

124, 3, 6, nos, qui nescimus a legibus discrepare,

nosci, 23, 2, 25, nec moram fas est incurrere iussionem, quae devotos maxime noscitur adiuvare.

49, 2, 32, qui pro generali quiete finalibus locis noscitur insudare

202, 5, 4, unde iam videtur paene debitum, quod vobis a tanta auctoritate ultro noscitur fuisse promissum.

oportere, 63, 2, 24, unum sibi ex negotiatoribus urbis suae desiderant oportere praestari,

83, 1, 19, quarum pretium sibi postulat oportere restitui.

posse, 61, 5, 23, ne genus hominum, quod vivit lucris, ad necem possit pervenire dispendiis

80, 4, 11, foris hoc agatis, ne in vestris provinciis dimicare possitis.

100, 1, 16, nec minor nobis est cura rerum moralium quam potest esse bellorum.

127, 2, 21, ita fit, ut, quod per incuriam poterat labi, manentum videatur diligentia sustineri,

137, 4, 17, quid Campania pati possit, agnoscitur, quando malum eius in orbis alia parte sentitur.

Leumann-Hofmann, 557, speaks only of *posse* as a circumlocution for the future. In 137, 4, 17, quoted above, the indirect question seems to be contemporaneous with the main verb, which is present indicative. *Possit* appears therefore to be quite redundant, as the present subjunctive of *pati* seems to be required.

probari, 40, 6, 29, quae vocem propriam nesciunt habere, dulcedinem probantur emittere cantilenae.

52, 1, 22, quanto magis suis bonis abundare debet Italia, cum nulla in parendo probetur sentire detrimenta?

53, 1, 12, si pietatis nomina probantur esse crudelia

93, 1, 24, perpetuum obsidem dederunt amoris sui qui apud nos probati sunt studere virtuti.

sentiri, 102, 2, 29, nec imminuit, quod resolvi posse sentitur:

valere, 98, 2, 5, instructam personam ad comitatum nostrum dirigere se promittat, qui . . . valeat praebere responsum. Cf. *posse*.

velle, 41, 10, 23, in quibusdam etiam nititur velle superare.

118, 3, 6, crudelitatis enim genus est ultra naufragium velle desaevire

222, 1, 28, quia nullas se captare velle profitetur insidias.

Leumann-Hofmann, 557, discusses the use of *velle* as a circumlocution for the future. The future idea does not appear clearly in the example in 118, 3, 6, quoted above. Apparently nothing would be lost from the thought if *velle* were omitted altogether.

videri, 17, 2, 15, ne nos huius modi factum cogas legibus vindicare, qui nunc videmur omnia mansuetudine temperasse.

18, 2, 27, qui nostrae aulae videntur iugiter excubare,

34, 2, 31, quia maiora nos decet tribuere, quam videmur a servientibus accepisse.

39, 1, 10, pro quibus ita videmur esse solliciti, ut nihil ammonitionis patiamur omitti.

47, 2, 15, sic enim decebat crescere, qui meliora visus est elegisse.

49, 7, 8, cuius est proprium quodcumque videtur esse praecipuum.

63, 3, 29, unum eis, quem sibi visi fuerint eligere, deputabit,

CHAPTER VIII

The Syntax of Subordination

I. *The Moods in Subordinate Clauses*

In independent clauses the various moods are employed in the Variae with little deviation from classical norms.

In subordinate clauses, however, the same consistency is not in evidence. In general we note an increase in the use of the subjunctive as compared with its use in classical prose, while in many types of subordinate clause (discussed below under the use of the various conjunctions) indicative and subjunctive occur at times apparently without distinction, as they are often joined by *et* or *nec* or other conjunctions which unite equal members. One example of this type which we shall not have occasion to mention elsewhere is 85, 3, 15, Quid erit suavius quam . . . protulisse iudicium, ubi tot patriciorum corda provocantur ad gratiam, ubi bonum factum celebretur ore sapientium? While the subjunctive in the second *ubi-* clause may be classed as potential, there appears to be no logical difference between its use and that of the indicative in the previous *ubi . . . provocantur.*

With regard to the subordinate clause in indirect discourse, Cassiodorus manifests a certain indifference to the mood he employs. It is true that many of his subordinate clauses are in the subjunctive, but it is also apparent that many subordinate clauses occurring in the indicative constitute an essential part of an indirectly quoted statement.

It is impossible also to discern any certain plan in his use of the so-called subjunctive by attraction. Very frequently an indicative occurs dependent upon a subjunctive and forming so intimate a part of the thought of the main clause that we naturally are led to expect a subjunctive. Where the subjunctive does occur dependent upon another subjunctive, usually some reason for this mood is apparent other than its mere dependence upon a subjunctive.

The influence of rhythm and similarity of sound is no doubt a

204

factor in the author's preference for the subjunctive in some instances. This is mentioned below in connection with certain uses of the subjunctive.

II. *The Sequence of Tenses*
(L.-Hof. 701-705)

Late Latin in general uses the tenses of the subjunctive in subordinate clauses with much more freedom than does classical prose. Even the classical authors, however, do not hesitate to disregard the usual sequence when a special point of clearness or emphasis can be gained by departing from it, e. g., by the use of the perfect subjunctive in secondary sequence in a result clause to emphasize the reality of the result, or by the use of the figure *repraesentatio* in indirect discourse, i. e., using the tense of the original statement no matter what tense would be required by strict sequence.

Cassiodorus avails himself of these licenses and others typical of Late Latin usage. His chief departure from classical sequence is his use of the pluperfect subjunctive to express incomplete action.

In Late Latin final and consecutive clauses were affected by a tense-shift which permitted the use of the pluperfect subjunctive instead of the imperfect. Examples occur in Fronto, Apuleius, and later writers (L.-Hof., 562).

Thus in final clauses, where in secondary sequence classical authors limited themselves to the use of the imperfect subjunctive, Cassiodorus employs the pluperfect also, e. g.

71, 10, 28, se vero soliditati arboris constrictis nexibus illigavit, ut et famosos cantus liberis auribus probare potuisset et pericula dulcisonae vocis unda rapiente vinctus evaderet.
306, 4, 27, utilitatis vestrae causas profunda cogitatione tractavimus, ut illud magis debuissetis efficere, quod vobis cognovimus expedire.
Cf. also 100, 3, 12; 121, 1, 19; 319, 1, 22; 350, 5, 27; 367, 1, 7.

In result clauses also, the pluperfect subjunctive often takes the place of the imperfect, e. g.

15, 12, 18, eius allegationes tanta veritate destruxit, ut voluisset gratiam quaerere.
Cf. also 89, 2, 1; 382, 7, 13; 384, 4, 14.

The pluperfect subjunctive occurs after a present indicative in clauses of various types, e. g.

50, 2, 15, ante suscipis electionis donum, quam tuum probare potuisses ingenium.

128, 2, 5, quid aptius quam ut . . . satiet quos etiam miraculis pascere debuisset?

372, 6, 10, tanta excurrentium laceratione deteritur, ut rationabiliter illi remitti debuisset vel quod apud ipsam nasci posse constaret.

Here, however, a contrary to fact idea is present in the subjunctive clause, and even classical prose allowed the tense of the condition to stand unchanged (Cf. K.-Steg., II, 2, 185).

III. *Relative Clauses*
(L.-Hof. 706-718)

Cassiodorus employs relative clauses with about the same frequency as do the writers of classical prose. In general his usage is classical. The following peculiarities may be noted.

1. The Relative Strengthened by a Demonstrative

In a few instances (noted by Traube, 579) the relative is strengthened by a following demonstrative. This usage occurs in all periods of Latin literature, even in Cicero, though the classical authors Caesar and Sallust avoid it. It becomes frequent only in Late Latin (L.-Hof., 714-715).

Typical examples from the Variae:

21, 1, 15, quicquid enim humani generis floris est, habere curiam decet: *quae* sicut arx decus urbium, ita *illa* ornamentum est ordinum ceterorum.

176, 7, 34, *quae* quantum diversis sollicitudinibus constringitur, tanto magis laudes amplissimas dignitas *haec* triumphat.

Traube adds also 82, 4, 32, where the reading *quae* is based upon the authority of one manuscript, *quae* cum audiret parentem, *illa* mox intendebat heredem. Mommsen reads *quasi* here instead of *quae,* an emendation apparently unsupported by manuscript authority.

The relative *quae* (neuter plural accusative = *sucina*) is supported by an appositive with a demonstrative in 143, 2, 27, *quae* ad vos Oceani unda descendens *hanc levissimam substantiam* . . . exportat.

2. Personal and Impersonal Constructions

A transition from a personal construction with the relative to an impersonal construction is made without repeating the pronoun in 65, 1, 24, quae fuerat fabricis deputata Romanis et nunc magnitudinis tuae discussione constitit abiuratam. . . . .

Classical prose usually employed a second relative in such cases, but transitions of this kind without the use of the second relative are found in rare instances in all periods and occur even in Cicero (Cf. L.-Hof., 714).

3. The Relative with Imperative or Jussive

Examples of a relative clause with the verb in the imperative or in an independent subjunctive, so that the relative clause is in effect not subordinate but coordinate, are rather frequent in the Variae. The usage occurs in classical Latin, but is more common later (Cf. L.-Hof., 718).

The following examples are typical of this usage of both imperative and subjunctive:

50, 28,   significamus nos . . . mille quingentos solidos destinasse, quos provincialibus . . . distribuas

182, 7, 22, Proinde, quod felicibus applicetur auspiciis, per indictionem illam comitivae privatorum te honore decoramus

    In this sentence and many similar ones the antecedent of *quod* is an entire sentence. Classical prose regularly used *id quod*. In the Silver period this gave way to *quod* alone.

217, 8,   comitivam . . . nos illi largitos fuisse noveritis, cui saluberrimam parientiam commodate

    Cf. similar uses of the imperative in 232, 5, 9; 275, 1, 13; 297, 3, 18; 313, 3, 15, *etc.*

4. The Moods in Relative Clauses

In general the indicative and the subjunctive occur in relative clauses in the same way as in classical prose. Thus the subjunctive is regular in relative clauses of purpose and result, in clauses of characteristic after *dignus,* and after indefinite, negative, and interrogative antecedents.

As in classical prose, so also in the Variae there are many clauses where it appears that the author's choice between indicative and subjunctive is influenced by very slight subjective reasons. This is especially true where the antecedent is omitted or is a mere indeterminate pronoun. In a few examples both moods occur, e. g.

5, 16, 15, neque enim tria genera dicendi in cassum prudens definivit antiquitas: humile, quod communione ipsa serpere *videatur*: medium, quod nec magnitudine *tumescit* nec parvitate *tenuatur*, sed inter utrumque positum, propria venustate ditatum suis finibus *continetur*: tertium genus, quod ad summum apicem disputationis exquisitis sensibus *elevatur*:

12, 2, 20, Nam si aequabilis credendus est quem iustus *elegerit,* si temperantia praeditus quem moderatus *ascivit,* omnium profecto capax potest esse meritorum, qui iudicem cunctarum *meruit* habere virtutum.

Elegerit may, however, be future perfect.

31, 4, 5, refugite tales familiares, qui *sint* iniuriarum ministri, qui amori vestro *nitantur* ascribere quod delinquunt et dum levitates suas exerere cupiunt, vestram reverentiam implicare *contendunt.*

50, 25,   Quis melius ad aequitatis iura deligitur quam qui sacerdotio *decoratur,* qui amore iustitiae personaliter *nesciat* iudicare et diligens cunctos in commune locum non *relinquat* invidiae?

248, 2, 5, Pater huic manu clarus ac summa fuit morum nobilitate conspicuus, quem nec ferventia bella *respuerunt* et tranquilla otia *praedicarent*

There are textual variants for *et,* chiefly *cum.*

Cassiodorus frequently uses the indicative in relative clauses which express or imply cause. The indicative was the original mood for the relative causal-clause. In the classical period the indicative gave way entirely to the subjunctive and was not revived in this usage until the Late Latin period (Cf. L.-Hof., 709, 713).

The following are typical examples of the indicative in the relative causal-clause in the Variae:

11, 4, 22, culpa nimirum artificis erit, cui se copia nulla subtraxit.

13, 8, 22, macte, summe vir, felicitate laudabili, qui ad hanc vocem dominantis animos impulisti, ut bonorum tuorum potius fateamur esse quod cedimus.

15, 12, 21, cuius legatio quid profecerit, datur intellegi, quae tantum est gratanter excepta, quantum et videbatur optata.

16, 1, 29, absit enim ut ornatui cedamus veterum, qui inpares non sumus beatitudine saeculorum.

20, 3, 28, atque ideo tanto iudicio laetare suscepto, qui pro labore honoris tui honorem alterum accipere meruisti.

36, 1, 12, Rationabiles petitiones supplicum libenter amplectimur, qui etiam non rogati iusta cogitamus.

92, 4, 6, deponite ferrum, qui non habetis inimicum.

IV. *Indirect Statements*
(Cf. L.-Hof. 586-587; 593; 720-721)
1. With the Infinitive

In the Variae as in classical prose the indirect statement is regularly in the accusative with the infinitive construction.

Here, as also in other types of clause, anacolouthon at times enters into the structure of the sentence. Thus in a long passage the infinitive construction is not always maintained throughout the statement, but the author reverts to the form of the independent clause.

Thus following the infinitives introduced by *cognovimus* in 60, 2, 17, he continues in 60, 2, 23, et, si dici fas est, cum alienis debitis sub truculentis compulsoribus urgerentur, possessionum quoque suarum amissione *privati sunt*.

Another striking example of this transition to the direct form is 267, 1, 5, quis enim nesciat divae recordationis Amalafridam, generis nostri decus egregium, violentum apud vos *reperisse* lucis occasum, et quam pridem habuistis dominam, *passi* non *estis* vivere nec privatam? Cf. also 126, 2, 8; 134, 2, 1; 203, 2, 7.

A list of verbs of saying and thinking used in the Variae in the accusative with the infinitive construction but not occurring in classical prose has been given on page 155. These verbs, when used, are generally followed by the classical construction.

The author, however, has not entirely avoided the use of *quod* and *quia* with a finite verb as a substitute for the classical infinitive.

2. The Use of *Quod*

The use of *quod* with *addere* occurs in Terence, Lucretius, and other poets. In prose it is first found in Pollio in the correspondence of Cicero, then in Livy and later writers. After verbs of saying and thinking *quod* occurs in the Bell. Hisp., then in Petronius, Tacitus,

and other Silver writers and becomes much more frequent in the
Late period. The subjunctive, as well as the indicative, is frequent in Late Latin (L.-Hof., 720-721).

Cassiodorus has several examples of *quod* and the indicative after
adde and *additur,* e. g.

175, 3, 21, additur quod leges tantam illis reverentiam detulerunt, ut,
          etc.
183, 8, 37, adde quod tempora nostrae laetitiae secretaria tua sunt,
          Cf. also 23, 2, 21; 188, 2, 9; 202, 3, 24; 272, 4, 34, etc.

Examples of *quod* and indicative with verbs of saying and
thinking:

217, 10,   scituri quod, si quis se probabili devotione tractaverit, simi-
            lia de nostris sensibus haud irrite postulabit.
363, 6, 22, nam quod acute sapit, quod cito reficit, commune illis
            intellegitur,
375, 3, 25, cogitate etiam, quod praesens facta vestra diiudico
377, 3, 25, vide quod tibi committitur antiqua fides et cotidiana
            diligentia.

The subjunctive with *quod* occurs only after *confido,* e. g.

241, 1, 22, Confido, patres conscripti, quod ad agendas optimo regi
            gratias omnium vestrum studia debeant concitari,
312, 3, 16, confidimus enim in virtute divina, quod et suis meritis vobis
            abunde placeat et desideria probae petitionis optineat,

However, when a *quod*-clause occurs in apposition with the subject, object, or modifier of a verb of saying or thinking, the clause
is regularly in the subjunctive, e. g.

59, 2, 27, multo acerbiora iungentes, quod pro sua quisque voluntate
            aliquid exigentibus dignetur abicere, *etc.*
68, 5, 22, illud quoque stupendum esse didicimus, quod una fluentorum
            natura diversis ministeriis videatur accommoda.
106, 10, 21, nec illud putetur irritum quod metarum circuitus ovorum
            ereptionibus exprimatur
106, 11, 25, hoc tamen dicimus omnimodis stupendum, quod illic supra
            cetera spectacula fervor animorum inconsulta gravitate
            rapiatur.
133, 2, 33, Arigerni suggestione comperimus Iudaeorum querela se
            fuisse pulsatum, quod in dominorum caede proruperit
            servilis audacia:
343, 5, 24, hoc autem iure putabitur stupendum, quod simile tantis
            qualitatibus elementum per pigrum stagnum videas ire
            celerrimum

3. The Use of *Quia*

Quia with the indicative after verbs of saying and thinking begins with Petronius and increases greatly in frequency in Late Latin. With the subjunctive it occurs first in the Late period (L.-Hof., 726).

I have noted only one example in the Variae, a subjunctive with *quia* in 34, 1, 24, debes enim advertere, quia vicissitudinem reddere studeamus vivis, qui mortuorum fidem non possumus oblivisci.

4. The Use of *Ut*

Indirect statements are occasionally expressed in the Variae by *ut* and the subjunctive instead of the classical accusative with the infinitive. Thus after the following verbs:

asserere, 51, 2, 10, asserens ut qui laetitiae publicae minister existit, mendicitate tristissima non debeat ingravari.

> Diom. gramm. I, 340, 17, and this passage are the only citations of this usage in T. L. L., II, 868, 24.
> A notable anacolouthon after the participle *asserens,* involving a transition from the classical infinitive construction to the subjunctive, which is added to the infinitive by *et,* occurs in 120, 2, 2 ff., asserens Aetheriam nurum suam, mariti postposita dilectione, cuidam se Liberio iugali foedere *sociasse* et cum ornatior cupit novis thalamis apparere, *studuerit* prioris viri facultates avertere. . . .

credere, 72, 15, 22, dicunt enim debere credi, ut beatitudo caelestis illis oblectationibus perfruatur

> *Credere ut* occurs in Tert., Comm., Hier., Cassiod. var. (this passage) and Ven. Fort. (T. L. L., II, 1145, 43 ff.).

depromere, 222, 1, 26, quapropter oblata supplicatione depromis, *ut,* cum tibi sit ratio firma prudentiae, actiones tuae non *relinquantur* ambiguae

> T. L. L. does not mention this usage, though it does (V, 616, 72) note the use of the accusative with the infinitive in 222, 2, 12, Oblata itaque supplicatione depromis *mulierem* quam tibi placitus illigavit amplexus, beneficio nostro iugali honestate *debere* sociari

dissimulare, 51, 1, 17, nec dissimulari potest salva communione qua vivitur, ut sollicitatores publicos habeat genialis tori reverenda societas et illud humani generis procreabile sacramentum scelerata temeritate profanetur.

> This passage and the similar one in 60, 5, 6, and Papyr. Wessely, 5, n. 1, are the only citations of this usage (T. L. L., V, 1484, 79 ff.).

promittere, 235, 2, 23, illum vero comitem vobis fecimus iurata voce promittere, ut, sicut nobis vestrum animum proditis devotissime, sic optata de nostris sensibus audiatis.
 Promittere ut occurs in Vulg. 2, Par. 21, 7 (Harpers'). Cf. use of *polliceri ut* beginning with Justinus (K.-Steg., II, 2, 222) and *sperare ut* beginning with Plautus (L.-Hof., 764).

V. *Indirect Questions*
(Cf. L.-Hof. 693-699)

 With the exception of a few instances in the early works of Cicero and in his Letters, classical prose uses the subjunctive in the indirect question. Livy and Tacitus are just as consistent in the use of the subjunctive, but Vitruvius and Petronius frequently use the indicative. Late Latin shows a great increase in the use of the indicative; in some authors it predominates (L.-Hof., 694).

 In the Variae both indicative and subjunctive occur, the indicative in 36 examples and the subjunctive in 127.[1]

 The two moods are employed side by side in two examples, 21, 4, 5, meministi, quotiens apud nos *laudati sint* innocentes, quotiens bonis actibus *reddidimus* vicem, and 192, 8, 18, requirant rudes, *quos visitant* aegrotantes si dolor *cessavit,* si somnus *affuerit.* In the first example Manuscripts K and M have the reading *sunt* instead of *sint.* In the second example there are no variants which would affect the mood. The context here shows plainly that *affuerit* must be a perfect subjunctive. Examples of the indicative in indirect questions:

19, 4, 7, Iuvat inspicere, quemadmodum denarius numerus more caeli
  et in se revolvitur et numquam deficiens invenitur.
19, 5, 17, animadvertendum est quanto tamen a veteribus ratione col-
  lectae sunt.
55, 5, 28, Iuvat nos referre quemadmodum . . . et possessiones iunxit
  et animos.
56, 6, 7, Perpendite, patres conscripti, si hanc subolem inremunera-
  tam relinquere debuimus

---

 [1] These numbers almost coincide with those given for the Confessions of St. Augustine, 35 indicative, approximately 120 subjunctive (Arts, p. 94). For the comparative frequency of indicative and subjunctive in a large number of Late authors the reader is referred to Bräunlich, A. F., *The Indicative Indirect Question in Latin* (diss., Chicago, 1920), 176-181.

67, 1, 25, ut intellegas, quo desiderio cupimus reficere quod de memoria nostra nescit exire.

82, 4, 31, libet referre quam magno tunc spectaculo totius scholae in eum convertebatur aspectus!

107, 7, 33, videant artis huius periti, quid de ipsis publica sentit auctoritas.

186, 1, 18, considerandum, quali labore servitum est,

201, 1, 5, vide quo iudicio frueris evectus,

205, 5, 3, vide ergo quanta debet nosse, qui possit tantos instruere.

The double or alternative question does not occur in the indirect form. The only near approach to it is in 340, 1, 14, nec interest talibus an sumere cibum an sustinere ieiunium. This remarkable sentence appears to be the result of contamination. The author prepares us for a use of *utrum . . . an* with the subjunctive but ends the sentence with the infinitives instead. After *non interest* we might even expect *an . . . an*, a usage which occasionally occurs in indirect questions from Vergil on (Cf. L.-Hof., 651; T. L. L., II, 9, 30), but the infinitives appear to take the place of the subjunctive.

This sentence is noted in T. L. L., II, 9, 42, without explanation under the heading *nota structuras has*. A similar use of *interest* and two infinitives is noted for Heges., 2, 9, 1, *interest lacessere hostem an excipere* in T. L. L., II, 11, 12.

VI. *Causal Clauses*

(With *quia, quod, quando, quoniam*)

(L.-Hof. 719-727; 740; 752-753)

The four causal conjunctions used regularly with the indicative, *quia, quod, quando,* and *quoniam,* occur in the following proportion with the indicative in the Variae: *quia* 507 times, *quod*[2] 13, *quando* 253, *quoniam* 62.

In Early Latin *quia* was frequent, *quod* was rare. In classical prose occurrences of *quod* outnumbered those of *quia*. Late Latin shows a preponderance of the use of *quia*, even to the total exclusion in certain authors of the causal use of *quod* (L.-Hof., 725-726).

---

[2] The expression *hinc est quod* has not been counted in the above, nor any other usage except that of *quod* in the purely causal subordinate clause. For the use of *hinc est quod*, cf. p. 217.

1. Causal *Quod*

The total number of occurrences of causal *quod* with the subjunctive is greater than that with the indicative. The subjunctive occurs 3 times stating a rejected reason. The subjunctive here is classical (Cf. K.-Steg., II, 2, 385). Examples:

90, 19,   indutias tibi postulas debere concedi, non quod habitatio tam clara pertaedeat, sed quo dulcior fiat renovata regressio.

191, 3, 29, non quod ad casum fecerit, sed quod legerit, ars dicatur:

372, 1, 19, civitas . . . pendet in collibus, non quod difficili ascensione turgescat, sed ut voluptuose campos virentes et caerula maris terga respiciat.

One of the indicative examples among the 13 mentioned above states a rejected reason. Only when the rejected reason is itself a fact, does classical prose use the indicative (K.-Steg., II, 2, 385). Cassiodorus' usage therefore is not classical in the following example:

135, 3, 25, per unum equum centum solidos multae nomine cogatur inferre: non quod tanti aestimanda est unius iumenti laesio, sed quia grandi damno reprimenda est importuna praesumptio.

The subjunctive with *quod* occurs 11 times as in classical Latin when the reason occurs in actual or implied indirect discourse (Cf. L.-Hof., 722). *Propterea quod* occurs thus in 106, 10, 17, Circus a circuitu dicitur, circenses quasi circuenses: propterea quod apud antiquitatem rudem . . . inter enses et flumina locis virentibus agerentur. *Eo quod* with the subjunctive occurs in 260, 1, 28, ad fontem Arethusae . . . elegit ponere mansionem, eo quod ipsa loca . . . fecunda sint et aquarum inundatione pulchrescant. Also in 314, 2, 4, significamus gloriae vestrae monasterium . . . laborare, eo quod ager eius . . . vitia . . . contraxerit.

Quod occurs alone in this usage in 138, 5, 24; 138, 8, 26; 205, 3, 27; 260, 1, 28; 261, 1, 31; 305, 1, 16; 326, 4, 20; 327, 8, 11; 344, 1, 18.

2. Causal *Quia*

As mentioned above, *quia* with the indicative is very frequent. Very rarely does a strengthening particle occur, e. g., 68, 6, 31, *propterea quia,* and 183, 6, 24, *vel quia.* Note the accumulation of

causal clauses (two with *quia* and one with *quando*) in 54, 5, 7,
legitimam sentiat ultionem: quia ideo elegimus mores vestros,
quia crudelibus parcere non potestis, quando genus pietatis est in
illos distringere, qui contra naturae ordinem sceleratis se docentur
actionibus miscuisse.

The subjunctive occurs only three times. One example is that of
the rejected reason, 185, 1, 3, sic relucent urbes lumine dignitatum: non quia fiat homo alter honoribus, sed quia modestior
efficitur . . .

In 101, 1, 19, quia nisi culparum occasiones emergerent, locum
pietas non haberet, the causal clause serves also as conclusion of a
contrary to fact condition.

In 284, 6, 9, Uno tempore duabus nemo copuletur uxoribus, quia
se noverit rerum suarum amissione plectendum, we have an example
of anacolouthon. The causal idea is submerged in that of an independent jussive subjunctive.

In a few examples the indicative occurs where we should expect
the subjunctive because of implied indirect discourse. Thus 284,
4, 6, ne . . . videantur comminationem iuris publici evadere, quia
vilissimae noscuntur subiacere fortunae, and 305, 1, 19, avari
quippe principis erat . . . nihil praestare, quia prius cognoscitur
summa meruisse.

3. Causal *Quando*

Quando in the Variae is usually causal. I have counted 253 occurrences with the indicative in the causal sense, as against 46 in
the temporal sense. Causal *quando* occurs thus in Early Latin,
also in Cicero and Sallust, though not in Caesar. It is found in
the Augustan poets, in Livy, and more frequently in late Latin (L.-
Hof., 740).

Four occurrences with the subjunctive are noted, viz., 90, 24;
106, 10, 21; 201, 1, 5; 202, 4, 1. The subjunctive in each of these
instances is due to implied indirect discourse or attraction.

4. Causal *Quoniam*

Quoniam occurs 62 times and is the most consistent of the
causal conjunctions. Cf. L.-Hof., 753. All occurrences are with
the indicative, except one where the imperative occurs, 121, 3, 29,

inter vos iustitiae consideratione corrigite . . . : quoniam nos specialiter iniunxisse cognoscite, ut error . . . legum districtione resecetur. Traube, 577, notes this use of *quoniam* = *nam,* and Leumann-Hofmann, 753, cites this sentence as an example of a usage of *quoniam* after the model of a similar usage of *quare.*

VII. *Quod-Clauses*
(L.-Hof. 719-724)
1. Substantive Clauses
A. WITH IMPERSONAL VERBS

In addition to the substantive use of *quod*-clauses after verbs of saying and thinking mentioned on p. 209 and the use of *quod* in the purely causal clause mentioned on p. 214, the following uses are noteworthy.

A substantive clause employing *quod* and the indicative often occurs as subject of an impersonal verb:

melius (est) 326, 5, 27, sed melius, quod eius fatigatione recreatus sic regalibus curis affui, ut non potuissem in arduis rebus deficiens approbari.
> The accusative with the infinitive is the regular classical construction with *melius est.* Cf. K.-Steg., II, 1, 695. The subjunctive without any introductory word occurs in the Variae, 161, 4, 27. Cf. p. 235.

proficit, e. g., 257, 4, 11, vobis proficit, quod Romani quieti sunt.
> With *proficere* the simple infinitive is classical. Cf. K.-Steg., II, 1, 670. The accusative with the infinitive occurs in the Variae, 67, 3, 19. Cf. p. 160.

sufficit, e. g., 258, 3, 8, sufficit enim quod ei relaxamus poenam qui facere praesumpsit iniuriam.
> The impersonal use of *sufficit* with the infinitive, with the accusative with the infinitive, and with *ut,* begins in the Silver period (K.-Steg., II, 1, 675, 695; II, 2, 242; cf. L.-Hof., 582, 588). The accusative with the infinitive occurs in the Variae, 48, 4, 24. Cf. p. 160.

vacat, e. g., 106, 10, 19, nec vacat quod XXIIII missibus condicio huius certaminis expeditur
> The infinitive occurs with impersonal *vacat* in another sense in 210, 2, 19. Cf. p. 155.

B. IN APPOSITION

Quod-clauses in apposition with a substantive in the main clause occur more frequently than in classical prose (Cf. K.-Steg., II, 2, 270-271). The following are typical examples:

115, 3, 33, fuit quoque in te pars altera vitae laudabilis, quod arcana nostra morum probitate claudebas

350, 3, 14, hac tamen interveniente distantia, quod illa opus suum finiunt

359, 2, 11, sed habemus iterum ex alia parte solacium, quod vestra bona nostra creduntur esse mandata

C. OTHER SUBSTANTIVE USES

Other substantive uses of *quod* in the meaning of *the fact that* are also relatively frequent as compared with classical prose. The following are typical examples. In several the *quod*-clause may be regarded as the equivalent of an abstract noun.

15, 14, 30, debuit itaque virtutibus eius res publica, quod illas provincias tam vicinas Gensericus non invasit

31, 4, 6, qui amori vestro nitantur ascribere quod delinquunt

31, 5, 17, crimini applicandum est, quod inde posteritas potuit interire.

69, 8, 9, sic medicabili substantiae venit a sulfure quod calet, a salsedine quod desiccat.

114, 4, 22, sed nihil maius persolvimus, quam quod vos tantae feminae decore copulavimus.

188, 2, 14, nam quid tibi debere possit, si nummis suis imputet quod evasit?

Substantive *quod*-clauses as subject of *est* occur frequently in the expression *hinc est quod,* e. g., 3, 5, 19, hinc est quod cogimur animo per cunctas ire provincias et iniuncta semper inquirere . . . This usage of *hinc . . . quod* occurs only in Varro before Late Latin (Cf. Kr.-Schm. I, 652).

2. Temporal Use of *Quod*

The following temporal uses of *quod* have been noted:

diu est quod, e. g., 282, 1, 25, diu est, quod diversorum querellae nostris auribus crebris susurrationibus insonarunt
Apart from a doubtful passage in Plautus, the use of *diu est quod* is Late Latin, beginning with Apuleius (L.-Hof., 722; cf. T. L. L., V, 1559, 32 ff.).

nunc est quod (with the present subjunctive), 312, 1, 26, nunc est potius quod regna coniungat promissio fixa et votiva concordia.

This appears to be a usage similar to the above *diu est quod*; the subjunctive is apparently potential. It is possible, however, to consider the *quod*-clause as optative and parenthetical, with the entire main clause serving as antecedent of *quod*.

The use of a *quod*-clause after the preposition *praeter* is Late, beginning with the archaists (L.-Hof., 724). Cassiodorus has such a usage in 363, 5, 16, praeter quod eius delectat dulcedo, in aspectu singularis eius est pulchritudo.

VIII. *Tamquam and Quasi*
(L.-Hof. 732-733; 783)

Quasi occurs much more frequently than *tamquam* in the Variae. This is to be expected, as in all periods *quasi* is the more frequent conjunction.

Curtius uses the two with about equal frequency, but after his time *quasi* gains at the expense of *tamquam* (Cf. L.-Hof., 733).

All occurrences are with the subjunctive. The sequence of tenses is regular, e. g.

20, 3, 26, dona reparat, quasi debeat omne quod praestat
54, 2, 20, sic fuit ad repentina sollicitus, quasi per moram crederetur instructus
69, 8, 8, et quasi aliquo desiderabili cibo refecti valentiores queant protinus inveniri, sic medicabili substantiae venit a sulfure quod calet, a salsedine quod desiccat.
106, 11, 29, ad inanes contentiones sic disceditur, tamquam de statu periclitantis patriae laboretur.
145, 3, 1, iussa, quasi scriberet per ordinem, retinuit
262, 6, 32, sic intrepidi veniunt, tamquam se noverint non esse capiendos
349, 6, sic enim unusquisque proprio usus est voto, tamquam de alieno non pependisset arbitrio.
384, 3, 8, ita prospera concertatione caesa est rebellium manus, quasi inde nudos, hinc stare contigisset armatos:

Quam si occurs less frequently than *quasi*. It is not used as the equivalent of *quasi* or *tamquam,* but to express inequality, e. g.

150, 18, Commodius enim sub expensarum lege tenetur exercitus, quam si cuncta fuerit vastare permissus.
183, 5, 19, quid enim maius cupias quam si te linguas nobilium laudare cognoscas?

IX. *Antequam and Priusquam*
(L.-Hof. 735-736)

The indicative with *antequam* and *priusquam* in clauses of fact even in the classical period begins to give way to the subjunctive. In the Silver Age the indicative is rare, and in the Late period many writers use only the subjunctive.

Cassiodorus has only the subjunctive. Usually it is found under circumstances where the classical writers also used the subjunctive, e. g., 36, 1, 28, et ideo ante distribuenda sunt arma quam possit flagitare necessitas.

Occasionally, however, it is used where classical prose might employ the indicative, e. g.

11, 4, 21, nescit ante subtrahi quam vestis possit absumi.
306, 3, 17, Ecce prius culpas ignoscimus quam devotiones aliquas sentiamus.

As in classical prose, *antequam* is the usual word employed; *priusquam* is rare.

There is also an occasional use of *ante . . . nisi,* e. g.

36, 2, 18, nec illis liceat ante discedere nisi hoc secunda iterum decernamus iussione.
117, 2, 21, nec illis liceat ante discedere, nisi hoc noster proloquatur affatus.

This usage appears to be analogous to that of *nisi = quam* after comparatives (Cf. L.-Hof., 732).

X. *Postquam*
(L.-Hof. 733-735)

Postquam, which rarely occurs in the Variae, is usually employed in the classical manner. The present, the perfect, and the pluperfect indicative occur, all of which tenses were used in classical prose. Most of the examples are purely temporal; in only a very few is there an implication of a causal idea, e. g.

64, 2, 20, nihil utile nutriens sub liquore spoliatum est solum fructibus, postquam obnoxium coepit esse paludibus.
365, 9, 6, mihi enim propria cura dilapsa est, postquam generalem coepi cogitare custodiam.

The indicative and the subjunctive connected by *nec,* and apparently used without distinction, occur in 306, 1, 7, Postquam venerabiles viros episcopos agnita legatione *remisimus* nec petitionibus vestris, quamvis essent quaedam reprehensibilia, noster animus *obviasset,* venientes ad nos aliqui retulerunt civitatem Romanam adhuc inepta sollicitudine laborare, *etc.*

The use of the subjunctive after *postquam* follows the analogy of its use after *cum.* It is not found in classical prose, but occurs in the Bellum Africanum, Vitruvius, and Valerius Maximus, and is more frequent in Late Latin (L.-Hof., 734).

XI. *Concessive Clauses*
(L.-Hof. 736-739; 780-781)

1. *Quamquam*

In classical prose *quamquam* is followed by the indicative. The subjunctive occurs once in Nepos, rarely in Livy and earlier Silver prose. Tacitus and Pliny use it frequently, and it is quite general in place of the indicative in Late Latin (L.-Hof., 736-737).

Quamquam is relatively rare in the Variae, but when it is used it is usually with the subjunctive, e. g.

5, 14, 1, ut, quamquam diversitate causarum legentis intentio concitetur, efficacius tamen rapiatur animus, cum tendit ad terminum.

20, 1, 18, quamquam potestati nostrae deo fovente subiaceat omne quod volumus, voluntatem tamen nostram de ratione metimur

39, 3, 18, et quamquam praefecturae urbanae hanc potestatem dederint leges, nos tamen specialiter delegavimus,

48, 5, 31, et quamquam omnium gratiam indiscreta fuerit electione sectatus . . . se ornavit

62, 5, 28, Sed quamquam tibi praesenti remuneratione digna solvamus, futuris tamen votis spem maximam pollicemur.

103, 3, 31, et quamquam deo iuvante nostris temporibus provinciam securam credamus, tamen prudentiae nihilominus est cavere etiam quae non putantur emergere.

258, 2, 16, cui operi, quamquam vos urgere debeat civicus amor, virum spectabilem Genesium praecipimus imminere

In one example indicative and subjunctive are found joined by *-que* with no apparent difference in the meaning of the two moods,

24, 4, 16, De percussore tantummodo, non etiam peremptore fratris, quamquam omnium communi lege *damnatur* solumque *sit* parricidium quod totius tragoediam reatus exsuperet, tamen humanitas nostra . . . definit

For *damnatur* the reading in MZNXEFA is *damnetur*.

2. Quamvis

In classical prose *quamvis* is always followed by the subjunctive. No certain example of the indicative is found before the Silver Period, and even in Silver and Late Latin the indicative is rarely used (Cf. L.-Hof., 737-738).

In the Variae *quamvis* is fairly frequent. It is followed by the subjunctive in all examples but one, viz.

318, 1, 20, Quamvis omnis provectus ad divinitatis *est* munera *referendus* nec aliquid *constat* bonum . . . tamen quam maxime causa regiae dignitatis supernis est applicanda iudiciis. The readings *sit* and *constet* are found in EF.

In 51, 2, 9, nunc autem quamvis histrio honesta nos supplicatione permovit . . . , the author gives us one of his rare examples of brevity. *Permovit* is the main verb, and the verb with *quamvis* is omitted. The meaning is: *Though an actor, he has moved us by an honest prayer.*

3. Licet

In classical and Silver Latin *licet* is always followed by the subjunctive. The indicative does not occur until the Late Latin period (L.-Hof., 738-739).

Licet with the subjunctive is rather frequent in the Variae; the only example of the indicative occurs in 28, 3, 14, quia licet nostra iussa pro sua reverentia in nullo violanda sunt, ea tamen custodiri volumus maxime, quae urbis faciem videntur ornare.

The reading *sint* is found in KEA.

4. Etsi and Etiamsi

Etsi occurs in concessive clauses in all the classical prose writers with the exception of Sallust. Its use continues in Silver and Late Latin, though in the Late period it is altogether avoided by certain authors. *Etiamsi* in concessive clauses is found in the clas-

sical authors with the exception of Caesar. It becomes frequent in
the Silver Age (L.-Hof., 780-781).

The mood following both conjunctions in classical prose is the
same as that following *si*. The subjunctive, however, begins to
usurp the previous functions of the indicative in Petronius, and
frequently does so in Late Latin (L.-Hof., 781).

Cassiodorus uses both moods, as a rule, in the classical manner,
but the subjunctive is much the more frequent. In the following
examples it appears to be used in place of the indicative:

11, 6, 1, caritatem, quam ego sperare debui, etiamsi aliis non videre-
tur posse concedi.

15, 9, 5, quod vocabulum etsi per alios videatur currere, proprium
tamen eius constat esse familiae.

183, 7, 29, Nam et si epulas nostras sollicita ordinatione disponas, non
solum nostro palatio clarus, sed et gentibus necesse est
reddaris eximius.

246, 2, 12, nam etsi persona summota sit, nihil tamen a fidelibus
amittitur

279, 9, 14, quod non creditur a suspicione longinquum, etiamsi non sit
actione vitiosum.

5. Concession Implied

In addition to clauses of concession introduced by various particles, Cassiodorus occasionally expresses concession by a paratactical use of the indicative, e. g., 380, 6, 29, potest aurum aliquis
minus quaerere, nemo, est qui salem non desideret invenire.

The jussive subjunctive also implies concession when it is used
as in 351, 3, 14, erudiatur quis forensibus litteris: alter qualibet
disciplina doceatur: ille tamen instructior redditur, qui actu con-
tinuae devotionis eruditur. The usage is classical. Only a few
examples occur in the Variae.

XII. *Quotiens*
(L.-Hof. 739)

Quotiens occurs at times in Late Latin as the equivalent of *cum*
or *si*. Several such examples occur in the Variae, e. g.

22, 1, 13, Gratum nobis est, quotiens de magnitudinis tuae meritis
aestimatio talis procedit, ut, *etc.*

23, 1, 18, res proeliorum bene disponitur, quotiens in pace tractatur.

26, 1, 17, Solida laus est regiae largitatis, quotiens conveniunt indulta
  iudiciis
217, 1, 14, tunc ordines vestros agitis, quotiens vobis non defuerit praesentia iudicantis.

The mood is consistently the indicative, unless the above word
defuerit is to be taken as a perfect subjunctive. The use of the
iterative subjunctive after *quotiens* begins with Quintilian.

XIII. *Dum-Clauses*
(L.-Hof. 741-746)

The conjunction *dum* is of very frequent occurrence in the
Variae, especially in a temporal sense, but also as a causal or concessive conjunction. In the causal and concessive uses and in many
of the temporal, it competes with *cum,* and thereby greatly dimin-
ishes the number of possible *cum*-clauses.

1. *Dum* Meaning *As Long As*

Dum meaning *as long as* occurs in only a few examples, chiefly
with the present indicative, e. g., 27, 1, 24, dum se probandi non
habet spatium, occulta est lux tota meritorum. The usage is
classical.

2. *Dum* Meaning *While*

Dum meaning *while* is very frequent with the present indicative
when the clause also depends upon a present, e. g., 69, 11, 26,
loquitur illic tacita natura, dum iudicat. Examples of *dum*
with the present dependent on a past tense are rare, e. g., 58, 3, 12,
Domitii viri spectabilis vitio, dum immemor iussionis tenaciter
parcit expensis, ad initium revocatus est labor operantium.

3. *Dum* Meaning *When*

Dum is frequently used in a temporal sense where classical
prose regularly used *cum.* The two conjunctions appear to be used
indifferently, sometimes appearing side by side as in the following:

363, 5, 14, defluit, dum aqua durescit: fecunda est, cum omnis agrorum
  fructus abscedit.

Indicative and subjunctive appear to be used indifferently in the
following temporal use of *dum:*

379, 5, 6, amplius pareat, dum speratur, quando gratissime faciebat, dum minime quaereretur.

4. Causal Use of *Dum*

In Silver Latin *dum* with the indicative is used in clauses that are clearly causal. In Late Latin the subjunctive is also used.

A. WITH THE INDICATIVE

Examples of causal *dum* with the indicative are frequent in the *Variae*. The following are typical:

4, 6, 3, cui ideo leges visae sunt inmensum onus imponere, dum ad ipsam honoris gratia maluerunt paene omnia pertinere.

16, 3, 25, nam et medendi peritus invitum frequenter salvat aegrotum, dum voluntas recta in gravibus passionibus non est.

B. WITH THE SUBJUNCTIVE

The following are typical examples of the causal use of *dum* with the subjunctive, which occurs less frequently than the indicative:

11, 5, 26, miramur tua te pericula minime cogitasse, dum sacrilegus sit reatus neglegentiae in tali veste peccare.

15, 10, 9, honor qui tunc dabatur egregiis, dum ad imperiale secretum tales constet eligi, in quibus reprehensionis vitium nequeat inveniri.

27, 2, 11, nec tardari volumus . . . sententiam, dum velimus omnia inter eos esse decisa

106, 11, 24, Cetera circi Romani longum est sermone decurrere, dum omnia videantur ad causas singulas pertinere.

122, 2, 8, versari nolumus in ecclesiae dispendio praesumptiones illicitas, dum nostra deceat tempora sedare confusa.

220, 1, 24, serena ipsa . . . iugiter adepta sordescunt: non immerito, quia dum sit homo commutabilis, naturae suae desiderat habere qualitates.

5. Explicative Use of *Dum*

Very frequently in the *Variae* *dum* adds an explicative clause to a previous statement. The indicative is used, chiefly the present. These clauses are not precisely causal, but *dum* is used in the manner of *nam* or *enim*. In many instances the effect is almost that of a coordinate clause, so that *dum* is practically the equivalent of *et*.

The following are typical examples of this usage:

24, 1, 25, indigentiam iuste fugimus, quae suadet excessus, dum perniciosa res est in imperante tenuitas.

26, 1, 1, unicuique patria sua carior est, dum supra omnia salvum
fore quaeritur, ubi ab ipsis cunabulis commoratur.

35, 2, 7, Feris insitum est copulam suam extrema concertatione de-
fendere, dum omnibus est animantibus inimicum, quod
naturali lege damnatur.

36, 2, 20, mora potest esse proficua, dum interdum expedit patriam
neglegere

47, 4, 26, celsos currus nisi confidentia magna non appetit, dum
generosi est animi optare quod summum est.

48, 1, 4, solent initia portendere meliora, dum a parvis inchoant,
quae in sequentibus magna se ammiratione sublimant.

70, 4, 22, miseratio quippe divina localiter sparsit gratiam, dum
omnia sua valde fecit esse laudanda.

73, 2, 14, is enim vincit assidue qui novit omnia temperare, dum iu-
cunda prosperitas illis potius blanditur, qui austeritate
nimia non rigescunt.

81, 2, 12, paulatim provehi mediocris probatur esse virtutis, dum
morosius agnoscitur quod sub lenitate praeparatur.

6. Adversative Use of *Dum*

An adversative use of *dum* developed along with the causal use.
A few examples with the indicative occur in Early Latin, in Lucre-
tius, and in Late Latin. The use of the subjunctive begins with
Tertullian (L.-Hof., 744).

No certain examples appear in the Variae. The following may,
however, be considered adversative:

Indicative, 373, 4, 8, pascit homo delicias suas et dum habet in potestate quod capiat, frequenter evenit, ut repletus omnia dere-
linquat.

Subjunctive, 69, 10, 19, quin etiam ardentis aquae fertilitate laetatur
miroque modo dum proxime salem generet sterilem, nutriat
pariter et virores.

XIV. *Dummodo*
(L.-Hof. 745)

Proviso is expressed in the Variae in the classical manner by
dummodo and the subjunctive. *Modo* alone does not occur. Examples of *dummodo* are rare, e. g.

22, 2, 9, quid enim interest, quo nomine possessor inferat, dummodo sine imminutione quod debetur exsolvat?

182, 5, 18, hinc optamus non adquirere, dummodo sint qui relicta debeant possidere.

Non occurs as the negative in a proviso clause in 166, 12, 2, habeant liberum unum tantum de duobus expetere, dummodo geminata exactione fortunas alienas non debeant ingravare.

The classical negative is *ne*. The use of *non* begins in poetry with Ovid and in prose with Livy.

XV. *Cum-Clauses*
(L.-Hof. 746-752)

1. Frequency

Traube, 529, makes the following statement concerning Cassiodorus' use of the conjunction *cum:* " *cum* coniunctio apud Cassiodorum prope obsolevit, cuius vice fungi solent *quando, dum,* cet." The words " prope obsolevit " are altogether an overstatement of the facts of the case. While it is true that *cum* encounters strong competition, especially from *dum* and *quando,* and is relatively far less frequent than in classical prose, still it is far from being an obsolete conjunction itself. By actual count the 46 documents of book I. are shown to contain 34 occurrences of the conjunction. The same book contains 21 occurrences of *dum* and 14 of *quando.* (All occurrences of each particle, temporal, causal, *etc.,* are counted.) While this proportion may vary considerably in the later books, where *quando* is more frequent, the number of occurrences of *cum* throughout the Variae is far too great for it to be regarded as nearly obsolete.

2. Correlations

While Cassiodorus uses the correlation *tunc-cum* rather frequently, he also makes use of other adverbs as the correlative of *tunc* where *cum* would be expected. I shall quote one example of each correlation. For citations of other examples, both of *tunc-cum* and other correlations with *tunc,* cf. Traube, 529.

tunc-dum, 33, 1, 13, tunc de exteris cogitandum, dum se ratio propriae necessitatis expleverit.

tunc-postquam, 181, 1, 29, actibus urbanis tunc se felicius occupavit, postquam agrestium causas decenter amisit.

tunc-quando, 23, 1, 20, male constructio loci tunc quaeritur, quando iam pericula formidantur.

tunc-si, 23, 1, 19, munitio quippe tunc efficitur praevalida, si diutina fuerit excogitatione roborata.

tunc-ubi, 108, 3, 27, ubi supra terram volitare spissitudinem minutissimarum conspexerint omnino muscarum, tunc promittunt laetificale quod quaeritur inveniri.

However, *tunc-cum* is itself frequent, e. g., 21, 4, 2, tunc fiat gratius labores anxios fuisse perpessum, cum te fructum eorum intellegis invenisse.

3. Tense and Mood Employed in Temporal Use

The most frequent examples of *cum*-temporal are those with the present indicative, where the *cum*-clause follows a present indicative of general or gnomic nature, e. g., 14, 5, 20, excessus tunc sunt in formidine, cum creduntur iudicibus displicere.

A similar use of the present indicative occurs dependent upon a subjunctive (chiefly the jussive). Attraction does not take place, e. g., 39, 1, 30, sit ergo pro re publica et cum ludere videmur.

The present indicative also occurs denoting a particular time or circumstance. Often it is dependent upon a subjunctive, e. g., 13, 8, 24, ut, cum haec pro remuneratione tribuimus, meliora iterum tuis meritis exigamur.

The perfect indicative occurs in rare instances, e. g., 29, 4, 21, teneatur ad culpam quisquis . . . iniuriam protervus inflixit, si male optavit, cum bene loqui debuit. It occurs where we should expect the subjunctive because of the subordination, e. g., 103, 5, 10, Memorant . . . hanc insulam ante aliquot annos undarum rupto terrore imitus erupisse, cum Hannibal apud Prusiam Bithyniae regem veneno secum ipse pugnavit, ne tantus dux ad Romanorum ludibria perveniret.

The future perfect occurs at times, following a future in the main clause, e. g., 30, 2, 3, quod tunc magis verius possidebit, cum hoc utilitati suae civitatis indulserit.

It also occurs in connection with a present indicative, e. g., 53, 1, 13, neglegitur levis reatus, cum tragoedia criminis magna tonuerit.

. . . Here, as elsewhere in subordinate clauses (Cf. p. 223), it is impossible to distinguish with accuracy between the future perfect and the perfect subjunctive.

The imperfect and pluperfect indicative after *cum*-temporal do not seem to occur. The subjunctive is also rare in these tenses, owing especially to the extended use of *dum* and *quando*.

The following are typical of this use of *cum* with the subjunctive, which is rare in the Variae, though frequent in classical prose:

> 12, 3, 27, cum adhuc fluctuantibus rebus provinciarum corda vagarentur et neglegi rudem dominum novitas ipsa pateretur, Siculorum suspicacium mentes ab obstinatione praecipiti deviasti
>
> 12, 7, 8, cum fame canis avida in Tyrio litore proiecta conchylia impressis mandibulis contudisset, illa naturaliter umorem sanguineum defluentia ora eius mirabili colore tinxerunt.

4. *Cum*-concessive.
(L.-Hof. 752)'

Cum denoting concession appears to follow classical norms consistently. Various tenses of the subjunctive are used according to regular sequence, e. g.

> 40, 5, 21, facti detrahit fidem, cum ostentet et oculis visionem.
> 47, 3, 19, conservasti divitias, cum ad eas praeter laboris studia pervenisses.
> 62, 2, 19, cum multis praeberes officia nulli tuam operam venditabas.

Cum is not frequent as a concessive conjunction. Concession is usually expressed by *quamquam, quamvis, etsi,* or *licet.* Cf. p. 220 ff.

5. *Cum*-causal
(L.-Hof. 752)

The majority of the causal uses of *cum* are classical, i. e., the subjunctive is used and follows regular sequence. The stereotyped *Quae cum ita sint* occurs, e. g., 80, 2, 18. *Praesertim cum* is also found, e. g., 25, 1, 10, praesertim cum beatitudo sit temporum laetitia populorum.

The indicative with *cum* in a causal sense is regular in Early Latin. After giving way entirely to the subjunctive in the classical period it is revived in Late Latin (Cf. L.-Hof., 747, 752). Cassiodorus has a number of examples, e. g.

33, 1, 19, Cum siccitas praesentis anni . . . abortivos messium fetus
non tam edidit quam imperfecta ubertate proiecit, maiori
nunc studio quaerenda sunt quae etiam in abundantia
expeti consuerunt.

62, 2, 17, placere siquidem meruisti cunctis, cum semper diligenda
custodis,

65, 1, 25, pecunia . . . cum nec reddita suo tempore nec docetur ex-
pensa, resumatur

120, 2, 4, cum ornatior cupit novis thalamis apparere, studuerit
prioris viri facultates evertere

The indicative and the subjunctive are found joined by *et* in
177, 1, 9, Cum de dignitate commissa laus semper iudicis *aestimetur*
et potior *habendus est* quam sunt illi quibus praeesse cognoscitur,
nemo amplius videtur erigi quam cui potuit Roma committi.

XVI. *Donec*
(L.-Hof. 754-755)

1. Meaning *As Long As*

Donec meaning *as long as* occurs rarely. The indicative, which
is the classical usage, is the mood employed. The subjunctive,
which begins with Livy in clauses of an iterative nature or in indirect discourse, does not occur in the Variae.

Examples:

158, 15,   curam . . . peragendam ad te decernimus pertinere ita, ut,
. . . donec vixeris, numquam tibi successorem tribuat
cuiusquam plectenda praesumptio

286, 5, 25, donec suscepti operis idoneus reperitur, neque de transferendis neque de imminuendis annonis a quolibet patiatur
improbam quaestionem,

2. Meaning *Until*

Donec in the meaning of *until* very rarely has the indicative, e. g.,
217, 1, 17, tam diu vos militare facimus, donec iudices destinamus.

The subjunctive, which is regular in the Variae, developed under
the influence of *dum*. It occurs rarely in Early Latin, is avoided
in classical prose, but occurs a few times in poetry and Silver prose
and more frequently in Late Latin (Cf. T. L. L., V, 1996, 4; K.-
Steg., II, 2, 380-382).

The following are typical examples:

78, 3, 10, Quapropter sustinete, donec ad Francorum regem legatos
nostros dirigere debeamus
270, 3, 16, minuta quaeque graviora discernentibus aquis a genetrice
terra separant ac fictilibus recondita vasta fornace deco-
quunt, donec solvantur utiliter in liquorem
349, 2, Petitionem tuam retinebit officium, donec consensum se-
quentium, dum facultas fuerit, inquiramus
363, 5, 9, Trahitur ad mensem Decembrem, donec fluxum eius hiemis
tempus aperiat

In Late Latin frequently a clause with *donec* implies purpose.
The following examples from the Variae seem to have such an
implication:

91, 4, 22, quapropter consuetudo nostra feris mentibus inseratur,
donec truculentus animus belle vivere consuescat.
105, 1, 10, dudum siquidem Thomati aurigae ex Orientis partibus advenienti annonas rationabiles consideratio nostra largita
est, donec eius artem probaremus et animum.

XVII. *Mox Ut* and *Mox*
(L.-Hof. 759)

While Cassiodorus uses at times the classical *ut primum* to express
as soon as, his regular method of expressing this idea is by the use
of *mox ut*. The indicative is used, chiefly the perfect and the future
perfect, the latter in a weakened sense equivalent to the present.
The usage of *mox ut* is called colloquial, but it occurs at times in
all the classical authors with the exception of Caesar. Examples
are numerous in the Variae. The following are typical:

3, 4, 13, mox ut coepero, clamoribus imminetur et festinatione nimia
geritur, ne cautius coepta peragantur.
175, 2, 17, nam mox ut datus fuerit, in vitae tempus reliquum homini
fit coaevus:
292, 10, 19, Mox autem ut tempus clausit navium commeatum bellique
cura resoluta est, ingenium suum legum potius auctor
exercuit
377, 4, 7, mox ut rei causam habita interrogatione cognovit, sacris
liminibus deportari diripientium manibus imperavit,

Much less frequently he uses *mox* alone. This usage occurs only
in Late Latin. Examples:

68, 4, 15, quae mox ad thermarum aedificia decora pervenerit, illisa
cautibus unda descendens et aera sua qualitate succendit
et tactu fit habilis, cum recepta fuerit in lavacris:

206, 1, 23, cautela quidem tua, mox adhibita fuerit, per patriciorum
et consulum ora discurrit:

239, 3, 21, qui mox inter parentes infantiam reliquit, statim rudes ·
annos ad sacri cubiculi secreta portavit

260, 6, 5, mox foro potuerint esse digni, statim incipiunt agresti habi-
tatione nesciri:

Note the correlation *mox-statim* in the last two examples.

XVIII. *Consecutive Clauses*
(L.-Hof. 760-761)

Affirmative clauses of result conform to classical norms. Negative clauses occasionally have *ne* instead of *ut non,* e. g.

54, 3, 25, ut sic accipientibus satisfaceret, ne dantes locum querimoniis
invenirent;

221, 2, 28, tuitionem tibi . . . nostra concedit auctoritas: ita tamen,
ne, his praesumptionibus sublevatus, civile despicias praebere responsum et tu videaris insolens calcare iura
publica

Ne instead of *ut non* in consecutive clauses is found first in
Tacitus and is frequent in Late Latin and in inscriptions (L.-Hof.,
762).

XIX. *Final Clauses*
(L.-Hof. 762)

Final clauses with *ut* and *ne* in general conform to classical
norms in the Variae. While several minor irregularities are to be
mentioned here, each of these occurs in only a few instances, and
the total number of such occurrences forms only a small percentage
of the total of affirmative and negative final clauses in the work.

Quo, which occurs several times with a comparative as in classical
prose, is also used occasionally without a comparative in place of *ut,*
e. g., 352, 5, 13, copiosa semper assistit et quo fiat habilis, in se
revoluta colligitur, dum magnis tractatibus explicetur. *Quo = ut*
occurs without a comparative occasionally in classical prose. It
occurs thus also in poetry and in the prose of the Silver Age,

especially in Tacitus, and is frequent in Late Latin (L.-Hof., 787; cf. K.-Steg., II, 2, 233).

Ut non occurs in several examples instead of *ne*, i. e., where the entire clause is negative, e. g., 30, 1, 13, adhibenda cautela est, ut qui ad continuos excursus constituti sunt, turpi macie non tabescant. Cf. also 33, 2, 8; 59, 2, 1; 149, 1, 8; 349, 3, 21; 349, 1, 29, etc.

A similar use of *ut nullus* occurs, e. g., 50, 30, ut nullus a nostra munificentia reddatur alienus.

The usage of *ut* with a negative instead of *ne* begins in Late Latin, being cited for Lactantius and later writers in L.-Hof., 762.

The classical method of adding a negative purpose clause after an affirmative one is by *ut . . . neve*, and from Cicero on *ut . . . neque* is also in use (L.-Hof., 693).

Cassiodorus frequently uses the latter, e. g., 48, 5, 25, Nunc ad candidatum ora convertite, ut paternarum laudum in hunc recognoscatis esse vestigium, nec tantum pater imaginem dedisse corporis quam signa iudicetur transfudisse virtutis. Cf. also 201, 4, 22; 203, 3, 34, etc.

There is also a less frequent usage of *ut . . . et ne*. Cassiodorus shows a variation of this in his usage of *ut . . . et minime*, e. g., 86, 2, 6, ut et ille augeatur fascibus et vobis tanti iudicis minime subtrahatur ornatus.

A second negative purpose clause is added to a first in various ways in classical prose. Frequent combinations are *ne . . . neve, ne . . . ne, ne . . . aut ne, ne . . . et ne, ne . . . et*.

Cassiodorus uses several of these and also *ut nec . . . nec*, e. g., 32, 1, 13, ut nec libertati pereat honesta licentia nec desit moribus disciplina. He has *ut et non . . . et non*, e. g., in 217, 1, 27, ut et improborum non pateat adventibus et bonorum non retardet accessus.

Classical prose added an affirmative purpose after a negative one by means of *ne . . . et ut* (K.-Steg., II, 1, 211). Cassiodorus has *ut nec . . . et*, e. g., 202, 1, 7, ut nec diutina potestate unus insolesceret et multorum provectus gaudia reperirent. Also *ne . . . et non*, e. g., 212, 5, 19, ne inter illa nimis ingeniosa priscorum ipse videatur esse metallicus et intellegere non possit, etc.

The occasional use of the perfect and pluperfect subjunctive in final clauses is mentioned under Sequence of Tenses, p. 205.

XX. Substantive Clauses of Result
(L.-Hof. 763)

Substantive clauses of result are very frequent in the Variae both after verbs and after phrases composed of adjectives with *est*.

1. After Verbs

Besides such classical uses as *accidit* (e. g., 23, 3, 29), *contigit* (55, 5, 31), *efficit* (55, 4, 20), *evenit* (117, 1, 5), *fit* (22, 1, 16), *restat* (93, 3, 17) with *ut,* the same construction is found with other verbs which do not occur with *ut* in classical prose. Thus:

absit, e. g. 16, 1, 29, absit enim ut ornatui cedamus veterum.
  The use of *absit ut* begins with Lucan (T. L. L., II, 210, 74).
convenit, e. g. 10, 2, 8, potentiae vestrae convenit et honori, ut concordiam vestram quaerere debeamus
  An *ut*-clause as subject of *convenit* occurs in Sen. ep., 90, 4; then Iulian. dig., Afric. dig., Ulp. dig., Tert., Hil., Hier., Aug., Cassiod. in psalm. (T. L. L., IV, 835, 81).
decet, e. g. 59, 6, Decet nostri temporis disciplinam, ut, qui publicis utilitatibus serviunt, superfluis oneribus non graventur.
  The subjunctive without a conjunction occurs in Plautus. *Ut* occurs in Late Latin, beginning with Ps. Quint. decl. (T. L. L., V, 135, 5 ff.).
nefas est, e. g. 278, 3, 22, nefas est enim, ut, quod a nobis praecipitur, a te nostro nomine per iniuriam vindicetur
necesse est, e. g. 56, 5, 4, necesse est enim, ut inter eos suavis crescat affectus
  Necesse est ut is rare in classical prose, but is more frequent in Silver and Late Latin (L.-Hof., 763; K.-Steg., II, 2, 236). Cassiodorus more frequently, however, uses *necesse est* and the subjunctive without *ut*. Cf. 13, 5, 13; 83, 1, 31; 119, 2, 12; 136, 30; 159, 2, 7; 177, 4, 24; 183, 7, 30, etc.
oportet, e. g. 58, 4, 19, oportet enim, ut, si ipse postulata nequit efficere, consortem beneficii gloriam nostri temporis permittat implere.
  Oportet ut is not found until Late Latin (L.-Hof., 763; K.-Steg., II, 2, 236).
pudet, e. g., 249, 3, 16, nimis in quaestore pudendum est, ut qui eligitur ad principis consilium, solacium expectet alienum.
tantum est, e. g., 31, 3, 30, tantum est, ut animis compositis peragatis laetitiam civitatis.
  Traube, 589, notes that in this example *tantum est = sufficit.*
trahi, e. g., 106, 9, 15, hinc tractum est, ut ostensa mappa certa videatur esse promissio circensium futurorum.

9

2. With Conjunctions, Adverbs, etc.

Other substantive uses of the *ut*-clause noted are the following:
With *esse* and the genitive, e. g., 98, 1, 30, cuius constat esse
propositi, ut debeat ex liberalitate laudari.

After *quam*, e. g., 128, 2, 4, Nam quid aptius quam ut sitienti
plebi provideat aquas sanctissimus sacerdos . . . ?

After *nisi*, e. g., 117, 1, 16, quid est enim dignius quod die
noctuque assidua deliberatione volvamus, nisi ut rem publicam
nostram sicut arma protegunt, aequitas inviolata custodiat?

This differs from the use of *nisi ut* as a condition in Silver and
Late Latin (Cf. L.-Hof., 761). Here *nisi* = *quam* after the comparative, and the *ut*-clause is substantive.

With the adverb *paene* and *est*, 176, 3, 14, paene est, ut leges
possit condere. . . . The meaning is *He is almost able to make
laws.*

3. With Adjectives and *Est*

The following non-classical examples have been noted:

absurdum est, e. g., 51, 2, 26, nimis enim absurdum est ut, quos poena
  meruit consumere, etiam lucra sibi valeant vindicare.
  The use of *absurdum est ut* begins with Gaius (T. L. L., I, 225, 10).
dignum est, e. g. 42, 2, 9, dignum est, ut bonis nostris vestra gratia
  perfruatur
  The use of *dignum est ut* begins with Vitruvius and is rather frequent in Late Latin (T. L. L., V, 1143, 52 ff.; L.-Hof., 763).
fas est, e. g., 287, 2, 20, neque enim fas erat, ut quem familia tanta pro-
  duxerat, sententia nostra in eo corrigendum aliquid inveniret.
  Cited for Quintilian, Florus and Ps. Quint. (T. L. L., VI, 294, 24).
grave est, e. g., 58, 1, 2, Grave nimis est, ut fructu laboris sui fraudetur
  industrius
indignum est, e. g., 36, 2, 7, indignum est ut ad vitam suam disponendam
  dicantur infirmi et putentur domum suam non regere
  No record of *indignum*. Cf. *dignum est* above.
iniquum est, e. g., 17, 3, 21, iniquum est enim, ut de una substantia . . .
  alii abundanter affluant, alii paupertatis incommodis ingemiscant.
  Iniquum est ut is a Late Latin usage. Cited for Lactantius (K.-
  Steg., II, 2, 242-243).
iniustum est, e. g., 96, 2, 16, iniustum est ut viles pecunias exigantur qui
  gloriosas conscientias obtulerunt.
  Iniustum est ut is a Late Latin usage. Cited for Augustine (K.-
  Steg., II, 2, 242-243).

iustius est, e. g., 33, 1, 12, iustius est, ut incolis propria fecunditas serviat
quam peregrinis commerciis studiosae cupiditatis exhauriat.
No record of *iustius est,* but *iustum est ut* occurs in Plautus (K.-
Steg., II, 2, 242-243).

melius est (without *ut* after analogy of *necesse est*) 161, 4, 27, sed melius
est paucorum damno malorum corrigatur intentio,
Melius est quam ut occurs in Plautus (K.-Steg., II, 2, 242-244).

mirabile est, e. g., 103, 5, 12, plus inde mirabile, ut mons . . . marinis
fluctibus haberetur absconditus
Accusative with infinitive is classical (L.-Hof., 588). Usage of *ut*
with *mirum est,* however, begins with Plautus (L.-Hof., 763).

4. In Apposition
(L.-Hof. 763)

In Early and Classical Latin an *ut*-clause is frequently used as
an appositive to explain a preceding demonstrative or relative
pronoun. The usage continues in Silver and Late Latin, and in
Late Latin an *ut*-clause is frequently used also to explain a previous
noun.

This usage is frequent in the Variae both with pronouns and
with nouns, e. g.

With Pronouns.

14, 2, 1, Illud . . . appetimus, ut collegium vestrum ornent lumina
dignitatum
18, 2, 1, quod nos . . . commovit, ut largitas nostra . . . usurpata
praesumptionibus videatur illicitis.
25, 2, 13, hoc introductum est, ut populi de colore vocitentur.
100, 1, 27, utrumque humanitas nostra coniungit, ut et largitatis remedio civibus consulamus et ad cultum reducere antiqua
moenia festinemus.

With Nouns.

17, 1, 10, cognovimus in ea te, qua non decuerat, actione versatum, ut
eum . . . dispendio proprietatis affligeres.
25, 2, 2, ratione servata, ut . . . cum multa reddat quod debuit
33, 2, 27, quae ergo talis mora, ut . . . velocia necdum fuerint desti-
nata navigia . . . ?
33, 1, 4, praecepta nos dedisse retinemus, ut pantomimum prasini
partis eligerent
52, 3, 11, factum suum ipsa condemnans, quippe ut pauper diviti,
casto lubrica, prudenti viro donaret insipiens.

52, 1, 30, Commovemur . . . querela supplicum . . . ut quibus non
fuerunt in exigendo compendia, gravem subeant in reddendo iacturam
54, 1, 15, hanc condicionem sustinent cuncta manantia, ut sapor . . .
nesciat rivulis abnegari.
60, 4, 4, eveniatque detestabilis casus, ut qui functionem propriam
vix poterat sustinere devotus, alienis oneribus prematur
infirmus.
61, 4, 17, in illa quoque parte . . . ut, si pensionem huius tituli sili-
quatorio praestat, monopolium quoque negotiator exerceat.
64, 3, 21, miramur priscae confidentiae virum, ut quod diu virtus
publica refugit, manus privata susceperit.
68, 3, 8, o magistri mirandum semper ingenium, ut naturae furentis
ardorem ita ad utilitatem humani corporis temperaret
132, 1, 11, hoc habet beneficium mediocritatis suae, ut probatione salva
interim moveat ad dolorem
177, 2, 15, Verum haec quoque modestia cognoscitur esse praedicanda,
ut optent se legibus teneri, quae ab ipsis sciuntur potuisse
constitui.

XXI. *Substantive Clauses of Purpose*
(L.-Hof. 764)

Substantive clauses of purpose occur frequently. Many examples
follow verbs which are used in classical prose in the same manner,
as *ammonere* (e. g., 27, 2, 25), *censere* (e. g., 17, 2, 13), *circum-
spicere* (e. g., 32, 1, 12), *cogere* (e. g., 16, 3, 23), *commonere* (e. g.,
33, 2, 16), *concedere* (e. g., 65, 1, 4), *decernere* (e. g., 22, 2, 18),
eniti (e. g., 86, 2, 28), *expetere* (e. g., 163, 1, 7), *hortari* (e. g., 10,
3, 15), *mandare* (e. g., 57, 2, 10), *persuadere* (e. g., 98, 1, 29),
postulare (e. g., 40, 2, 1), *praecipere* (e. g., 24, 2, 28), *praestare*
(e. g., 11, 2, 15), *precari* (e. g., 331, 2, 8), *providere* (e. g., 350,
1, 30), *sancire* (e. g., 30, 2, 1), *sperare* (e. g., 304, 11), *statuere*
(e. g., 102, 4, 6), *videre* (e. g., 179, 5, 3).

The use of an *ut*-final clause after the following verbs occurs
chiefly in the Silver and Late period:

annuere, e. g., 64, 4, 27, annuimus, ut ad loca ipsa Decemnovii duos ex
vestro corpore dirigatis,
Annuere ut occurs in Vergil and Silius (T. L. L., I, 792, 41).
avertere, e. g., 78, 4, 21, avertant enim divina, ut supra vos iniquitas illa
praevaleat.
Avertere ne occurs in Vitruvius. *Avertere ut* is cited only for this
place and Bened. reg. 38 (T. L. L., II, 1323, 47).

constringere, e. g., 267, 1, 2, constringimur, ut quos ante dulces parentes diximus, nunc eis causas amarissimas imputemus
Constringere ut occurs once in Cicero. Also in Seneca, Curtius, and Late Latin (T. L. L., IV, 544, 82 ff.; cf. K.-Steg., II, 2, 219-220).

custodire, 249, 5, 23, custodi, ut semper laeteris veritate vocabuli.
Custodire ut occurs in Colum., Quint., Mart. Brac. (T. L. L., IV, 1564, 60).

dare, e. g., 354, 6, 30, illa dedit ut eligeres iam perire.
Dare ut is rare in classical prose. Occurs in Verg., Ov., Liv., and Silver and Late Latin (T. L. L., V, 1690, 57 ff.; cf. K.-Steg., II, 2, 224-225).

debere, e. g., 21, 3, 30, debetis enim bene gerentibus, ut eos laudis vestrae comitetur assensus.
One example of *debere ut* in Cicero. Also Frontinus (T. L. L., V, 92, 80).

declarare (as a verb of command), e. g. 84, 2, 26, declaramus, ut marmora . . . ad Ravennatem urbem per catabolenses vestra ordinatione dirigantur. Cf. 58, 1, 24 (Cod. Iust. and Cassiod. var. only citations in T. L. L., V, 187, 41).

definire (as verb of command), e. g. 24, 4, 19, definit, ut huius modi portenta provinciae finibus abigantur.
Definire ut is Late Latin. Ulp., Vulg., Cod. Theod., Cassiod. var., Conc. Aurel., Cod. Iust. (T. L. L., V, 347, 47 ff.).

delegare, e. g., 98, 2, 25, Atque ideo praesenti auctoritate delegamus, ut in Avinione, qua resides, nulla fieri violenta patiaris.
Delegare ut is Late Latin. Aug., Leo M., Vict. Vit., Cassiod. var. (T. L. L., V, 431, 45 ff.).

deposcere, e. g., 10, 6, 26, deposcimus, ne suspendatis . . . caritatem.
Deposcere (ut) ne is Late Latin. Vopisc., Symm., Schol. Verg. Veron., Veg., Mectar., Ps. Aug., Cassian., Leo M., Avell., Ruric., Ven. Fort. (T. L. L., V, 590, 61 ff. Cassiod. not cited).

dictare, e. g., 56, 1, 20, Priscarum legum reverenda dictat auctoritas, ut nascendo curialis nullo modo possit ab originis suae muniis discrepare
This passage is the only example of *dictare ut* cited in T. L. L., V, 1013, 3.

iniungere, e. g., 121, 3, 30, nos specialiter iniunxisse cognoscite, ut error . . . legum districtione resecetur.
Iniungere ut occurs in Pliny and Sidonius (Georges).

instruere, e. g., 61, 2, 6, illustrem magnificentiam tuam . . . duximus instruendam, ut . . . non iterum ab eisdem . . . solidorum quantitas exigatur.
After analogy of *docere ut.* Cf. T. L. L., V, 1736, 18.

iubere, e. g., 99, 3, 28, Quapropter iubemus ut studium devehendi supradictae speciei commune subeatur

Iubere ut occurs in classical prose only in stereotyped formulae.
Iubere with the subjunctive alone occurs in personal commands in
Early Latin. With *ut* this usage begins in the Silver period
under the influence of *imperare ut* and is continued in the Late
period, when *iubere ne* was also used (L.-Hof., 764; K.-Steg.,
II, 1, 717-718; cf. II, 2, 228-229).

quaerere, e. g., 82, 4, 32, quaerens, ut quae auctorem cognoverat dicere,
per huius posset similitudines approbare.

Quaerere ut occurs in Vitruvius and in one doubtful passage in
Cicero's Letters. *Quaerere id, ut* is classical (K.-Steg., II, 2,
215).

spectare, e. g., 79, 1, 3, Grave malum est . . . dissimulando spectare, ut
de uno aliquid dolendum possit emergere.

Spectare ut occurs in Cic. epist. 5, 8, 3. The regular classical use
is *spectare id (illud, eo, huc,* etc.), *ut* (K.-Steg., II, 2, 215).

studere, e. g., 251, 2, 5, tu stude, ut iustitia reddaris acceptus.

Less frequent than accusative with infinitive in classical prose.
Occurs also in Early, Silver, and Late Latin (Cf. K.-Steg., II, 2,
214-215).

XXII.   *Anacolouthon in Ut-Clauses*
(Cf. L.-Hof. 760)

In several instances Cassiodorus either fails to complete a clause
beginning with *ut* or completes it in such a way that we feel that
he has lost sight of the dependent nature of the clause he has
begun and is determined to give emphasis to his verb by the use
of a future indicative in a jussive sense, or even an imperative.
Various types of *ut*-clauses are represented in this usage in the
Variae.

Examples of the use of *ut* with the indicative in result clauses
in several Late authors including Cassiodorus are mentioned in
Leumann-Hofmann 760. Stangl (I, 264) discusses an example
from Cassiodorus' Ad Corinthios Prima and refers to the similar
use in Variae, 240, 5, 13, which I quote below. An example of *ut*
followed by the imperative in a long periodic sentence is cited for
Ennodius, opusc. 9, p. 418, 19 ff. *quaesumus te ut . . . da . . .
fructus.*

A mild form of anacolouthon occurs in 308, 1, 21, Cognoscite,
Quirites, quali vos princeps vester firmitate dilexerit, *ut* temptatus

asperis rebus non vos *pateretur* esse sollicitos, *nec voluimus* amplius vota vestra differri, quos semper optamus in summa rei publicae celebritate laetari. Here the clause *nec voluimus,* etc., is logically on a par with the clause *ut . . . pateretur,* but the author changes to the indicative and puts it grammatically on a par with *cognoscite,* i e., as a second independent verb.

The two successive sentences beginning in 20, 2, 7, are, Quapropter Moniarii supplicatione commoti praesentibus te affamur oraculis, *ut,* si re vera mancipia eius Breones irrationabiliter cognoveris abstulisse, qui militaribus officiis assueti civilitatem premere dicuntur armati et ob hoc iustitiae parere despiciunt, quoniam ad bella Martia semper intendunt, dum nescio quo pacto assidue dimicantibus difficile est morum custodire mensuram. Quapropter omni protervia remota, quae de praesumptione potest virtutis assumi, postulata *facies* sine intermissione restitui : ne per dilationis incommoda eorum videatur supplex odisse victoriam.

If we take the text just as it is in the Monumenta edition, the *ut* is left without completion. By dropping the second *quapropter* (which is omitted in EFA e) and making one sentence of all this material we can complete the *ut* by means of the future indicative form *facies.* A variant reading *facias* occurs for this in KF, but in view of the use of *facies* and other future forms in the examples to be discussed below it is not necessary to reject this form.

Facies occurs elsewhere after *ut,* alone once, and twice in conjunction with a present subjunctive form. Thus 158, 1, 4, ammonemus, ut huius rei veritate discussa, si re vera, ut ad nos perlatum est, nullus ei aut testamento heres extitit aut proximitatis iure successit, fisci nostri eam *facies* compendiis aggregari; 51, 2, 24, decernimus, ut a tempore, quo iugalem copulam animo vitiata dereliquit, omni contractu, qui levitatis errore firmus esse non potest, legum ratione cassato, quicquid a retentatoribus constiterit possideri, sine ulla *facies* dilatione restitui, nec scelerati ad irrisionem iustitiae fraudum suarum *valeant* compendia vindicare; 155, 1, 7 ff., tibi praesenti iussione delegamus, ut secundum ordinationem magnificorum virorum Abundantii praefecti praetorio atque Wiliae comitis patrimonii ad loca designata cum artificibus incunctanter *accedas* et, sive in domo regia seu in privata reperta fuerint, sine aliqua *facies* tarditate procurari. . . .

Examples of the future indicative in conjunction with a present subjunctive after *ut,* in which first and second conjugation future forms occur and for which no variants are given, are 256, 3, 11 ff., corroboramus, ut saepe dicta domus . . . in tua vel heredum tuorum possessione *permaneat,* et quicquid de hac facere malueris, *habebis* liberam potestatem . . . ; 379, 1, 22, experientiam tuam . . . ad Histriam provinciam iubemus excurrere, ut in tot solidos vini, olei vel tritici species de tributario solido *debeas* procurare, in aliis vero tot solidis, quos a nostro arcario praecepisti, tam a nego-tiatoribus quam a possessoribus emere *maturabis.* . . .

Leumann-Hofmann, 760, Stangl (I, 264) and Löfstedt (Komm. 254, footnote), suggested *Gleichklang,* i. e., similarity of sounds in the verb endings, as an influence in the use of the indicative. It does not seem to be evident in the examples I have given, although it would seem to be an influence in the use of the indicative in the result clause from the Variae mentioned by Stangl (loc. cit.), 240, 5, 13, cum ipso negotiorum aequabilia *disponebat* et in tantam se similitudinem eius cogitationis *adiunxerat, ut* causis recognitis, quod ille velle *poterat,* iste sua sponte *peragebat.*

Through a similar anacolouthon the imperative occurs after *ut* in two examples, 159, 3, 31 ff., decernimus, ut, si in iudicio supra memorati Pitziae se probavit ingenuum, calumniantes protinus *amovete:* 275, 4, 23 ff., concedentes, ut, cum deo propitio supra dictum virum ad nostra obsequia venire fecerimus, tales homines *destinate,* per quos, *etc.*

XXIII. *The Subjunctive After Verbs of Fearing*
(Cf. L.-Hof. 691)

After verbs of fearing the subjunctive occurs as in classical prose. *Ut* and *ne* are regularly employed in the classical manner. The only unusual example is 233, 1, 28, Si vos externus heres imperii suscepisset, dubitare forsitan poteratis, ne, quos prior dilexerat, invidendo subsequens non amaret. . . . Here the verb *dubitare* seems to be used as a verb of fearing (Cf. Traube, 537). The usage of *ne* . . . *non* after a verb of fearing is classical, and the context lends itself to the interpretation of *dubitare* in the sense of *fear. Dubitare* in the sense of either *doubt* or *hesitate* does not admit of the use of *ne* . . . *non* in classical prose.

XXIV. Clauses With Quemadmodum
(L.-Hof. 765-766)

The interrogative use of *quemadmodum* is rare in the Variae. It occurs, however, both in direct and in indirect questions, e. g., 352, 3, 3, nam quemadmodum velociter potuisset scribi, quod repugnante duritia corticis vix poterat expediri? 26, 3, 28, non ergo quotiens superes, sed quemadmodum vincas, inquirimus.

In the relative use of this word there are a few examples where it seems to be a definite substitute for *ut* in clauses of result or purpose. Leumann-Hofmann, 766, refers only in a general way to the use of *quemadmodum* in place of *ut* in Late Latin, discussing its temporal usage. Cassiodorus, however, appears to make *quemadmodum* a definite substitute for *ut* in either a final or consecutive sense. It is usually found in correlation with *sic,* and the distinction between final and consecutive uses must depend upon the exact interpretation which is to be given to that word. Usually it appears to be final, and the transfer of *quemadmodum* from a mere relative function to a final one may be compared with the similar development of *qualiter* cited for certain very late authors in L.-Hof., 766.

The following are typical examples of this use of *quemadmodum* following *sic*.

202, 2, 16, praesidatum tibi concedimus . . ., ut sic debeas agere, quemadmodum nobis possessor gratias cum tributis videatur exsolvere.

209, 3, 17, tribunum te . . . nostra facit electio, ut omnia sic agas, quemadmodum tibi vota civitatis adiungas

215, 24, curas . . . te habere censemus, ut omnia ad tuum titulum pertinentia sic agas, quemadmodum ad meliora pervenias.

In the following example *quemadmodum* without the correlative *sic* appears to be used in a final sense:

361, 1, 23, Oportet quidem cuncta sub tranquillitate peragi, quemadmodum pote sit bonis moribus convenire.

While it is possible to regard *quemadmodum* as interrogative in the following example, the existence of the final use mentioned above is an argument for calling this a substantive final use:

376, 3, 13, vide quemadmodum reliqua ad te pertinentia praepares, qui te occursurum esse cognoscis.

XXV. Clauses With *Quatenus*
(L.-Hof. 769-770)

Quatenus is a very frequent word in the Variae. Very rarely does it denote local extent, either literal or figurative, in which usages it is classical, e. g., 61, 1, 31, petitionibus vestris eatenus licentiam commodantes, quatenus constituta divalia permiserunt.

Quatenus with the subjunctive occurs in the Variae introducing causal, final, and consecutive clauses. The causal usage begins with Lucretius, in prose, with Valerius Maximus, and continues in Late Latin. Final *quatenus* begins with Tertullian, and consecutive *quatenus*, with Ambrose. The consecutive usage is not frequent in any author. In the Variae both the causal and the consecutive uses rarely occur, while the final usage is frequent.

1. Examples of the use of causal *quatenus:*

108, 9, 10, talem eligite, post quem partes erubescant impudenti fronte litigare, quatenus possessorum iura confusa esse non debeant

108, 2, 17, Hoc nobis gratum fuisse cognosce, quatenus industria illa maiorum libris exposita nostris temporibus venerit approbanda.

2. Examples of the use of final *quatenus*. Cf. final *ut*, p. 231.

25, 4, 25, constituatur a vobis prasini pantomimus, quatenus sumptum . . . electis contulisse videamur.

27, 2, 28, ut ad expeditionem . . . moveatis, quatenus et parentum vestrorum in vobis ostendatis inesse virtutem et nostram peragatis feliciter iussionem.

29, 3, 18, instructas destinare non differant te instante personas, quatenus legibus examinata cognitio eorum sententia terminetur.

57, 2, 12, mandamus, ut in famulos . . . resecetis, quatenus qui exemplis provocantur pessimis, poenis arceantur aspectis.

64, 5,   nostra praecepit auctoritas, ut in Hostiliensi loco constitui debeatis, quatenus . . . excursus . . . solito more faciatis

90, 22,   ut . . . redire festines, quatenus habitatio Romana . . . non rarescat.

118, 14,   ut . . . trabes sine aliqua dilatione devehatis, quatenus et nostra ordinatio sortiri possit effectum et perceptis mercedibus nec vos videamini sustinere dispendium.

119, 26,   causam diligenti examinatione discutiat, quatenus inter eos sopiatur querela

126, 30,   hoc te et legitima volumus disceptatione cognoscere et probabili sententia terminare: quatenus nullus temptare ausus
sit, quod nobis displicere cognoscit.
(Note the use of the perfect subjunctive. Cf. p. 205.)

3. Examples of consecutive *quatenus:*

34, 4, 13, ut per hastam . . . ita manum percutientis inficiat, quatenus vivae substantiae pars sine sensu aliquo immobilis
obstupescat.
63, 3, 30, qui ita commercium negotiationis exerceat, quatenus nec
. . . aliquid pensionis impendat vel quodlibet gravamen
ex permissa nundinatione sustineat.
179, 5, 4, sed vide ut tantum doctrinae deferas, quatenus probabiliter
omnia perquisitus exponas.

4. *Quatenus* also occurs in various types of substantive clauses.
Cf. substantive uses of *ut,* p. 236.

Examples:

16, 2, 19, praesentibus effamur oraculis, quatenus . . . quae sunt
decreta serventur.
28, 2, 27, magnificentiam tuam duximus admonendam, quatenus super-
indicticiorum onera titulorum praefata ecclesia in ea
summa non sentiat
89, 2, 2, sancimus, quatenus . . . sine aliqua recuperet tarditate,
147, 2, 24, sub hac condicione . . . quatenus . . . praedicta substantia
Iohanni viro clarissimo contradatur

XXVI. *Conditional Sentences*
1. Indicative Conditions
(L.-Hof. 772-773)

While the subjunctive has to some extent replaced the indicative
in the conditional sentences in the Variae, the indicative is still
employed in a large number of examples. A large variety of tense-
combinations appear, but for each example a parallel one can be
found in classical prose. Cassiodorus' use of the indicative condition is therefore generally classical.

A. TYPES OF INDICATIVE CONDITION

The following are the chief types represented in the Variae:

(a) *si est — est* e. g., 29, 5, 25, si tranquillos *optant* adversarios suos,
certe *volunt* eos esse victores.

244   STUDIES IN MEDIEVAL AND RENAISSANCE LATIN

(b) *si est — erit* e. g., 11, 4, 21, Quod si conchyliorum qualitas non *mu-tatur* . . . , culpa nimirum artificis *erit*
This type, which is very frequent before and after Cicero, gave way largely to the type *si erit — erit* in Cicero and in some other authors both earlier and later.

(c) *si fuit — est* e. g., 56, 1, 22, si eos vel ad honores transire iura *vetue-runt,* quam *videtur* esse contrarium curionem rei publicae . . . servire . . . ?

(d) *si est — fuit* e. g., 4, 9, 17, tanta regum beneficia, si *pateris* ignorari, frustra *maluisti* benigna festinatione concedi.
For discussion of a similar use of the perfect in the conclusion of a future condition, cf. Tense, p. 184.

(e) *si erat — fuit* e. g., 131, 3, 32, dum civiliter *oportuit* recipi, si iure *videbatur* exposci.

(f) *si erit — erit* e. g., 126, 3, 14, nam quae *erunt* refugia supplicantibus, si et nostra beneficia *vulnerabunt?*

(g) *si erit — est* e. g., 28, 1, 5, Nil *prodest* initia rei solidare, si *valebit* praesumptio ordinata destruere.
In the greater number of examples the future indicative appears to be used in the general or gnomic sense. Cf. p. 184.

(h) *si fuerit — est* e. g., 12, 6, 6, non compulsorem ad te *mittimus,* sed ultorem, si aliqua *credideris* ludificatione tardandum.
While this type occurs in Cicero's Letters, it is especially charac-teristic of colloquial speech, occurring in such writers as Vitru-vius and especially in Late Latin.

(i) *si fuerit — erit* e. g., 69, 12, 29, si opus non *potuerit* implere sus-ceptum, quantum adhuc expendendum esse credideris, missis nobis brevibus *indicabis*
While we may consider the word of the *fuerit*-type in the above examples as a future perfect, it appears that the Late authors did not sharply distinguish between the perfect subjunctive and the future perfect in conditional and in other types of subordi-nate clause. (Cf. L. Hof., 564.)

B. THE IMPERATIVE IN APODOSIS

In the Variae very frequently the apodosis of different types of conditions is an imperative or an independent subjunctive, usually jussive, e. g., 38, 4, 12, Roma si habet parem, aestima nos et aliis similia credidisse; 56, 2, 28, si desideria petitorum veritate sub-sistunt, pro implendis muniis eos ad curiam suam remeare permittat.

While this usage occurs in all periods, even the Classical, it is especially a characteristic of colloquial speech (Cf. L.-Hof., 775).

C. THE INDICATIVE AND THE SUBJUNCTIVE PAIRED IN CONDITION

While many indicative conditions of the type *si est* . . . *est* occur in the Variae, there is a tendency to express such conditions by the subjunctive in the form of the present general *si sit* . . . *est*. Occasionally the two moods are found side by side in a condition, e. g., 37, 1, 21, ornatus enim ipsorum est, si, quae solent illi deligere, nos *iubemus* et si, quod ab illis cottidie petitur, nos magnopere *postulemur*; 11, 5, 25, Haec si omnia *constiterint,* si in nulla parte praetermissa *videtur* esse sollemnitas, miramur tua te pericula minime cogitasse . . . ; 35, 5, 19, Si quis tibi autem calumniantium damna *generavit* et Agnello . . . extortam *constiterit* fuisse pecuniam, nostra iussione conventus secundum leges ablata restituat.

D. PARATAXIS = CONDITION

Occasionally Cassiodorus combines a paratactical use of the indicative, imperative, or jussive subjunctive with an indicative in such a manner as to produce the effect of a condition and conclusion. Such a use of parataxis, especially without *et* or any similar conjunction, is common to all periods of the language (Cf. L.-Hof., 688 and 770). The usage with *et* first becomes frequent in the Augustan Age (Cf. L.-Hof., 660).

Examples of this usage:

106, 11, 26, transit prasinus, pars populi maeret: praecedit venetus et ocius turba civitatis affligitur.
108, 7, 1, arithmeticam indicas, auditoriis vacat.
115, 3, 9, proba tuum animum et opus non habebis obsequium
202, 3, 25, horre vitium et principis mereris affectum
202, 3, 26, illis obtempera et nostra cognosceris implere mandata.
232, 4, 1, pueritia tuitionem gratiae consequatur et non in totum a parentibus destituimur.
272, 2, 23, nam fac invalidum gaudere, sanatus est.
290, 9, 29, utere moribus tuis et omnium vota complesti.

2. The Subjunctive in General and Less Vivid Conditions
(L.-Hof. 773-774)

The type of condition which we know as the less vivid future or vague future condition, is lacking in the Variae except with *forsitan.* Cf. p. 193. This is to be expected, as its place, even from the

Early period, was gradually being taken by the conditions in the forms *si sit* . . . *est* and *si sit* . . . *erit,* and in Late Latin these have almost entirely displaced the type *si sit* . . . *sit* (L.-Hof., 774).

Where the subjunctive occurs in the conclusion it can usually be explained as jussive or deliberative; so the following and similar examples really represent the type *si sit* . . . *est.*

29, 1, 10, ubi enim quaeratur modestus animus, si foedent violenta patricios?

64, 3,   quid enim agat homo, si professo desit obsequio . . . ?

The type *si sit* . . . *est* is very frequent both in the sense of a present general condition and as a substitute for the less vivid form with subjunctive in the conclusion. The following are typical examples of the present general condition:

3, 5, 21, non sufficit agenda militibus imperare nisi haec iudicis assiduitas videatur exigere.

18, 1, 12, quae numquam desiderantibus absconditur, si suis vestigiis perquiratur.

18, 1, 24, quae sic nominis sui obtinet dignitatem, si aequabili moderatione per potiores currat et humiles

19, 6, 28, cuncta turbantur, si integritas cum fraudibus misceatur.

26, 4, 31, nam si dominus vincat, oppressionis invidia est: aequitas vero creditur, si supplicem superare contingat.

27, 1, 4, ad laudem regnantis trahitur, si ab omnibus pax ametur.

The following serve for the less vivid future type:

37, 1, 7, si robora primis scintillis adhibeas, igniculum opprimis

67, 3, 20, quibus magis prospicimus, si ad mutuata sustinendo pervenire faciamus.

The type *si sit* . . . *erit* occurs less frequently. The future indicative in this type appears to be used in a general sense and not to differ essentially in sense from the present, as in the example previously given, p. 244. Examples:

16, 1, 16, quae enim *dabitur* discordantibus pax, si nec legitimis sententiis *adquiescant?*

17, 1, 26, sic enim aequitatis libra *servabitur,* si auxilium largiamur imparibus et metum nostri pro parvulis insolentibus *opponamus.*

35, 1, 5, *erit* detestatio cunctorum, si se *servet* innoxium.

119, 1, 4, quid enim a bellica confusione pax tranquilla *distabit,* si per vim litigia *terminentur?*

204, 3, 20, ad quae sic *poteris* idoneus inveniri, si frequenter geometram
legas Euclidem, si schemata eius . . . in tuae mentis con-
templatione *condideris*
Note the second condition, *si condideris.*

In a few examples the present subjunctive in the condition has a
conclusion in the perfect indicative, e. g.

4, 9, 20, quos si celebrandos posteris tradas, abstulisti, consuetudine
maiorum, morientibus decenter interitum.
25, 3, 21, nam si honorum omnium causa pensetur, pro illorum
utilitate delecti sunt,

For discussion of this use of the perfect indicative, cf. Tense,
p. 184.

3. Contrary to Fact Conditions
(L.-Hof. 773-774)

Cassiodorus' use of the condition contrary to fact is generally classical. The indicative occurs very frequently in the conclusion in such
verbs as *posse, debere,* and in the periphrastic conjugations, e. g.

127, 1, 2, Si loci vestri cogitaretur auctoritas, si reverentiae cura
Romanae, ultro debueratis expetere, in quibus arguimini.
168, 5, 5, qui multo amplius crescere potuit, nisi fides eius sub avi-
dissima remuneratoris sterilitate iacuisset.

Cassiodorus in conformity with Silver and Late Latin usage
extends this classical construction to other verbs also, e. g.

11, 2, 11, si perscrutator Hydrontini maris intusa conchylia sollemniter condidisset apto tempore, acervus ille Neptunius . . .
imbrem aulicum flammeo liquore laxaverat.
243, 7, 14, evaserat Caecilius pondus verecundiae, si hunc provectum
saecula priora genuissent.

In one example, following a condition contrary to fact expressed
by the subjunctive, a causal clause with *quia* occurs with two verbs
in the pluperfect indicative. But as the *quia* assigns reasons for
an unreal state of affairs, it is itself the apodosis of an understood
condition contrary to fact and we should expect the subjunctive.
The example is 170, 3, 19, hoc si voluisses cum sorore nostra tractare, utique vobis non potuisset accidere, quia nec fratrem *per-
miserat* laedi nec maritum *fecerat,* in rebus talibus inveniri.

As in classical prose, the condition is often implied in a partici-
pial or other phrase rather than expressed, e. g., 36, 2, 21, Ulixes
Ithacus *in laribus propriis* forte *latuisset.*

Frequently too, as in other types of condition, a clause which is in the subjunctive for other reasons serves also as conclusion of a contrary to fact condition, e. g., 40, 4, 16, ut potuissent et illi opus tuum praeferre, si utrumque didicissent.

4. The Iterative Subjunctive in Conditions
(L.-Hof. 774-775)

At least two conditions occur with the pluperfect subjunctive in the condition and the imperfect indicative in the conclusion where the condition is not contrary to fact, viz., 155, 1, 29, nam si te iudicis suspicio saeva tetigisset, laudando iustitiam leni ac penetrabili remedio eius animam corrigebas, obtinens suavi persuasione, quod superiori non potuisses imponere; 247, 4, 5, quod si amoeni recessus et provinciale otium forte libuissent, ad te catervae causantium et anxia currebant vota laesorum. These are examples of an iterative use of the subjunctive in the condition. This usage of the subjunctive began in the classical period, but is frequent only from Livy on, and in Late Latin almost entirely supplanted the indicative (L.-Hof., 774-775).

XXVII. *Siquidem*
(L.-Hof. 782-783)

Siquidem, which is frequent in Late Latin, occurs in only a few places in the Variae. The use is generally explicative, as in 342, 2, 5, Romanum si quidem nomen vos commendatis, si nostris dominis benigna conceditis; 347, 18, digne siquidem eius integritati committimus quae custodienda esse censemus.

It is used in a more definitely causal manner in 91, 1, 5, Iuvat probatis ordinanda mandare, siquidem et de talibus iudicium gaudet eligentis et eorum secura substantia est, quae committitur approbatis.

Both the explicative and the causal usages are classical.

XXVIII. *Quominus*
(L.-Hof. 788)

Quominus, which almost vanished from use in Late Latin, occurs very rarely, its place being regularly taken by *ne.* Where it does occur, the usage is classical, i. e., the subjunctive after a verb of hindering etc., e. g., 132, 3, 21, si non nihil est, quod pro suis partibus possit opponere, quominus in hac causa pulsetur, vestris intentionibus responsurus occurrat. . . .

The conjunction *quin* seems to be lacking in the Variae. All expressions of hindering are extremely rare.

XXIX. *Anacolouthon*
(Cf. L.-Hof. 806-807)

Besides the various occurrences of anacolouthon mentioned under participles, p. 177, under *ut*-clauses p. 238, and elsewhere in this work, there remain a few other sentences where, if the text is correct, the author has lost the logical sequence of his phrases or clauses. Traube, 515, has a list of the chief anacolouthic sentences of the Variae, including a number to which attention has been called in the previous pages. The following are a few of the more striking examples which I have not had occasion to mention elsewhere:

104, 2, 31, Et ideo praesentibus decernimus constitutis, ut Alamannorum boves, qui videntur pretiosiores propter corporis granditatem, sed itineris longinquitate defecti sunt, commutari vobiscum liceat, *minores quidem membris, sed idoneos ad laborem,* ut et illorum profectio sanioribus animalibus adiuvetur et vestri agri armentis grandioribus instruantur.

170, 2, 10, Sed stupeo *vos* his beneficiis obligatos Gesalecum, qui nostris inimicis, dum a nobis foveretur, adiunctus est, in vestram defensionem sic fuisse susceptum, ut qui ad vos viribus destitutus privatusque fortunis venerat, subita pecuniae ubertate completus ad gentes exteras probetur esse transmissus:

314, 2, 2, Et ideo significamus gloriae vestrae *monasterium famularum dei,* quod vobis insinuatum est tributorum gravi sorte laborare, eo quod ager eius nimia inundatione perfusus sterilitatis vitia de inimica humectatione contraxerit:

315, 1, 4, et ideo *arcarios prorogatores tritici, vini et casei, macellarios, vinarios, capitularios horreariorum et tabernariorum, fenerarios et cellaritas, qui ad urbem Romam vel ad mansionem pertinent Ravennatem, sed et eos, qui ripam Ticinensem et Placentinam sive per alia loca quicumque publicos titulos administrare noscuntur, quos a vobis conperimus ordinatos,* cuius iudicia sic libenter amplectimur, sic servari desideramus, tamquam a nobis facta esse credantur, nec sinimus contra illos cuiusquam praevalere malitiam, qui vestro iudicio amministrationes publicas susceperunt.

SUMMARY AND CONCLUSION

It may be well in concluding this study to summarize briefly the results of the investigation which have been given in detail in the previous pages and to make a few general observations on the syntax of Cassiodorus.

GENDER AND NUMBER

A few nouns occur in a gender differing from the normal one. The form *alphabeti* occurs followed by a masculine relative *quem*. *Exormiston* is found once with neuter modifiers and once with feminine. *Praedium* occurs once followed by a masculine pronoun, though it occurs elsewhere in the Variae in its regular gender, the neuter. The form *agelli* is followed by the neuter relative *quod*. A masculine pronoun (the form is *ipso*) in one example seems to refer to the noun *divinitas*. A masculine pronoun is used once in agreement in sense with *persona*.

A few plural abstracts occur which are unknown to classical prose. Of these plurals, *aspectus, integritates, iussiones,* and *nuditates* are not cited in the lexica even for Late Latin. The words *frumenta* and *commercia* are used in the plural in meanings not found for these words in classical prose. The ablatives *tempore* and *temporibus* occur at times with no distinction in meaning. *Cordi,* no doubt because of the analogy of its frequent use in the singular in the stereotyped *cordi nobis est,* etc., occurs in the singular also in other phrases referring to a plurality of persons. *Bella* occurs in the sense of *bellum,* i. e., war in general or in the abstract. The plurals of *sinus* and *animus* occur in the meaning of their respective singulars. The use of nouns with certain adjectives and indefinite pronouns sometimes results in singular for plural and vice versa. Plural of majesty and plural of reverence are very frequent, but the use of the plural is not sustained throughout, and inconsistencies in number are in this usage the rule rather than the exception.

THE CASES

The use of the vocative requires no further comment than to

250

note its rarity, 124 examples in the entire Variae. There are no notable peculiarities in its use.

Pronoun subjects are sometimes omitted at the expense of clearness. The nominative occurs once as the subject of *opus est*. The nominative in exclamation occurs about as frequently as the accusative. Various anacolouthic nominatives occur, including a few examples of the nominative absolute.

Many verbs, ordinarily intransitive, take the accusative in the Variae. A few verbs are added to the classical list of those that take the double accusative. Accusative of inner object is avoided in the use of nouns; a few pronouns are so used. Accusative of limit of motion and accusative of extent of time and space are totally lacking. Accusative in exclamation is not frequent.

The partitive genitive and genitive of possession are regularly classical. The classical genitive of definition is represented by numerous examples, the genitive of apposition by a few, while the Late Latin genitive of identity is frequent. The genitive occurs in a few temporal and local expressions according to classical usage. The use of the objective genitive is in general classical. The genitive of quality has almost entirely supplanted the ablative; in a few examples this genitive appears without an attribute. The verb *impetere* takes the genitive of the charge in addition to the classical *accusare*, etc. The genitive occurs with a few adjectives with which it is not used in classical prose. The genitive after verbs is rare. The genitive with *causa, gratia,* and *instar* is rare; the Late Latin use of *propter* with the genitive occurs once.

The dative occurs with many verbs, both prepositional compounds and simple verbs, with which it was not used in classical prose. The dative of possession seems less frequent than in classical prose, but it occurs not only with *esse,* but also with *existere* and *emergere*. Many adjectives which come into use only in Silver and Late Latin occur in the Variae with the dative. A number of adjectives which take other constructions in classical prose take the dative in the Variae. The dative of advantage and disadvantage and the sympathetic dative follow classical norms. The ethical dative and the dative of the person judging do not occur. The dative of agent is used in the classical manner, but in a few examples the ablative occurs with the passive periphrastic. The dative of purpose has largely given way to the prepositions *ad* and *in*. A few classical examples of the double dative construction occur. There are several examples of the dative of goal or limit, a poetic and Late prose usage. Some of these examples include an added idea of advantage or disadvantage, but others are purely goal or limit.

The ablative without a preposition occurs with a few verbs indicating departure with which classical prose used a preposition; one example of this usage indicates temporal point of departure. Source or origin is usually expressed by prepositions, rarely by the simple ablative. Several verbs not in use in the Classical period take the ablative of separation; others used in classical prose with a preposition to express separation express it without the preposition in the Variae. The ablative of comparison is more frequent than the corresponding use of *quam*. In several examples the author follows the Silver and Late Latin custom of using the preposition *ab*. The ablative of agent occurs occasionally with the passive periphrastic. One certain example of the omission of *ab* with the ablative of agent has been noted. Accompaniment or association is regularly expressed by the preposition *cum*. The ablative alone occurs in one example with *copulare*. Attendant circumstance and accordance are usually expressed by *cum* or *sub;* a few instances of the simple ablative occur. The ablative of manner without a preposition is somewhat rare; the only unusual word is *astu*. *Potiri* and *perfungi* are found both with the ablative and the accusative. A few verbs govern the ablative of means, which did not do so in classical prose.

The adjective *plenus* is always used with the ablative. *Dignus* is regularly with the ablative, but takes the dative in one example. The ablative of means gives way somewhat to the use of *per,* but is still the regular method of expressing means. Two examples with *ab* seem to be ablative of means. The ablative of price is rare, but the usage is regularly classical. The use of the ablative absolute is regularly classical, except that in a few cases the noun in the ablative absolute is identical with the subject of the main clause. The ablative of place without a preposition is usually found only in stereotyped expressions; however, it occurs in two instances of proper names indicating provinces. The ablative occurs several times for the locative; the locative itself occurs only three times. The ablative of cause is used in the classical manner, but is somewhat rare, owing to the extended use of prepositions. The ablative of *time when* is classical; however, the ablative is in regular use also for duration, taking the place of the accusative of duration, which does not occur. One analogous usage of the ablative for extent of space has been noted.

The Adjective and the Adverb

Cassiodorus reflects Late Latin tendencies in his frequent use of adjectives instead of objective genitives or prepositional phrases, also in the great frequency of adjectives and participles used substantively. He also uses *magis* and other comparative words with an adjective already in the comparative. A number of comparative and superlative forms in *-ior, -issimus,* etc. occur where classical Latin used *magis,* etc., with the positive. Moreover, the degrees of comparison are not as sharply distinguished as in classical prose. The adjective *festinus* in agreement with the subject occurs where classical prose used an adverb. *Quondam, retro, iugiter,* and *tunc* are employed at times as adjectives.

Unus and *mille* occur in some non-classical usages, notably one example of *unus* in a sense approaching that of an indefinite article. *Tot* occurs in a Late Latin usage as an indefinite numeral. Some poetical uses of numerals are found.

Many adverbs are used in meanings which they did not have in classical prose. There are some Late Latin peculiarities in the comparison of adverbs.

The Pronoun

Personal pronoun subjects are rarely expressed unnecessarily. The genitive of personal pronouns occasionally occurs in place of the corresponding possessive adjectives, a Silver and Late Latin characteristic. The forms *nostrorum* and *vestrorum* occur occasionally for *nostrum* and *vestrum.* A tabulation of the demonstrative pronouns shows their relative frequency in this order, *ille, hic, is, ipse, iste, idem.* The relative infrequency of *is* is due as much to its total omission as the antecedent of *qui* as to the substitution of other demonstratives for it. *Hic qui* occurs for *is qui* with the usual Late Latin frequency. Stereotyped phrases using forms of *hic* are rare. *Ille* is the most frequent demonstrative, being used for *is* and for *hic* and occurring often in an indefinite sense. *Ipse* is usually intensive in the Variae, but also substitutes for *ille, is,* and *idem,* and sometimes serves as a reflexive. *Iste* ceases to be a " pronoun of the second person " and substitutes for *hic, ille,* and *is.* An *iste-ille* correlation is regular. *Idem* is very rare and shows in some examples a weakening of the concept of identity. *Sui* occurs for the possessive *suus* in some examples. *Suus* serves for *eius,* etc. Also *proprius* for *suus, tuus,* etc. The reflexive is used as a reciprocal pronoun as in poetry and Late prose. *Aliquis* (unemphatic) is used for *quis* after *si, nisi,* and *ne*; it also substitutes for *quisquam.* Both these usages are only Late Latin.

THE PREPOSITION

Prepositions in general are more frequent than in classical prose, and their frequent use tends to eliminate certain case constructions in the oblique cases and to diminish the number of occurrences in others. Many prepositions are used to express ideas for which they were not employed in classical prose. In the prepositions governing the accusative, exceptions to classical usage or notable extensions of classical norms have been observed chiefly in the use of *ad, apud, iuxta, ultra, intra, supra, circa, secundum,* and *per.* The use of *ante, post, penes, propter, ob, contra, extra, praeter, adversus,* and *erga,* apart from minor variations, is classical.

The prepositions *ab, de,* and *ex* with the ablative occur almost indiscriminately to express separation and departure. Some of the distinctions in the use of these prepositions had been lost in the classical period. There is an increase in the use of *de* as in all Late Latin. *Ab* occurs in certain non-classical combinations with adjectives. It is sometimes used with the ablative of comparison. Extensions of *de* are noted in the partitive sense; also in its use denoting origin, cause, means, and agent. Extensions of the classical use of *ex* to denote origin, cause, material, means, and agent are found. It is also used in various fixed adverbial phrases and with a noun in the ablative in such a combination as *ex principe.*

Sine is used with *aliquis*, a Late Latin usage. An instrumental use of *cum* occurs; the rarity of the modal use is noteworthy. Extensions of *pro* in the sense of *according to*, in *proportion to*, giving rise to a causal and a final usage of this preposition, are noted. Also one example in a wide extension of the proportional sense to a temporal one. The prepositions *absque* and *prae* occur rarely, but are chiefly found in the classical manner.

With regard to the prepositions which govern either accusative or ablative, there is some confusion in the use of the two cases, particularly with the preposition *in*. Thus the accusative occurs at times with verbs of rest, the ablative at times with expressions of motion and in a final sense. In expressions denoting an exchange both cases occur. Extensions of the final and consecutive uses of *in* with the accusative and of adverbial phrases with *in* and the accusative occur.

In with the ablative occurs once in a locative sense with the name of a town. It also occurs in place of the simple ablative with *confidere, gaudere, gravari, implicare, miscere,* and *praesumere.* A few extensions of the temporal use of *in* with the ablative occur, and numerous examples of its use as the equivalent of an ablative of respect. Adverbial phrases with *in* and the ablative are frequent.

Sub occurs only with the ablative. In two examples the ablative seems to be used for an accusative. Various modal uses of *sub* are frequent, and it is the regular preposition in the Variae for the simple ablative of manner in place of the infrequent *cum. Super* with the accusative occurs a few times in the sense of *praeter. Super* with the ablative occurs only in a few stereotyped phrases.

THE NOMINAL FORMS OF THE VERB

The infinitive occurs rather frequently as a simple noun, often with a modifier. The usage is chiefly Late. One infinitive occurs after the preposition *cum*, a Late Latin peculiarity. A few infinitives depend directly on adjectives or substantives. These occurrences are poetic, Silver, and Late. There are a few examples of the infinitive to express purpose. As can be seen from the lists, many verbs are followed by the complementary infinitive, the accusative with the infinitive, and the nominative with the infinitive, which did not take these constructions in classical prose. The tenses of the infinitive show some deviations from classical usage. The gerundive occurs as an attributive and as a predicate adjective in the classical manner, but showing extensions in the words used. Numerous gerundives are used substantively, a usage beginning with Horace; one such example is, in effect, a plural gerund. The gerundive with *esse* serves as a future infinitive passive; less frequently the gerundive alone serves as a future participle passive. The gerundive in agreement with a direct object to express purpose occurs frequently. The use of the gerundive in the oblique cases and with prepositions is mostly classical, as are nearly all uses of the gerund. One example of a genitive of the gerund with a feminine noun in apposition occurs, a usage mostly Early and Late. There is a frequent use of the ablative of the gerund instead of the present participle.

The supine in *-um* does not occur. The supine in *-u* is found only in a few stereotyped uses.

The present participle as an attribute conforms to classical usage. The predicate uses show several divergences. Present participles at times indicate action prior to or subsequent to that of the main verb. The use of the present participle for purpose is very rare. *Constitutus* and *positus* occur as substitutes for a present participle of *esse*. The use of the perfect participle in agreement with a substantive as the equivalent of a verbal noun is frequent and occurs chiefly in the nominative. The use of the perfect participle instead of a relative clause is more frequent than in classical prose. A few future participles are used attributively which are not so used in classical prose. The predicate use of the future participle is more frequent than in classical prose. This participle is used to imply purpose both after verbs of motion and verbs of rest. Participles are frequently employed in anacolouthic constructions.

THE SYNTAX OF COORDINATION

Agreement in person is sometimes according to sense. A few impersonal verbs are used personally. Some intransitive verbs are used transitively; a few transitive verbs are used absolutely. One example of a passive as middle voice is noted. A few deponents have passive meaning. The Late form *deberemur* occurs once. Tense-shifting affects many tenses in independent clauses. Inconsistencies occur in the use of epistolary tenses.

Num is totally lacking. *Numquid* takes its place, but is itself rare. *Nonne* and *-ne* are rare. There are some pecularities, chiefly Late, in the use of *-que, atque, nec, sive,* and *vel.*

Rhetorical and exclamatory questions occur, usually in the classical manner. The use of the optative subjunctive is generally classical; *utinam* rarely occurs. The potential subjunctive is usually classical; the imperfect tense, rare in Late Latin, occurs in a few examples. *Forsitan* (the most common), *fortasse, fortassis,* and *forte* show some Silver and Late peculiarities. The indefinite second person occurs, usually with the subjunctive, but sometimes with the indicative; this use of the indicative is largely colloquial. The use of the hortatory subjunctive is classical; but it occurs rarely. The future indicative often has imperative force; the future imperative occurs only in stereotyped expressions. The jussive subjunctive is frequent, sometimes alternating with the imperative. Prohibition is rarely expressed by the classical *noli* and *cave,* more frequently by *ne,* and particularly *non,* with the subjunctive. *Posse, debere, videri,* and other verbs occur at times as auxiliaries or in a weakened sense, a usage which is characteristic of Cassiodorus' style.

The Syntax of Subordination

Both the moods and the tenses in subordinate clauses are used with a certain amount of freedom in the Variae. The chief divergence in the use of the tenses is in the use of the pluperfect subjunctive for the imperfect. Relative pronouns are in a few instances strengthened by a demonstrative. The imperative and jussive subjunctive in relative clauses is more frequent than in classical Latin. Distinctions between the uses of the indicative and the subjunctive in relative clauses are not always clearly marked; sometimes both moods occur in the same sentence without apparent reason for the change. Relative clauses of cause often have the indicative. Indirect statements are sometimes expressed by *quod, quia,* or *ut*-clauses, but the classical use of the infinitive is more common. Indirect questions occur in the proportion of more than three subjunctives to one indicative.

Causal *quia* and *quando* are frequent, *quod* and *quoniam* are rare. The subjunctive occurs in the same sense as the indicative in occasional examples with all these conjunctions except *quoniam*. *Quod*-substantive clauses are especially frequent. *Quod* occurs in a few temporal phrases, *diu est quod,* etc. *Tamquam* and *quasi* are classical in their use; of the two, *quasi* is much more frequent. *Antequam* is frequent, *priusquam* is rare; the uses are generally classical. The use of *postquam* is generally classical, but both the indicative and the subjunctive occur in one example with no apparent distinction in meaning. *Quamquam* is nearly always followed by the subjunctive; *quamvis* in one example has the indicative. Both these divergences from classical usage begin in the Silver Age. The subjunctive is especially frequent with *etsi* and *etiamsi*. *Quotiens* occurs in place of *cum*; the usage is Late. *Dum* is frequent as a substitute for *cum*; the explicative use of *dum* is very frequent. *Dummodo* is used in the classical manner, except for the occurrence of a negative *non* for *ne*. *Cum*-clauses, in spite of yielding to *dum* and *quando,* are fairly frequent. Causal *cum* sometimes has the indicative; both the indicative and subjunctive occur in one example with no apparent distinction in meaning. *Donec* meaning *until* regularly takes the subjunctive; the usage is not classical. A few examples of final *donec* occur. *Mox ut* occurs regularly in the meaning of *as soon as*. Less frequently *mox* occurs alone, a Late usage.

Pure final and consecutive clauses are generally classical; *non* sometimes occurs in a final clause. Substantive final and consecutive clauses follow many verbs which did not take the substantive clause in classical prose. *Ut*-clauses present some notable anacoloutha. The usage after verbs of fearing is classical. *Quemadmodum* sometimes serves as a final particle. I have found no parallel for this use. *Quatenus* is a frequent substitute for *ut* in causal, final, and consecutive clauses. Its use as a causal particle is Silver Latin, its use in the final and consecutive senses is Late.

Indicative conditions are generally classical; many tense-combinations occur. The subjunctive occurs in the protasis along with the indicative in a few examples without distinction in the meaning of the two moods. A paratactical construction often is equivalent to a condition. Less vivid conditions of the classical form are almost entirely lacking; the present general of the type *si sit-est* is frequent.

There is an extension of the classical use of the indicative in the apodosis of contrary to fact conditions. The pluperfect subjunctive occurs in the protasis in a few conditions not contrary to fact, but as an iterative subjunctive.

Clauses with *siquidem* explicative and causal are frequent. *Quominus* is rare; *quin* is apparently lacking.

Anacolouthon occurs in various types of clauses so frequently that it may be considered a general characteristic of Cassiodorus' style.

The preceding summary of the syntax of the Variae reveals a considerable number of points in which the syntax of Cassiodorus differs from that of the authors of the Classical Age. And yet, when we consider that a period of over five hundred years separates these writers from the author of the Variae, a period which witnessed social, political, and religious changes of the greatest importance in the Roman world, we may well be surprised that the literary language of the Romans still remained so largely in the days of Cassiodorus what it had been in the days of Cicero. For the groundwork of Cassiodorus' syntax is the syntax of the prose of the Classical and Silver periods, and his divergences therefrom arouse our wonder, not because of their frequency or radical nature, but rather because, on the whole, they are so few and so conservative.

The nominal syntax of the Variae differs from classical syntax, as we have seen, only in minor shiftings of gender and irregularities of number, in the loss of a few case-constructions and the substitution of prepositions for a few declensional forms, in the extended substantival use of adjectives and participles, in a greater freedom of choice in the use of demonstratives, in additions to the functions of various prepositions and the greater relative frequency of their employment, in a more extended substantival use of the infinitive and an increase in the number of individual verbs introducing infinitive constructions, in the total absence of the supine in

-*um* and almost total absence of the supine in -*u,* and the frequent anacolouthic use of participles.

With regard to the verbal syntax, independent clauses remain basically the same in Cassiodorus as in the classical authors. His subordinate clauses show a certain freedom from restriction in the choice both of moods and tenses. The classical usages of mood and tense are not lost, but non-classical uses are added and sometimes appear side by side with the classical.

But in all instances of major importance where Cassiodorus' syntax, either nominal or verbal, and his vocabulary diverge from classical norms, a precedent can be found for his usage in the writings of the Silver Age or in the earlier Late Latin writers, profane and ecclesiastical. He deliberately, then, takes counsel of the past and adopts in the main the linguistic usage of earlier authors. The result is a work that is highly artificial. His vocabulary inevitably reflects to a certain degree the language of his day, but in its main features it is drawn from the writings of the past. His syntax can not neglect the popular element entirely, but in its main points it is the syntax of the classical and Silver writers and, in a word, is quite traditional.

As an author Cassiodorus stands at the end of a literary tradition of artificiality that goes back to the Classical Age. Even in the classical period there existed a divergence between the spoken language of the ordinary people and the written language of the literary elect. The Silver and Late writers in the full literary tradition do nothing to close the gap, but rather widen it. It is only the language of the Late inscriptions and of such authors as have a distinctly popular or vulgar style that gives us today a fair view of the colloquial speech of Cassiodorus' time. If we compare, for instance, the rhythmic periods of the *Variae* and the preservation of the classical morphological forms with the language of Gregory of Tours, Cassiodorus' younger contemporary, or with the popular style of the *Peregrinatio Aetheriae* of an earlier period, or with the unpolished language of many of the Late inscriptions, we realize how far away from the colloquial speech of the time is this stilted model of official correspondence.

INDEX VERBORUM ET LOCUTIONUM

261

10

unciae appellatio, 21
unde, uses of, 65
universus, in plural sense, 5
unus, with partitive gen., 19; = indefinite article, etc., 60; unus idemque, 85; unus-alter, reciprocal, 89
unusquisque, 60
urgeri, with nom. with inf., 162
ut, in indirect statement, 211 ff.; in final clauses, 231 ff; ut non = ne, 232; ut . . . neque, etc., 232; in substantive clauses of result, 233 ff.; in substantive final clauses, 236 ff.; with impv. by anacolouthon, 239; with indicative by anacolouthon, 240; after verbs of fearing, 240
uti, verb, with abl., 45
utillimus, 57
utinam, 190

vacare, with abl. of separation, 41; with ad, 92; impersonally, 155; with quod and indic., 216
vacuare, with abl. of separation, 41
valde, with comparative, 57
valere, as auxiliary, 203
valiturus, as attributive participle, 176
variarum (liber), variarum nomen, 22
vectigal fidei, 21

vehere, absolute use of, 181
vel = et, 189; vel . . . vel = et . . . et, 189
velle, substantively, 150; as auxiliary, 203
veniae locus, 37
venire, with de, 113; use of gerundive in agreement with subject of, 168
venturus, as attributive participle, 176
veracissimus, 57
vereri, with acc. with inf., 157
Vergilianum carmen, 52
vesci, with abl., 45
vester, in plural of reverence, 5
vestrorum = vestrum, 68
videre, use of passive as auxiliary, 203; with ut-substantive final clause, 236
viri virtutum, 26
virtutum radices, 21
vitalis vigor, 52
vitiorum humilia, 20
vituperatio nostra, 52
vivacius, 57
vocabulum principis, 21
vocitare de, 114
voluptatum laetitia, 23
vos, expressed as subject, 67
votum furoris, 23; votum puritatis, 23

VITA

Bernard Henry Skahill was born at Cascade, Iowa, December 19, 1890. His preliminary training was received in the public school, in St. Martin's parochial High School of Cascade, and in Columbia Academy of Dubuque, Iowa. In 1910 he enrolled at Columbia College, Dubuque, Iowa, and received from that institution the degree of Bachelor of Arts in June, 1914. From 1914 to 1917 he pursued theological studies at the Grand Seminary of Montreal and received the degrees of Bachelor of Theology and Bachelor of Canon Law. He was ordained to the priesthood at Dubuque, Iowa, September 1, 1917, and was immediately assigned to the faculty of Columbia Academy, teaching courses in English and Latin. During the Summer Session of 1918 he followed Latin courses in the Johns Hopkins University, and during the Summer Session of 1920, in the University of Minnesota. During the scholastic year 1920-1921 he attended the Catholic University of America, where he pursued courses in Latin, Greek, and Comparative Philology. After receiving the degree of Master of Arts from the Catholic University in June, 1921, he was assigned to the faculty of Columbia College, where he taught Greek and Latin until June, 1932. In September, 1932, he resumed his work at the Catholic University as a candidate for the degree of Doctor of Philosophy. His courses in the Catholic University were taken under Professor Roy J. Deferrari, Dr. Martin R. P. McGuire, Dr. James Marshall Campbell, Dr. J. P. Christopher, and Dr. James A. Geary.

THE CATHOLIC UNIVERSITY OF AMERICA STUDIES
IN MEDIEVAL AND RENAISSANCE LATIN

Edited by Roy J. Deferrari, Martin R. P. McGuire, and Brother Giles, C.F.X.